For Bethanne!
Fellow Smithie &
Albright buddy!

xo Cindy

If you're too innocent,
life has a way of coming in
and growing you up.

— Helen Hunt

For my children

— C. C.

To protect the innocent, the not-so-innocent, and me,
from those who might be feeling litigious, I changed nearly
everyone's name as well as a number of personal details about
these events, which happened more than a decade ago.

AN ILLUSTRATED MEMOIR OF DIVORCE

Good

RIDDANCE

CYNTHIA COPELAND
COLORS BY FRANK M. YOUNG

Abrams ComicArts, New York

Spring

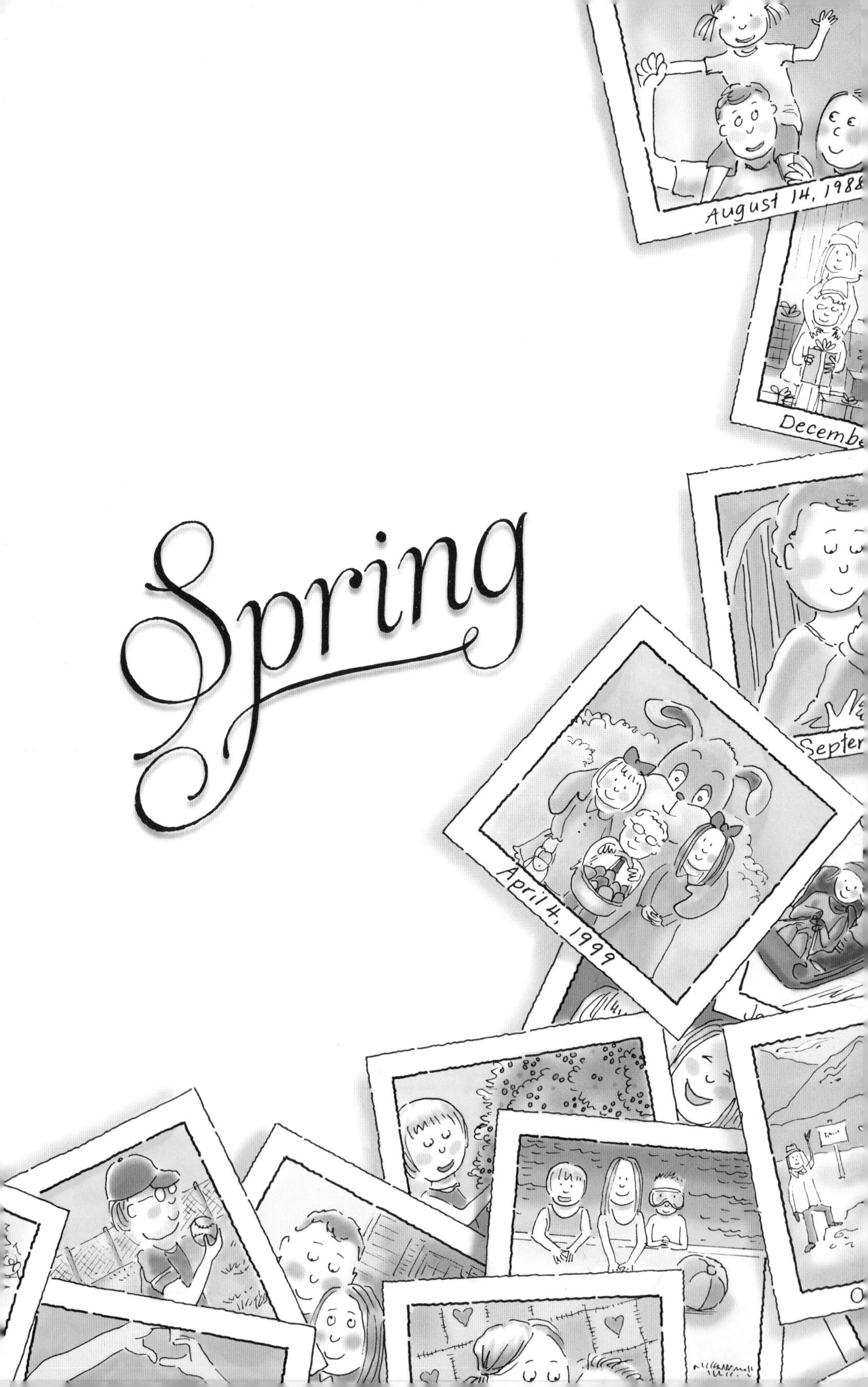
April 4, 1999

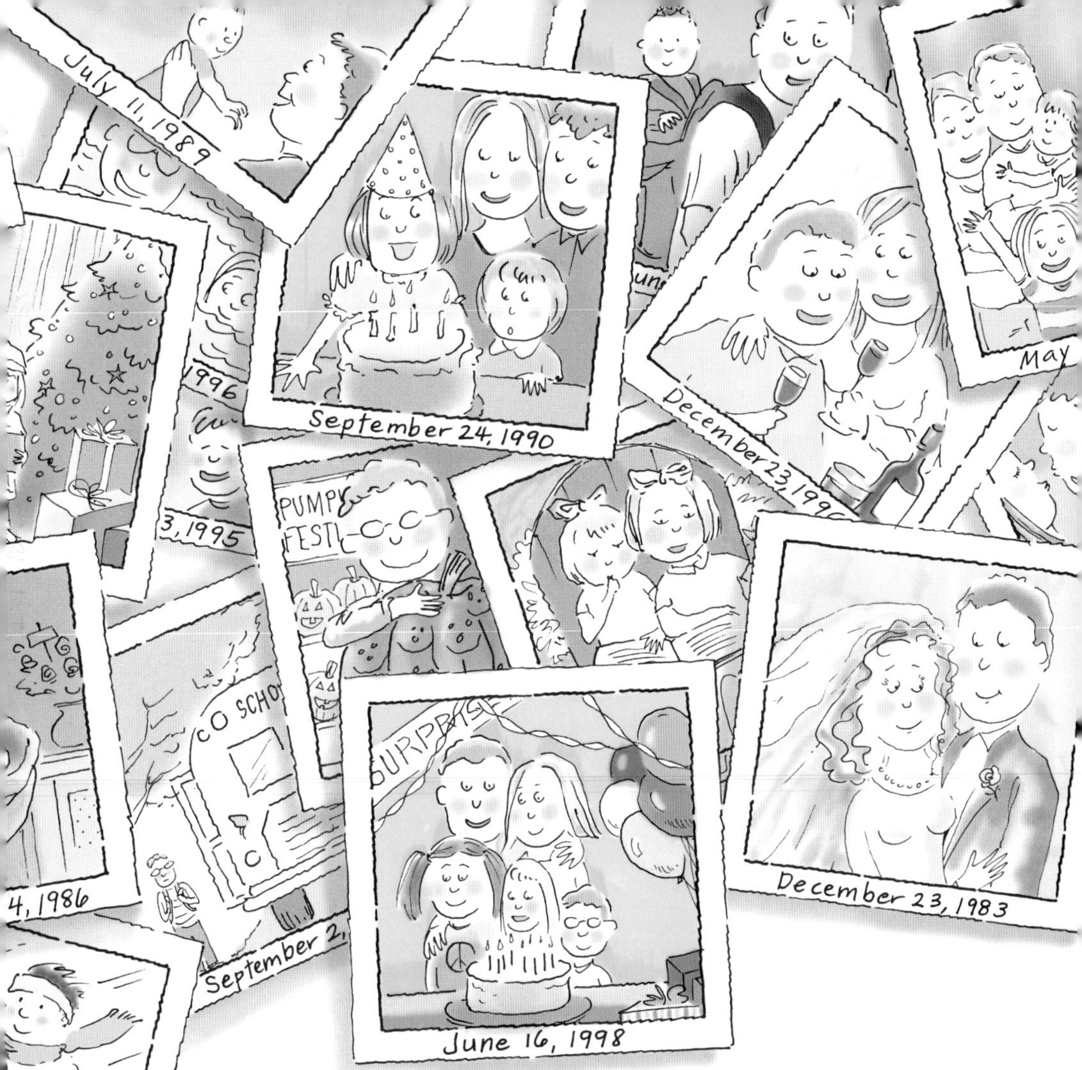
July 11, 1989
September 24, 1990
December 23, 1983
June 16, 1998

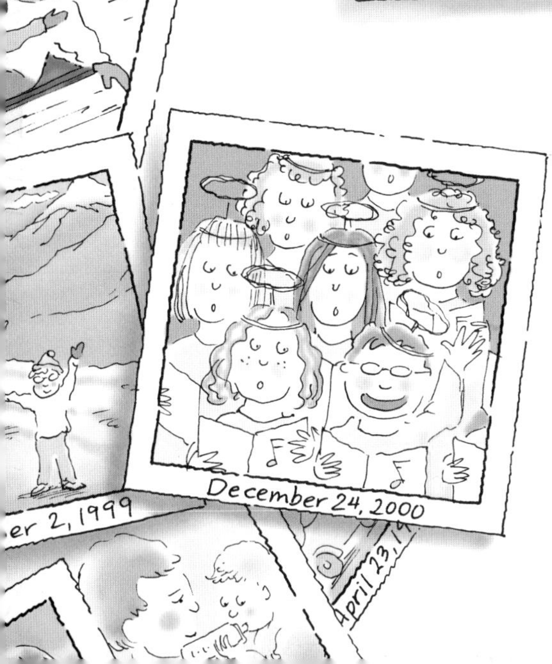
December 24, 2000

... and then it was
March 24, 2001,
the night before
everything changed...

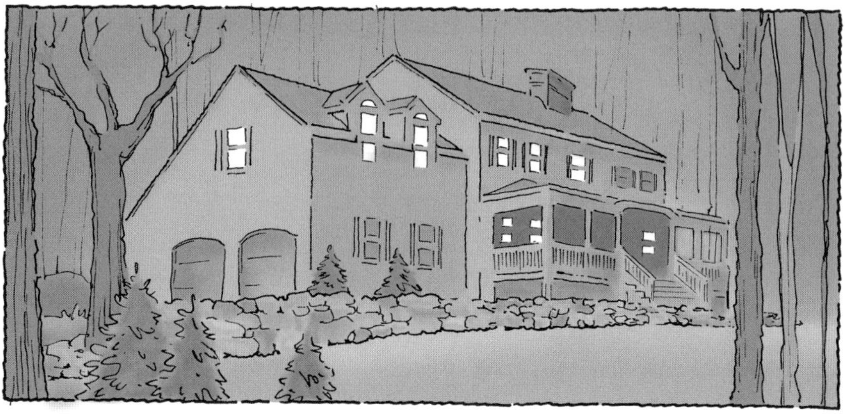

While the kids played, T.J. and I talked about what color to paint the bathroom, how cute Emma looked with her new haircut, and whether to plant cucumbers in the garden. (No one would eat them, but we loved hearing Jack say "cute cumbers.") Just contented and comfortable family talk.

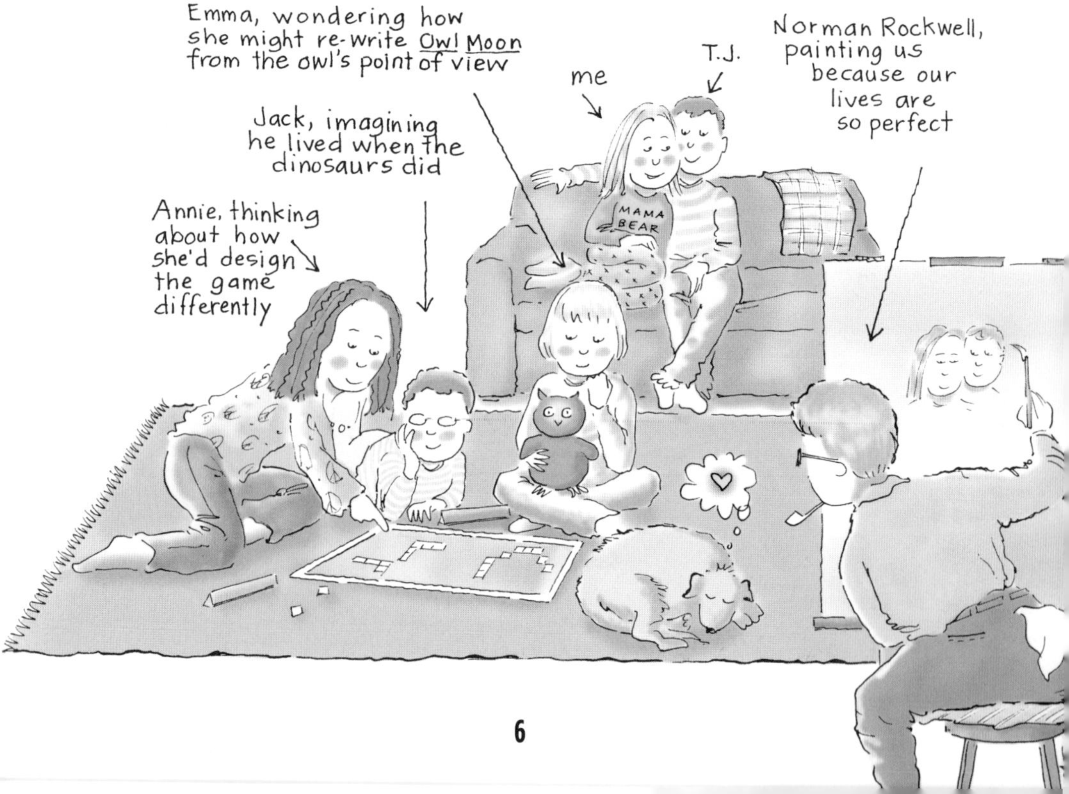
Emma, wondering how she might re-write Owl Moon from the owl's point of view
me
T.J.
Norman Rockwell, painting us because our lives are so perfect
Jack, imagining he lived when the dinosaurs did
Annie, thinking about how she'd design the game differently
MAMA BEAR

The girls let Jack win on

MEHR

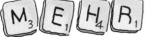

because he insisted it was a real word. ("It's the sound a baby triceratops makes!") Then, as Jack retreated into the Cretaceous Period, the rest of us played one of our favorite games: Turn-Down-The-Volume-on-the-TV-and-Make-Up-Your-Own-Words.

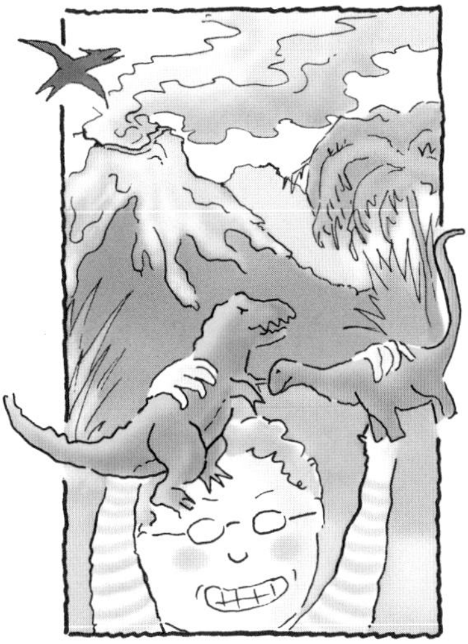

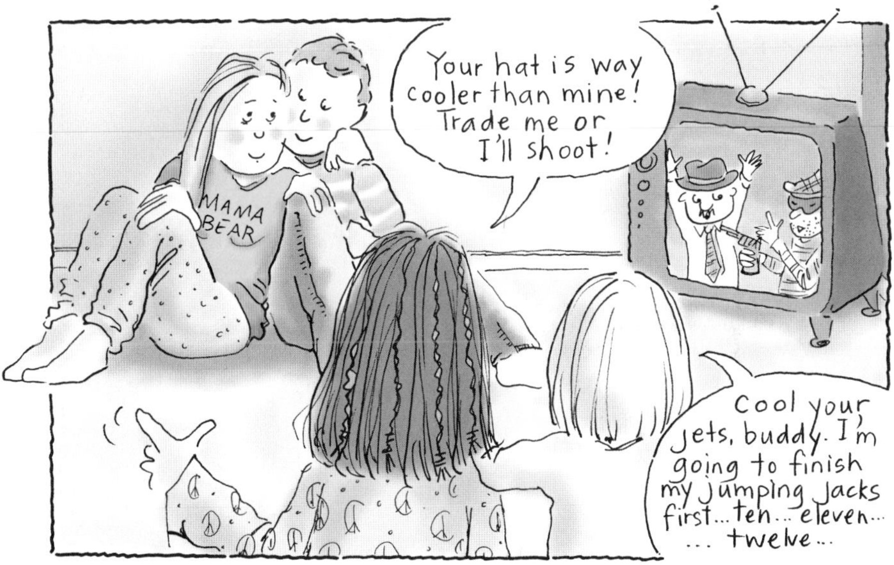
MAMA BEAR
Your hat is way cooler than mine! Trade me or I'll shoot!
Cool your jets, buddy. I'm going to finish my jumping jacks first... ten... eleven... ... twelve...

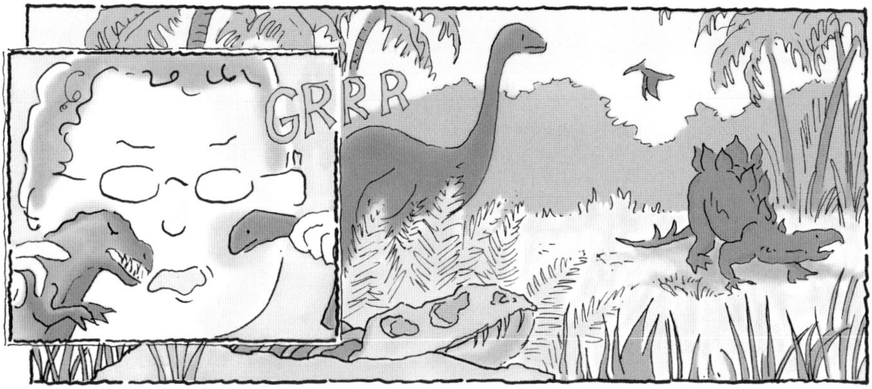
GRRR

We didn't play THIS game.

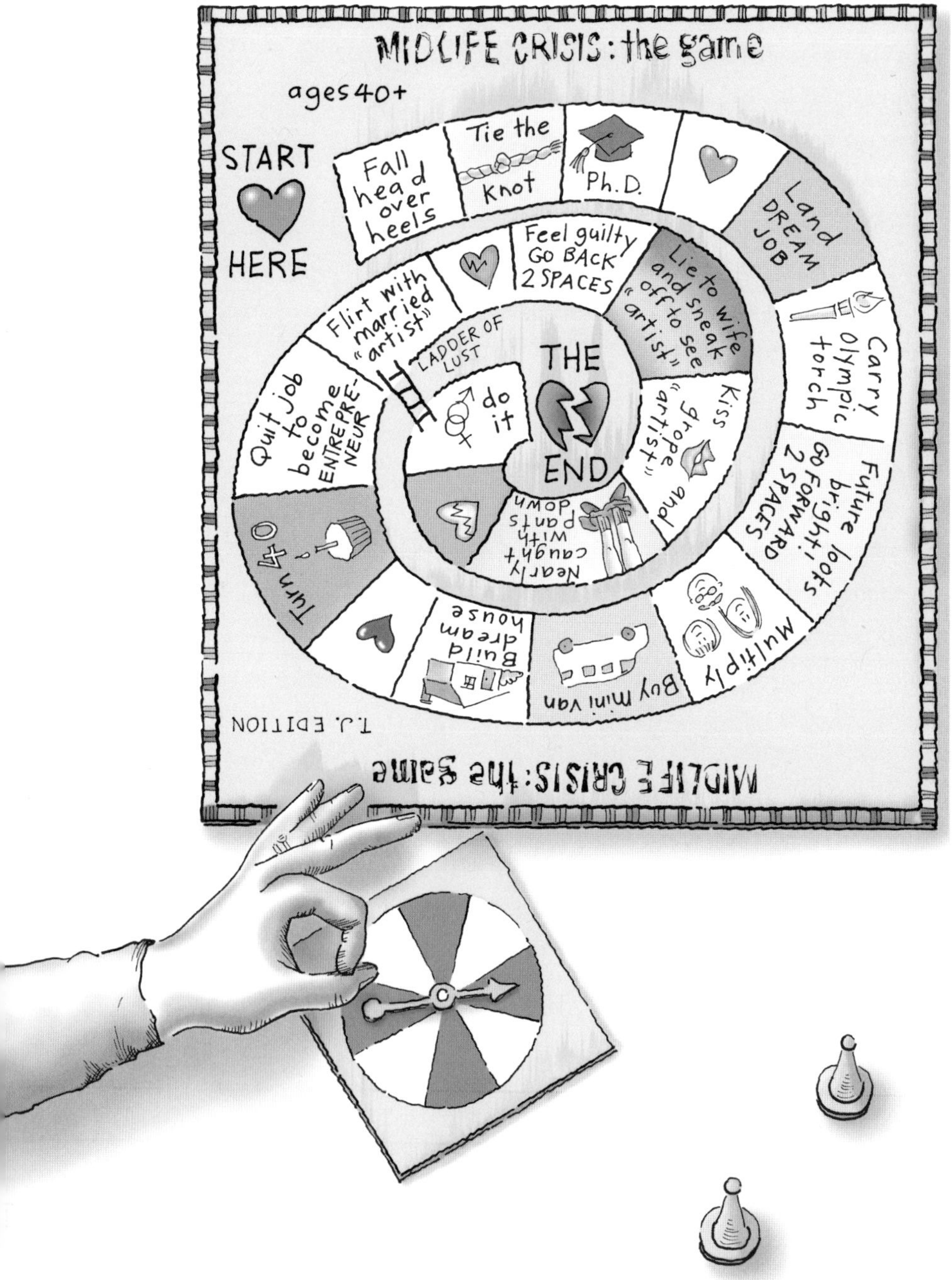
MIDLIFE CRISIS: the game
ages 40+
START HERE
Fall head over heels
Tie the Knot
Ph.D.
Land DREAM JOB
Carry olympic torch
Future bright: lots
Go FORWARD 2 SPACES
Multiply
Buy mini van
Build dream house
Turn 40
Quit job to become ENTREPRENEUR
Flirt with married "artist"
Feel guilty GO BACK 2 SPACES
Lie to wife and sneak off to see "artist"
Kiss, grope and "artist"
Nearly caught with pants down
LADDER OF LUST
do it
THE END
T.J. EDITION
MIDLIFE CRISIS: the game

If we had, the next day might not have come as such a shock.

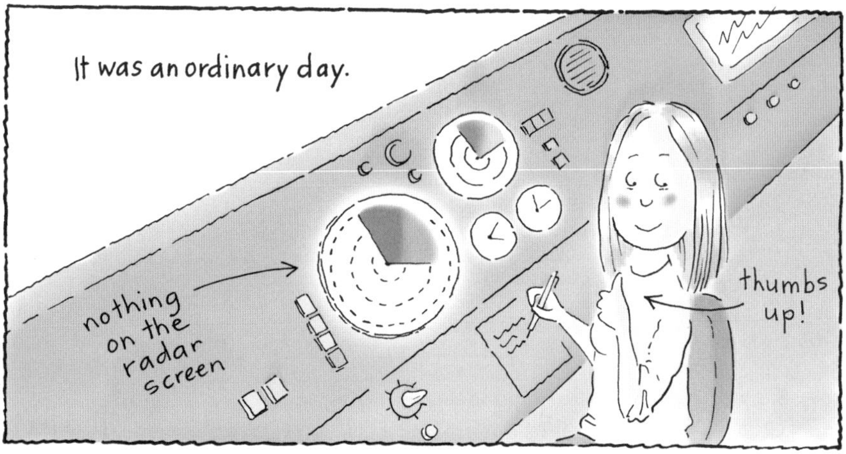
It was an ordinary day.
nothing on the radar screen
thumbs up!

(Beware of ordinary days.)

Annie was at hockey practice; Emma and Jack were upstairs playing. I had time to do some online research for a book that I was writing and check out recipes for dinner.

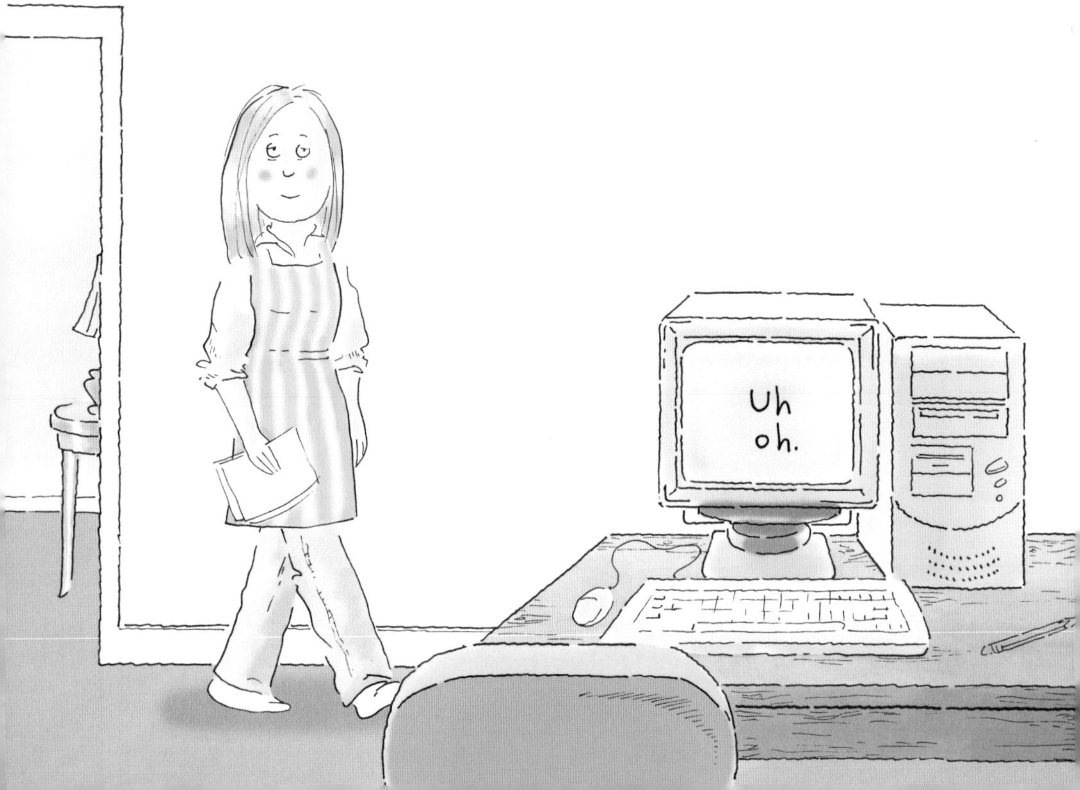
Uh oh.

It wasn't easy to find recipes that met all of the family requirements:

1. Heavy on carbs (T.J. was going on a long bike ride tomorrow.)

2. Vegetarian (Annie worked in a pet store after school and wouldn't eat animals.)

3. No squash, or anything resembling squash, including squash-colored cheese (Jack)

4. Nothing that required excessive chewing (Emma had just gotten braces.)

T.J. had left all sorts of pages up on the computer... Spreadsheets... chemical charts...financial calculations... I began clicking off of them...

GASP

Mom? Are you ok?

No.

The words on the computer screen didn't seem real. I must have hit the print button because suddenly the printer began clicking and whirring and spewing out paper. Page after page spilled out, one driving into the next like a pile-up on the highway. I prayed for the pages to be blank. Then maybe it wouldn't be true.

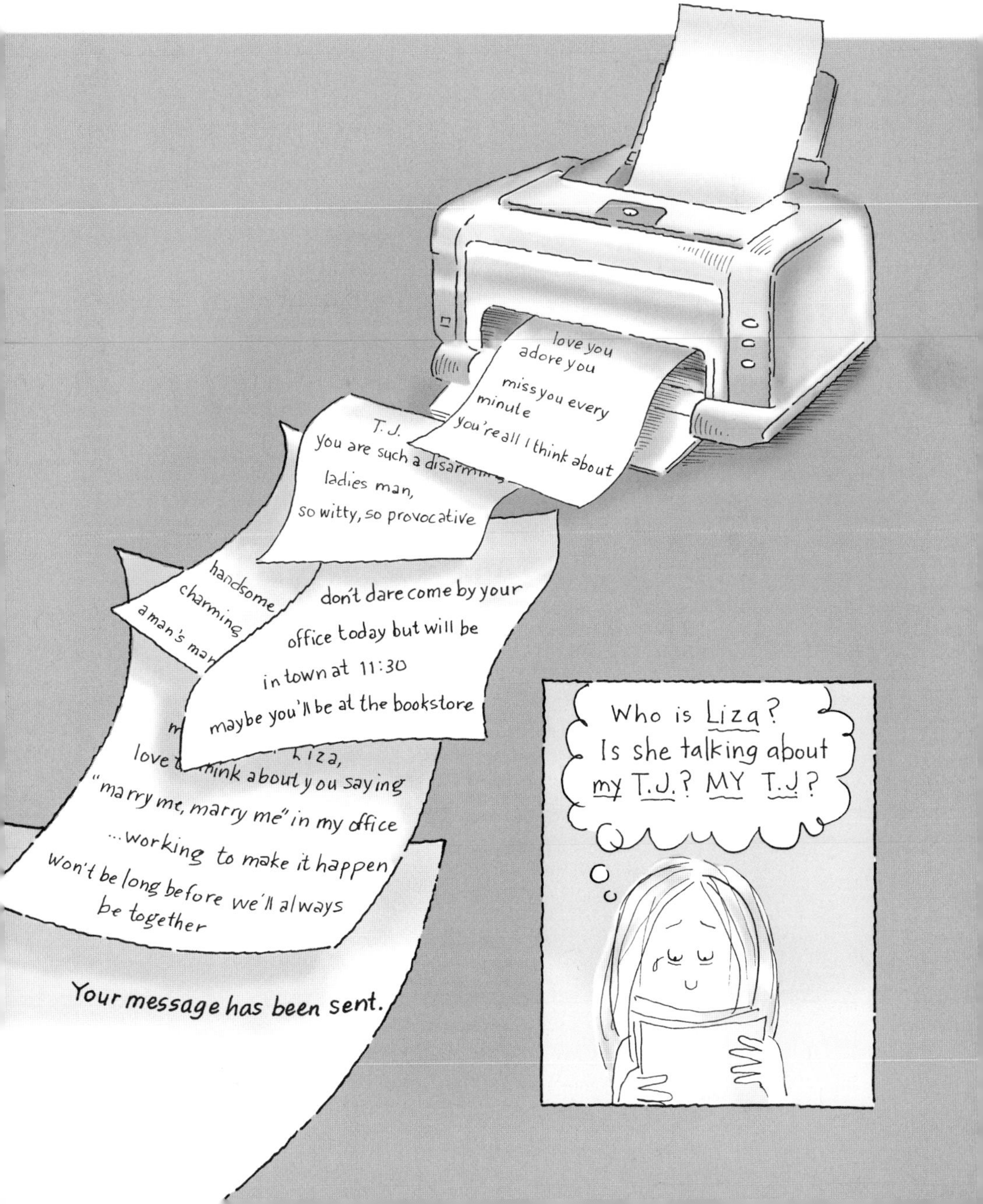
love you
adore you
miss you every minute
you're all I think about
T. J.
you are such a
ladies man,
so witty, so provocative
handsome
charming
don't dare come by your office today but will be in town at 11:30
maybe you'll be at the bookstore
"marry me, marry me" in my office
...working to make it happen
won't be long before we'll always be together
Your message has been sent.
Who is Liza?
Is she talking about my T.J.? MY T.J?

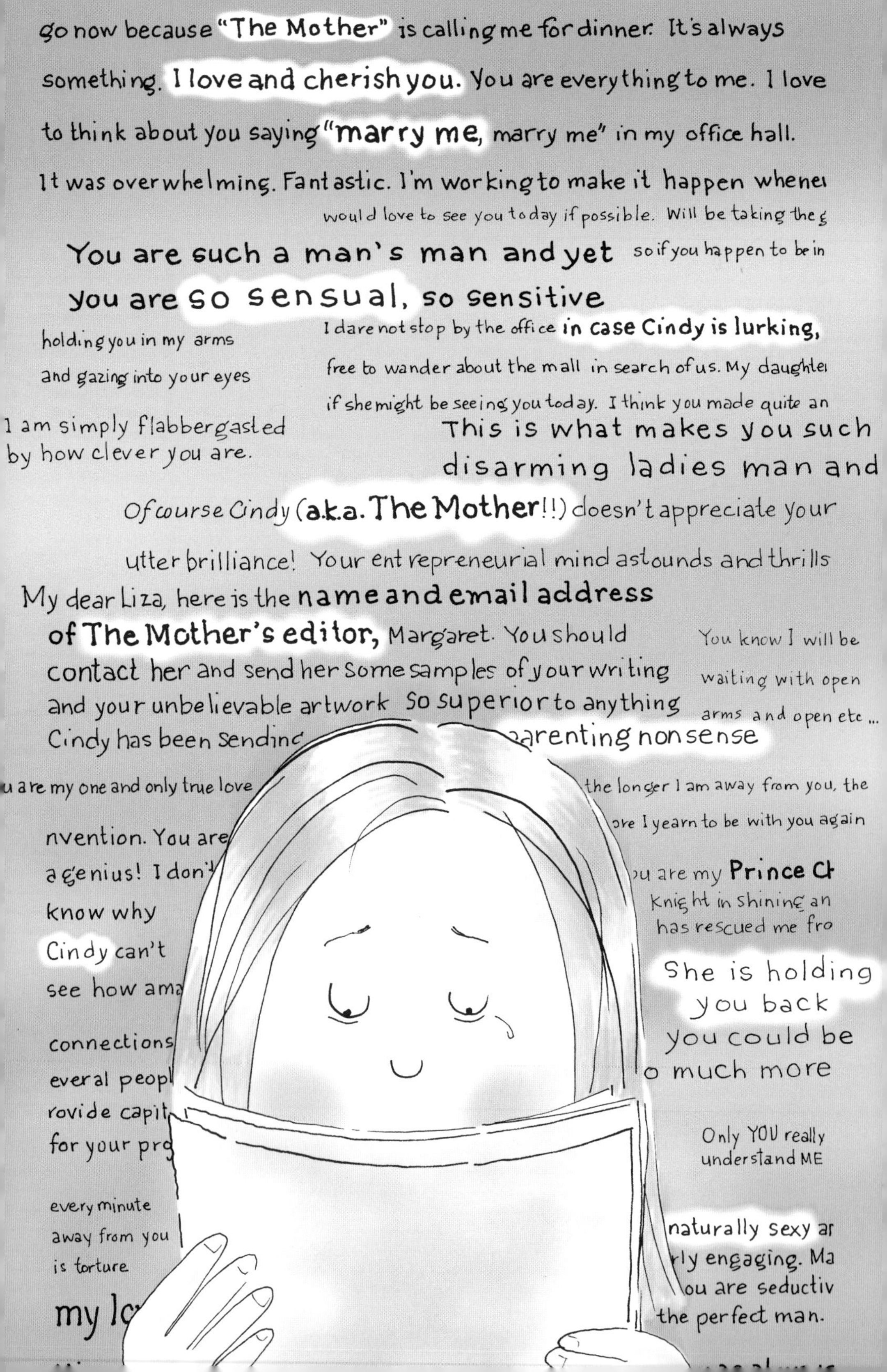
go now because "The Mother" is calling me for dinner. It's always
something. I love and cherish you. You are everything to me. I love
to think about you saying "marry me, marry me" in my office hall.
It was overwhelming. Fantastic. I'm working to make it happen whene
would love to see you today if possible. Will be taking the
You are such a man's man and yet
you are so sensual, so sensitive
so if you happen to be in
holding you in my arms
and gazing into your eyes
I dare not stop by the office in case Cindy is lurking,
free to wander about the mall in search of us. My daughte
if she might be seeing you today. I think you made quite an
I am simply flabbergasted
by how clever you are.
This is what makes you such
disarming ladies man and
Of course Cindy (a.k.a. The Mother!!) doesn't appreciate your
utter brilliance! Your entrepreneurial mind astounds and thrills
My dear Liza, here is the name and email address
of The Mother's editor, Margaret. You should
contact her and send her some samples of your writing
and your unbelievable artwork So superior to anything
Cindy has been sending
arenting nonsense
You know I will be
waiting with open
arms and open etc...
u are my one and only true love
the longer I am away from you, the
ore I yearn to be with you again
nvention. You are
a genius! I don'
know why
Cindy can't
see how ama
connections
everal peopl
rovide capit
for your pr
ou are my Prince C
Knight in shining ar
has rescued me fro
She is holding
you back
you could be
o much more
Only YOU really
understand ME
every minute
away from you
is torture
my lo
naturally sexy a
rly engaging. Ma
ou are seductiv
the perfect man.

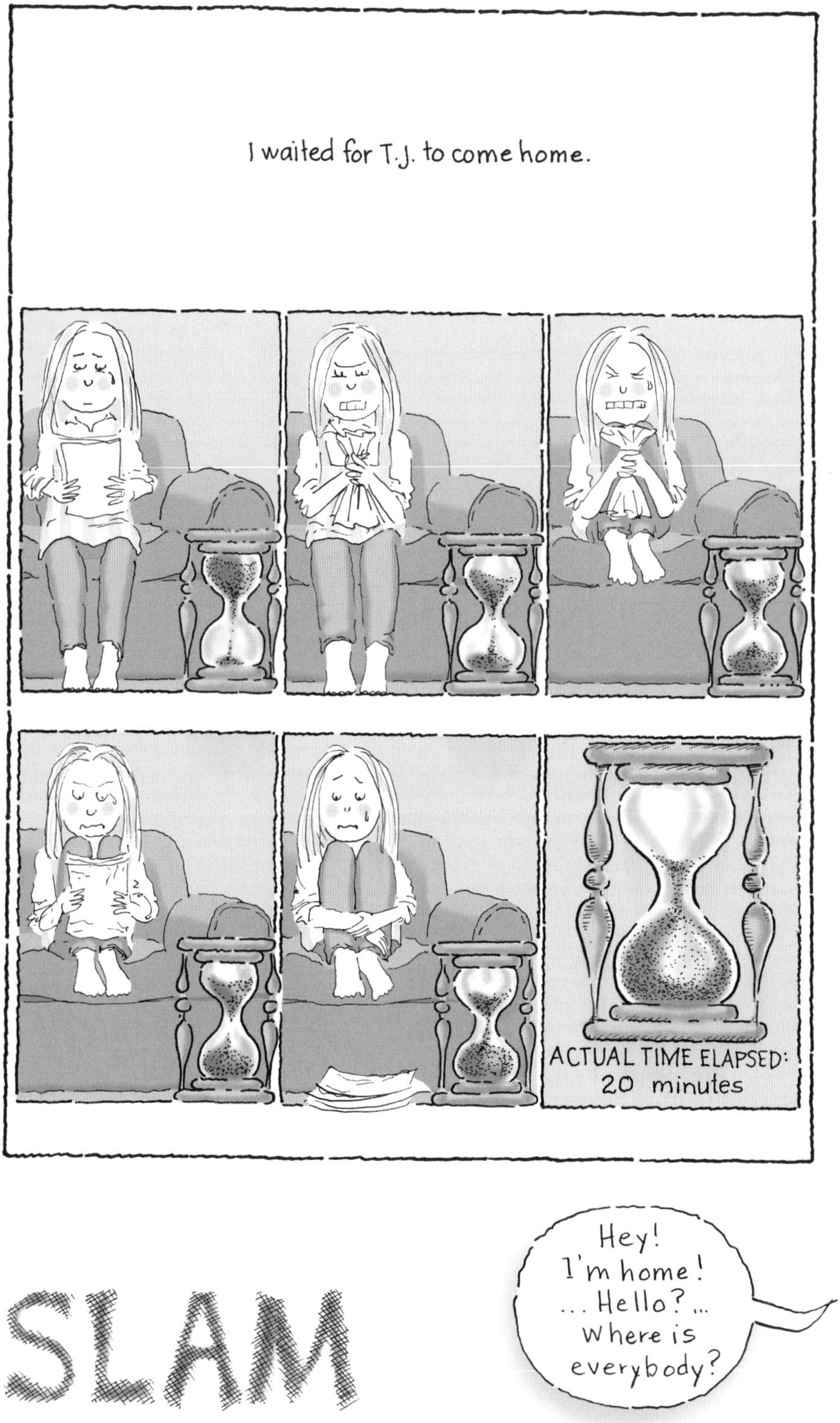
I waited for T.J. to come home.
ACTUAL TIME ELAPSED: 20 minutes
SLAM
Hey! I'm home! ... Hello? ... Where is everybody?

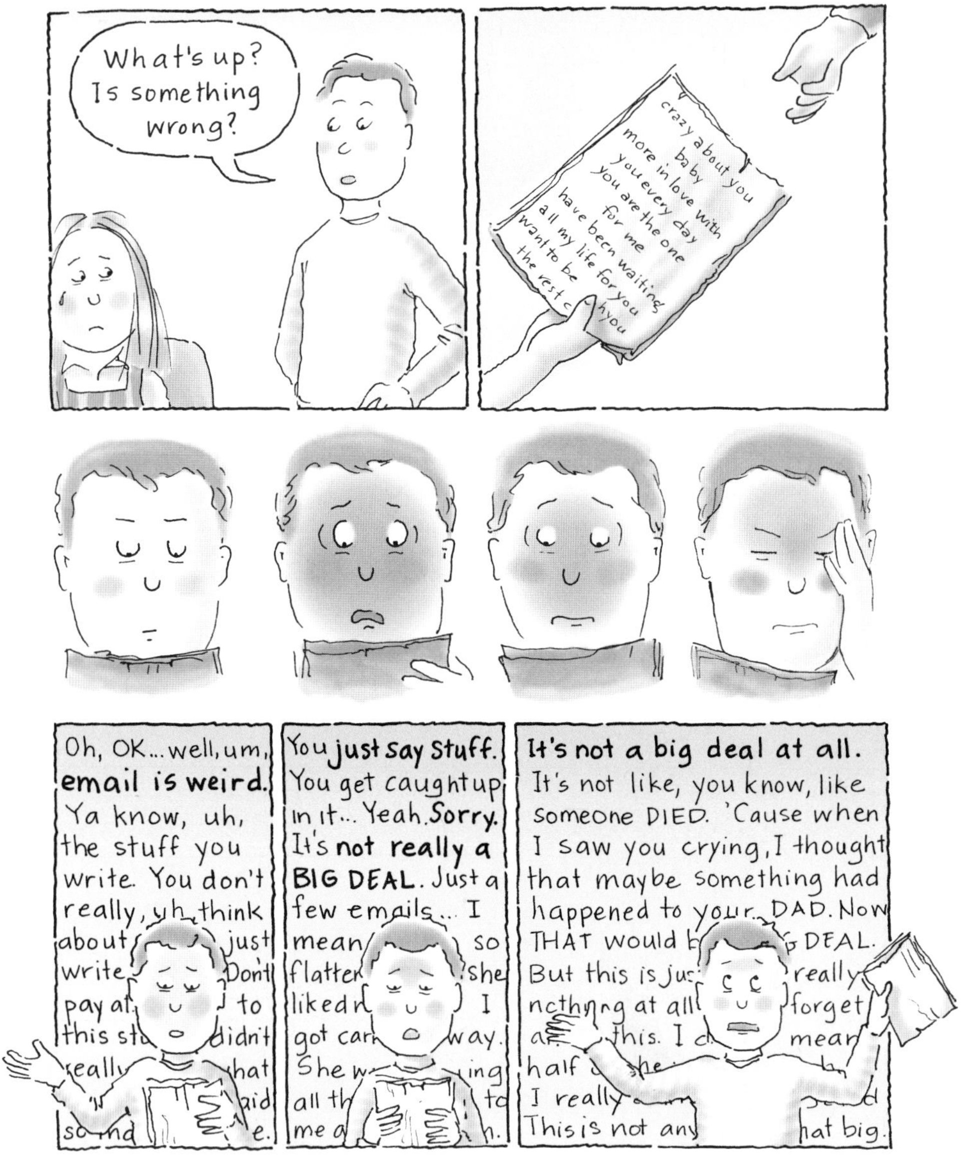
What's up? Is something wrong?
crazy about you
baby
more in love with
you every day
you are the one
for me
have been waiting
all my life for you
want to be
Oh, OK... well, um, email is weird. Ya know, uh, the stuff you write. You don't really, uh, think about
You just say stuff. You get caught up in it... Yeah. Sorry. It's not really a BIG DEAL. Just a few emails... I mean
It's not a big deal at all. It's not like, you know, like someone DIED. 'Cause when I saw you crying, I thought that maybe something had happened to your... DAD. Now THAT would

But it really was a big deal.

By any measure, it was a

MAJOR,

BIG-TIME,

SUPER COLOSSAL deal.

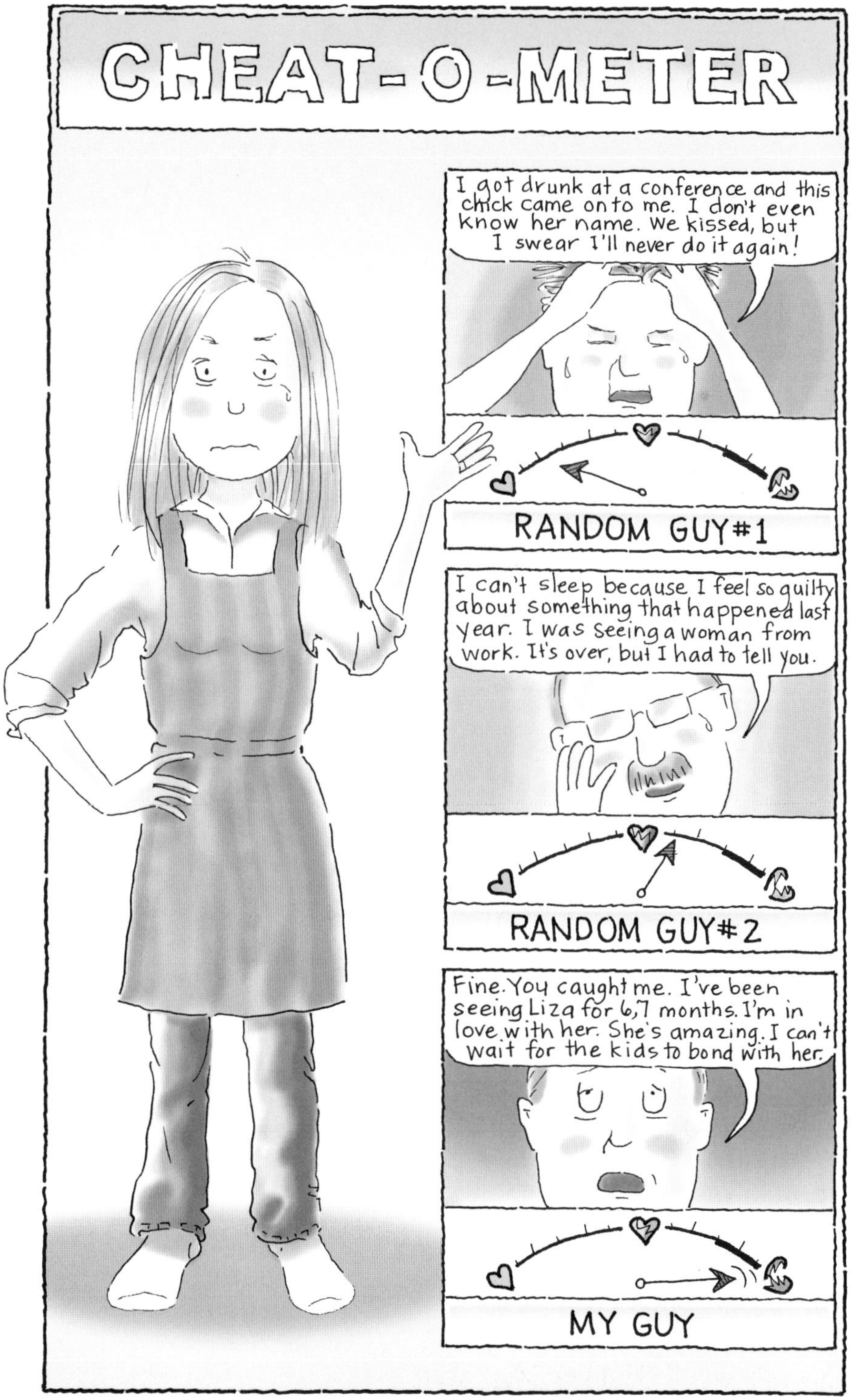
CHEAT-O-METER
I got drunk at a conference and this chick came onto me. I don't even know her name. We kissed, but I swear I'll never do it again!
RANDOM GUY #1
I can't sleep because I feel so guilty about something that happened last year. I was seeing a woman from work. It's over, but I had to tell you.
RANDOM GUY #2
Fine. You caught me. I've been seeing Liza for 6, 7 months. I'm in love with her. She's amazing. I can't wait for the kids to bond with her.
MY GUY

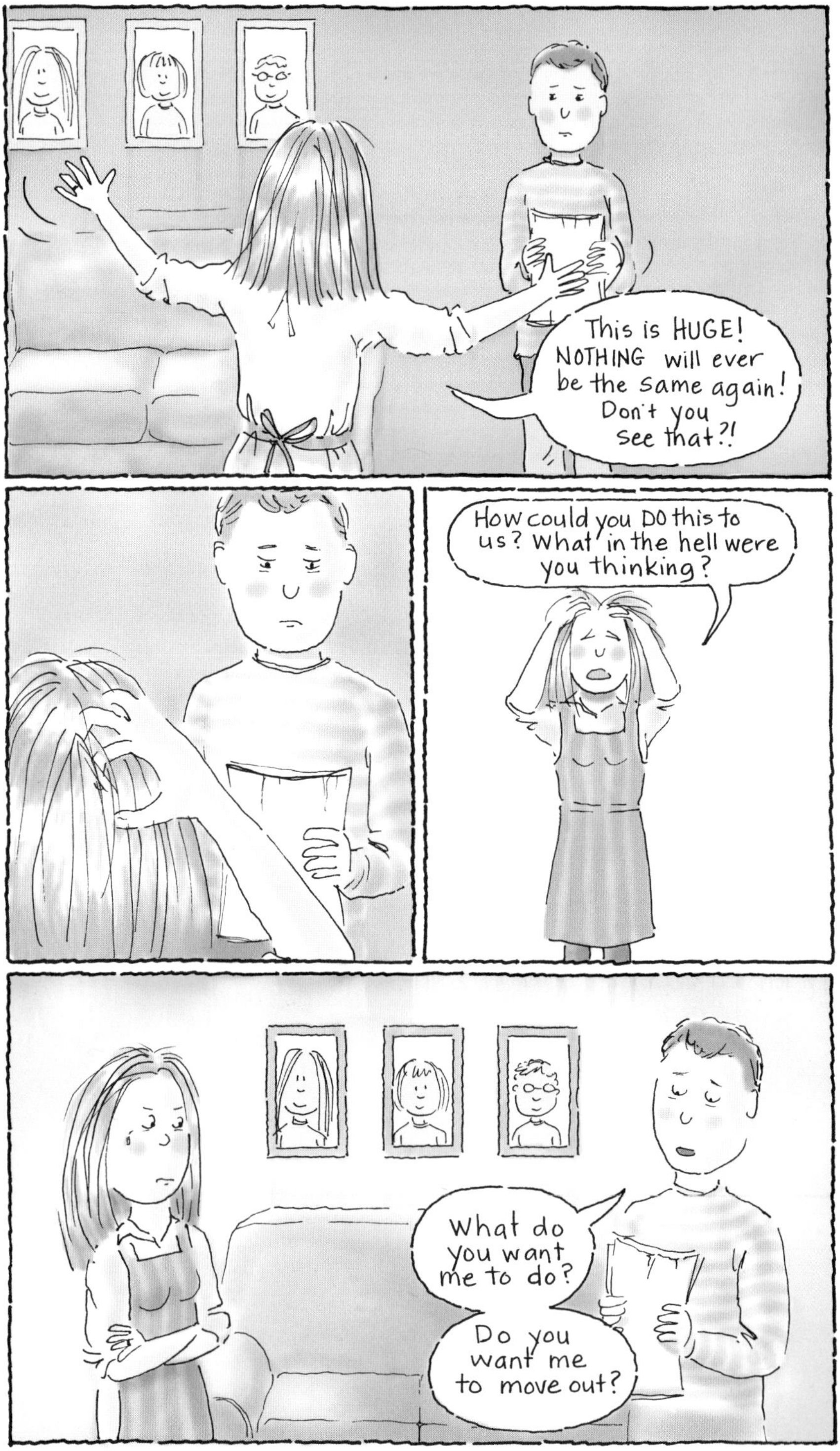
This is HUGE! NOTHING will ever be the same again! Don't you see that?!
How could you DO this to us? What in the hell were you thinking?
What do you want me to do?
Do you want me to move out?

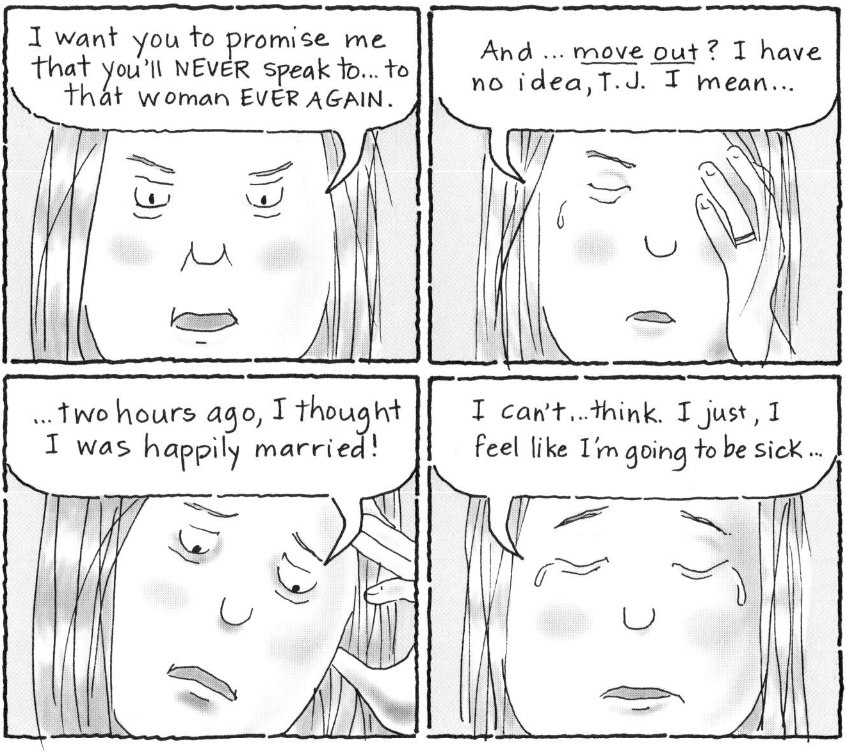
I want you to promise me that you'll NEVER speak to... to that woman EVER AGAIN.
And ... move out? I have no idea, T.J. I mean...
...two hours ago, I thought I was happily married!
I can't...think. I just, I feel like I'm going to be sick...

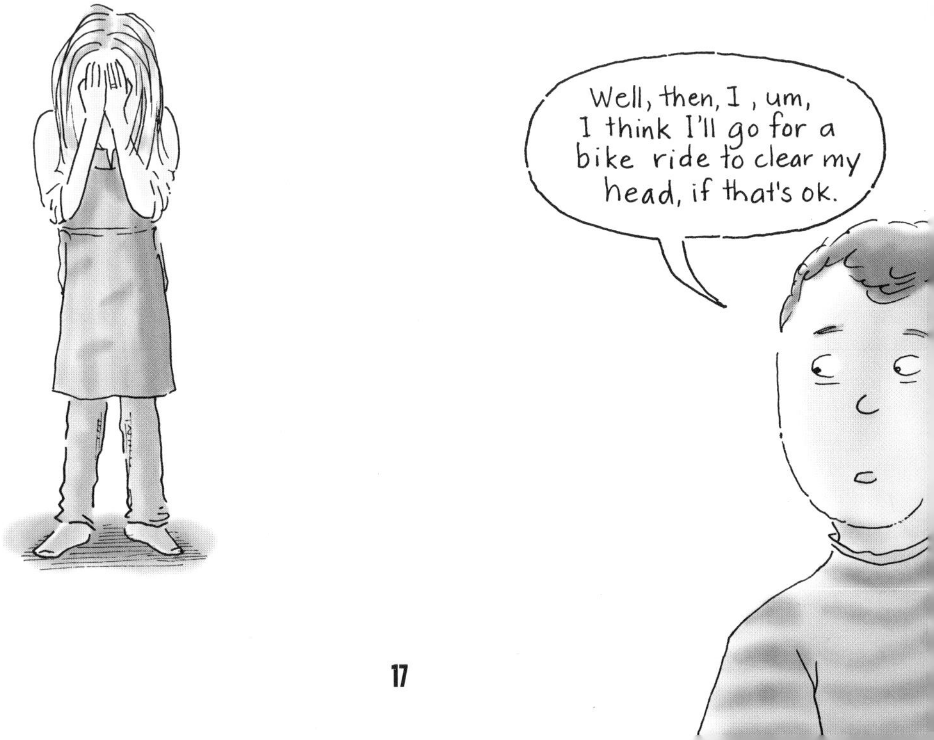
Well, then, I, um, I think I'll go for a bike ride to clear my head, if that's ok.

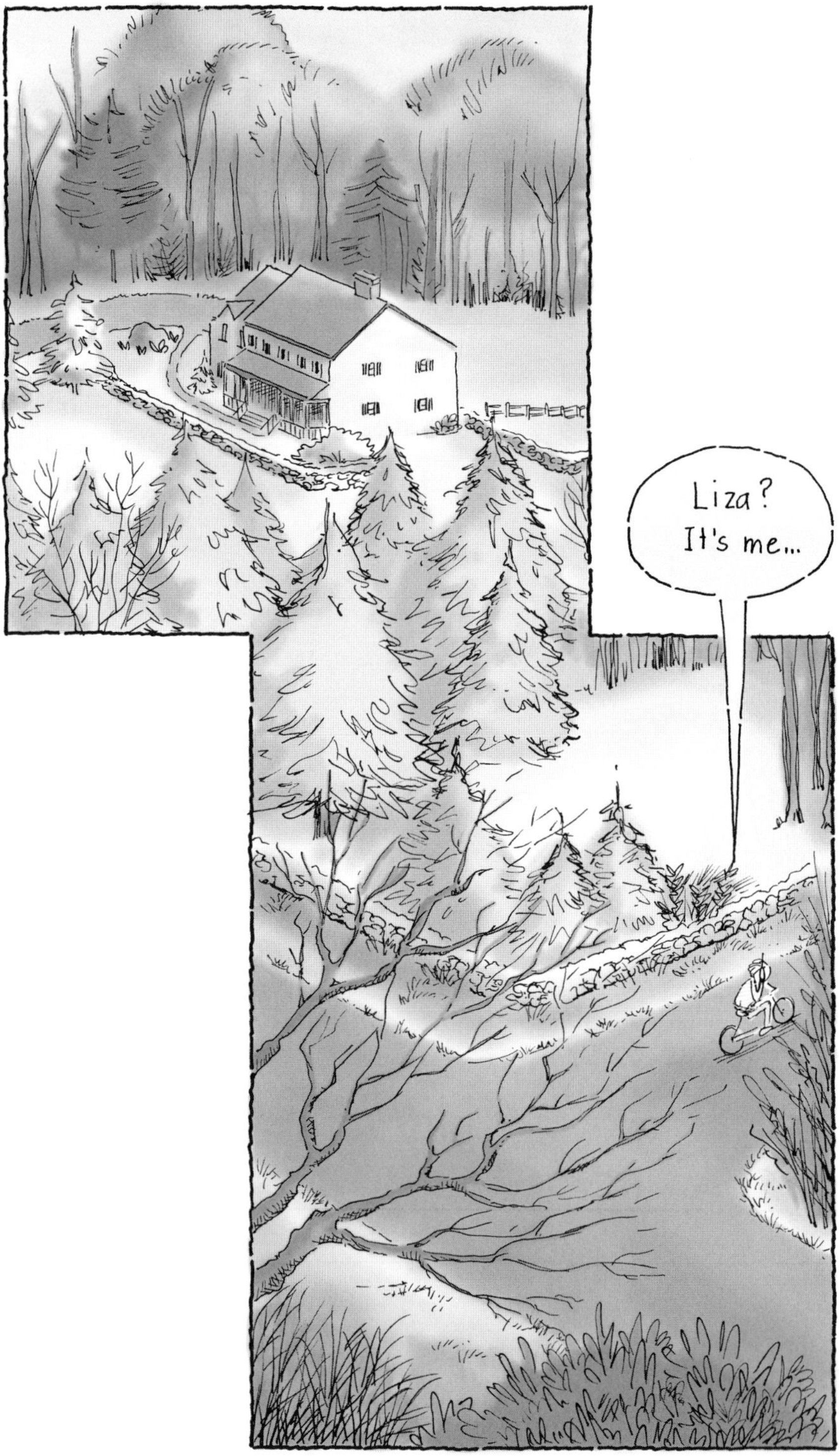
Liza? It's me...

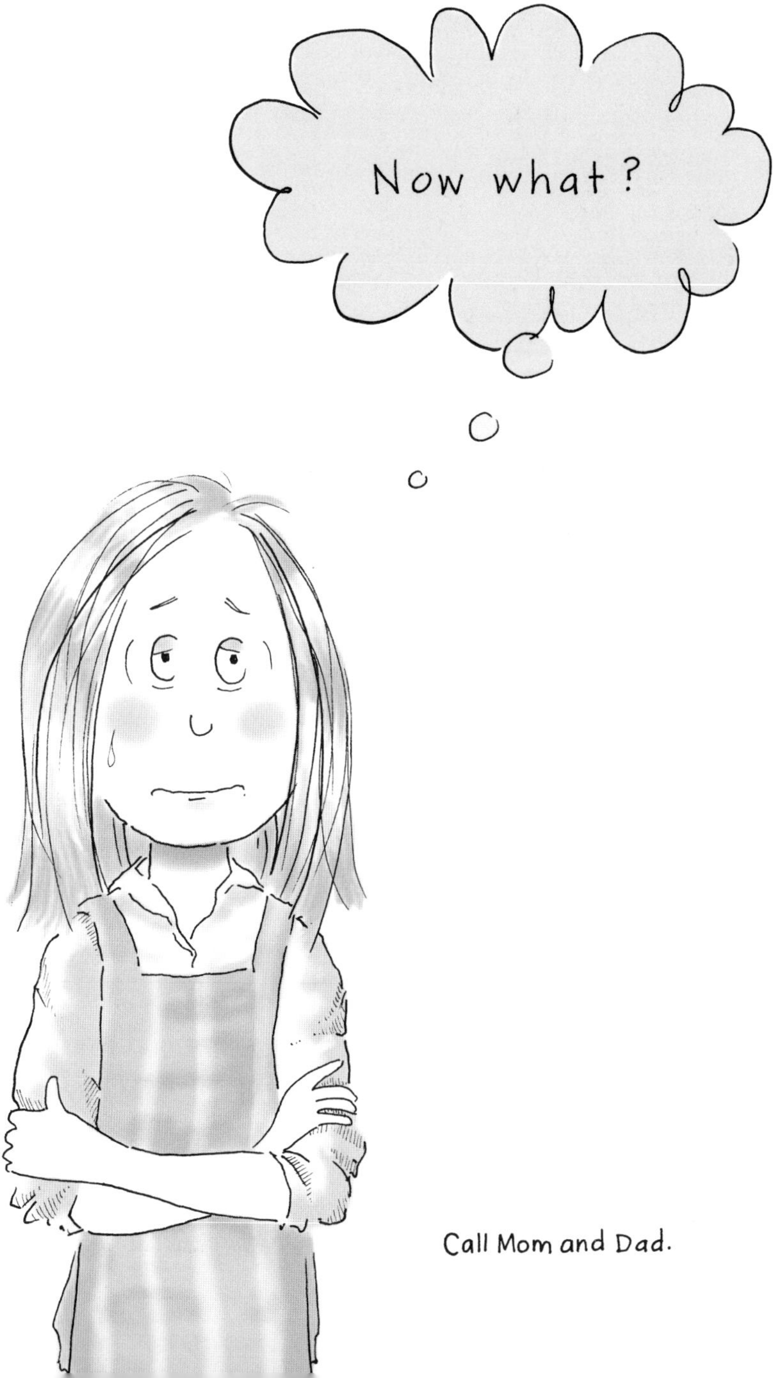
Now what?

Call Mom and Dad.

I call my parents whenever I'm in crisis. My mom administers the emotional remedy and my dad supplies the practical advice.

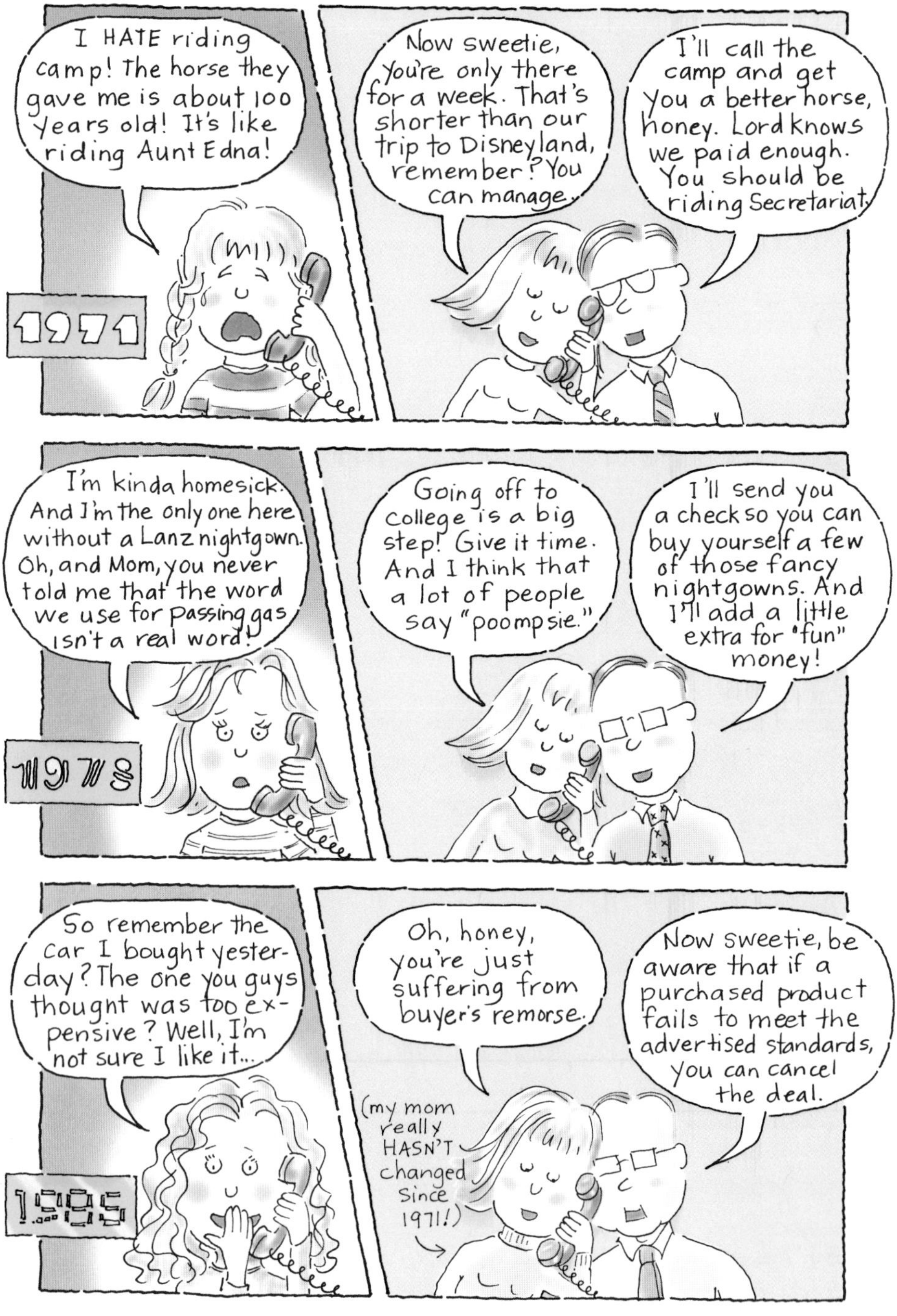
I HATE riding camp! The horse they gave me is about 100 years old! It's like riding Aunt Edna!
1971
Now sweetie, you're only there for a week. That's shorter than our trip to Disneyland, remember? You can manage.
I'll call the camp and get you a better horse, honey. Lord knows we paid enough. You should be riding Secretariat.
I'm kinda homesick. And I'm the only one here without a Lanz nightgown. Oh, and Mom, you never told me that the word we use for passing gas isn't a real word!
1978
Going off to college is a big step! Give it time. And I think that a lot of people say "poompsie."
I'll send you a check so you can buy yourself a few of those fancy nightgowns. And I'll add a little extra for "fun" money!
So remember the car I bought yesterday? The one you guys thought was too expensive? Well, I'm not sure I like it...
1985
Oh, honey, you're just suffering from buyer's remorse.
Now sweetie, be aware that if a purchased product fails to meet the advertised standards, you can cancel the deal.
(my mom really HASN'T changed since 1971!)

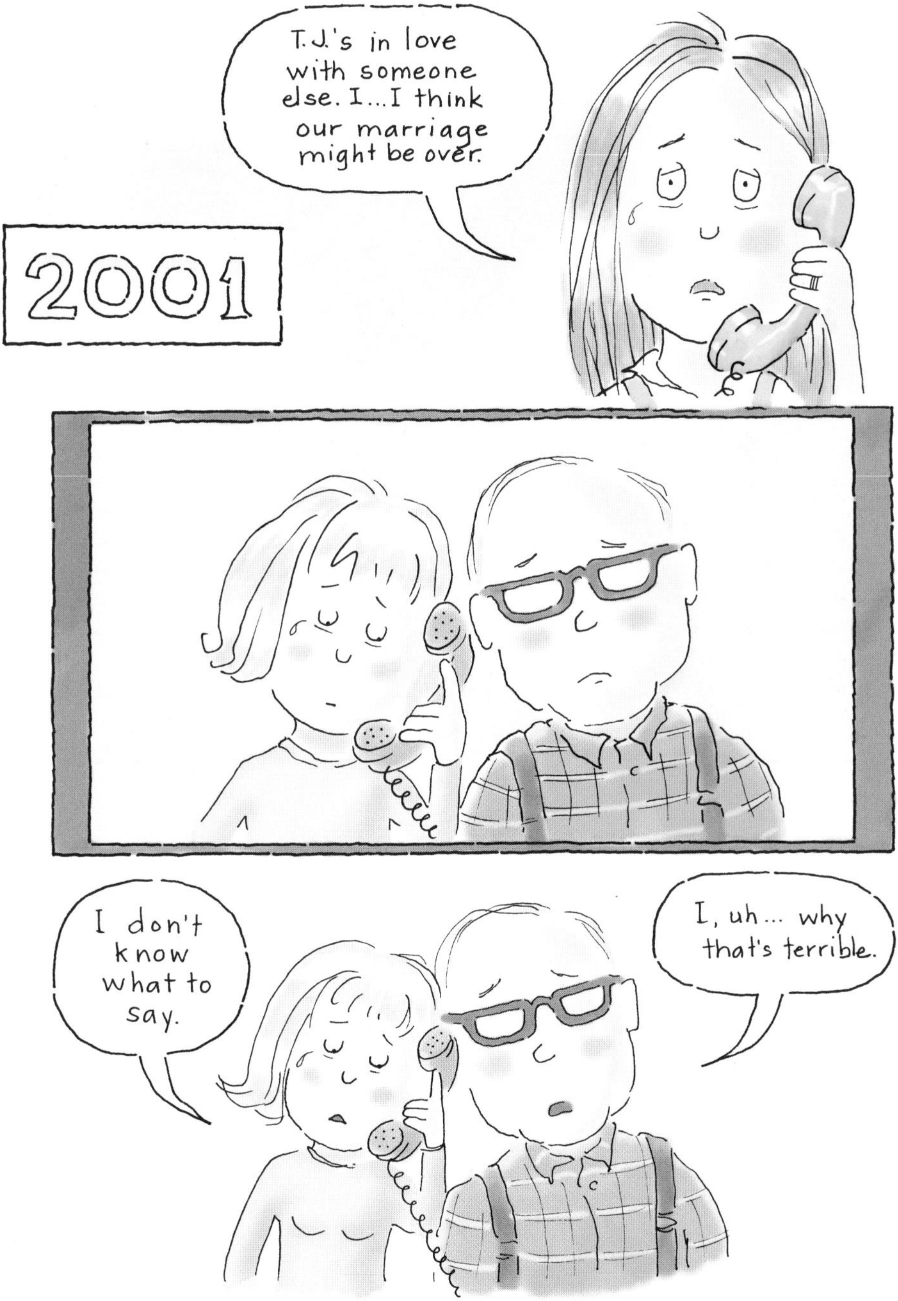
2001
T.J.'s in love with someone else. I...I think our marriage might be over.
I don't know what to say.
I, uh... why that's terrible.

But this one was just too big. My parents had no answers for me. I didn't know where else to turn.

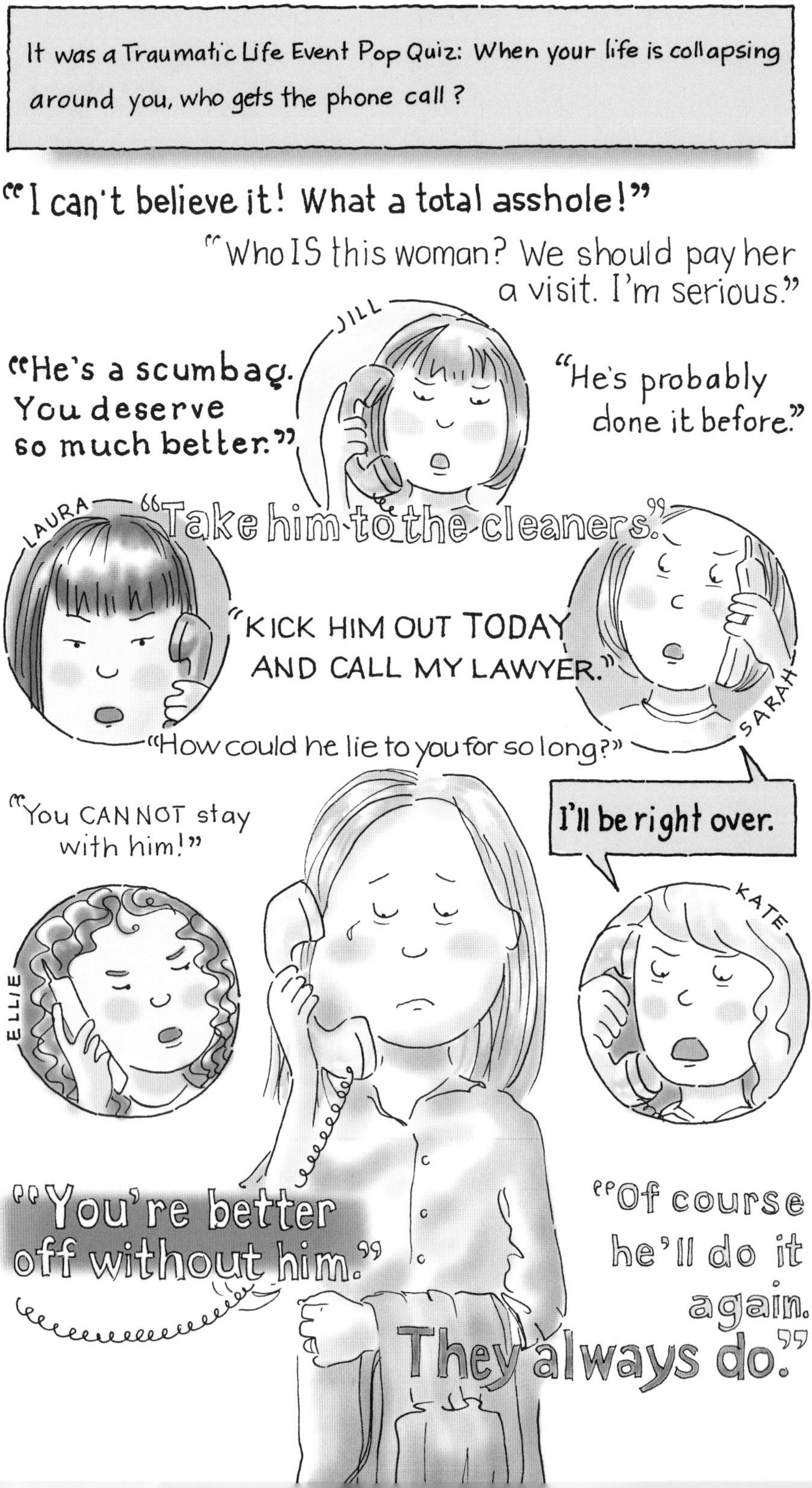
It was a Traumatic Life Event Pop Quiz: When your life is collapsing around you, who gets the phone call?
"I can't believe it! What a total asshole!"
"Who IS this woman? We should pay her a visit. I'm serious."
JILL
"He's a scumbag. You deserve so much better."
"He's probably done it before."
LAURA
"Take him to the cleaners."
"KICK HIM OUT TODAY AND CALL MY LAWYER."
SARAH
"How could he lie to you for so long?"
"You CAN NOT stay with him!"
I'll be right over.
KATE
ELLIE
"You're better off without him."
"Of course he'll do it again. They always do."

I waited outside for Sarah and Kate. I wanted to talk to them in the driveway so that the kids wouldn't overhear our conversation.

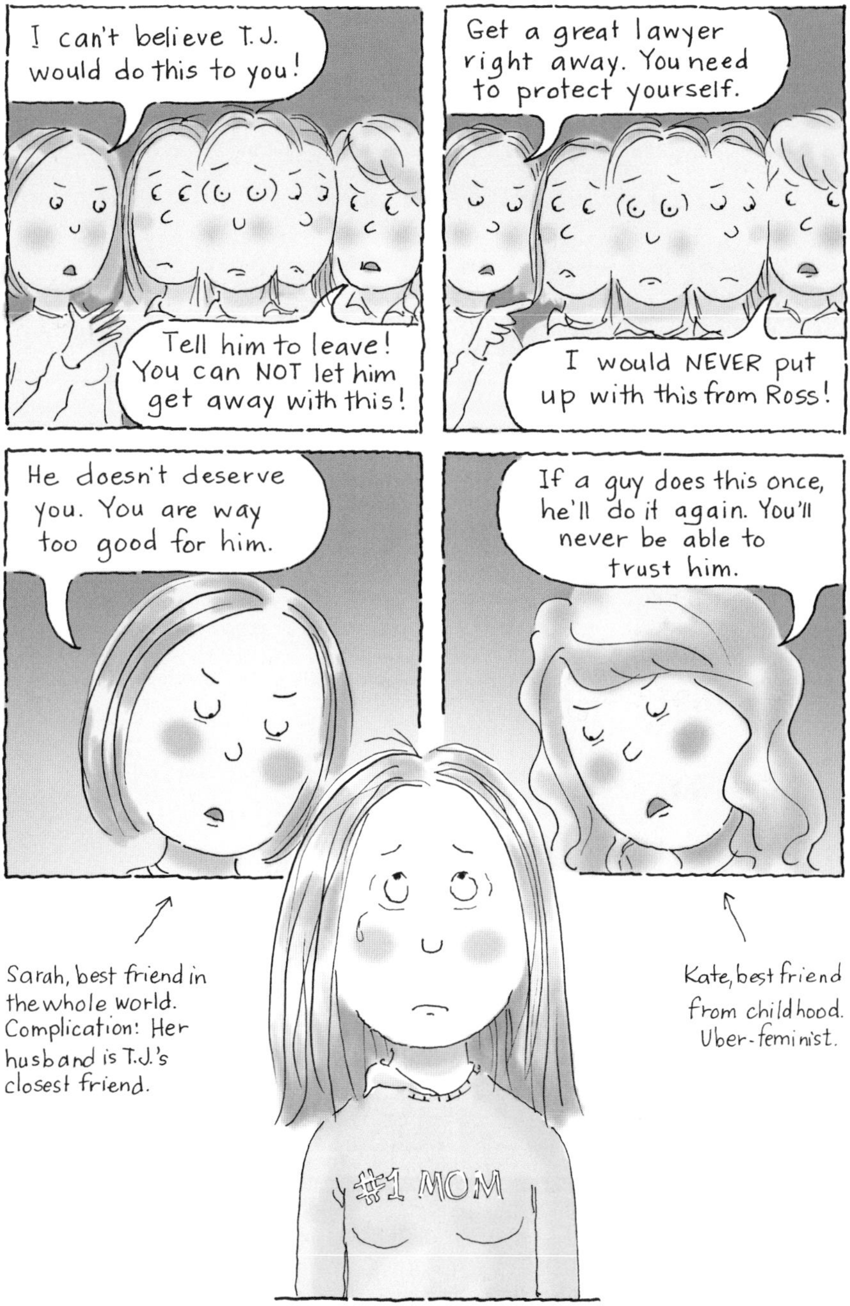
I can't believe T.J. would do this to you!
Tell him to leave! You can NOT let him get away with this!
Get a great lawyer right away. You need to protect yourself.
I would NEVER put up with this from Ross!
He doesn't deserve you. You are way too good for him.
If a guy does this once, he'll do it again. You'll never be able to trust him.
Sarah, best friend in the whole world. Complication: Her husband is T.J.'s closest friend.
Kate, best friend from childhood. Uber-feminist.
#1 MOM

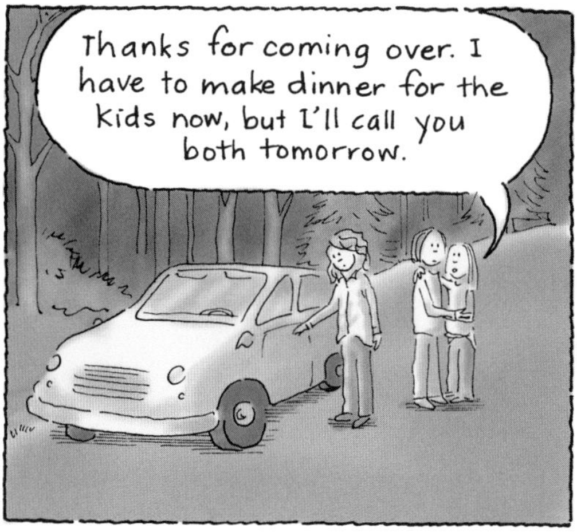
Thanks for coming over. I have to make dinner for the kids now, but I'll call you both tomorrow.

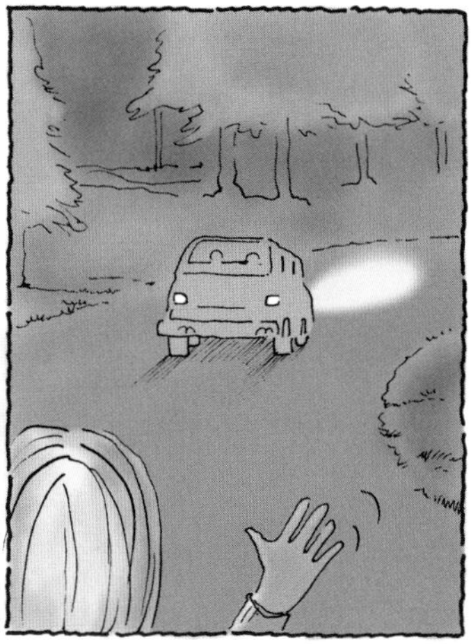

I normally listened to my own voice but that day my thoughts became entangled in everyone else's. After my friends left, their words stayed with me.

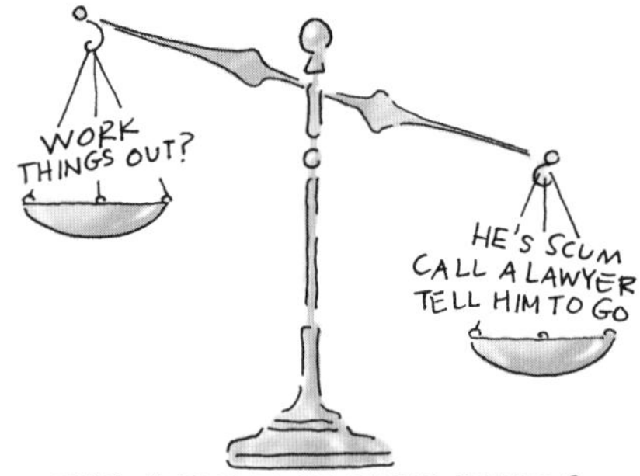
WORK THINGS OUT?
HE'S SCUM
CALL A LAWYER
TELL HIM TO GO

THE WEIGHT OF THEIR WORDS

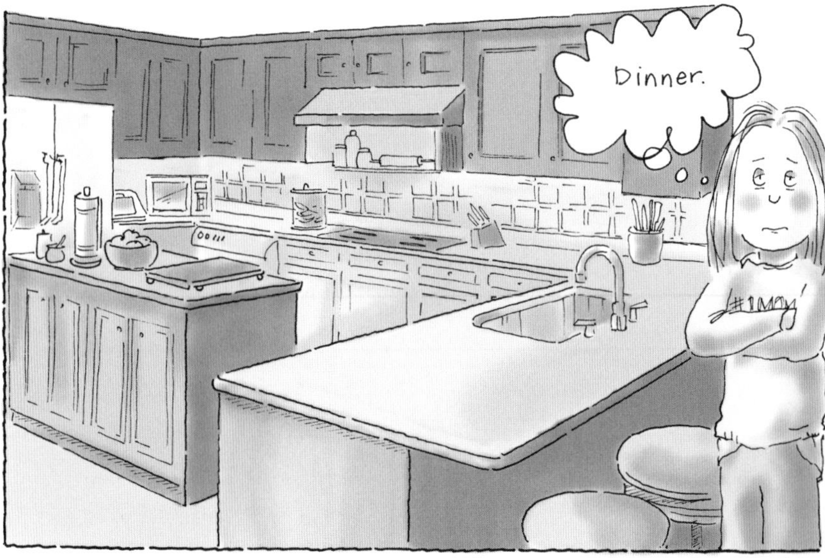
Dinner.
#1MOM

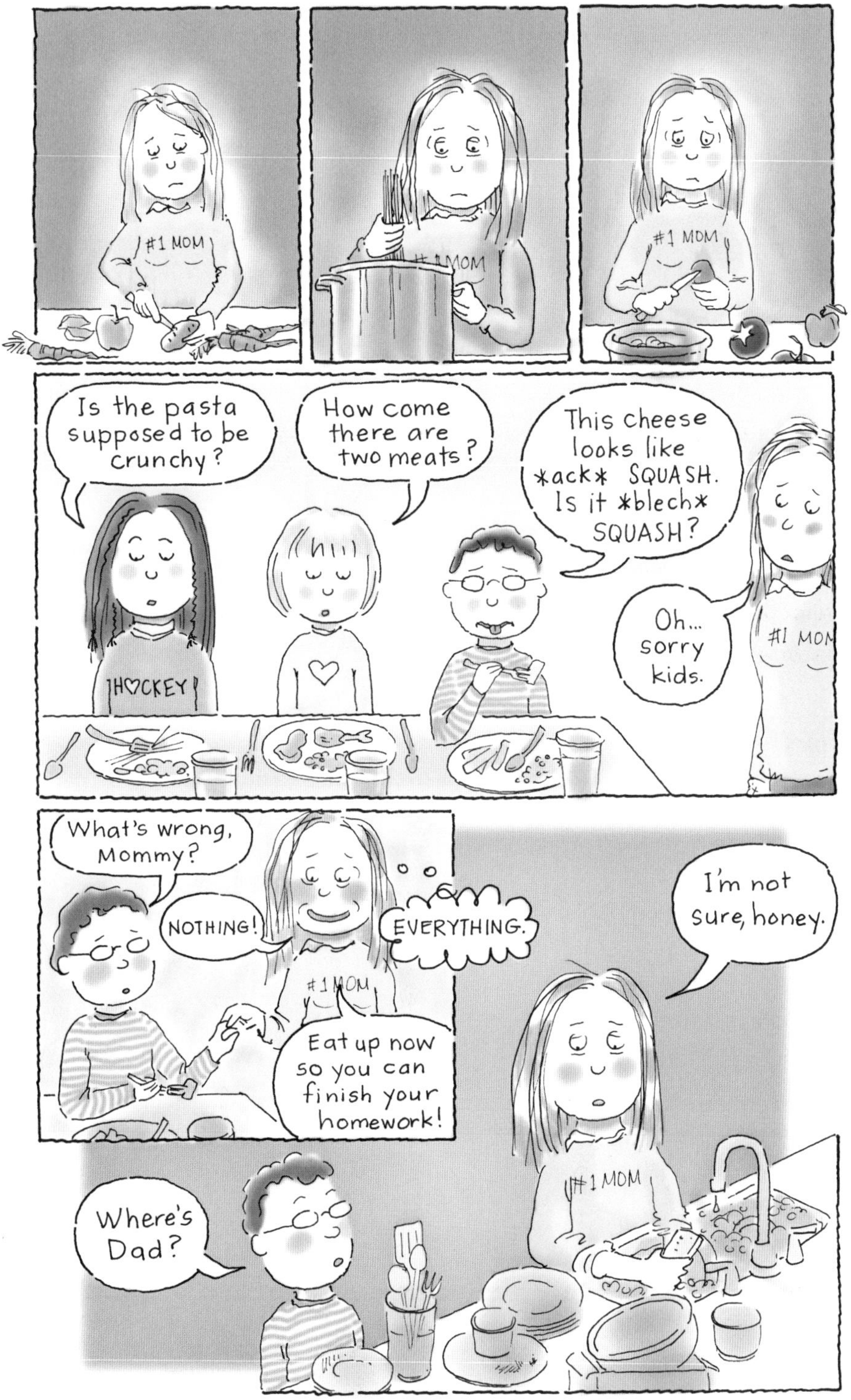
#1 MOM
#1 MOM
#1 MOM
Is the pasta supposed to be crunchy?
How come there are two meats?
This cheese looks like *ack* SQUASH. Is it *blech* SQUASH?
Oh... sorry kids.
HOCKEY
#1 MOM
What's wrong, Mommy?
NOTHING!
EVERYTHING.
#1 MOM
Eat up now so you can finish your homework!
I'm not sure, honey.
#1 MOM
Where's Dad?

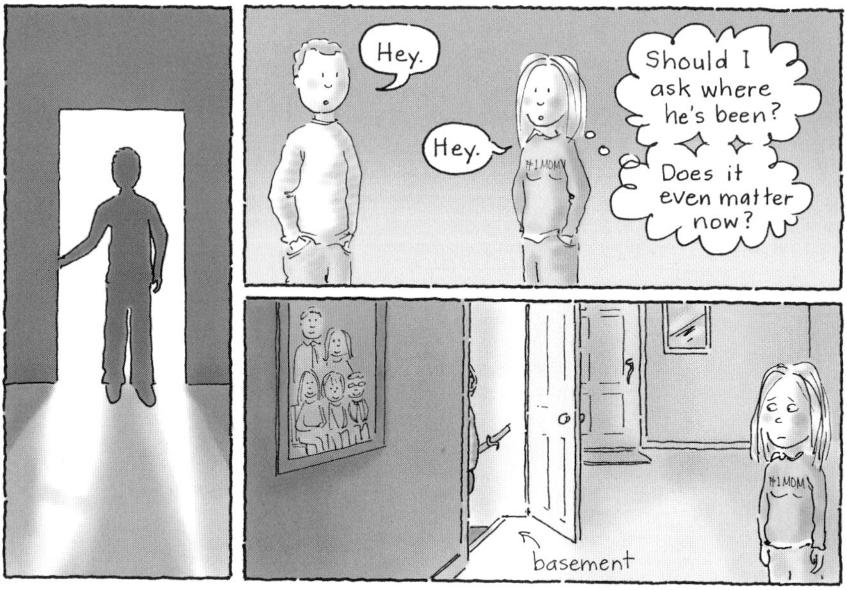
Hey.
Hey.
#1MOM
Should I ask where he's been?
Does it even matter now?
basement
#1MOM

After I tucked the kids in that night, I got into bed, exhausted. But sleep was not going to come easily.

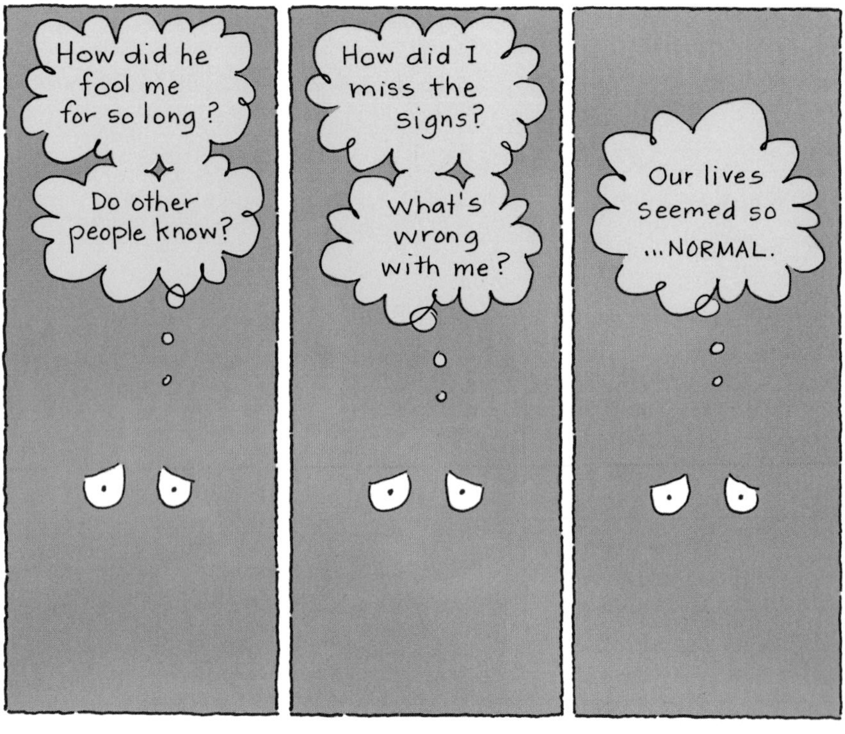
How did he fool me for so long?
Do other people know?
How did I miss the signs?
What's wrong with me?
Our lives seemed so ...NORMAL.

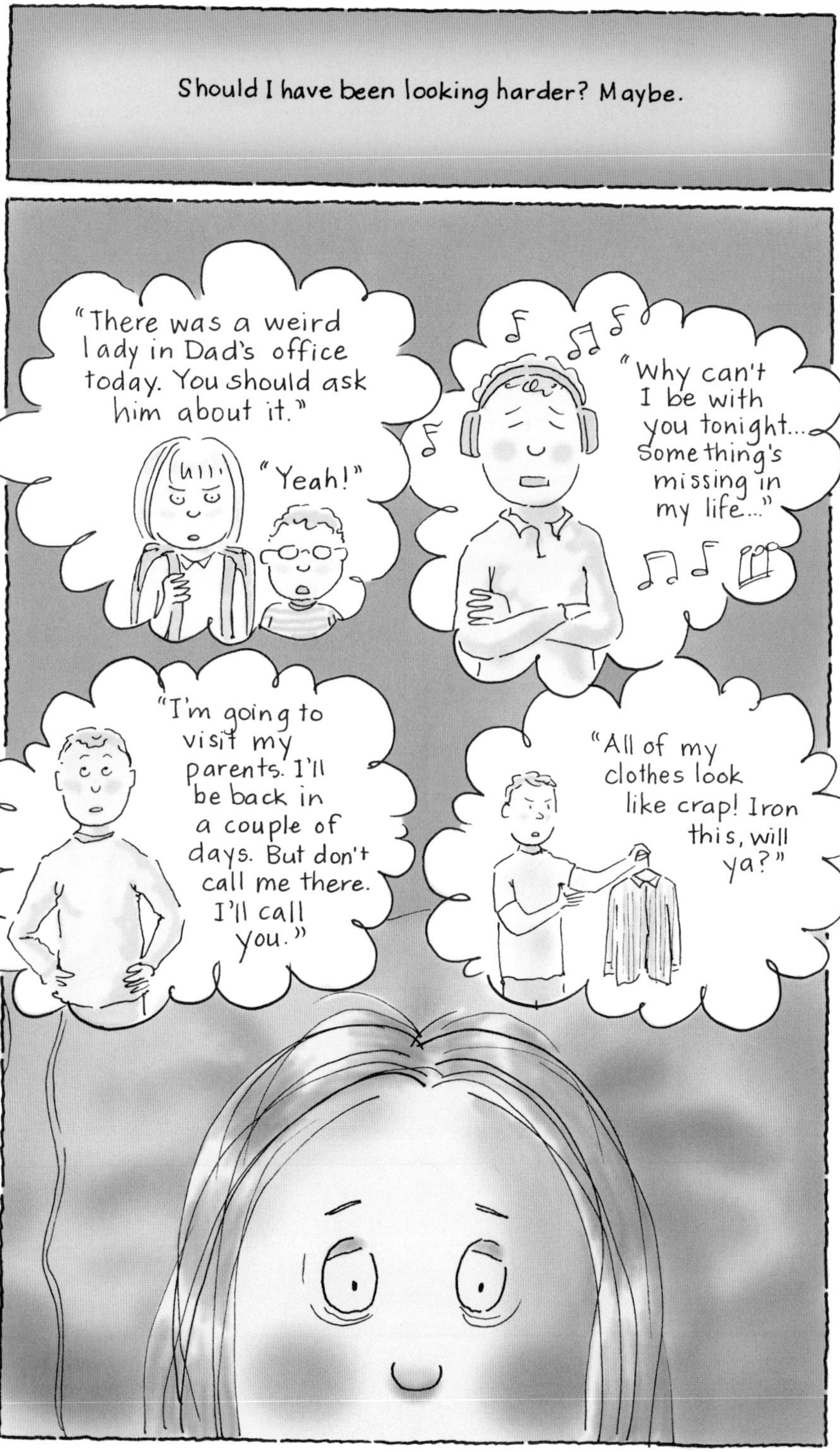
Should I have been looking harder? Maybe.
"There was a weird lady in Dad's office today. You should ask him about it."
"Yeah!"
"Why can't I be with you tonight... Something's missing in my life..."
"I'm going to visit my parents. I'll be back in a couple of days. But don't call me there. I'll call you."
"All of my clothes look like crap! Iron this, will ya?"

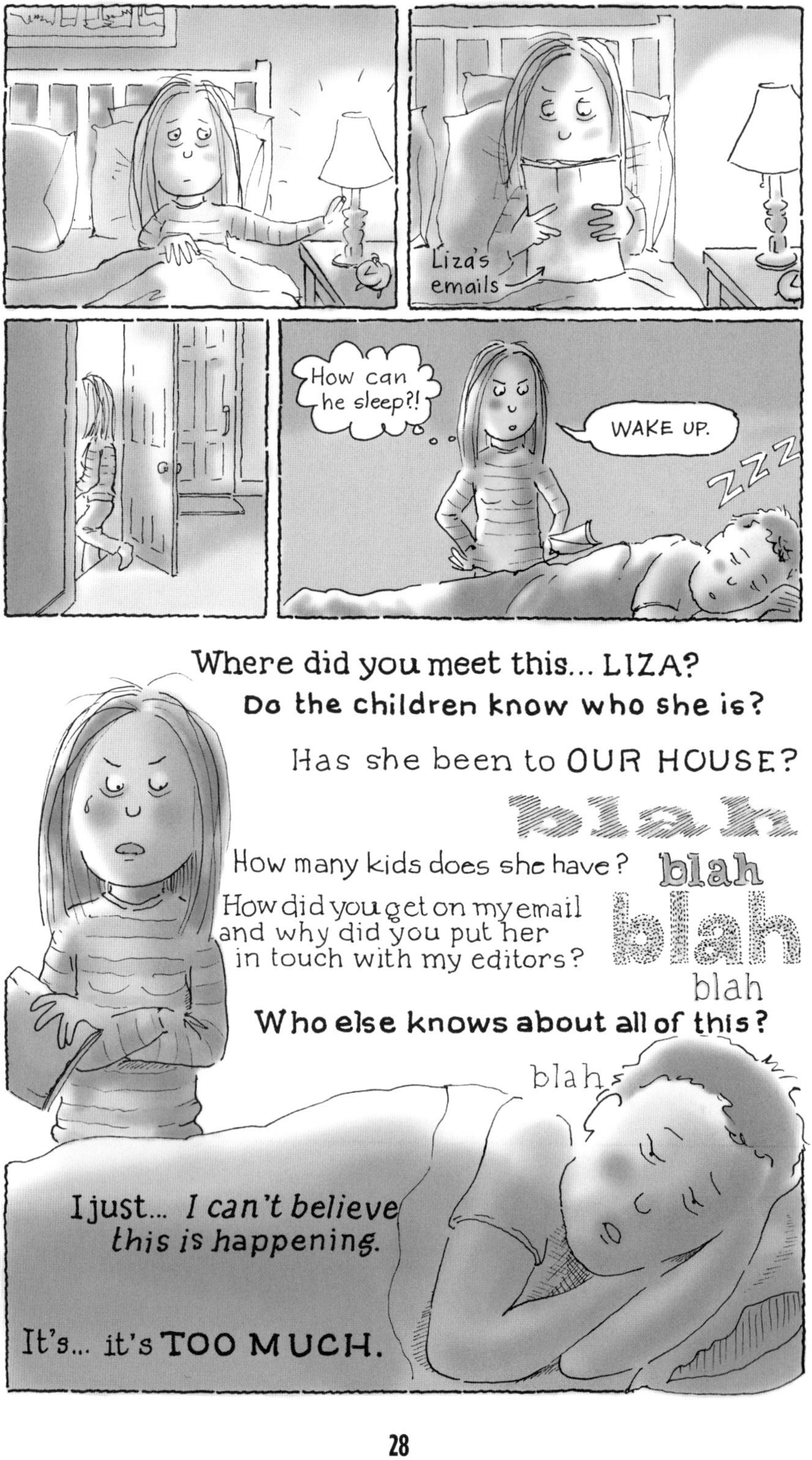
Liza's emails
How can he sleep?!
WAKE UP.
ZZZ
Where did you meet this... LIZA?
Do the children know who she is?
Has she been to OUR HOUSE?
blah
How many kids does she have?
blah
How did you get on my email and why did you put her in touch with my editors?
blah
blah
Who else knows about all of this?
blah
I just... I can't believe this is happening.
It's... it's TOO MUCH.

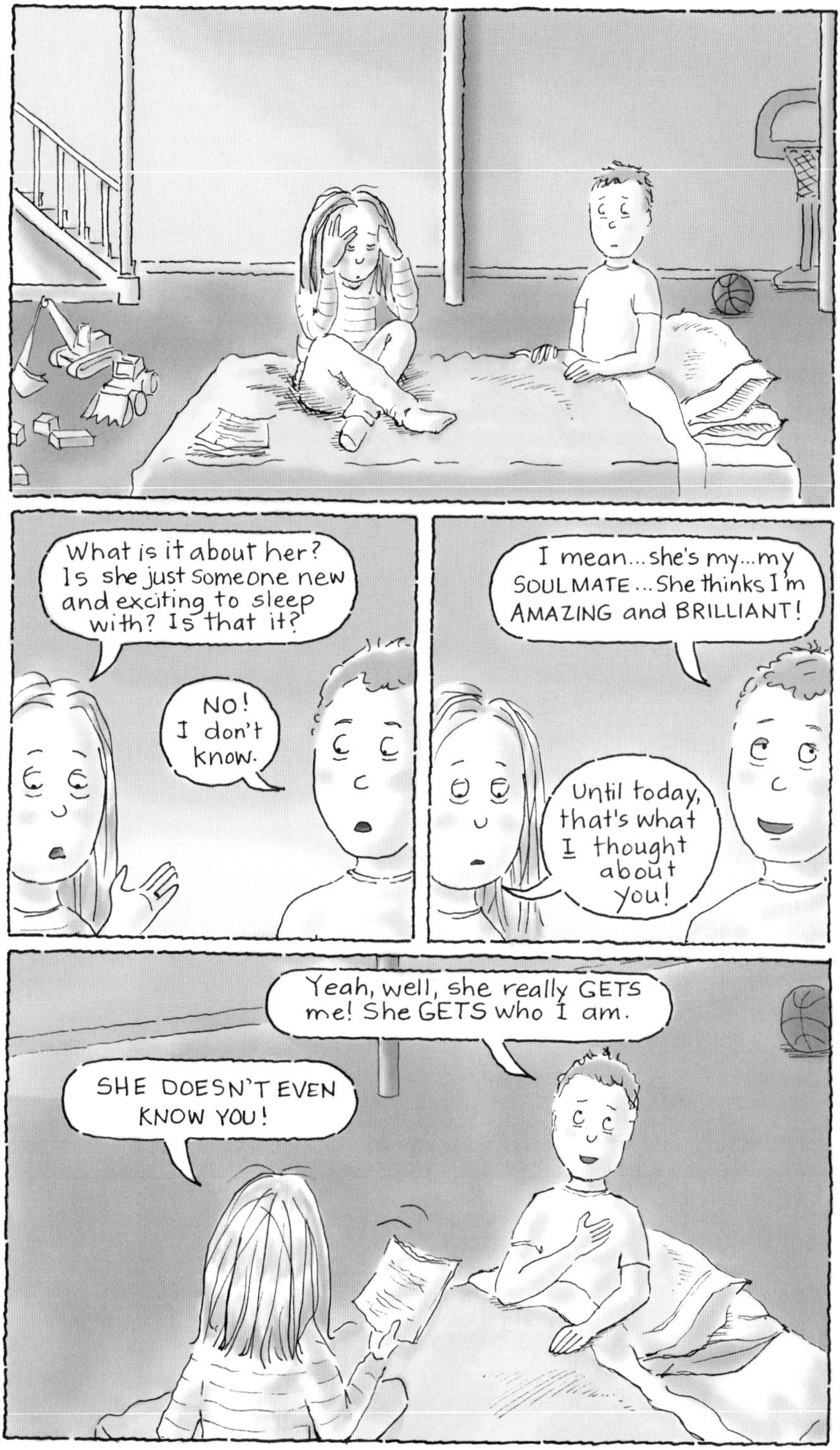
What is it about her? Is she just someone new and exciting to sleep with? Is that it?
No! I don't know.
I mean...she's my...my SOULMATE...She thinks I'm AMAZING and BRILLIANT!
Until today, that's what I thought about you!
Yeah, well, she really GETS me! She GETS who I am.
SHE DOESN'T EVEN KNOW YOU!

What is T.J.'s greatest fear?

Being buried alive.

Who does T.J. say was the smartest one in his family?

Pokey, his beagle.

What does T.J. say is his favorite movie?

Lawrence of Arabia.

What is really his favorite movie?

Miss Congeniality.

What record album does T.J.'s family always play at Christmas time?

Christmas with Ray Conniff by the Ray Conniff Singers.

Is anyone allowed to make fun of this?

No.

What is T.J.'s favorite book?

If I Ran the Zoo by Dr. Seuss.

Why is 25:59 an important number to T.J.?

It's the fastest he's ever climbed Mt. Monadnock.

Who was T.J.'s high school celebrity crush?

Chrissie Hynes of The Pretenders.

What was the worst thing that happened to T.J. while at MIT?

He drove off in his car with the only copy of his doctoral dissertation on the roof.

What was the second worst thing?

After a 20-hour stint in the lab, he walked a mile to a grocery store to buy black raspberry ice cream but when he got back to his apartment, he realized that it was mismarked and it was actually rum raisin ice cream, which he hates

What is the only thing T.J. remembers about first grade?

He had a crush on his teacher and when she made him stay after school because he had misbehaved, he thought it was because she liked him.

Could your "soul mate" answer ANY questions about you?

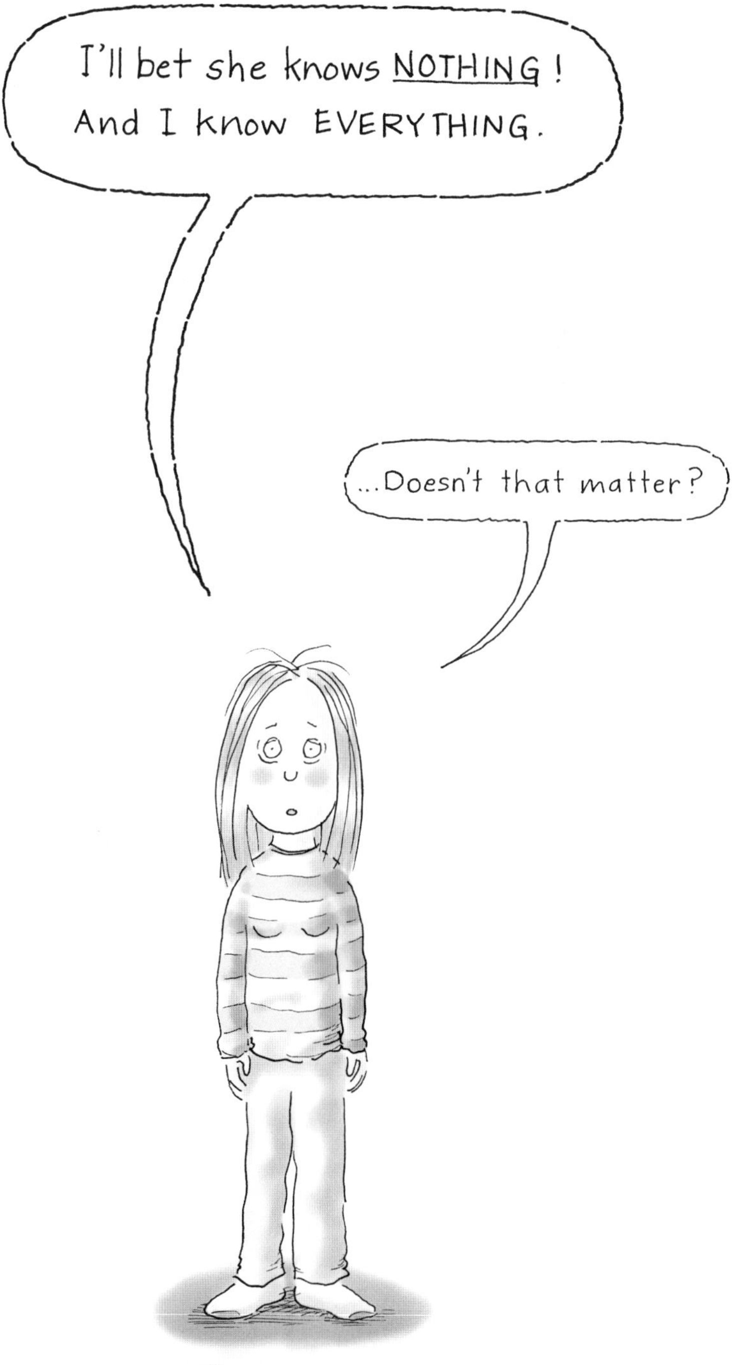
I'll bet she knows NOTHING!
And I know EVERYTHING.
...Doesn't that matter?

The next morning I woke up hopeful, but then my dreams dissolved.

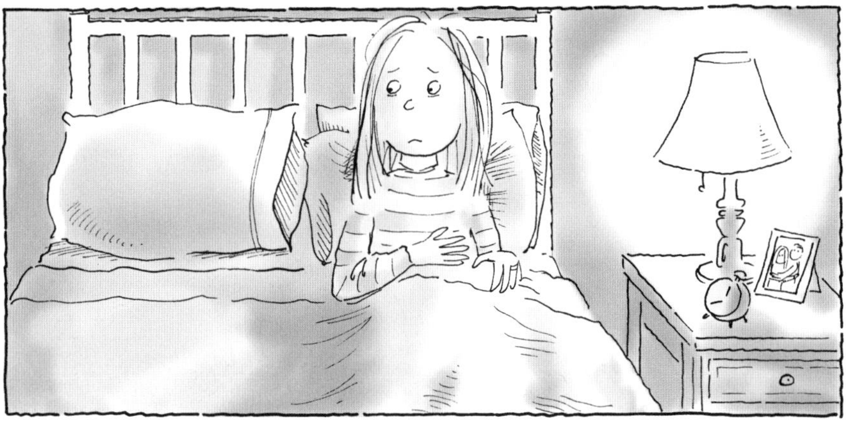

I looked for T.J. He owed me so many more answers.

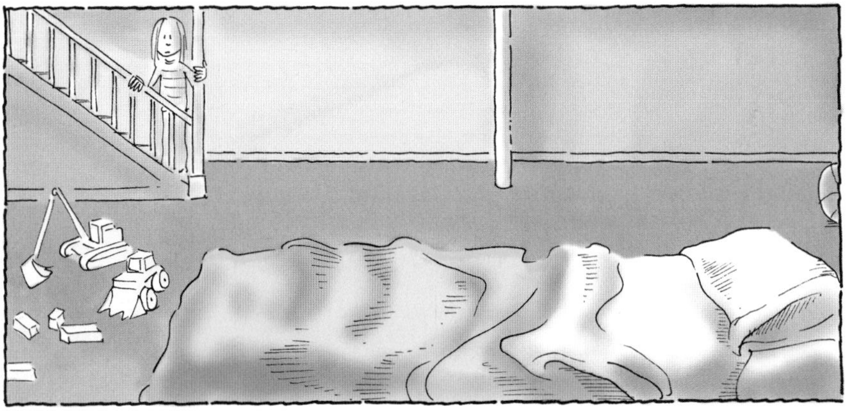

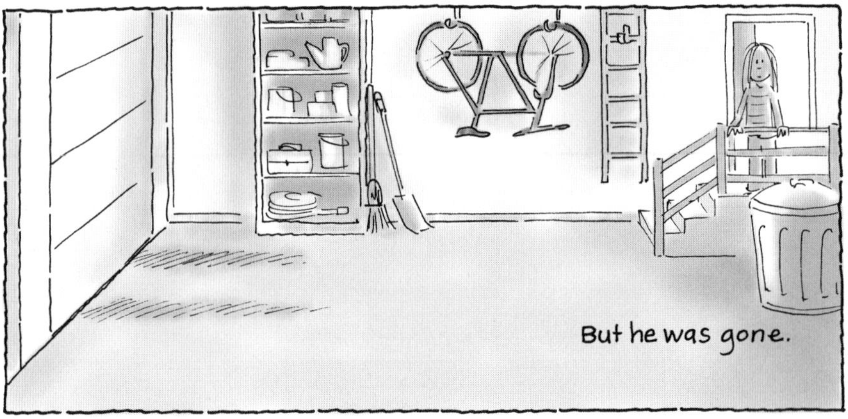
But he was gone.

I got the kids up, made them breakfast, and helped them pack for school.

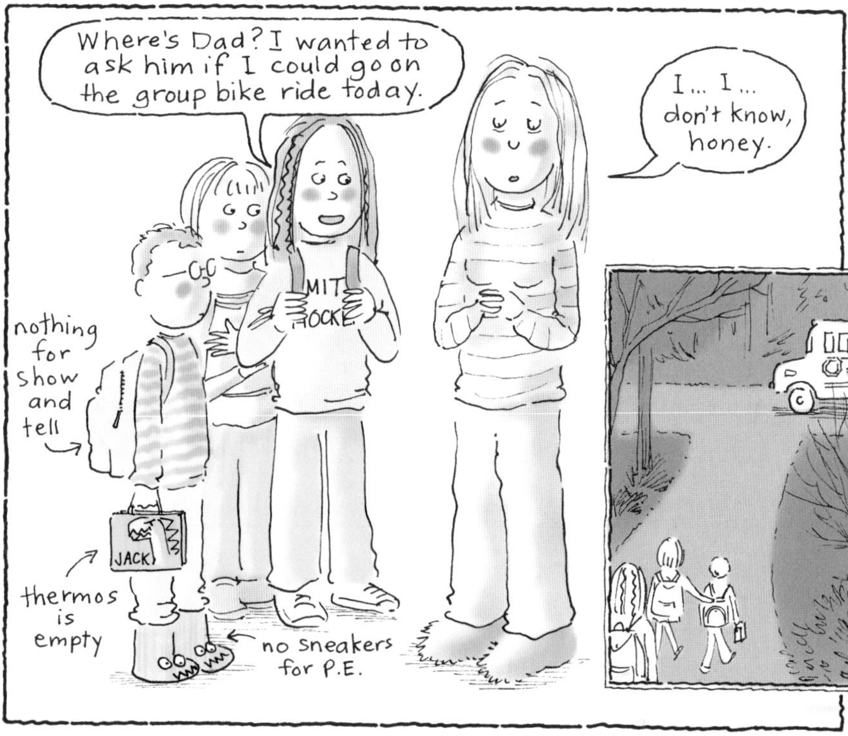
Where's Dad? I wanted to ask him if I could go on the group bike ride today.
I... I... don't know, honey.
MIT HOCKE
nothing for show and tell
JACK
thermos is empty
no sneakers for P.E.

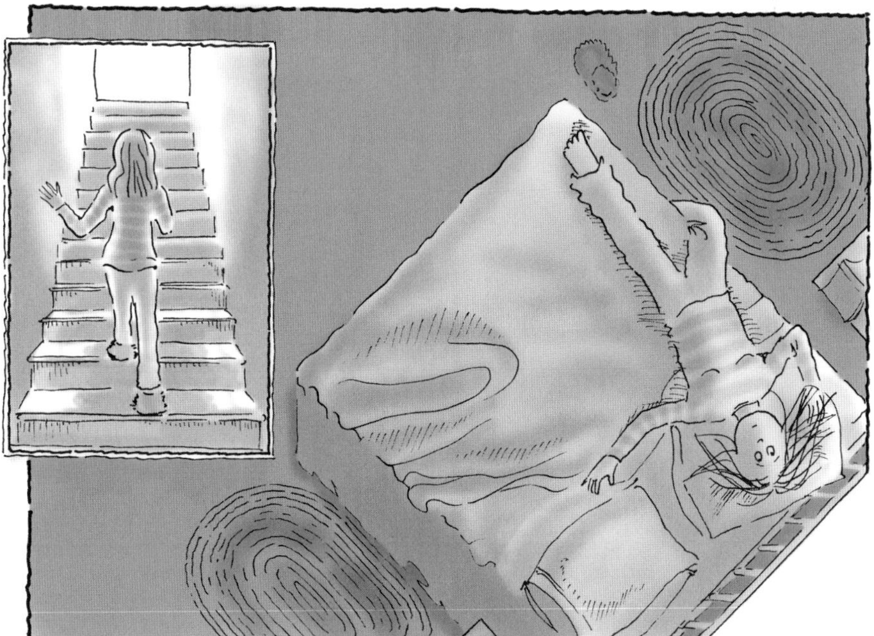

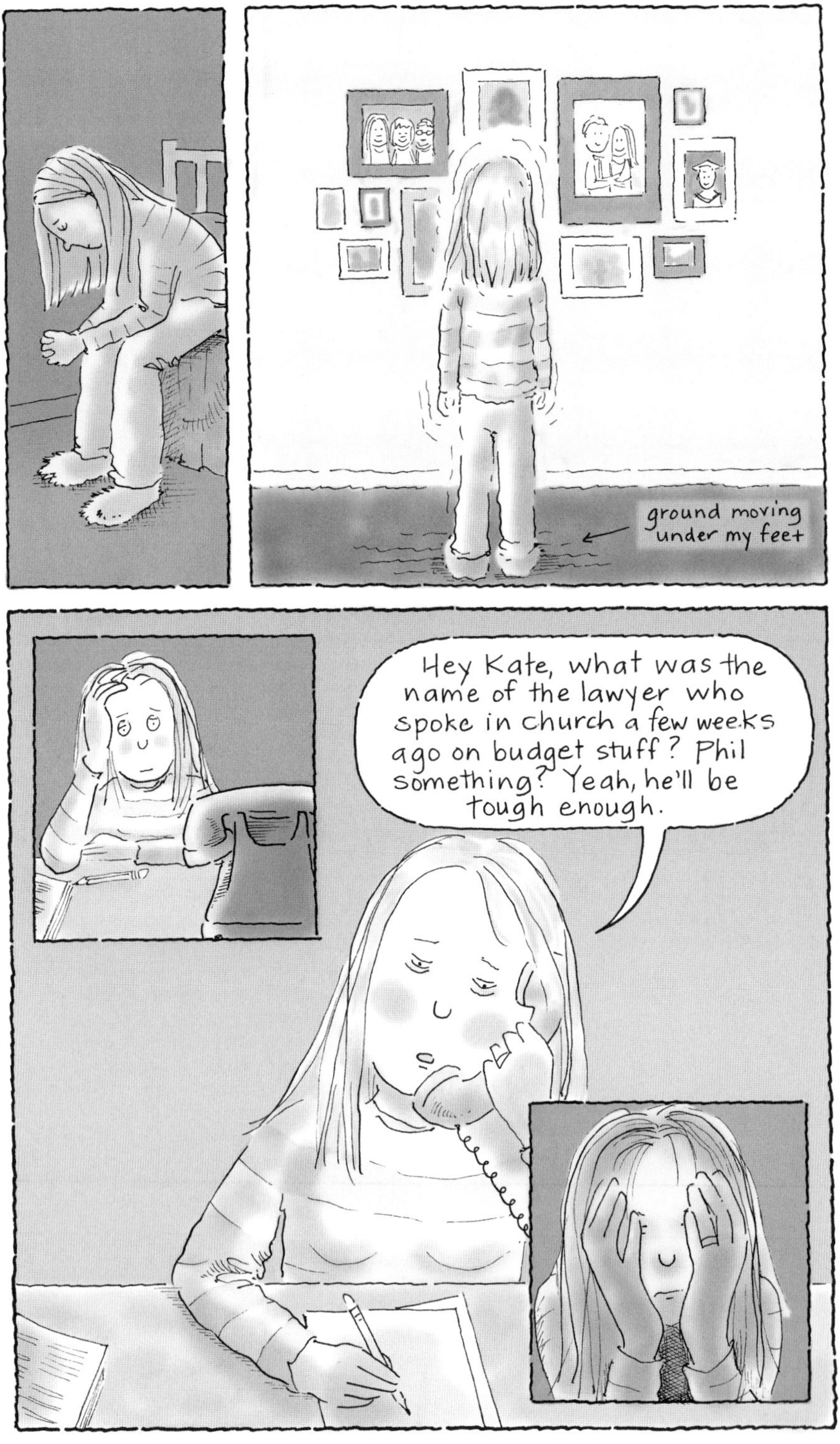
ground moving
under my feet
Hey Kate, what was the name of the lawyer who spoke in church a few weeks ago on budget stuff? Phil something? Yeah, he'll be tough enough.

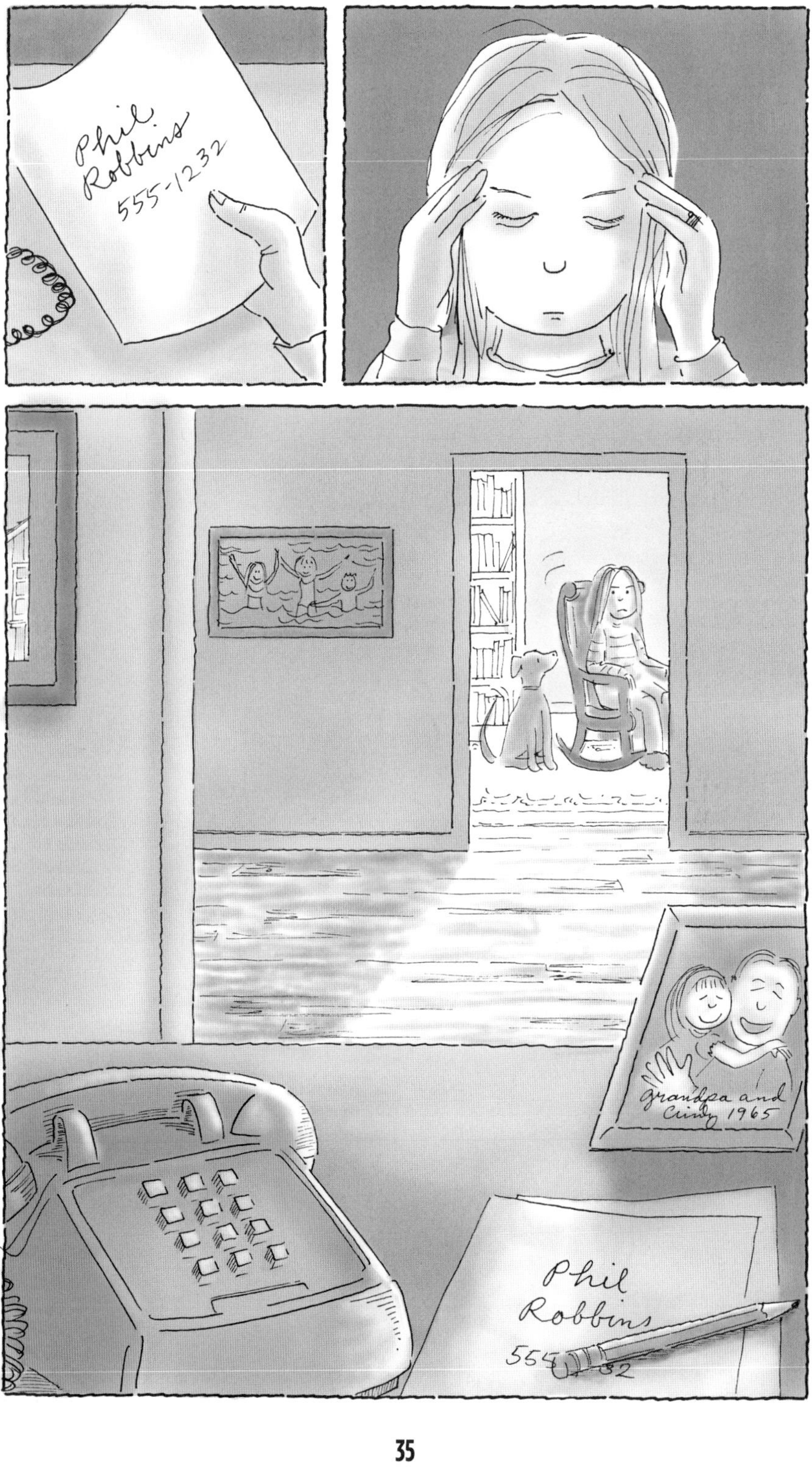
Phil
Robbins
555-1232
grandpa and
Cindy 1965
Phil
Robbins

The next day, I coped with my misery by watching a Saved By The Bell marathon on TV.

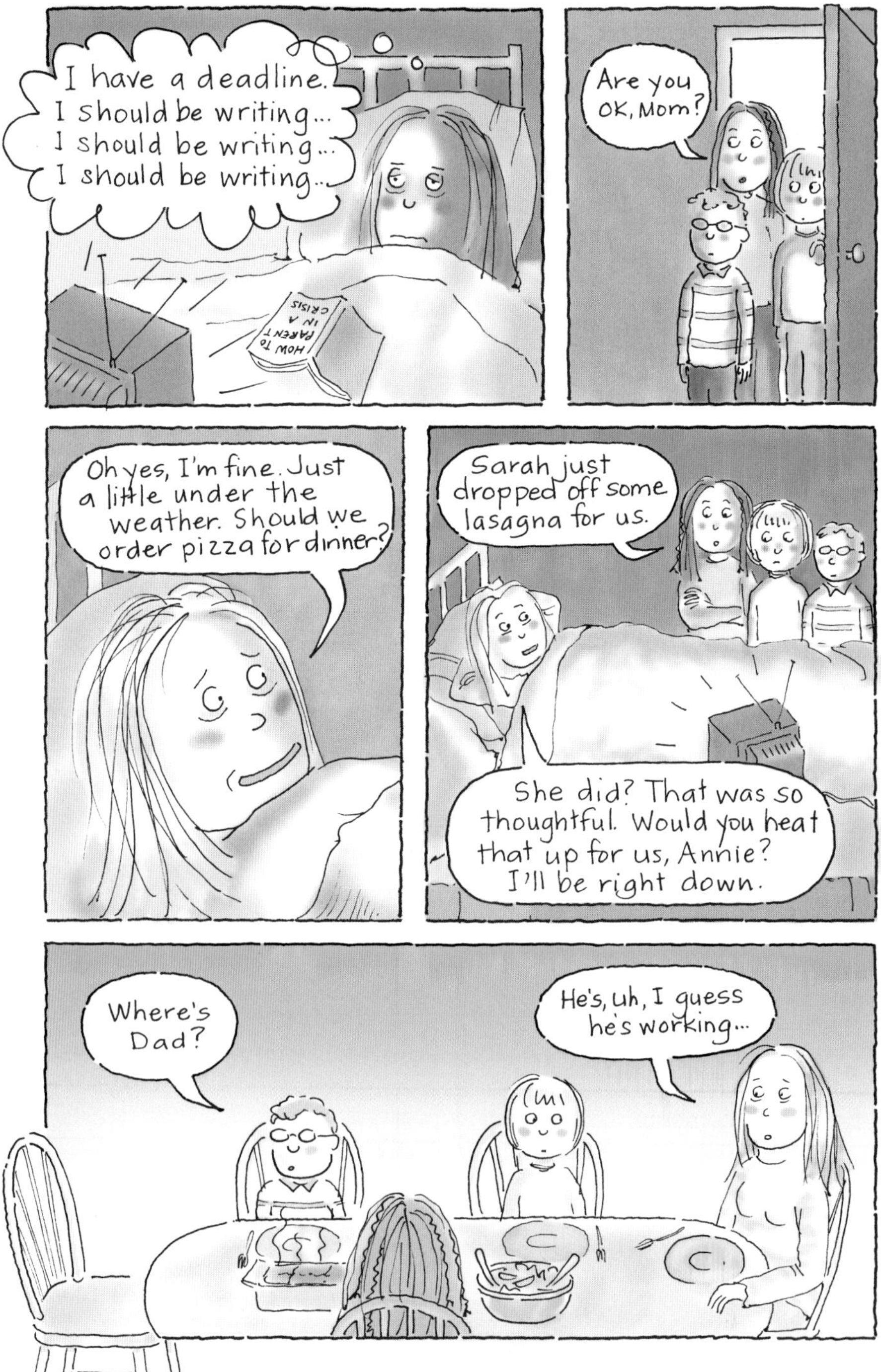
I have a deadline. I should be writing... I should be writing... I should be writing...
HOW TO PARENT IN A CRISIS
Are you OK, Mom?
Oh yes, I'm fine. Just a little under the weather. Should we order pizza for dinner?
Sarah just dropped off some lasagna for us.
She did? That was so thoughtful. Would you heat that up for us, Annie? I'll be right down.
Where's Dad?
He's, uh, I guess he's working...

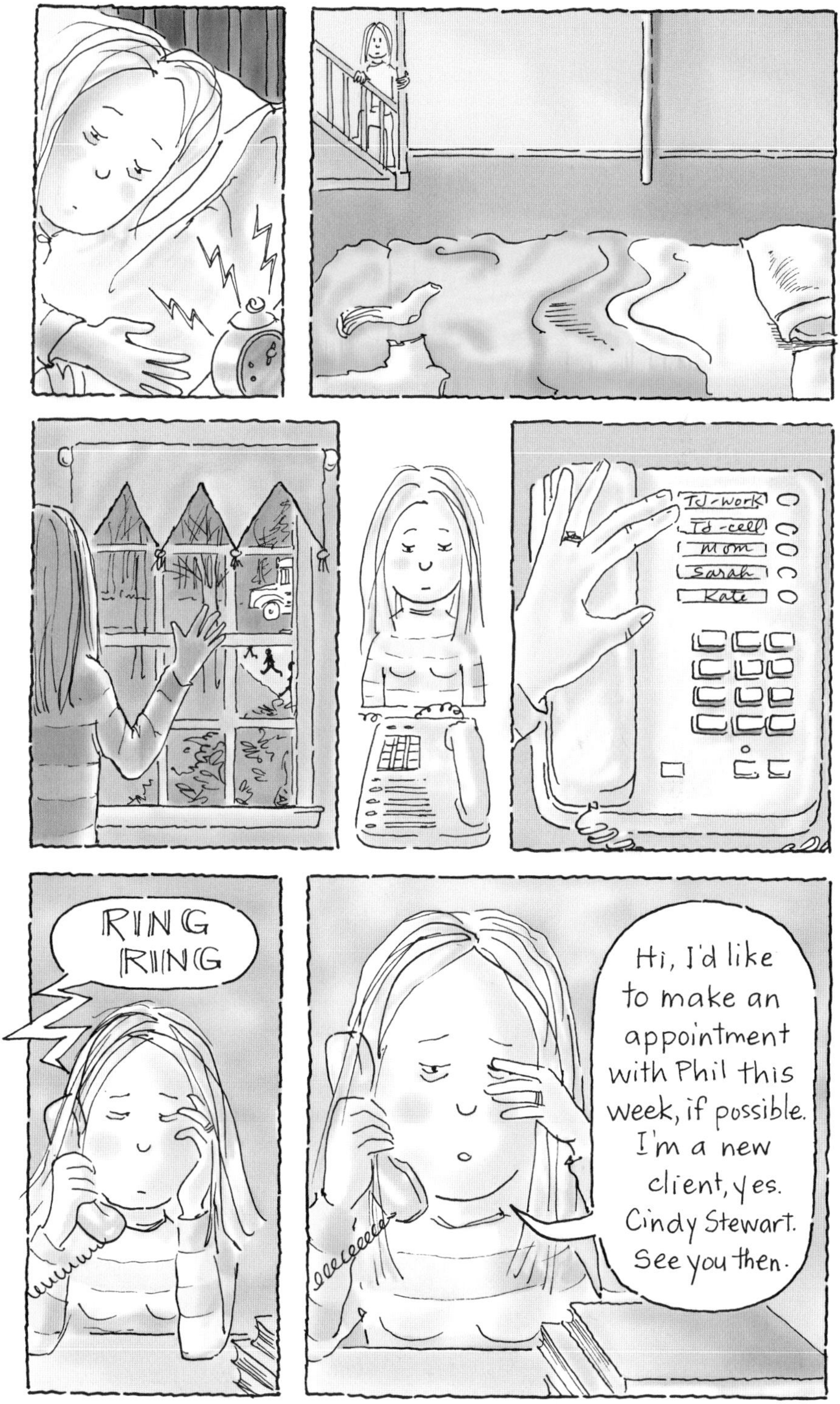
TJ-work
TJ-cell
Mom
Sarah
Kate
RING RING
Hi, I'd like to make an appointment with Phil this week, if possible. I'm a new client, yes. Cindy Stewart. See you then.

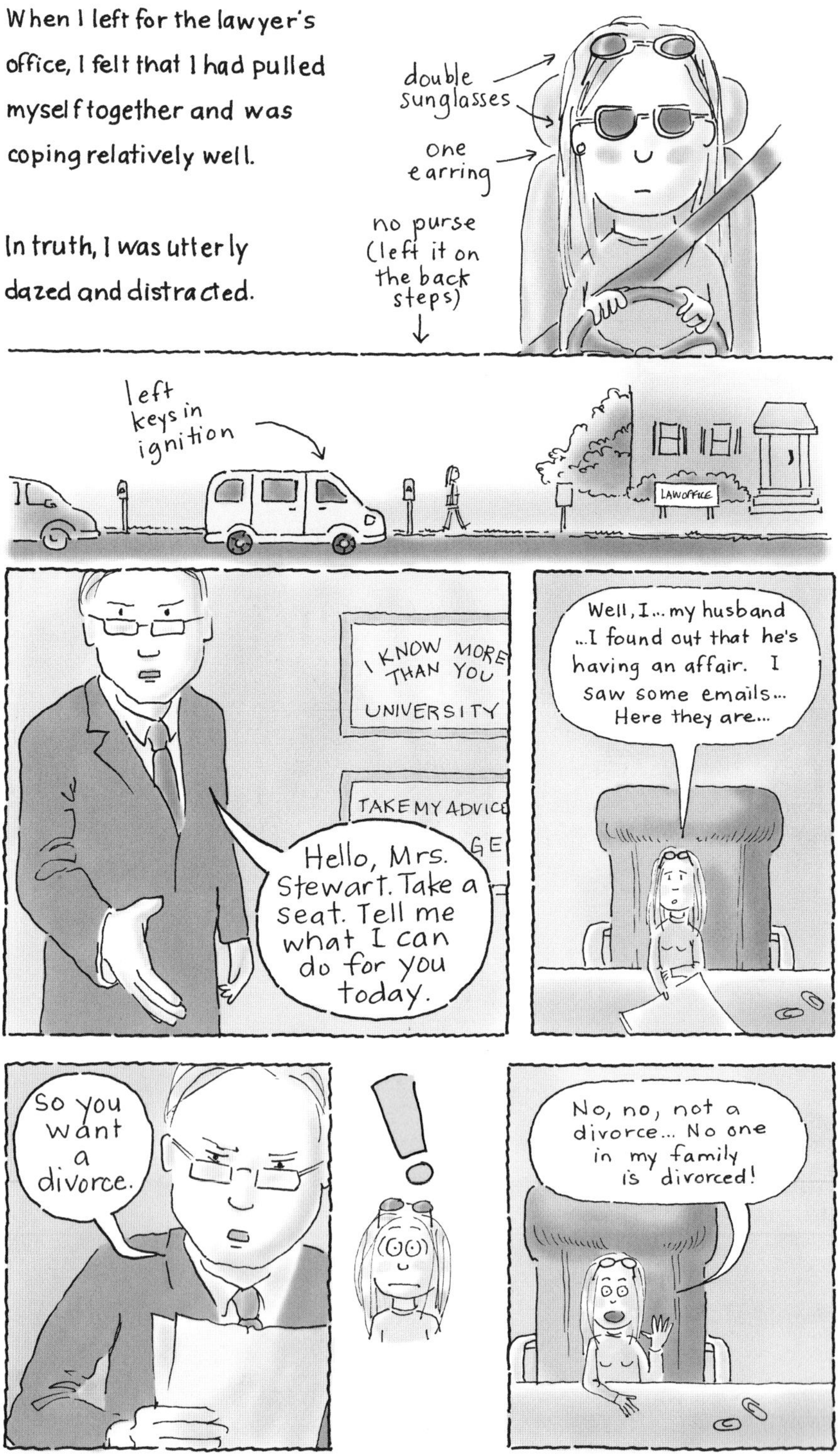
When I left for the lawyer's office, I felt that I had pulled myself together and was coping relatively well.
In truth, I was utterly dazed and distracted.
double sunglasses
one earring
no purse (left it on the back steps)
left keys in ignition
LAW OFFICE
I KNOW MORE THAN YOU UNIVERSITY
TAKE MY ADVICE
Hello, Mrs. Stewart. Take a seat. Tell me what I can do for you today.
Well, I... my husband ...I found out that he's having an affair. I saw some emails... Here they are...
So you want a divorce.
!
No, no, not a divorce... No one in my family is divorced!

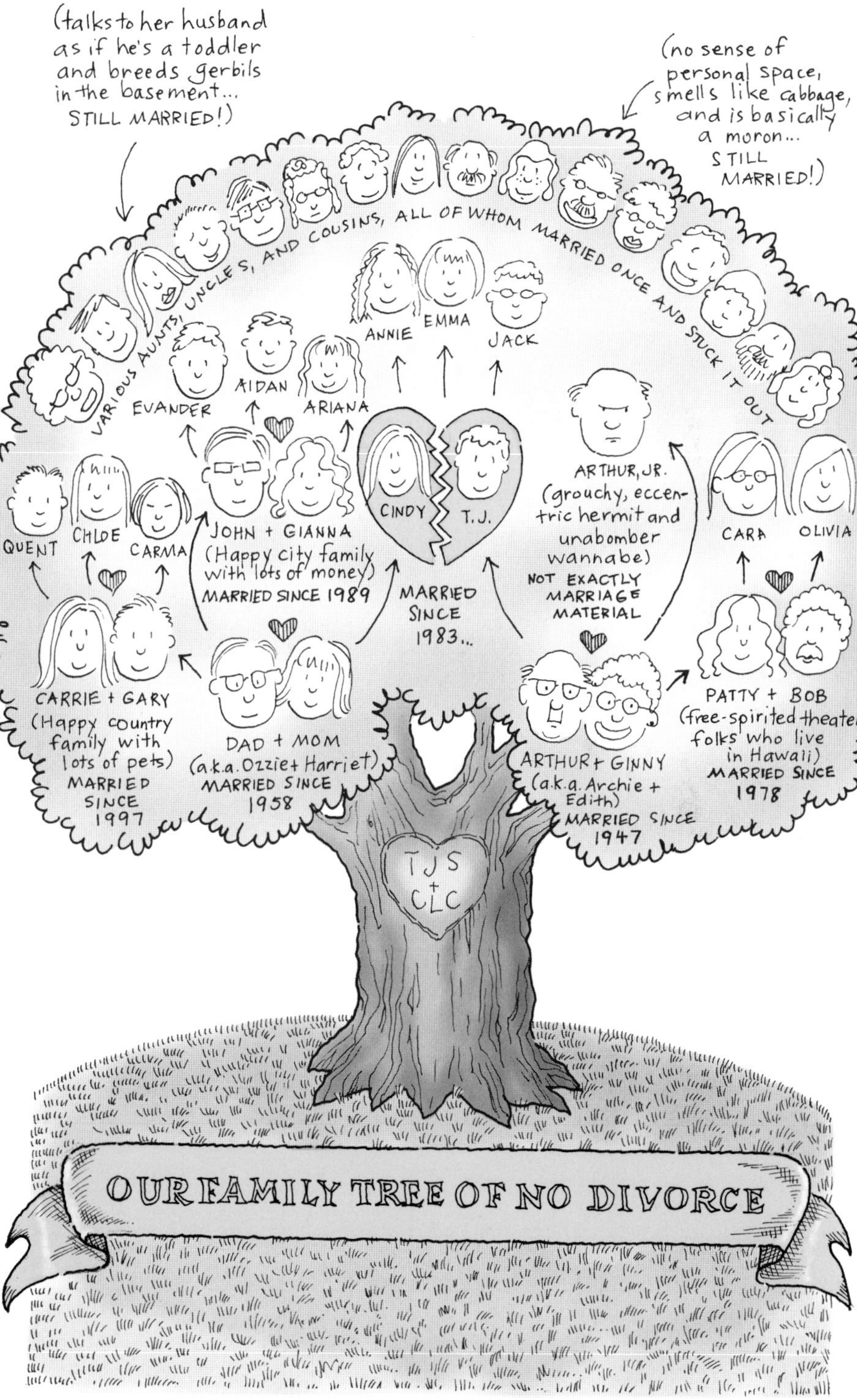
(talks to her husband as if he's a toddler and breeds gerbils in the basement... STILL MARRIED!)
(no sense of personal space, smells like cabbage, and is basically a moron... STILL MARRIED!)
VARIOUS AUNTS, UNCLES, AND COUSINS, ALL OF WHOM MARRIED ONCE AND STUCK IT OUT
ANNIE
EMMA
JACK
EVANDER
AIDAN
ARIANA
CINDY
T.J.
ARTHUR, JR. (grouchy, eccentric hermit and unabomber wannabe)
NOT EXACTLY MARRIAGE MATERIAL
QUENT
CHLOE
CARMA
JOHN + GIANNA (Happy city family with lots of money) MARRIED SINCE 1989
MARRIED SINCE 1983...
CARA
OLIVIA
CARRIE + GARY (Happy country family with lots of pets) MARRIED SINCE 1997
DAD + MOM (a.k.a. Ozzie + Harriet) MARRIED SINCE 1958
ARTHUR + GINNY (a.k.a. Archie + Edith) MARRIED SINCE 1947
PATTY + BOB (free-spirited theater folks who live in Hawaii) MARRIED SINCE 1978
TJS + CLC
OUR FAMILY TREE OF NO DIVORCE

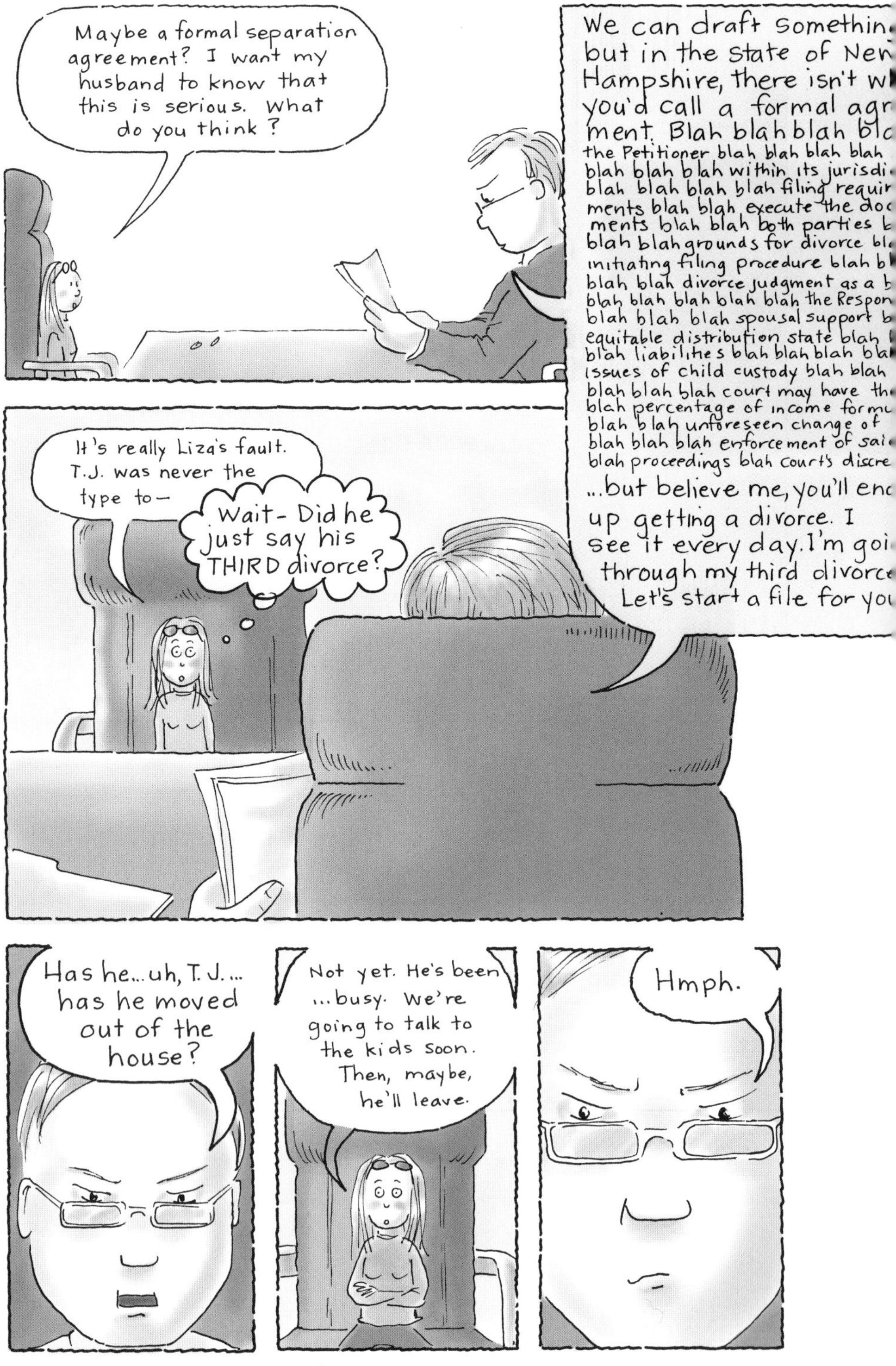
Maybe a formal separation agreement? I want my husband to know that this is serious. What do you think?
We can draft somethin but in the State of New Hampshire, there isn't w you'd call a formal agr ment. Blah blah blah bla
the Petitioner blah blah blah blah blah blah blah within its jurisdi blah blah blah blah filing requir ments blah blah execute the doc ments blah blah both parties b blah blah grounds for divorce bl initiating filing procedure blah b blah blah divorce judgment as a b blah blah blah blah blah the Respon blah blah blah spousal support b equitable distribution state blah blah liabilities blah blah blah bla issues of child custody blah blah blah blah blah court may have th blah percentage of income formu blah blah unforeseen change of blah blah blah enforcement of sai blah proceedings blah court's discre
...but believe me, you'll end up getting a divorce. I see it every day. I'm goi through my third divorce Let's start a file for you
It's really Liza's fault. T.J. was never the type to—
Wait- Did he just say his THIRD divorce?
Has he...uh, T.J.... has he moved out of the house?
Not yet. He's been ...busy. We're going to talk to the kids soon. Then, maybe, he'll leave.
Hmph.

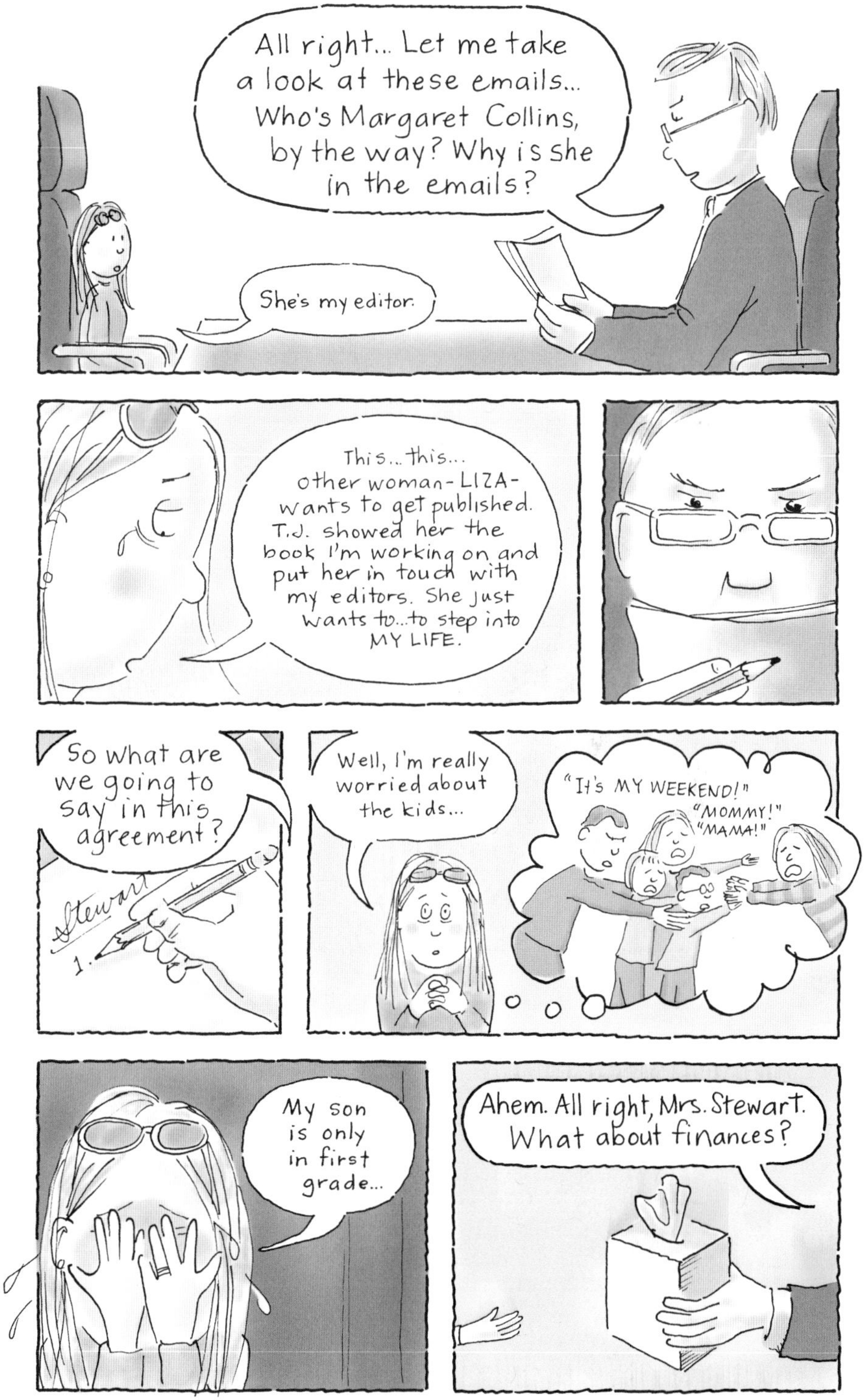
All right... Let me take a look at these emails... Who's Margaret Collins, by the way? Why is she in the emails?
She's my editor.
This... this... other woman- LIZA- wants to get published. T.J. showed her the book I'm working on and put her in touch with my editors. She just wants to... to step into MY LIFE.
So what are we going to say in this agreement?
Stewart
1.
Well, I'm really worried about the kids...
"It's MY WEEKEND!"
"MOMMY!"
"MAMA!"
My son is only in first grade...
Ahem. All right, Mrs. Stewart. What about finances?

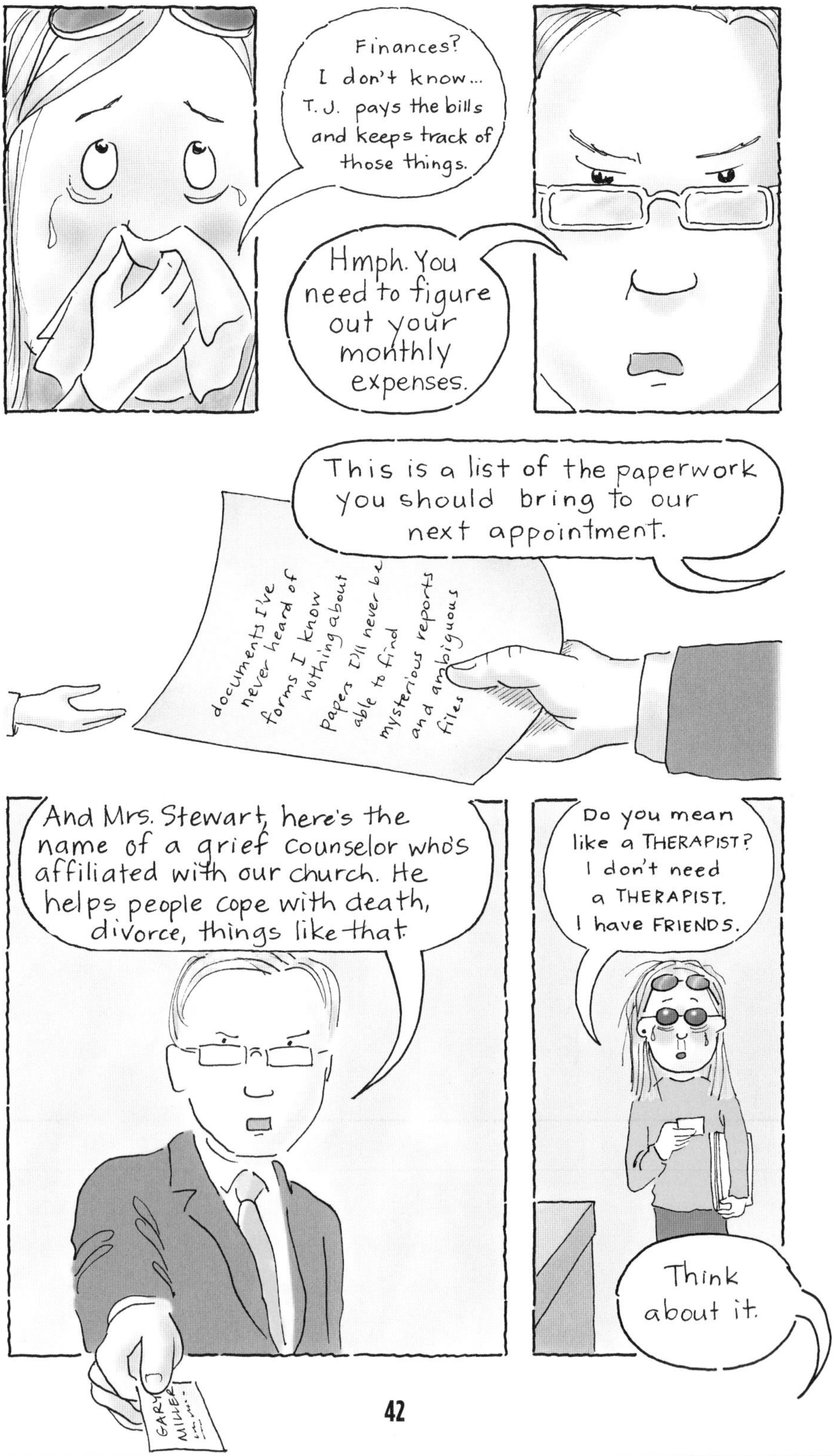
Finances? I don't know... T.J. pays the bills and keeps track of those things.
Hmph. You need to figure out your monthly expenses.
This is a list of the paperwork you should bring to our next appointment.
documents I've never heard of
forms I know nothing about
papers I'll never be able to find
mysterious reports and ambiguous files
And Mrs. Stewart, here's the name of a grief counselor who's affiliated with our church. He helps people cope with death, divorce, things like that.
GARY MILLER
Do you mean like a THERAPIST? I don't need a THERAPIST. I have FRIENDS.
Think about it.

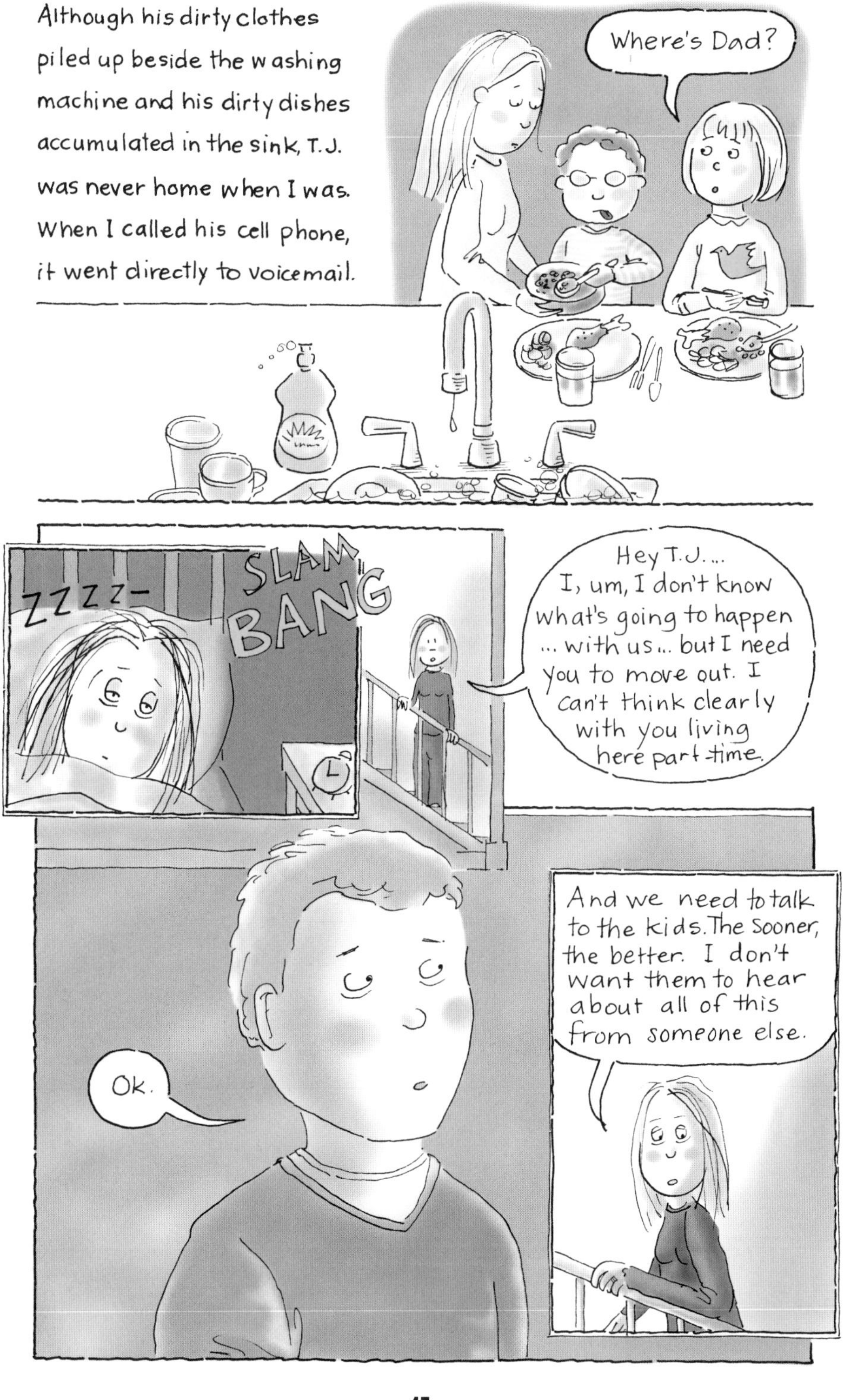
Although his dirty clothes piled up beside the washing machine and his dirty dishes accumulated in the sink, T.J. was never home when I was. When I called his cell phone, it went directly to voicemail.
Where's Dad?
ZZZZ-
SLAM
BANG
Hey T.J. ... I, um, I don't know what's going to happen ... with us... but I need you to move out. I can't think clearly with you living here part-time.
Ok.
And we need to talk to the kids. The sooner, the better. I don't want them to hear about all of this from someone else.

Two days later, we sat down with the kids to give them a G-rated version of what had happened. Things did not go as I expected.

SPEECH I HAD CAREFULLY PREPARED

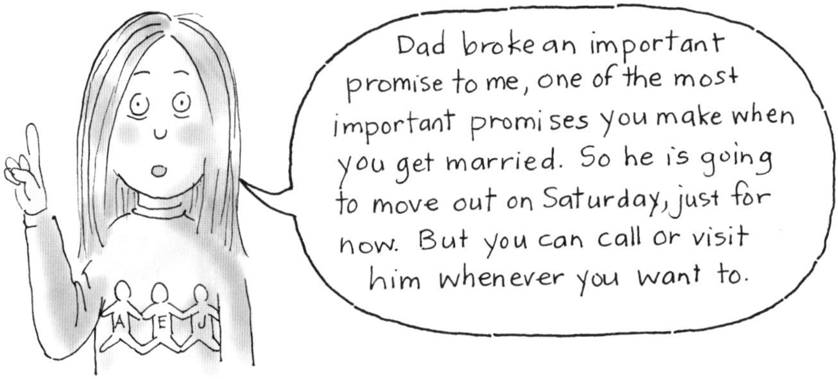
Dad broke an important promise to me, one of the most important promises you make when you get married. So he is going to move out on Saturday, just for now. But you can call or visit him whenever you want to.
A E J

HOW I IMAGINED IT WOULD GO

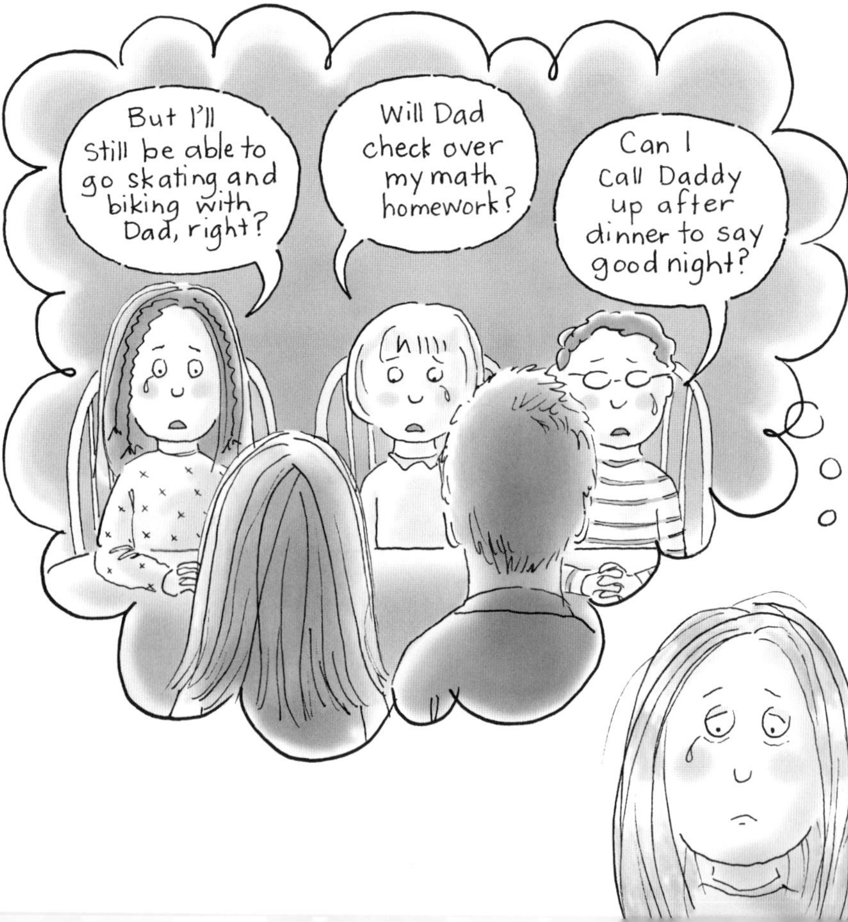
But I'll still be able to go skating and biking with Dad, right?
Will Dad check over my math homework?
Can I call Daddy up after dinner to say good night?

HOW IT ACTUALLY WENT

hee hee
hee hee
Does that mean I can get an indoor cat? Dad's the only one who's allergic!
Can we go to McDonald's* for dinner? The Happy Meal toy is a T-Rex right now!
*T.J. did not allow fast food

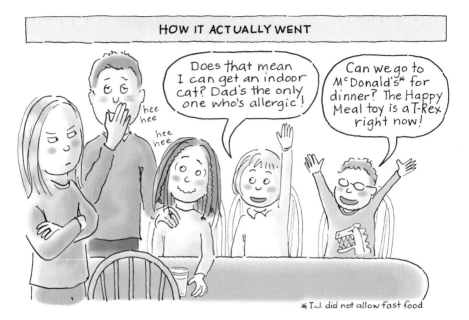

It wasn't that the kids didn't care, or weren't upset. But it was life, not a movie. And sometimes in life, girls ask about cats, but a few days later come down with mono, and then strep throat, and then the flu, and strep throat again. Boys ask about Happy Meals, but then drag a blanket and pillow into your room every night and sleep on the floor next to your bed.

And mothers act like everything will be fine, but then fall asleep in the bathtub and wake up hours later, when the water is ice cold and the house is dark.

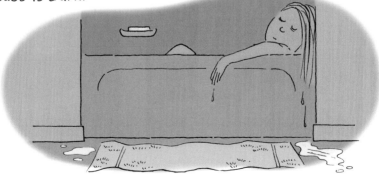

That Saturday, just before Emma's 12th birthday, T.J. moved out.

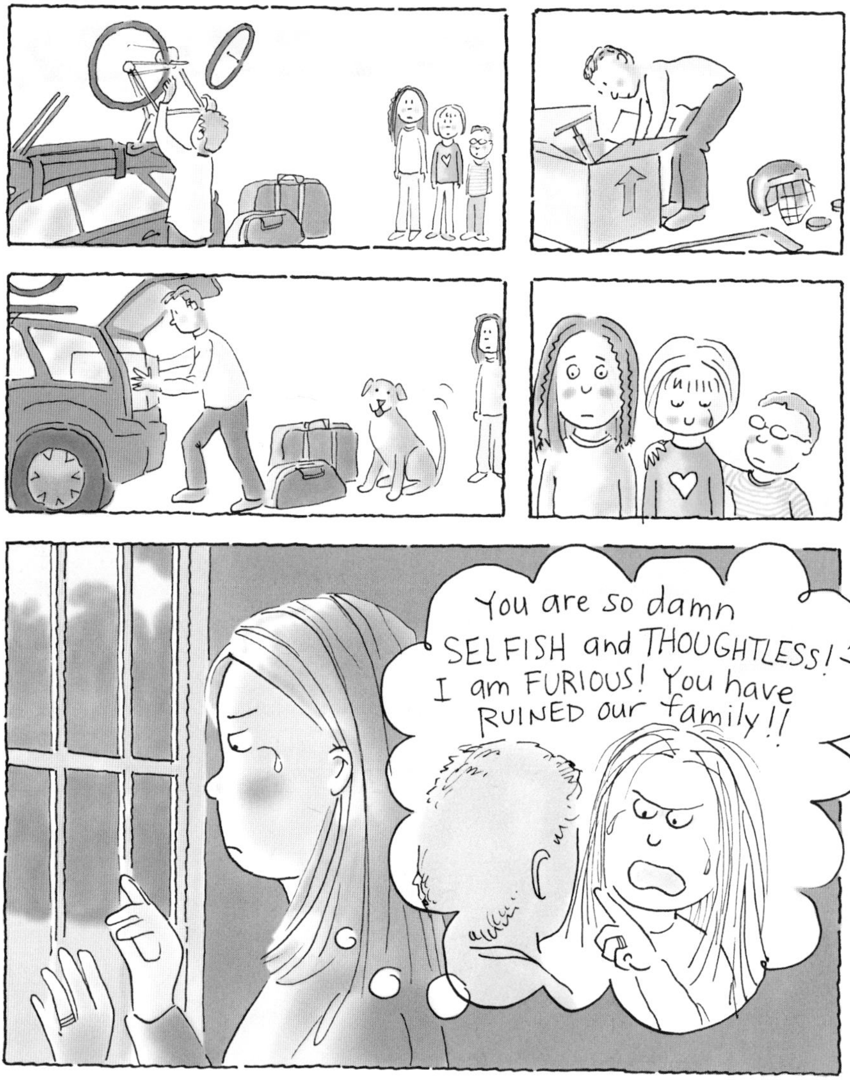
You are so damn SELFISH and THOUGHTLESS! I am FURIOUS! You have RUINED our family!!

There were so many things I wanted to say to him—things I had every right to say. But I couldn't feed the anger. If I did, it would grow stronger and take over, making it hard to distinguish right from wrong. I had to force myself to stay calm and focus on what was best for the kids.

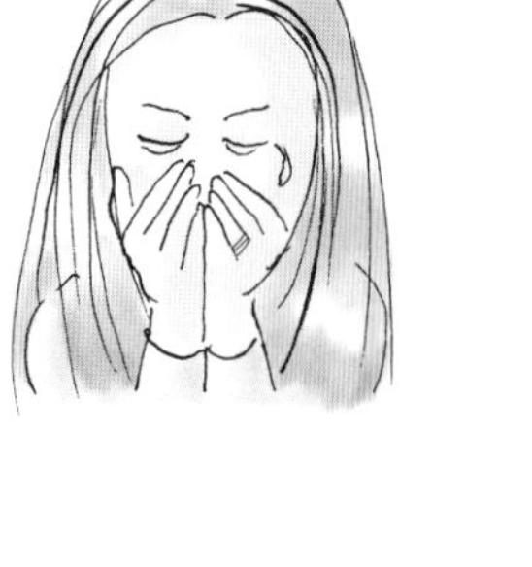

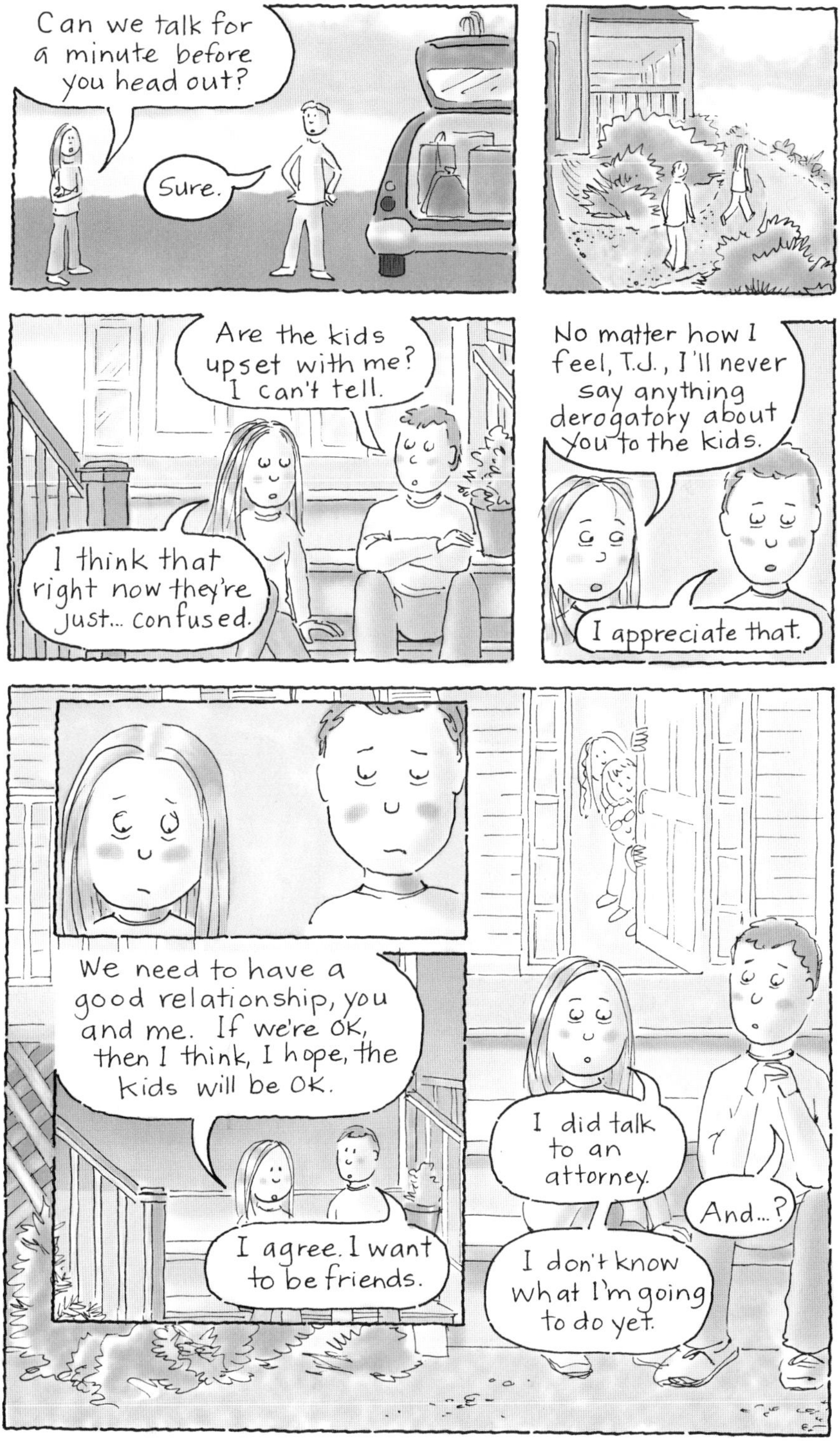
Can we talk for a minute before you head out?
Sure.
Are the kids upset with me? I can't tell.
I think that right now they're just... confused.
No matter how I feel, T.J., I'll never say anything derogatory about you to the kids.
I appreciate that.
We need to have a good relationship, you and me. If we're OK, then I think, I hope, the kids will be OK.
I agree. I want to be friends.
I did talk to an attorney.
And...?
I don't know what I'm going to do yet.

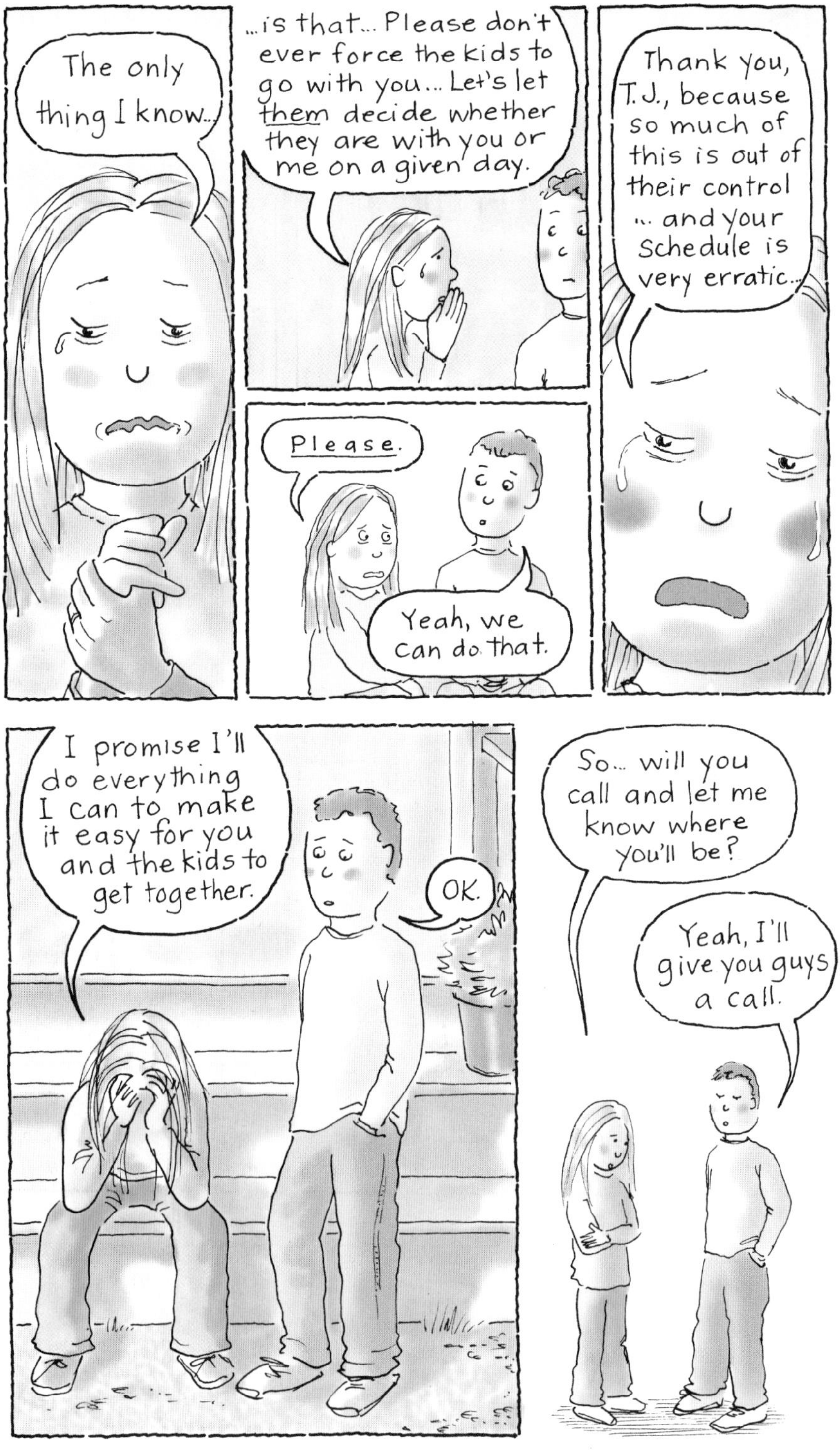
The only thing I know...
...is that... Please don't ever force the kids to go with you... Let's let them decide whether they are with you or me on a given day.
Please.
Yeah, we can do that.
Thank you, T.J., because so much of this is out of their control ... and your Schedule is very erratic...
I promise I'll do everything I can to make it easy for you and the kids to get together.
OK.
So... will you call and let me know where you'll be?
Yeah, I'll give you guys a call.

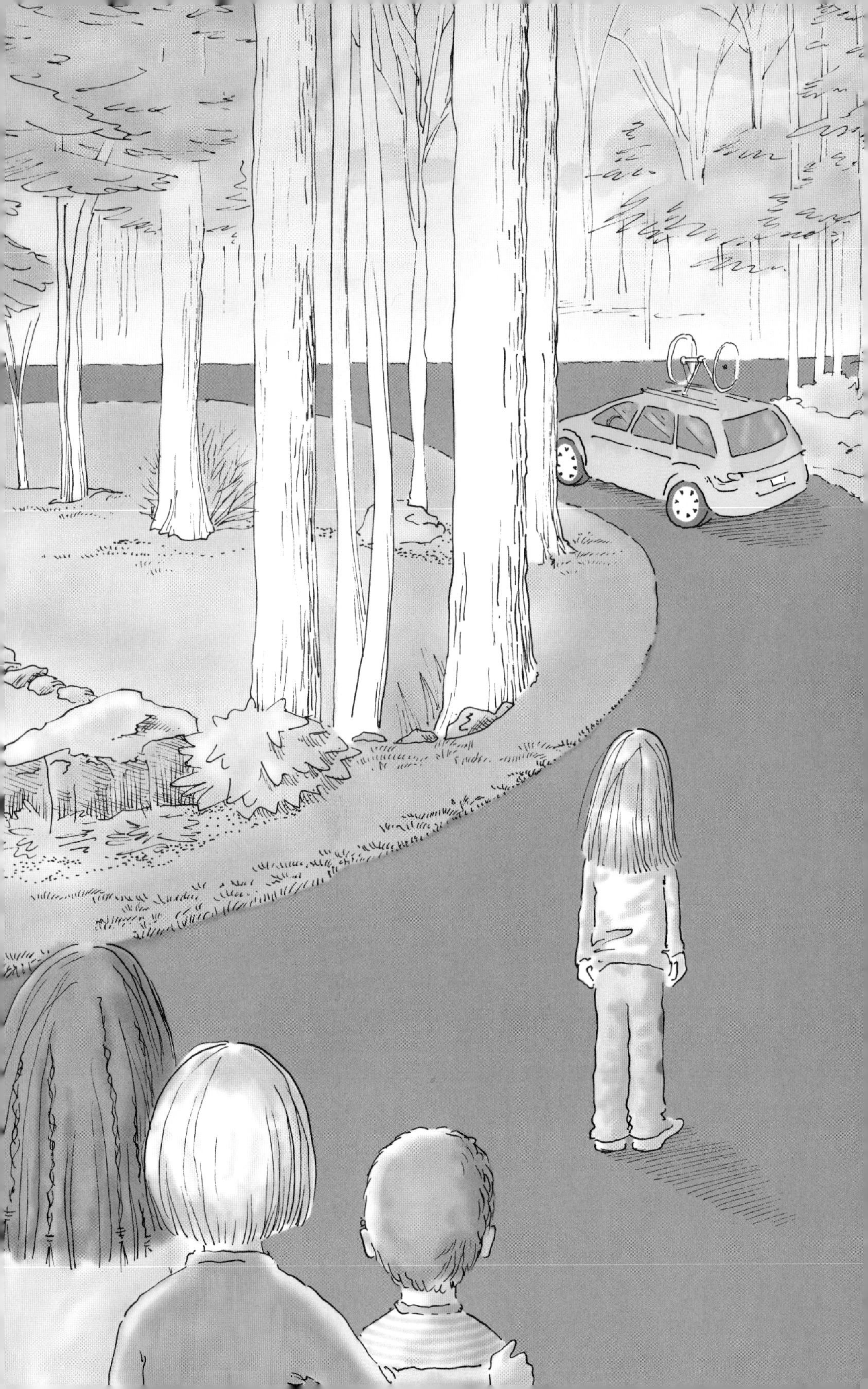

I had assumed T.J. would unpack at Liza's, but it seemed that her third husband was still living with her. So while he waited for that little hiccup to be worked out, T.J. decided to camp out in his office.

After a few surreptitious trips to his parents' basement (and a couple to the dumpster behind his building), he had everything he needed.

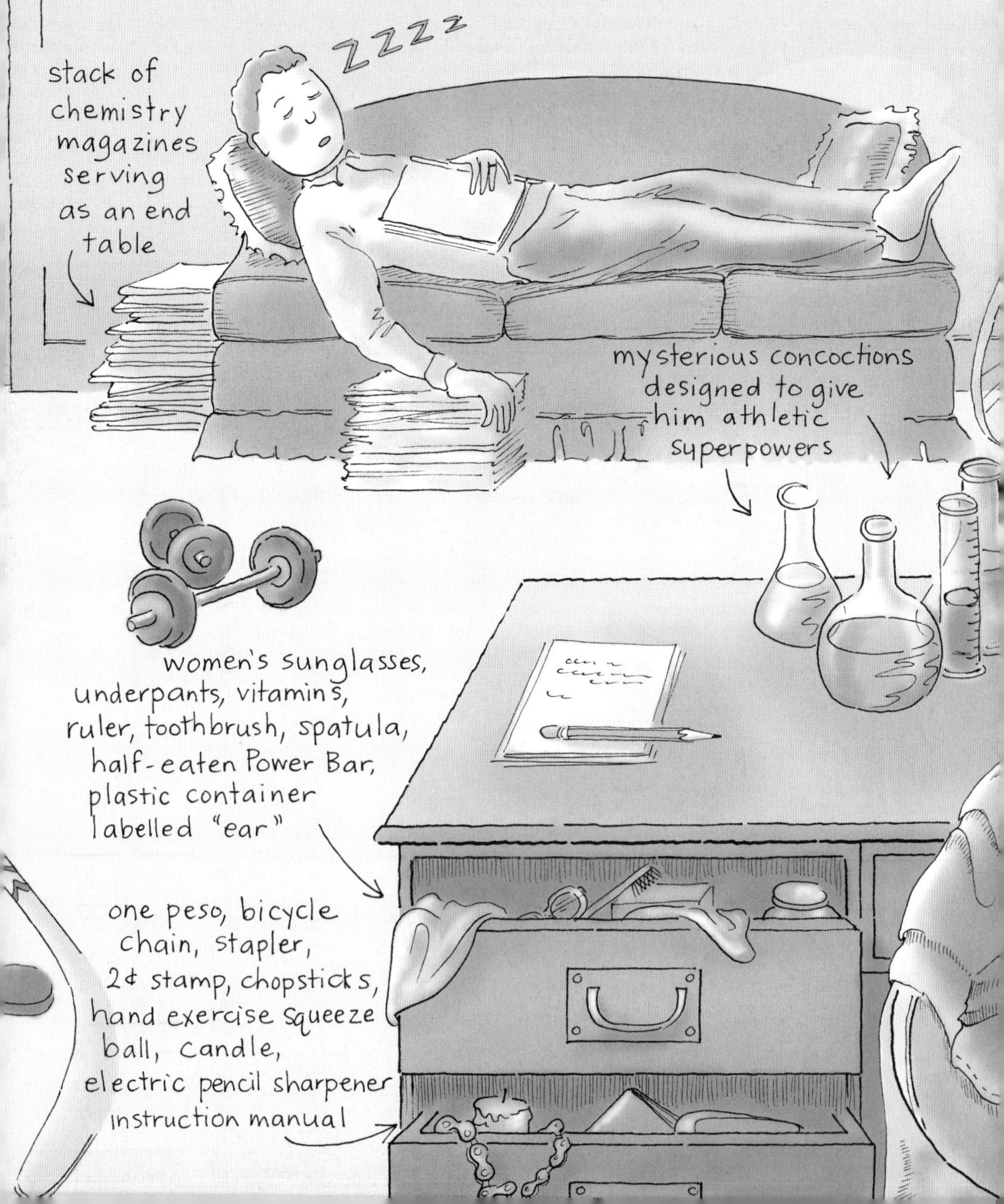
ZZZZ
stack of chemistry magazines serving as an end table
mysterious concoctions designed to give him athletic superpowers
women's sunglasses, underpants, vitamins, ruler, toothbrush, spatula, half-eaten Power Bar, plastic container labelled "ear"
one peso, bicycle chain, stapler, 2¢ stamp, chopsticks, hand exercise squeeze ball, candle, electric pencil sharpener instruction manual

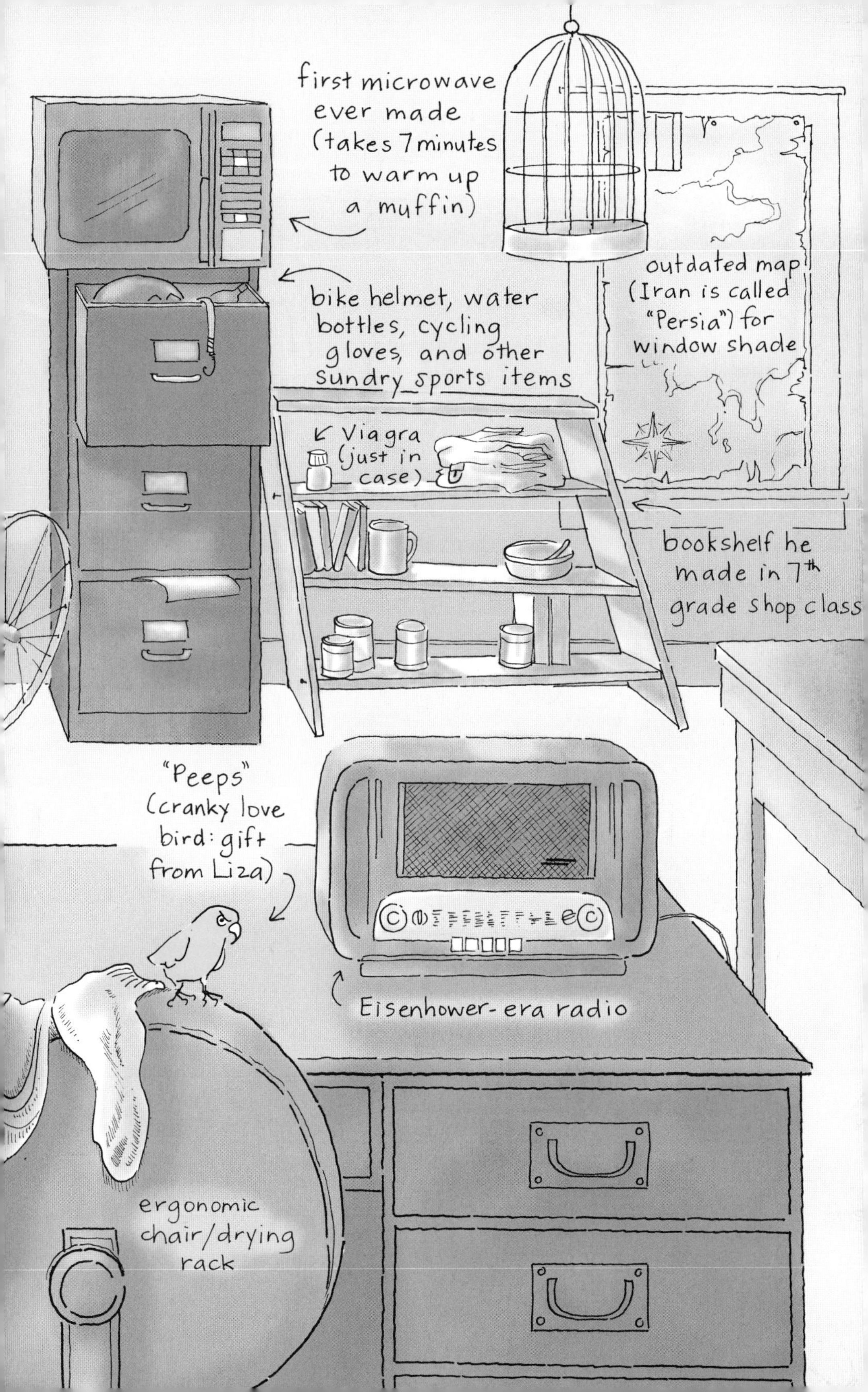

first microwave ever made (takes 7 minutes to warm up a muffin)
bike helmet, water bottles, cycling gloves, and other sundry sports items
outdated map (Iran is called "Persia") for window shade
Viagra (just in case)
bookshelf he made in 7th grade shop class
"Peeps" (cranky love bird: gift from Liza)
Eisenhower-era radio
ergonomic chair/drying rack

Despite the inconveniences (and illicitness) of living in his office, the arrangement appealed to T.J. He liked to flaunt his unconventional side. He also loved being thrifty. No matter how much money he made, he always insisted on living as cheaply as possible.

T.J.'s Tips for Thrifty Family Living

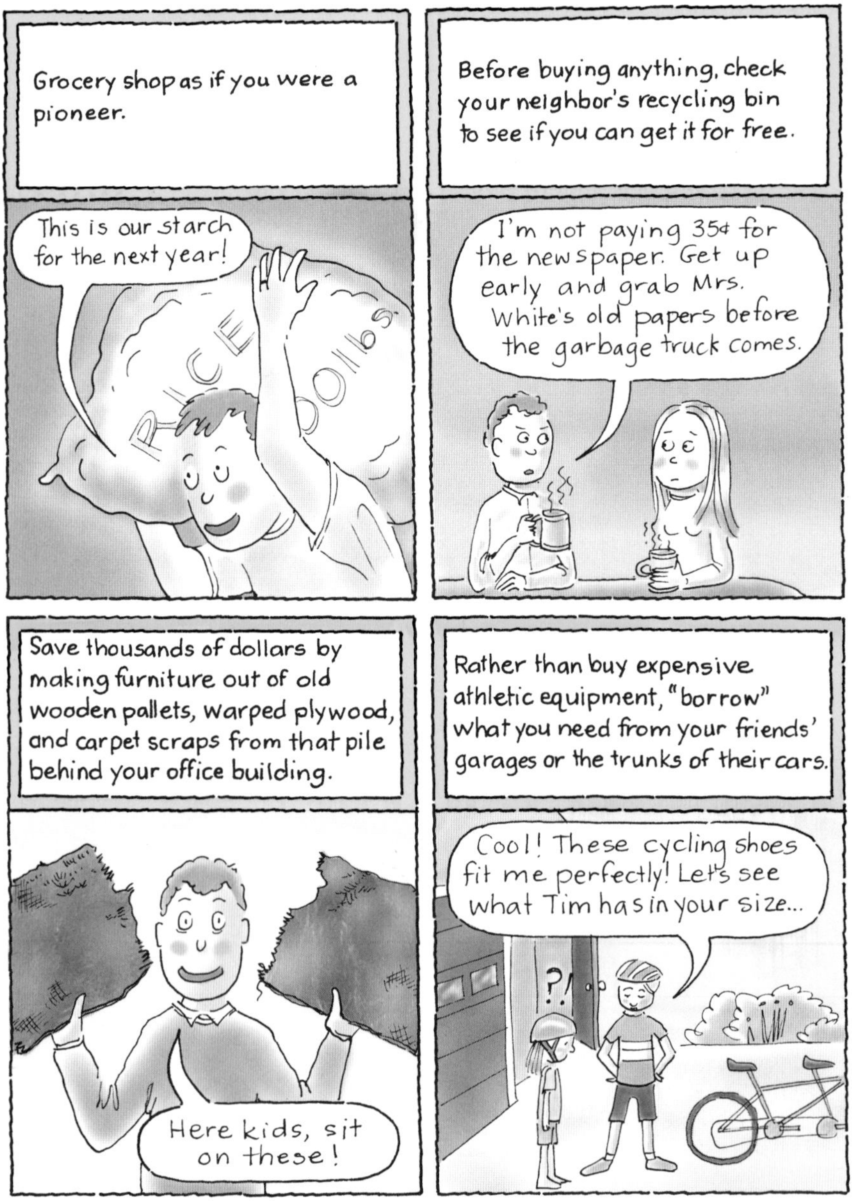
Grocery shop as if you were a pioneer.
This is our starch for the next year!
RICE
100lbs
Before buying anything, check your neighbor's recycling bin to see if you can get it for free.
I'm not paying 35¢ for the newspaper. Get up early and grab Mrs. White's old papers before the garbage truck comes.
Save thousands of dollars by making furniture out of old wooden pallets, warped plywood, and carpet scraps from that pile behind your office building.
Here kids, sit on these!
Rather than buy expensive athletic equipment, "borrow" what you need from your friends' garages or the trunks of their cars.
Cool! These cycling shoes fit me perfectly! Let's see what Tim has in your size...
?!

Out on his own, he took thriftiness to a new extreme.

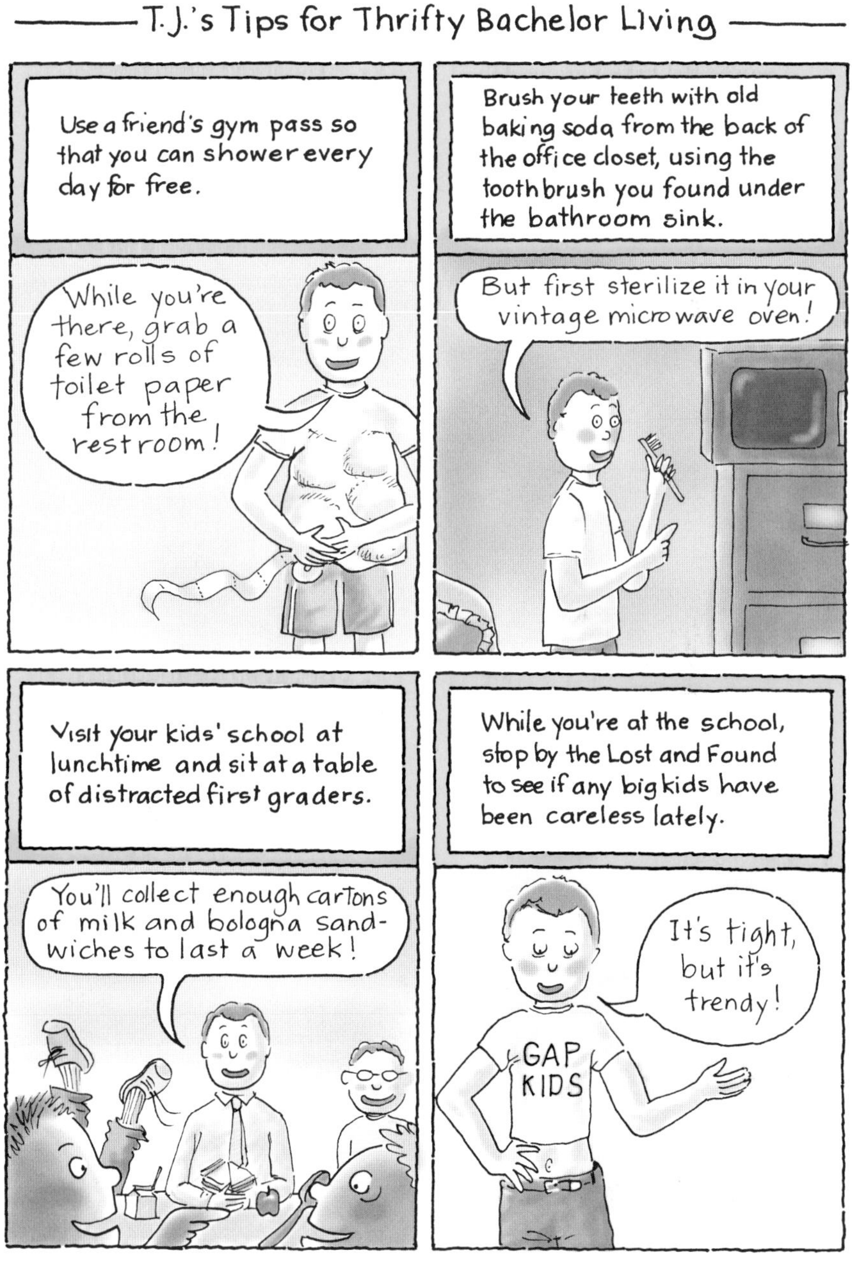
T.J.'s Tips for Thrifty Bachelor Living
Use a friend's gym pass so that you can shower every day for free.
While you're there, grab a few rolls of toilet paper from the restroom!
Brush your teeth with old baking soda from the back of the office closet, using the toothbrush you found under the bathroom sink.
But first sterilize it in your vintage microwave oven!
Visit your kids' school at lunchtime and sit at a table of distracted first graders.
You'll collect enough cartons of milk and bologna sandwiches to last a week!
While you're at the school, stop by the Lost and Found to see if any big kids have been careless lately.
It's tight, but it's trendy!
GAP KIDS

There were just a few essential items that he wasn't able to pilfer. But he soon realized that it didn't matter if HE had no T.V. ...

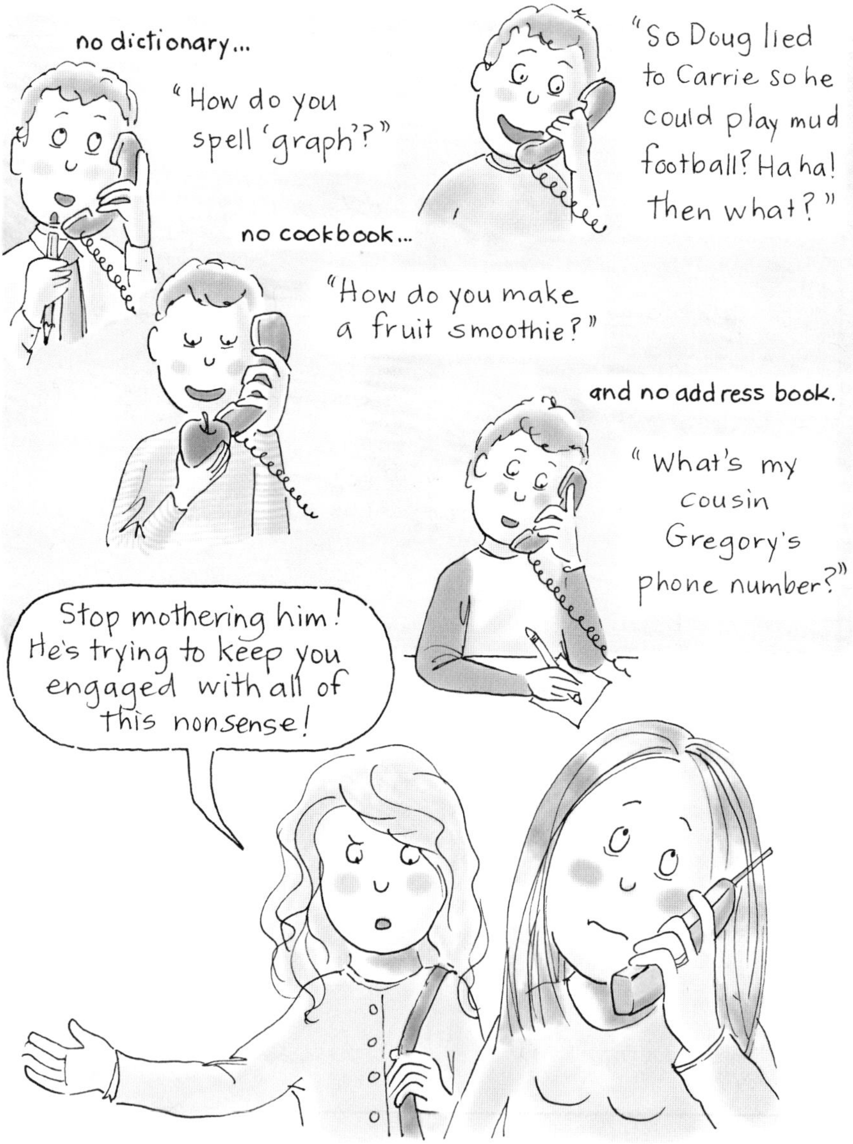
no dictionary...
"How do you spell 'graph'?"
"So Doug lied to Carrie so he could play mud football? Ha ha! Then what?"
no cookbook...
"How do you make a fruit smoothie?"
and no address book.
"What's my cousin Gregory's phone number?"
Stop mothering him! He's trying to keep you engaged with all of this nonsense!

I told myself that I had to take T.J.'s calls because we'd agreed to be friends. But it was more than that. There was a measure of comfort in those brief connections and conversations because the split had been so abrupt. It's hard to cut someone out of your life so suddenly when you've spent nearly every day with him for the past 18 years.

The kids, who were used to their dad's eccentricities, didn't seem to mind visiting him at the office. They always found interesting things to do.

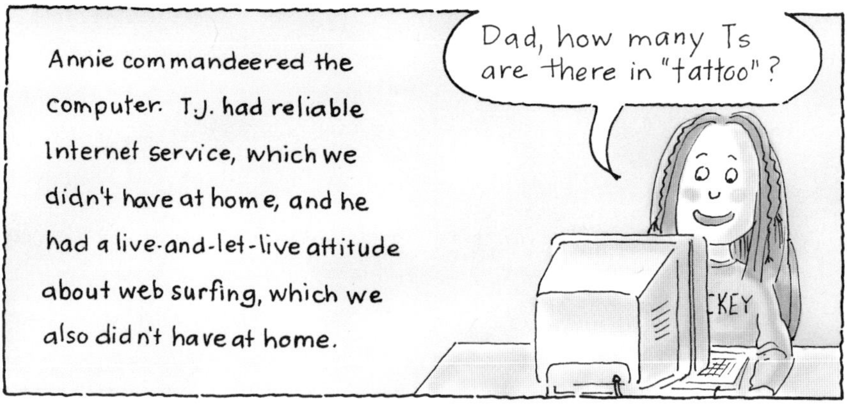
Annie commandeered the computer. T.J. had reliable Internet service, which we didn't have at home, and he had a live-and-let-live attitude about web surfing, which we also didn't have at home.
Dad, how many Ts are there in "tattoo"?
CKEY

Emma felt that it was her duty to straighten things up, tend to T.J.'s appearance, and provide constructive feedback.

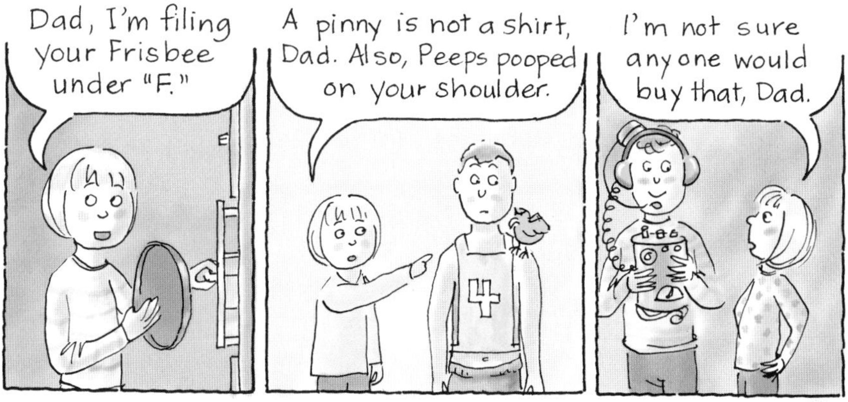
Dad, I'm filing your Frisbee under "F."
A pinny is not a shirt, Dad. Also, Peeps pooped on your shoulder.
I'm not sure anyone would buy that, Dad.

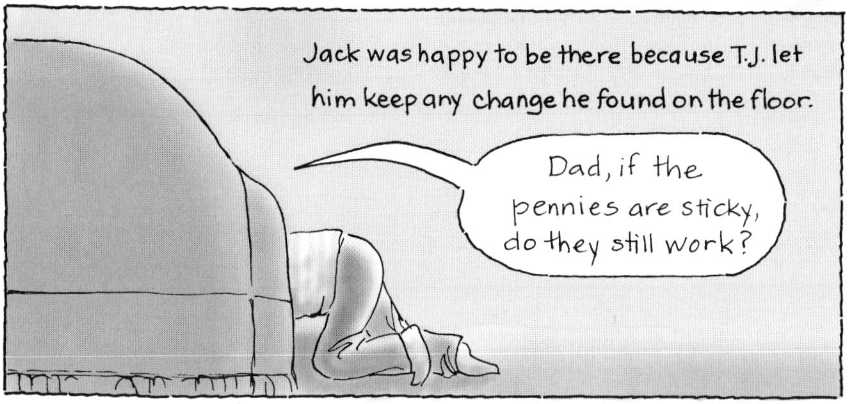
Jack was happy to be there because T.J. let him keep any change he found on the floor.
Dad, if the pennies are sticky, do they still work?

More than anything, the kids liked the idea that they could see their dad whenever they wanted to, rather than being restricted by a "divorce schedule." T.J. liked it, too. He popped in and out of our lives when it suited him.

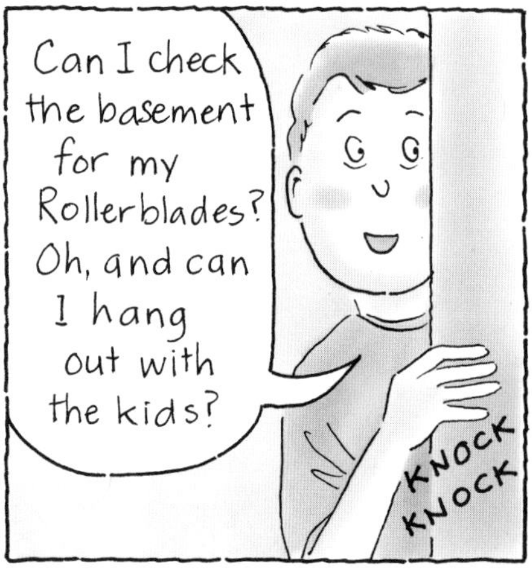
Can I check the basement for my Rollerblades? Oh, and can I hang out with the kids?
KNOCK KNOCK

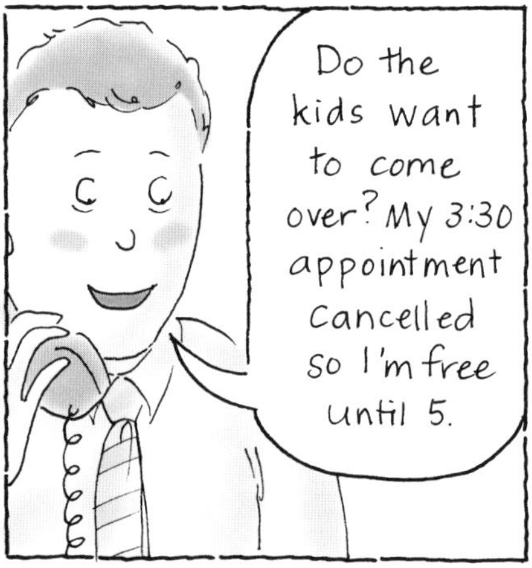
Do the kids want to come over? My 3:30 appointment cancelled so I'm free until 5.

The only downside to our kid-centered plan was that I was left with odd pockets of free time that I couldn't always anticipate.

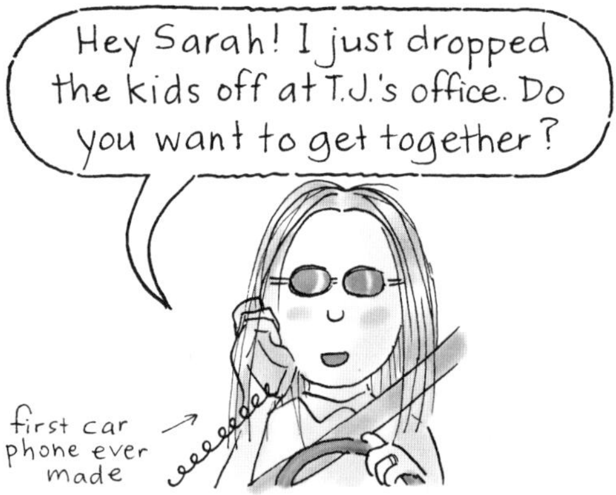
Hey Sarah! I just dropped the kids off at T.J.'s office. Do you want to get together?
first car phone ever made

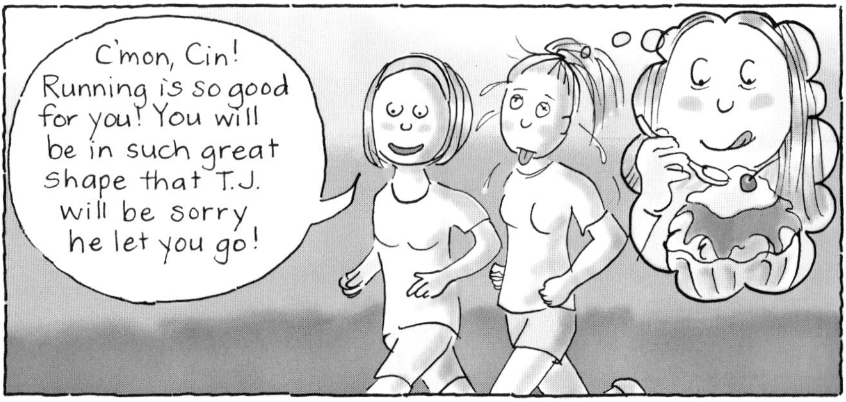
C'mon, Cin! Running is so good for you! You will be in such great shape that T.J. will be sorry he let you go!

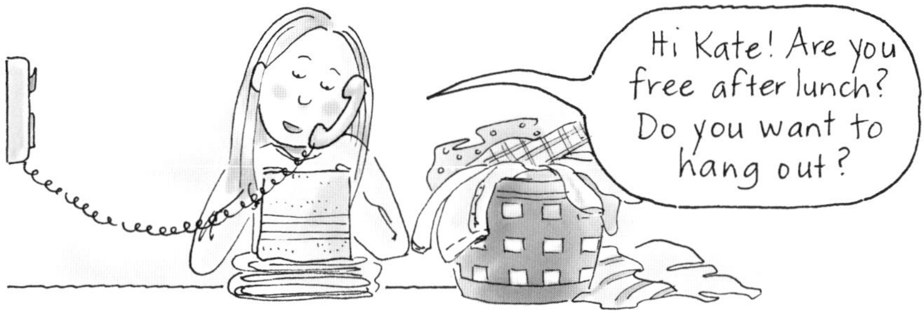
Hi Kate! Are you free after lunch? Do you want to hang out?

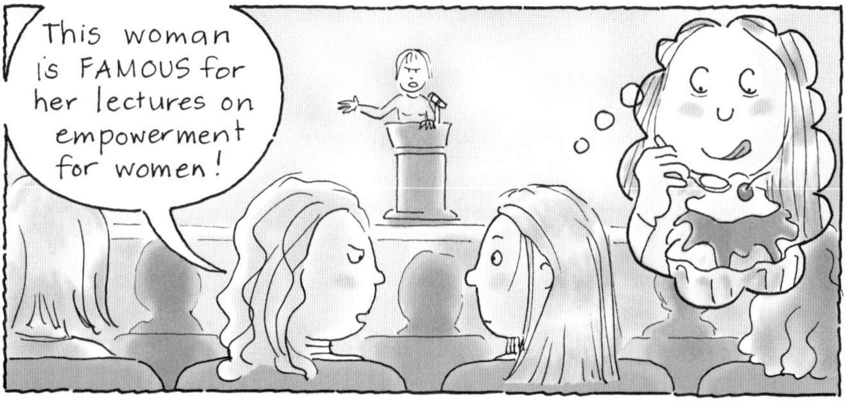
This woman is FAMOUS for her lectures on empowerment for women!

I was slogging through, one day at a time. But life was starting to feel like the board games I played with the kids when they were pre-schoolers. I used to let them make up the rules as we went along, so I never knew when a push on the pop-o-matic dice bubble would send me down a chute or back three spaces or into the thick and airless Molasses Swamp.

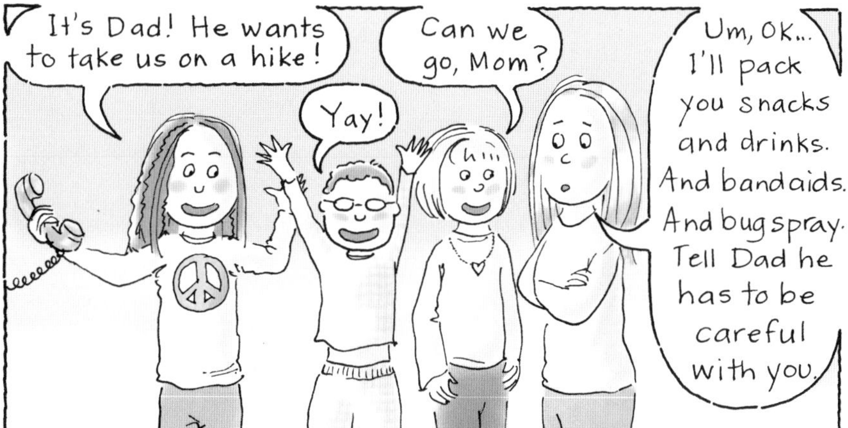
It's Dad! He wants to take us on a hike!
Yay!
Can we go, Mom?
Um, OK... I'll pack you snacks and drinks. And bandaids. And bug spray. Tell Dad he has to be careful with you.

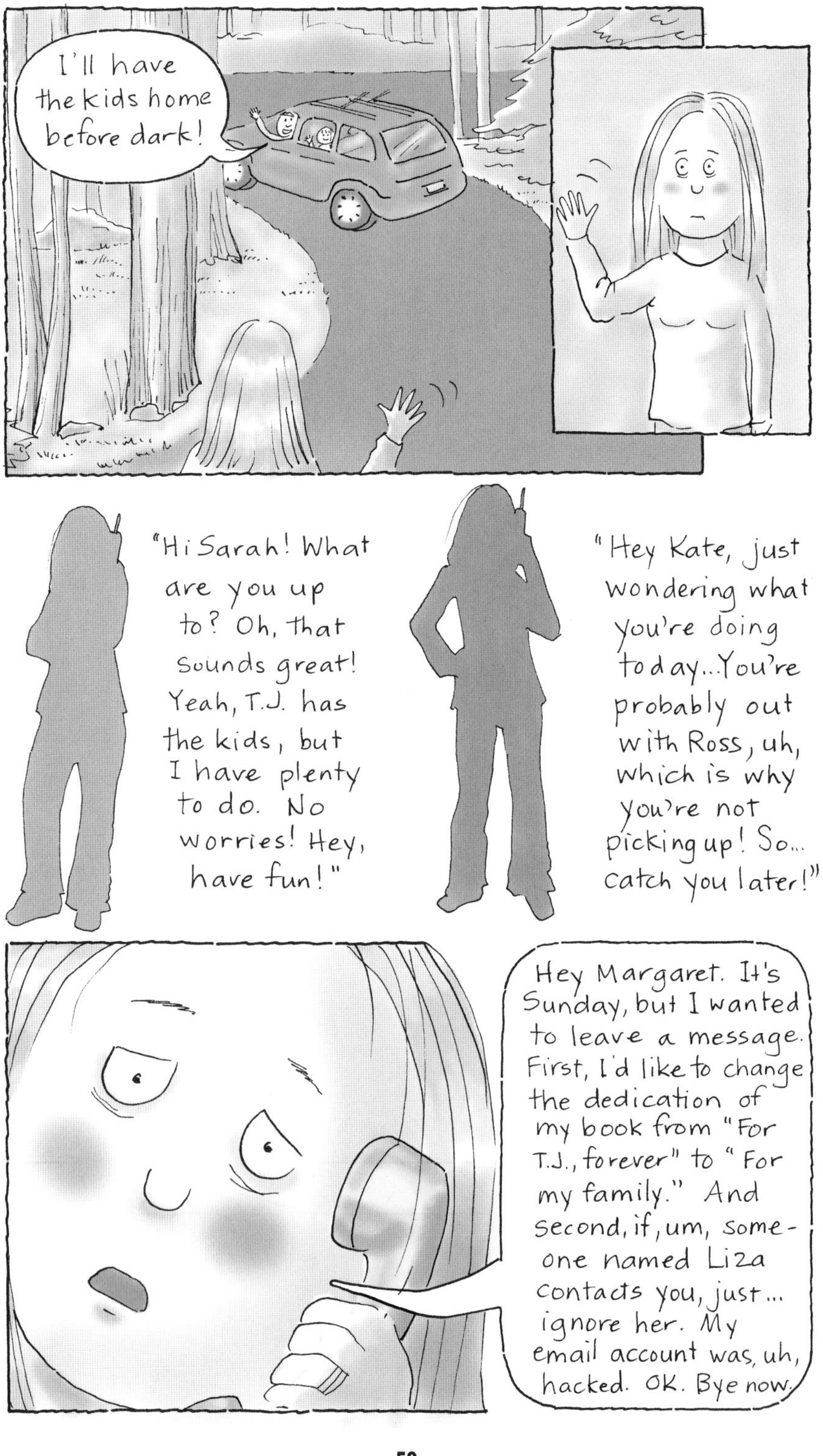
I'll have the kids home before dark!
"Hi Sarah! What are you up to? Oh, that sounds great! Yeah, T.J. has the kids, but I have plenty to do. No worries! Hey, have fun!"
"Hey Kate, just wondering what you're doing today...You're probably out with Ross, uh, which is why you're not picking up! So... catch you later!"
Hey Margaret. It's Sunday, but I wanted to leave a message. First, I'd like to change the dedication of my book from "For T.J., forever" to "For my family." And second, if, um, someone named Liza contacts you, just... ignore her. My email account was, uh, hacked. OK. Bye now.

I used to relish the days T.J. took the kids hiking or kayaking and I had time to focus on my work.

Why did today feel so different?

Today felt... claustrophobic... oppressive... like something heavy was pressing down on me, making it hard to breathe...

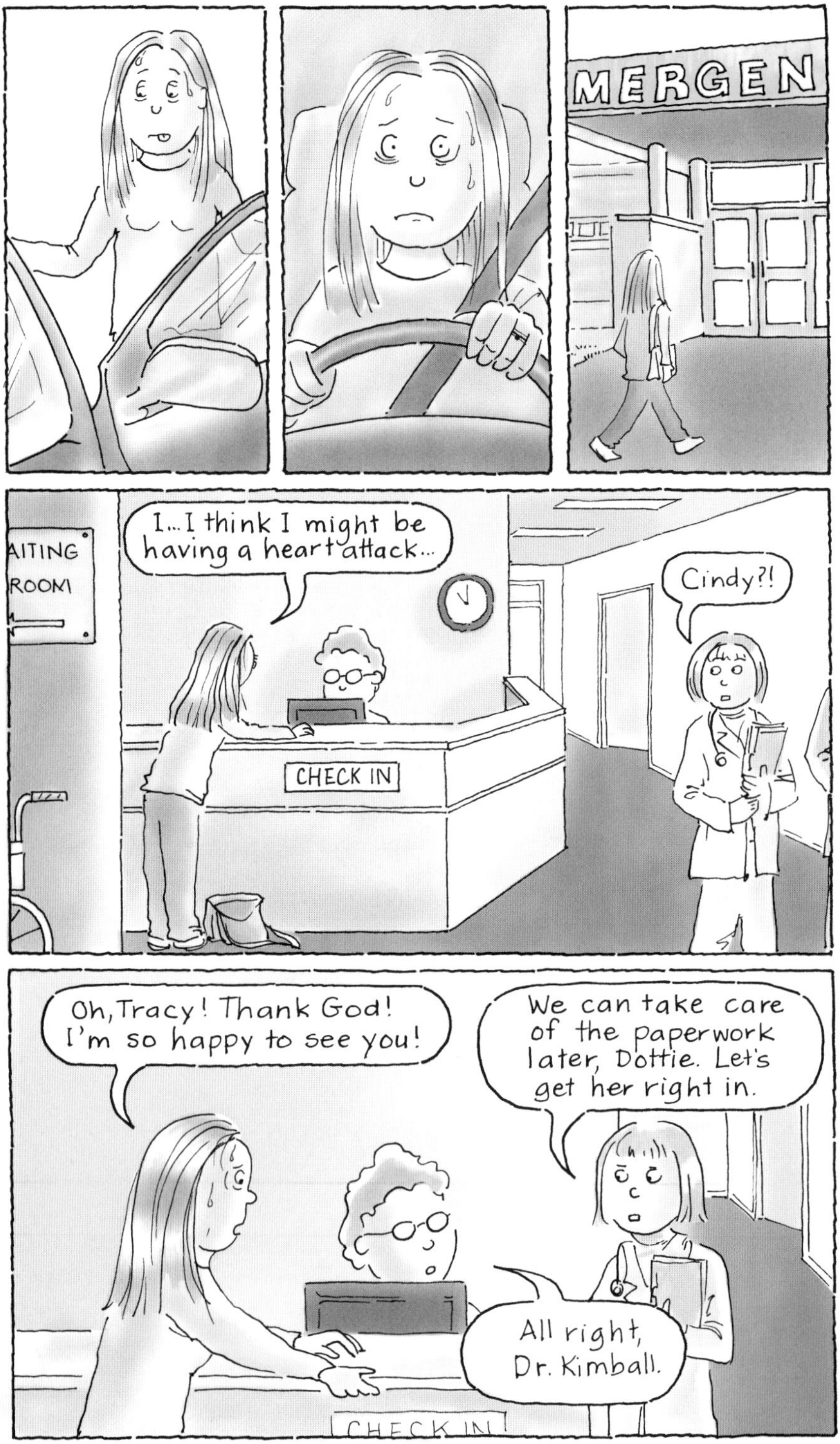
MERGEN
AITING ROOM
I...I think I might be having a heart attack...
CHECK IN
Cindy?!
Oh, Tracy! Thank God! I'm so happy to see you!
We can take care of the paperwork later, Dottie. Let's get her right in.
All right, Dr. Kimball.

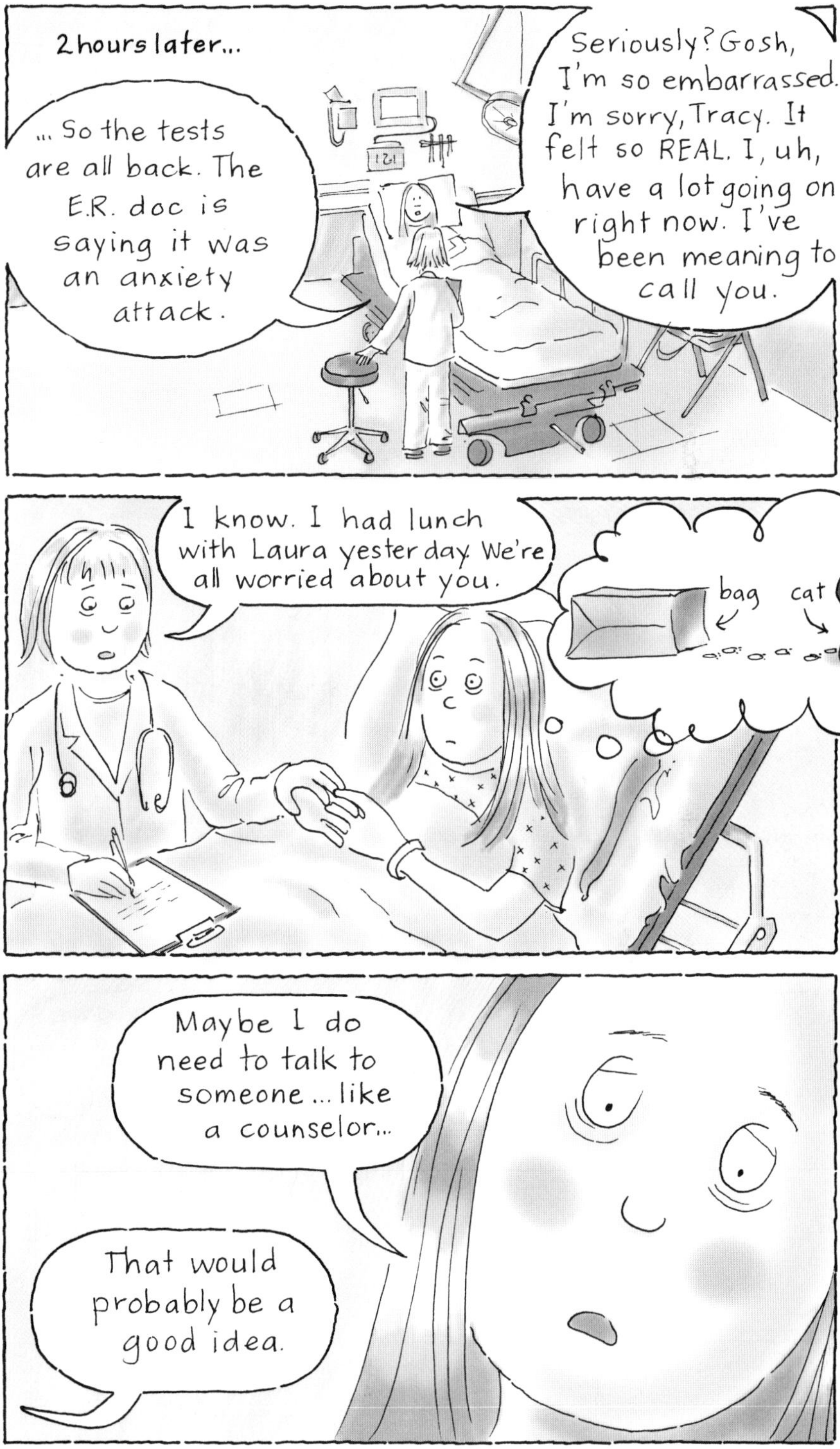
2 hours later...
... So the tests are all back. The E.R. doc is saying it was an anxiety attack.
Seriously? Gosh, I'm so embarrassed. I'm sorry, Tracy. It felt so REAL. I, uh, have a lot going on right now. I've been meaning to call you.
I know. I had lunch with Laura yesterday. We're all worried about you.
bag
cat
Maybe I do need to talk to someone ... like a counselor...
That would probably be a good idea.

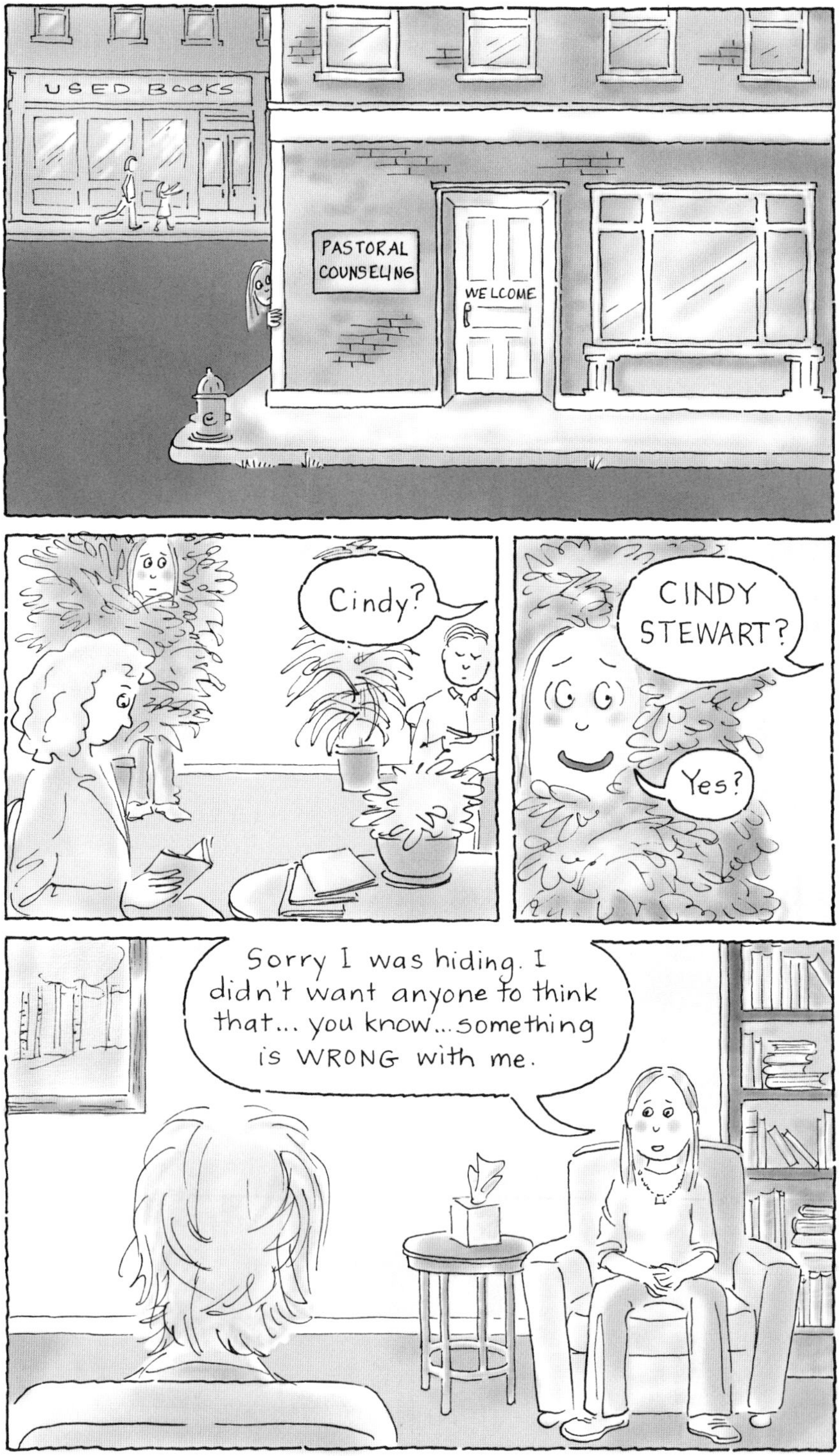
USED BOOKS
PASTORAL COUNSELING
WELCOME
Cindy?
CINDY STEWART?
Yes?
Sorry I was hiding. I didn't want anyone to think that... you know... something is WRONG with me.

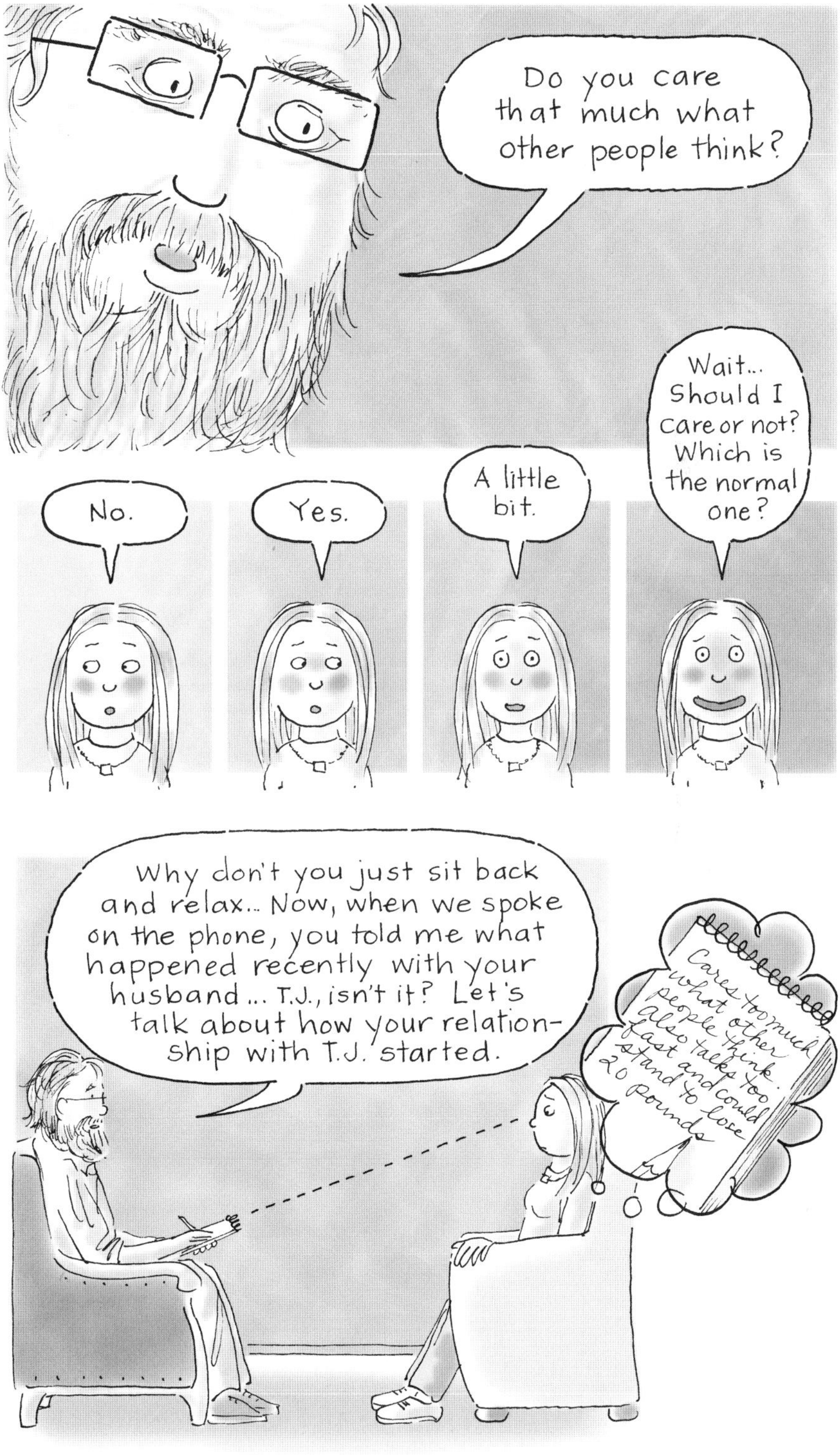
Do you care that much what other people think?
No.
Yes.
A little bit.
Wait... Should I care or not? Which is the normal one?
Why don't you just sit back and relax... Now, when we spoke on the phone, you told me what happened recently with your husband... T.J., isn't it? Let's talk about how your relationship with T.J. started.
Cares too much what other people think. Also talks too fast and could stand to lose 20 pounds

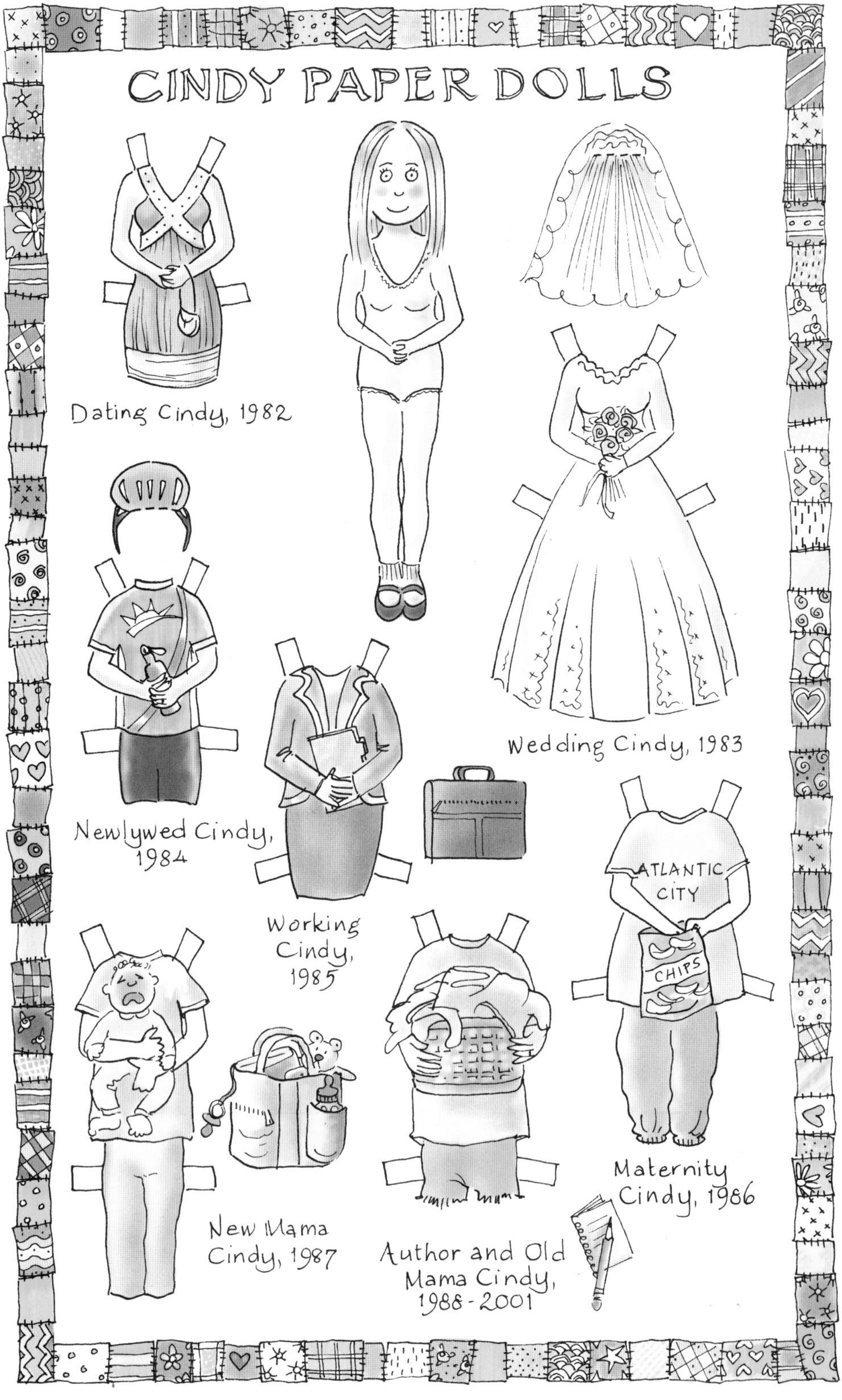
CINDY PAPER DOLLS
Dating Cindy, 1982
Wedding Cindy, 1983
Newlywed Cindy, 1984
Working Cindy, 1985
ATLANTIC CITY
CHIPS
Maternity Cindy, 1986
New Mama Cindy, 1987
Author and Old Mama Cindy, 1988-2001

Once upon a time

(1982), in a faraway land (Boston), Cindy was trying to find work as a freelance writer and artist so that she could pay the very high rent on her very tiny studio apartment.

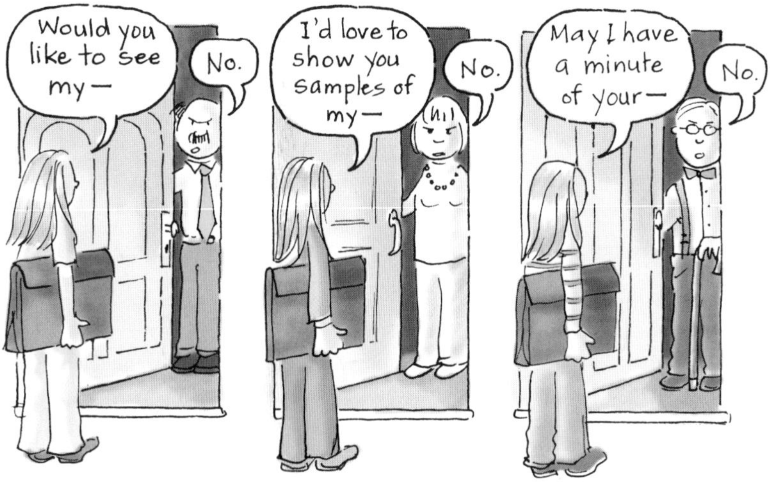
Would you like to see my—
No.
I'd love to show you samples of my—
No.
May I have a minute of your—
No.

Nearby, T.J. was mixing powders and potions in a laboratory at MIT, working toward his doctorate in Inorganic Chemistry.

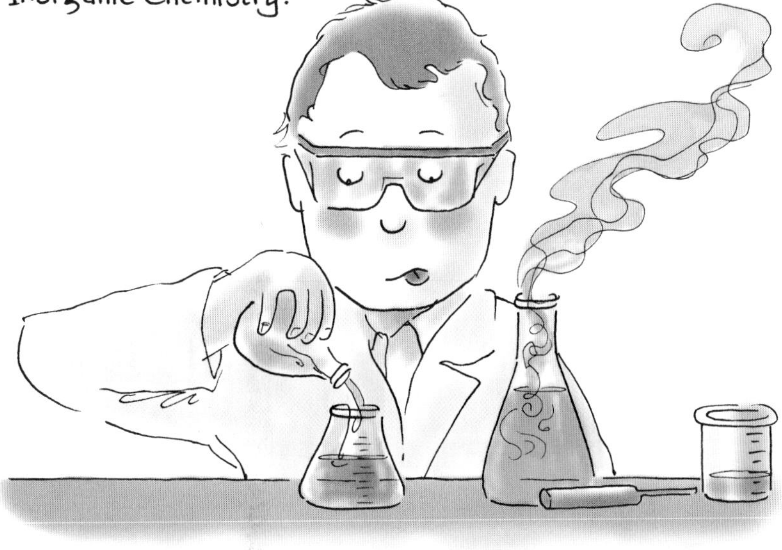

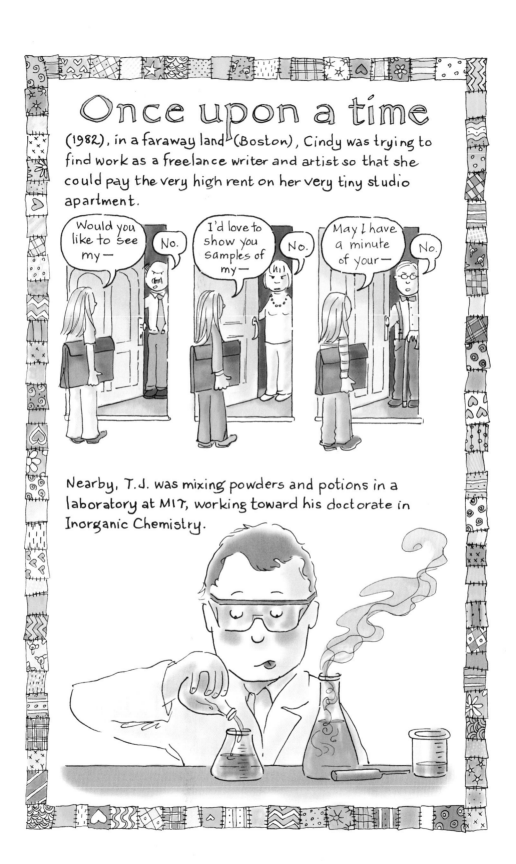

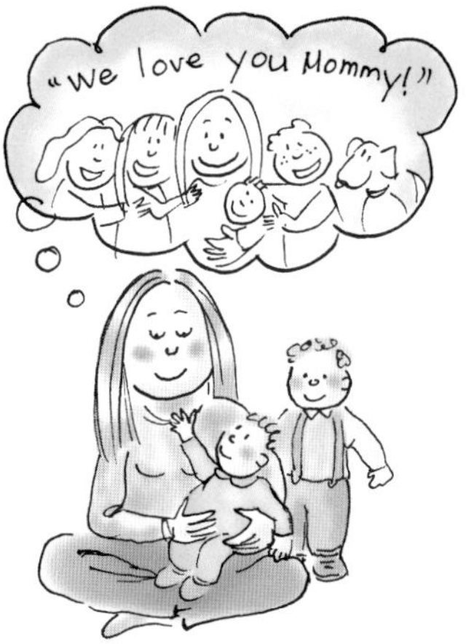
"We love you Mommy!"

Every Sunday, Cindy helped out in her church nursery because she loved playing with babies. Joan, another church member, had a boyfriend named Steve and Steve played hockey with T.J.

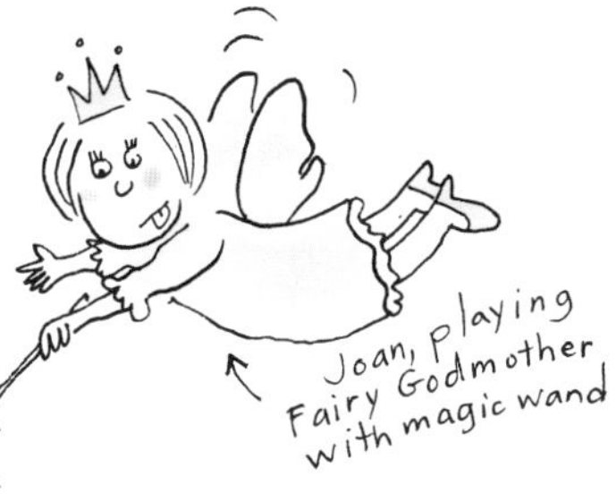
Joan, playing Fairy Godmother with magic wand

Joan decided to arrange a blind date between Cindy and T.J. just before Christmas.

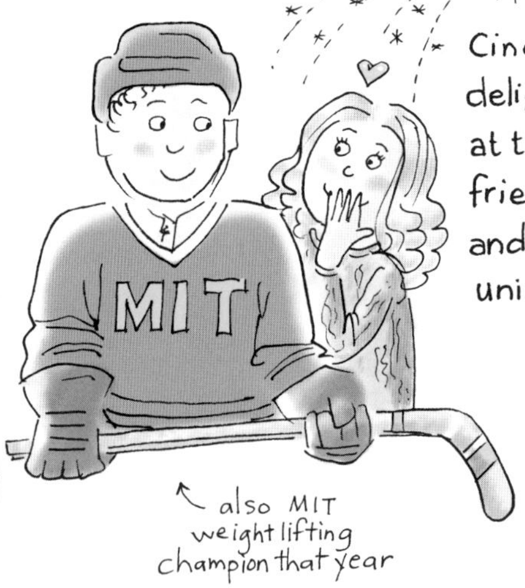
MIT
also MIT weight lifting champion that year

Cindy was both relieved and delighted when she met T.J. at the MIT ice rink. He was friendly and looked handsome and strong in his hockey uniform.

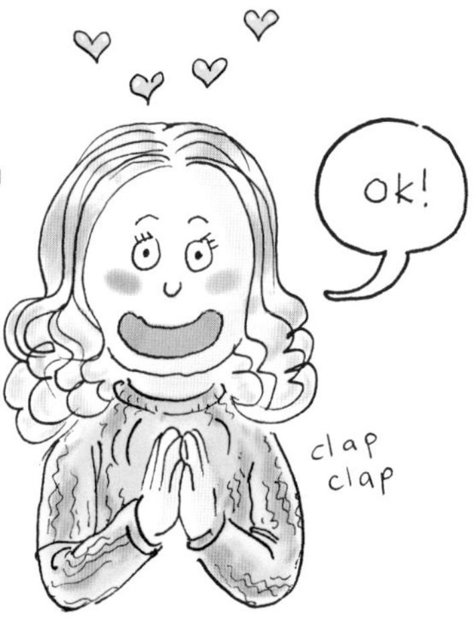
Ok!
clap clap

At the end of the night, T.J. asked Cindy if she would be his date for New Year's Eve.

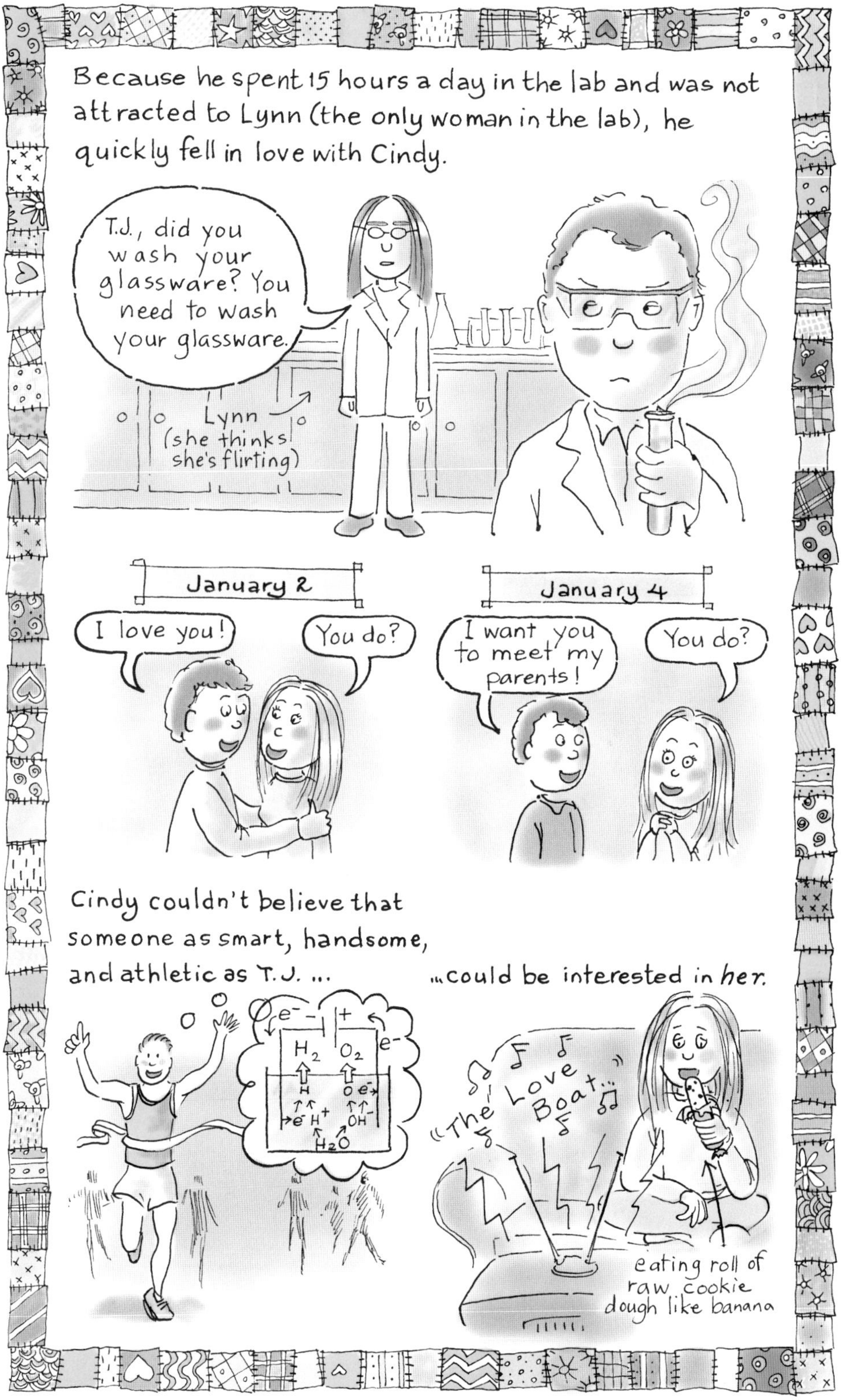
Because he spent 15 hours a day in the lab and was not attracted to Lynn (the only woman in the lab), he quickly fell in love with Cindy.
T.J., did you wash your glassware? You need to wash your glassware.
Lynn (she thinks she's flirting)
January 2
I love you!
You do?
January 4
I want you to meet my parents!
You do?
Cindy couldn't believe that someone as smart, handsome, and athletic as T.J. ...
e^-
H_2
O_2
OH^-
H_2O
...could be interested in *her*.
"The Love Boat..."
eating roll of raw cookie dough like banana

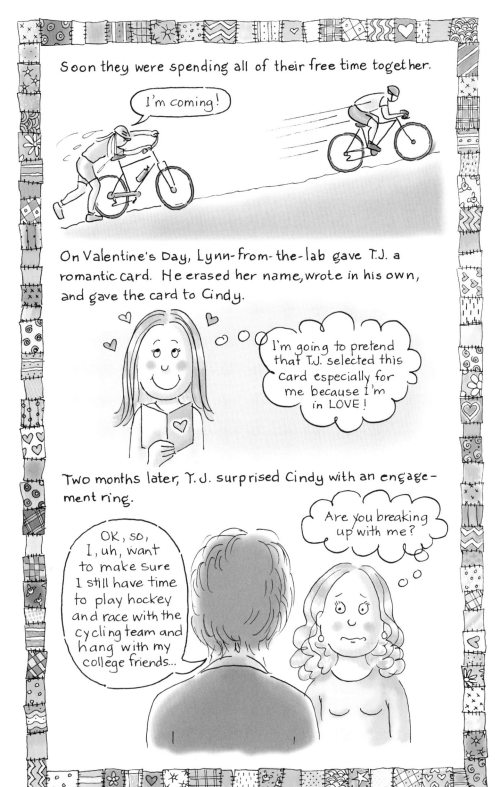

Soon they were spending all of their free time together.

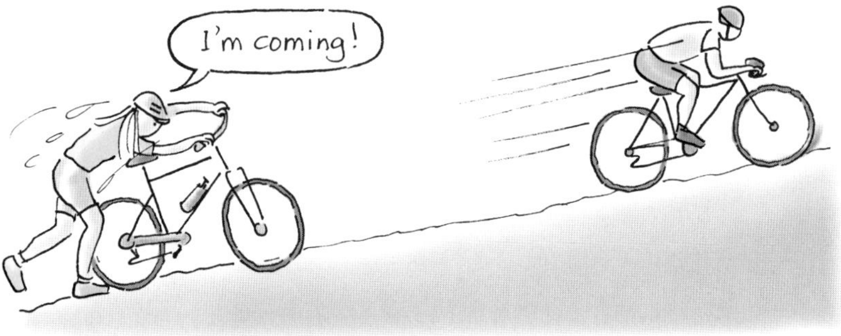
I'm coming!

On Valentine's Day, Lynn-from-the-lab gave T.J. a romantic card. He erased her name, wrote in his own, and gave the card to Cindy.

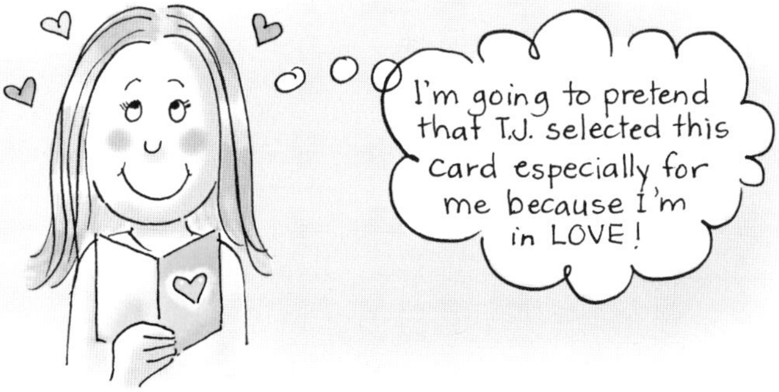
I'm going to pretend that T.J. selected this card especially for me because I'm in LOVE!

Two months later, T.J. surprised Cindy with an engagement ring.

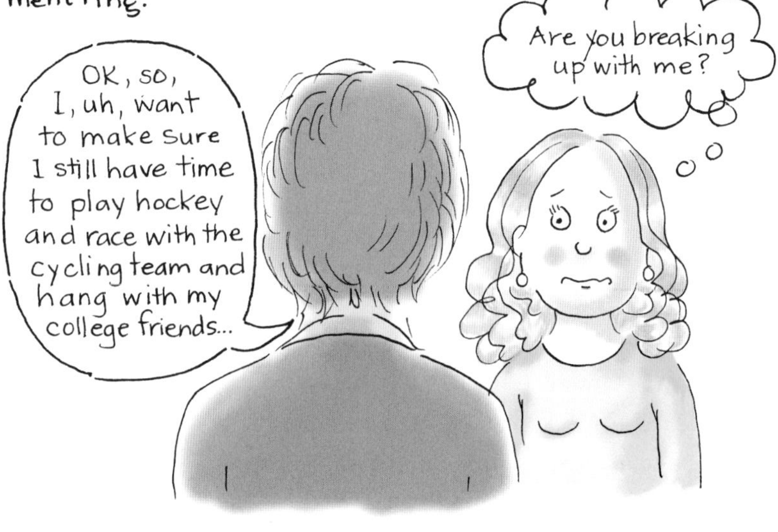
OK, so, I, uh, want to make sure I still have time to play hockey and race with the cycling team and hang with my college friends...
Are you breaking up with me?

They were married exactly a year from the day they met, on December 23, 1983.

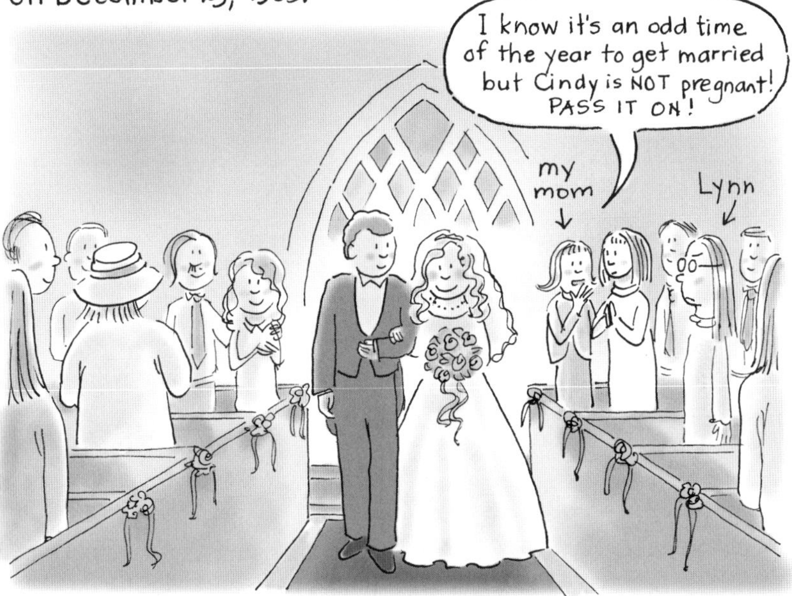
I know it's an odd time of the year to get married but Cindy is NOT pregnant! PASS IT ON!
my mom
Lynn

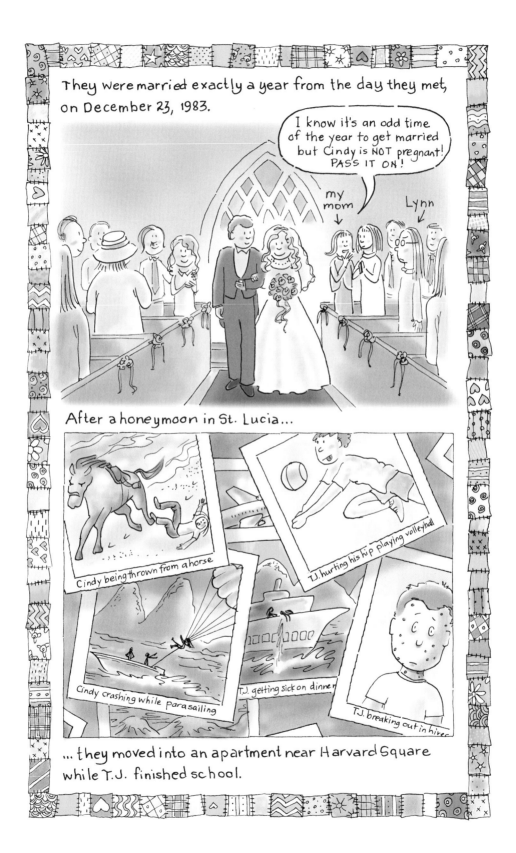

After a honeymoon in St. Lucia...

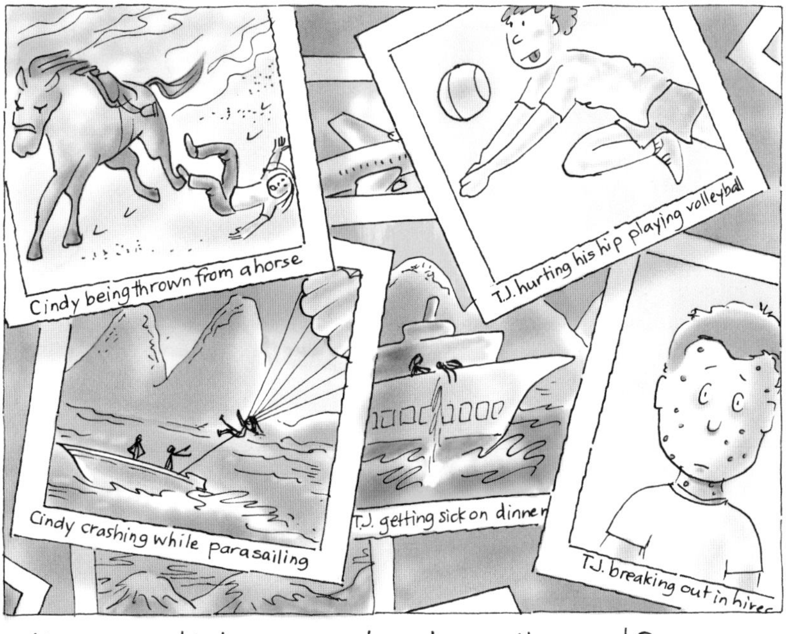
Cindy being thrown from a horse
T.J. hurting his hip playing volleyball
Cindy crashing while parasailing
T.J. getting sick on dinne
T.J. breaking out in

... they moved into an apartment near Harvard Square while T.J. finished school.

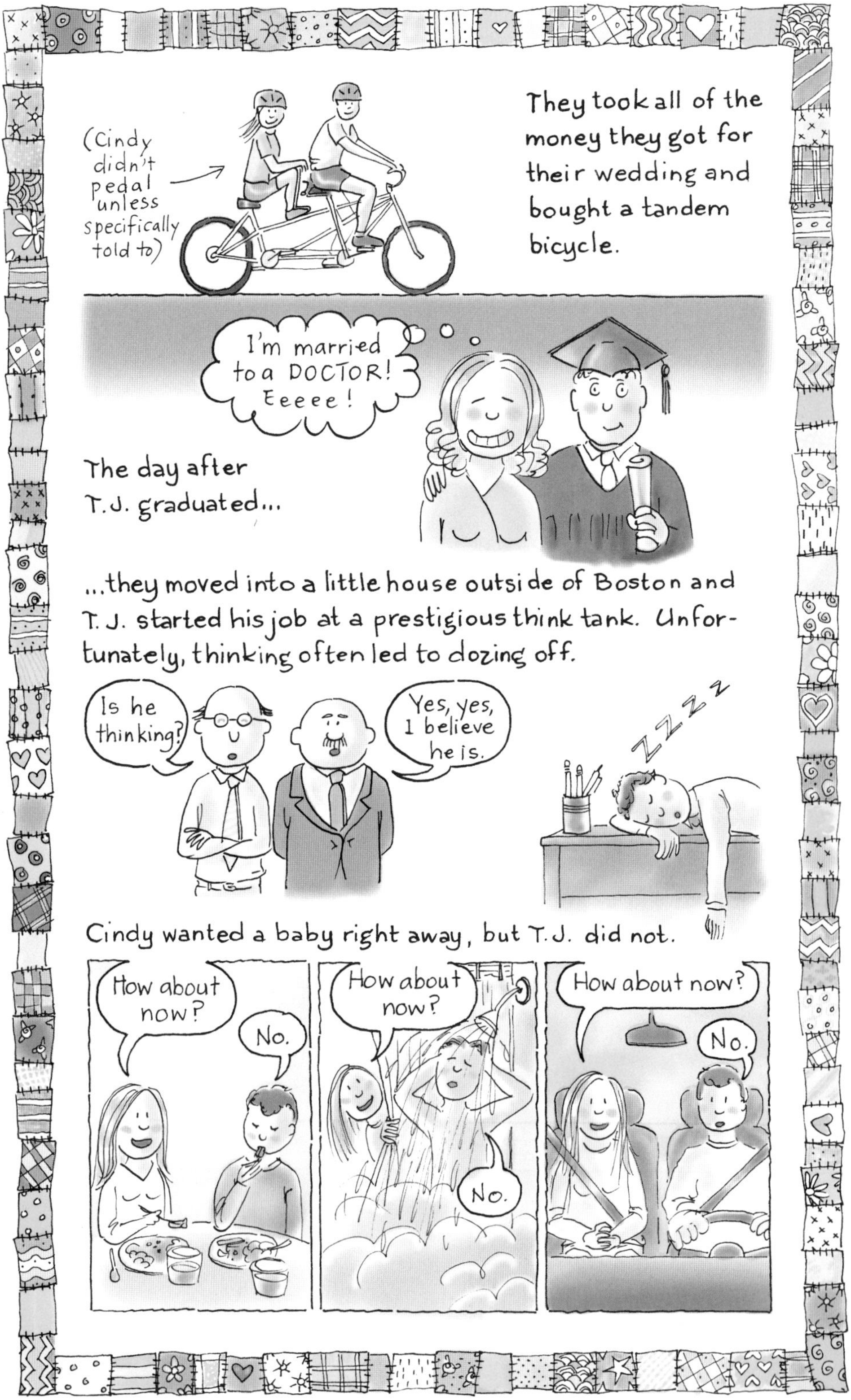
(Cindy didn't pedal unless specifically told to)
They took all of the money they got for their wedding and bought a tandem bicycle.
I'm married to a DOCTOR! Eeeee!
The day after T.J. graduated...
...they moved into a little house outside of Boston and T.J. started his job at a prestigious think tank. Unfortunately, thinking often led to dozing off.
Is he thinking?
Yes, yes, I believe he is.
ZZZZ
Cindy wanted a baby right away, but T.J. did not.
How about now?
No.
How about now?
No.
How about now?
No.

So Cindy got a job as an editor and they saved money while they hiked and biked and fixed things around the new house.

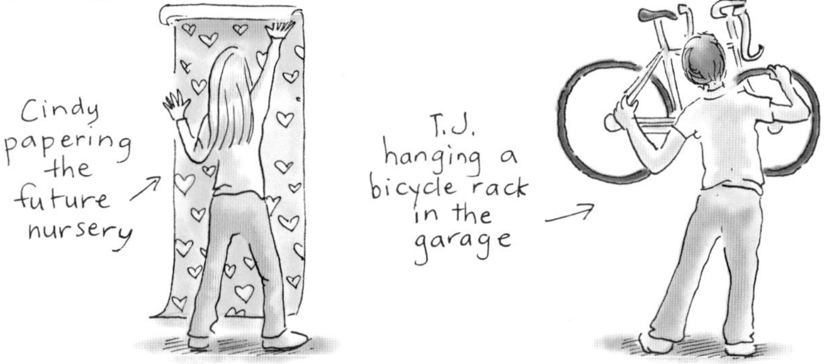
Cindy papering the future nursery
T.J. hanging a bicycle rack in the garage

Three years after they got married, T.J. relented.

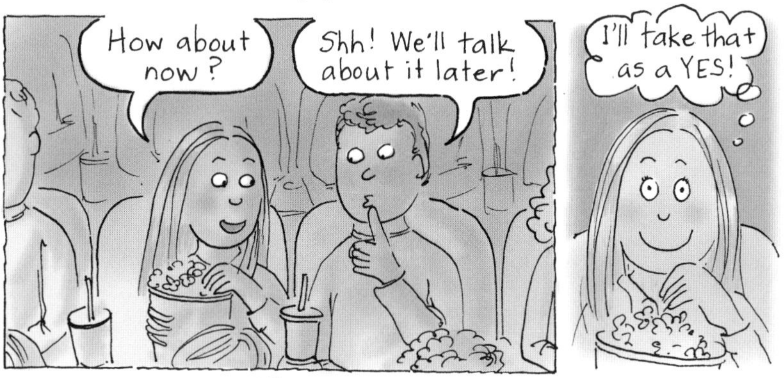
How about now?
Shh! We'll talk about it later!
I'll take that as a YES!

Nine months later, Cindy had a baby girl. They named her Annie.

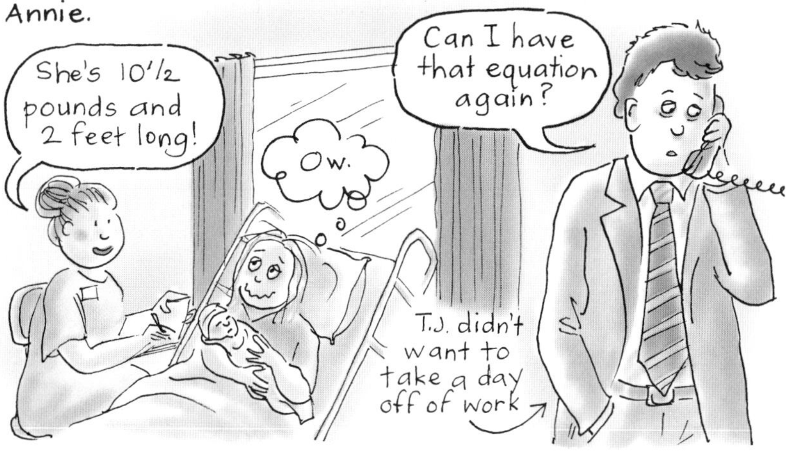
She's 10½ pounds and 2 feet long!
Ow.
Can I have that equation again?
T.J. didn't want to take a day off of work

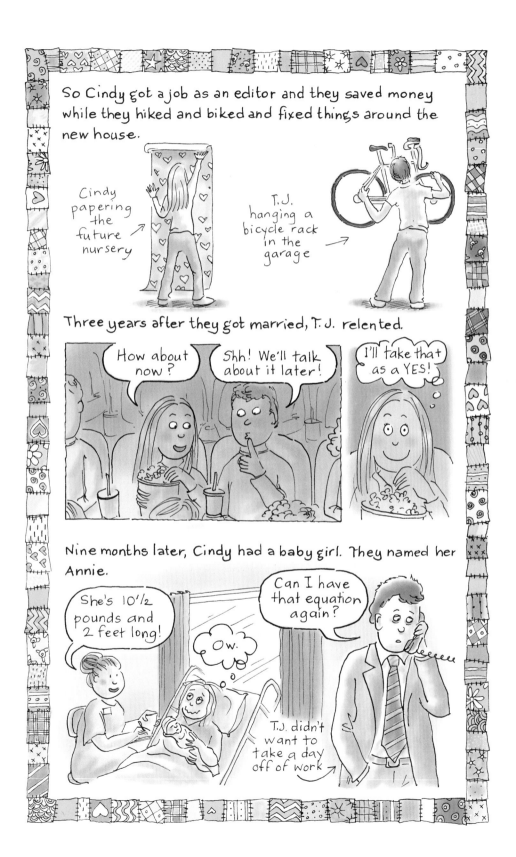

T.J. accepted a job as a research scientist and the family moved to an old farmhouse in New Hampshire on a stretch of meadow across from a pond. Cindy began writing a book about being a first-time mom.

Two years later (on the same day that Cindy's first book was published), Emma was born. Jack came along several years after that.

Smile everyone!

The years passed happily. When the children napped or slept, Cindy wrote books about raising a happy family. When the children were awake, they made board games...

I'll jump over the chicken coop to get to the hand-dug well with the dead squirrel floating in it!

baked bread...

planted green bean teepees and sunflower houses in the garden...

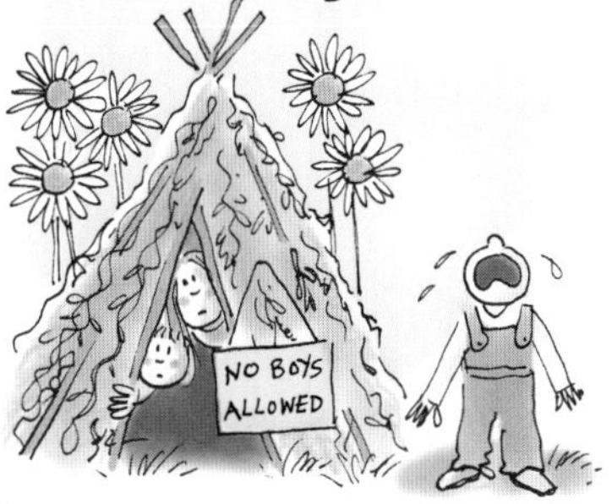
NO BOYS ALLOWED

and caught frogs and salamanders in the pond.

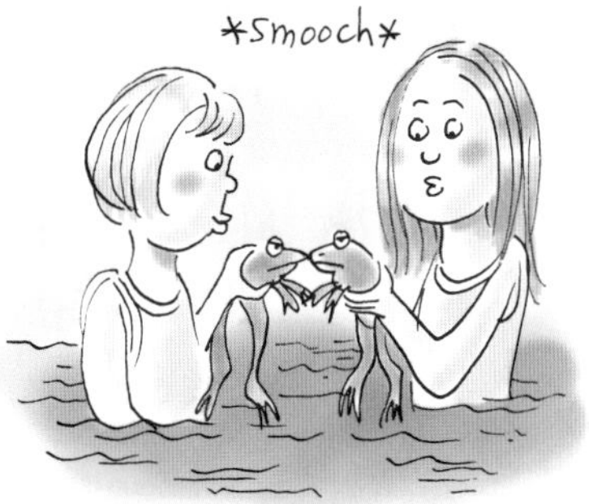
Smooch

They got a Golden Retriever and pet sheep.

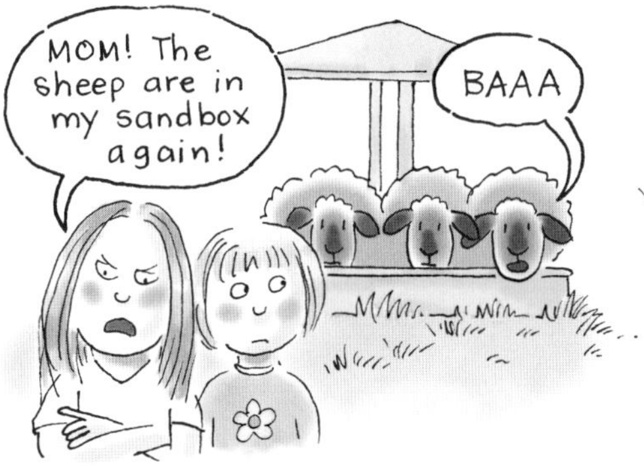
MOM! The sheep are in my sandbox again!
BAAA

They even had pet geese (although not for long).

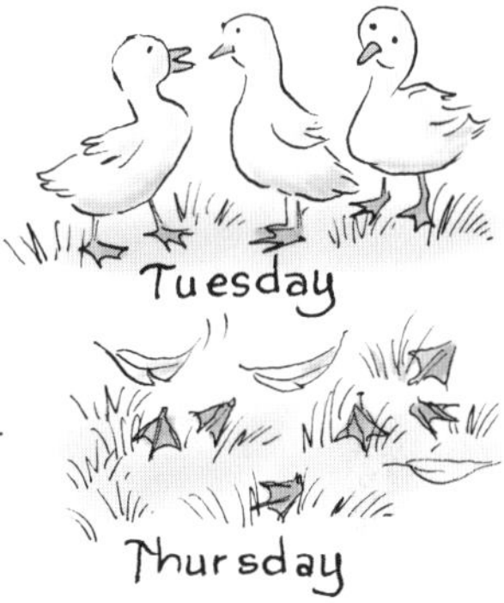
Tuesday
Thursday

T.J. and Cindy didn't always agree on parenting issues...

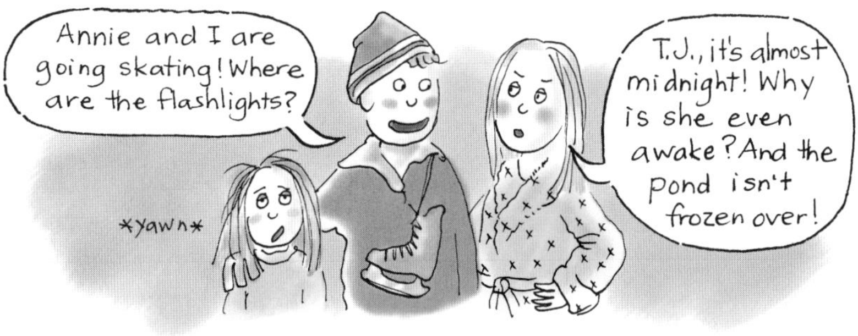
Annie and I are going skating! Where are the flashlights?
yawn
T.J., it's almost midnight! Why is she even awake? And the pond isn't frozen over!

... but T.J. left most of that to Cindy while he focused on his career and his extreme sports. Cindy and T.J. didn't have much time for each other, but Cindy wasn't worried: When the kids were older, they'd reconnect.

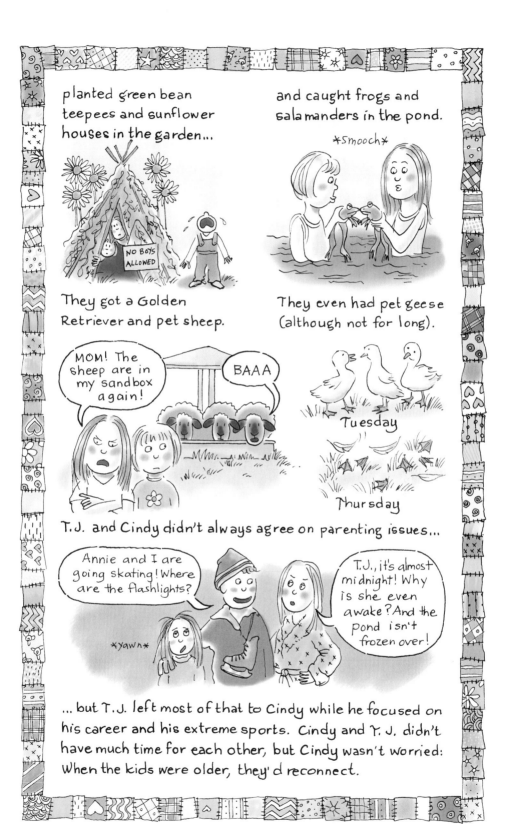

As the children's lives got busier, Cindy and T.J. realized that they needed to live closer to town. So they sold their farmhouse and built a big, new house in a fancy neighborhood. With her royalty checks, Cindy added a big, new addition to the big, new house.

chalkboard mural

Emma's room

Jack's room

gazebo on the hill

Annie's room

play loft

secret play house under the stairs

kids' craft corner

stage for the kids' shows

barn for kids' outdoor pets

frog pond

tree fort

sand box

vegetable garden

It was their dream house.

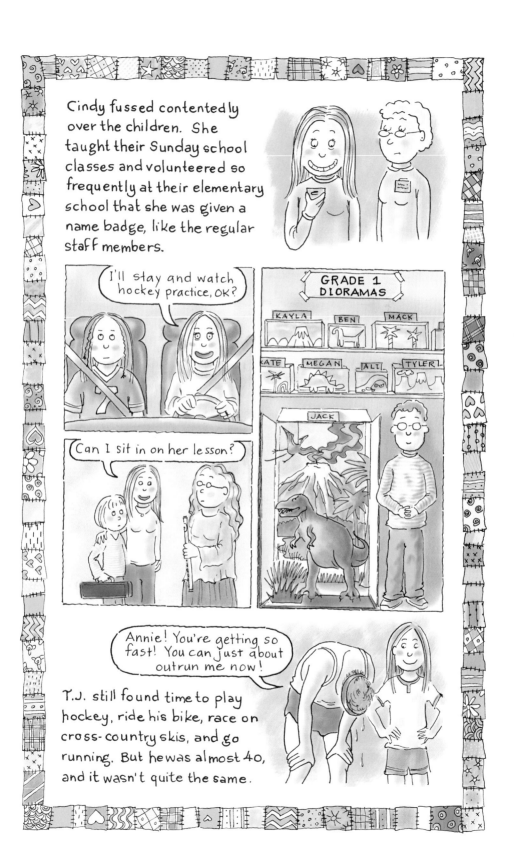

Cindy fussed contentedly over the children. She taught their Sunday school classes and volunteered so frequently at their elementary school that she was given a name badge, like the regular staff members.

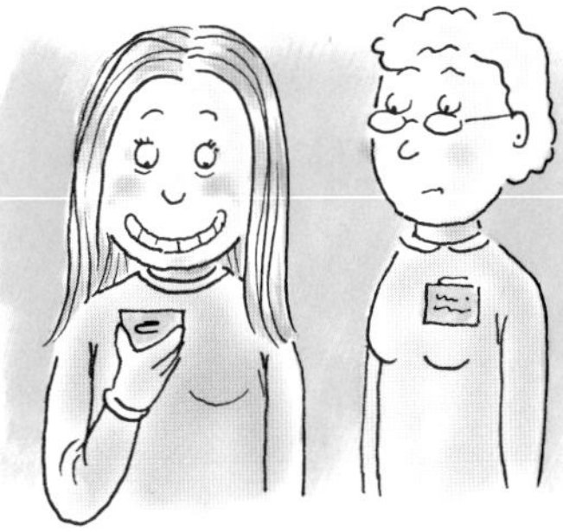

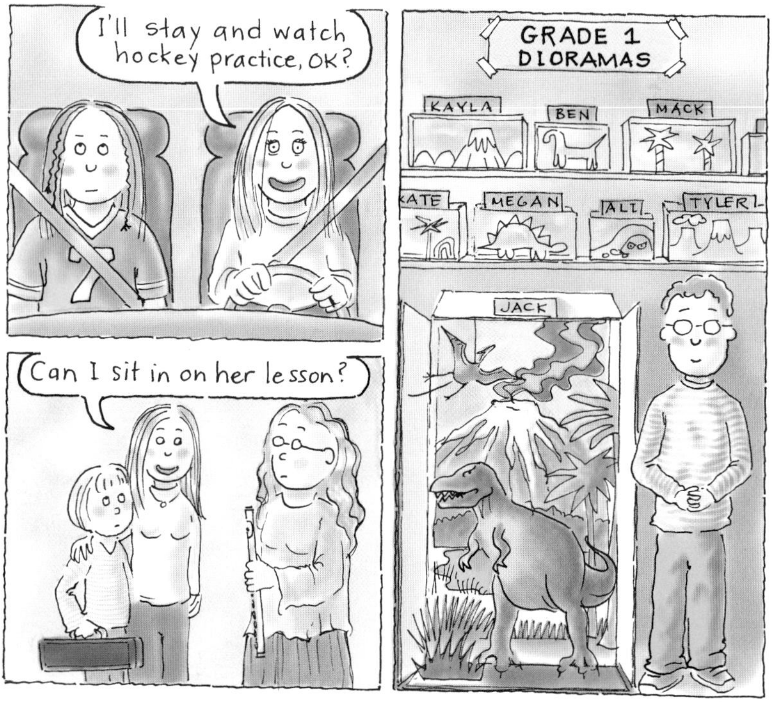
I'll stay and watch hockey practice, OK?
GRADE 1 DIORAMAS
KAYLA
BEN
MACK
KATE
MEGAN
ALI
TYLER
JACK
Can I sit in on her lesson?

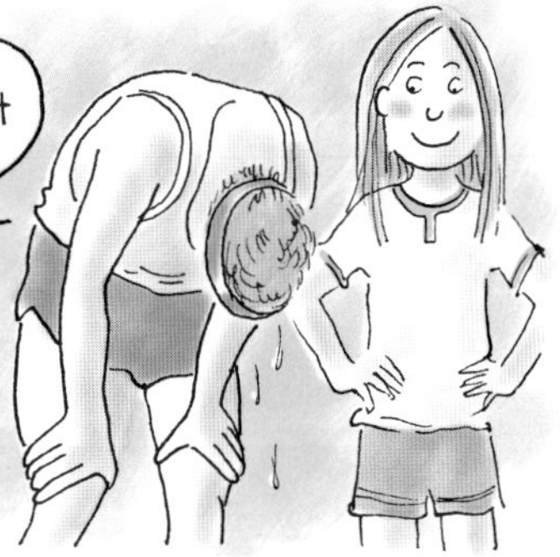
Annie! You're getting so fast! You can just about outrun me now!

T.J. still found time to play hockey, ride his bike, race on cross-country skis, and go running. But he was almost 40, and it wasn't quite the same.

T.J. grew restless at work. He decided to start his own consulting company. When it became clear that this new venture wouldn't make millions, he began spending evenings in the basement, experimenting.

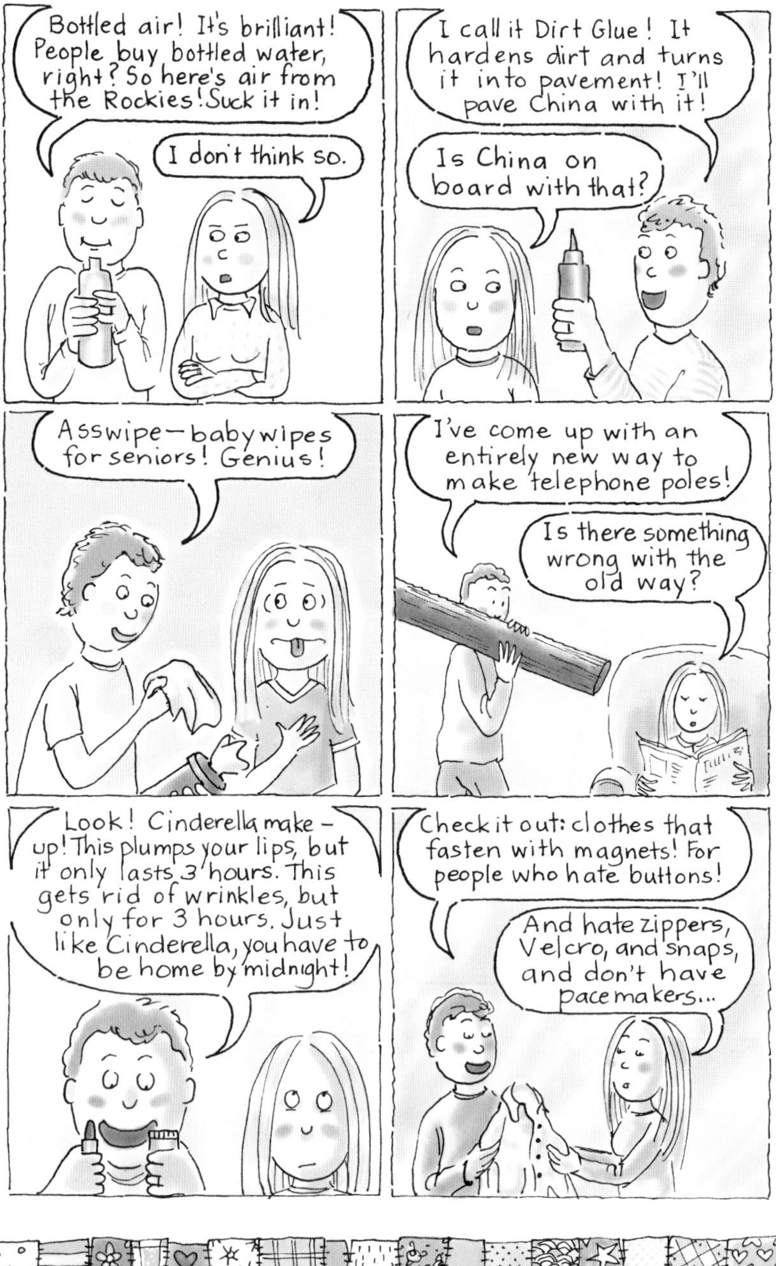
Bottled air! It's brilliant! People buy bottled water, right? So here's air from the Rockies! Suck it in!
I don't think so.
I call it Dirt Glue! It hardens dirt and turns it into pavement! I'll pave China with it!
Is China on board with that?
Asswipe—babywipes for seniors! Genius!
I've come up with an entirely new way to make telephone poles!
Is there something wrong with the old way?
Look! Cinderella make-up! This plumps your lips, but it only lasts 3 hours. This gets rid of wrinkles, but only for 3 hours. Just like Cinderella, you have to be home by midnight!
Check it out: clothes that fasten with magnets! For people who hate buttons!
And hate zippers, Velcro, and snaps, and don't have pacemakers...

T.J. wanted Cindy to pay more attention to him. He wanted her to show as much enthusiasm for his ideas as she did for the kids' ideas. Cindy was afraid that if she showed too much enthusiasm, she would discover that T.J. had invested their life savings in dirt glue or bottled air. Or something even weirder.

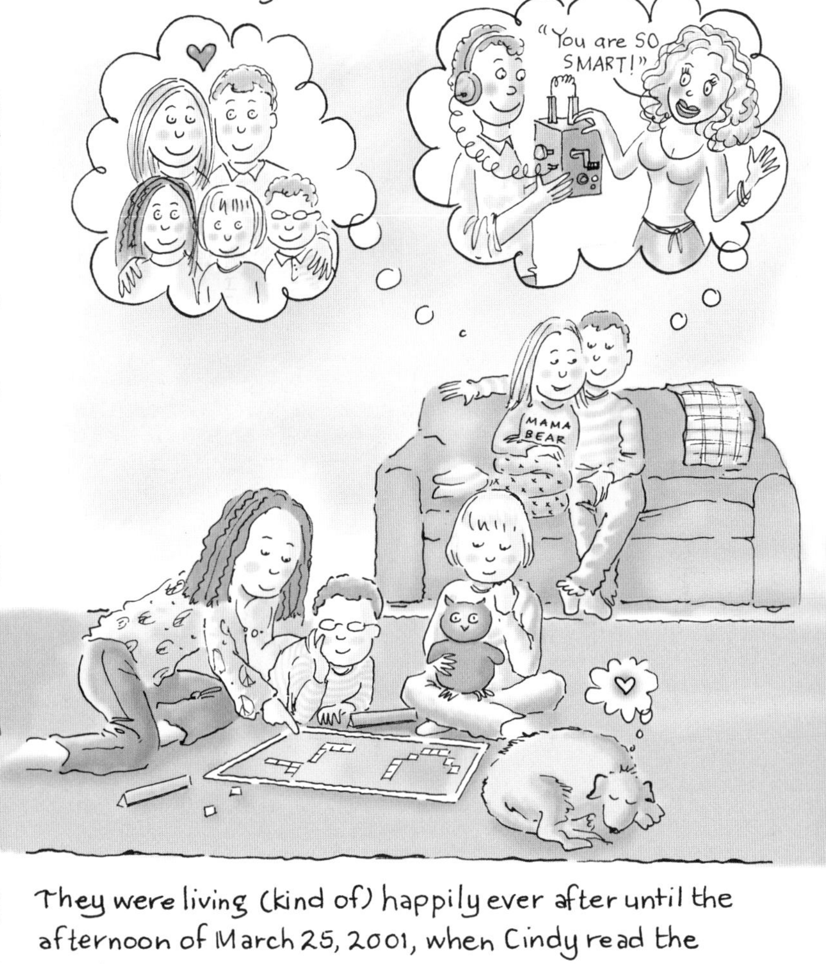
"You are SO SMART!"
MAMA BEAR

They were living (kind of) happily ever after until the afternoon of March 25, 2001, when Cindy read the emails.

THE END...

...isn't always where it should be.

It was the first time I'd gone back and analyzed the entire relationship. I guess I'd always put marriage in the same category as algebra and string theory: Things I Shouldn't Over-think.

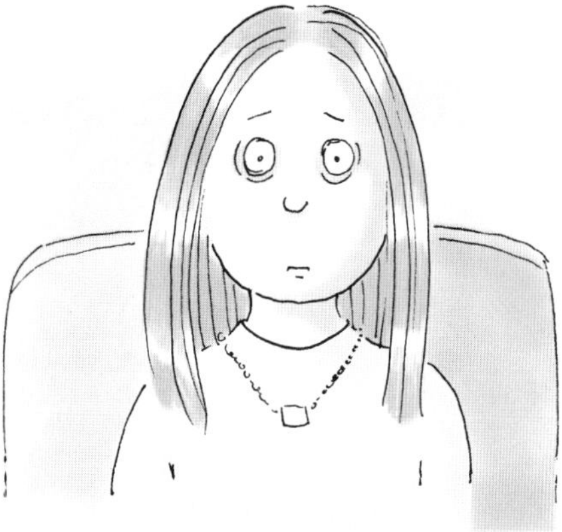

But now I had to face a new, altered reality. How much of our fairy tale would I have to re-write?

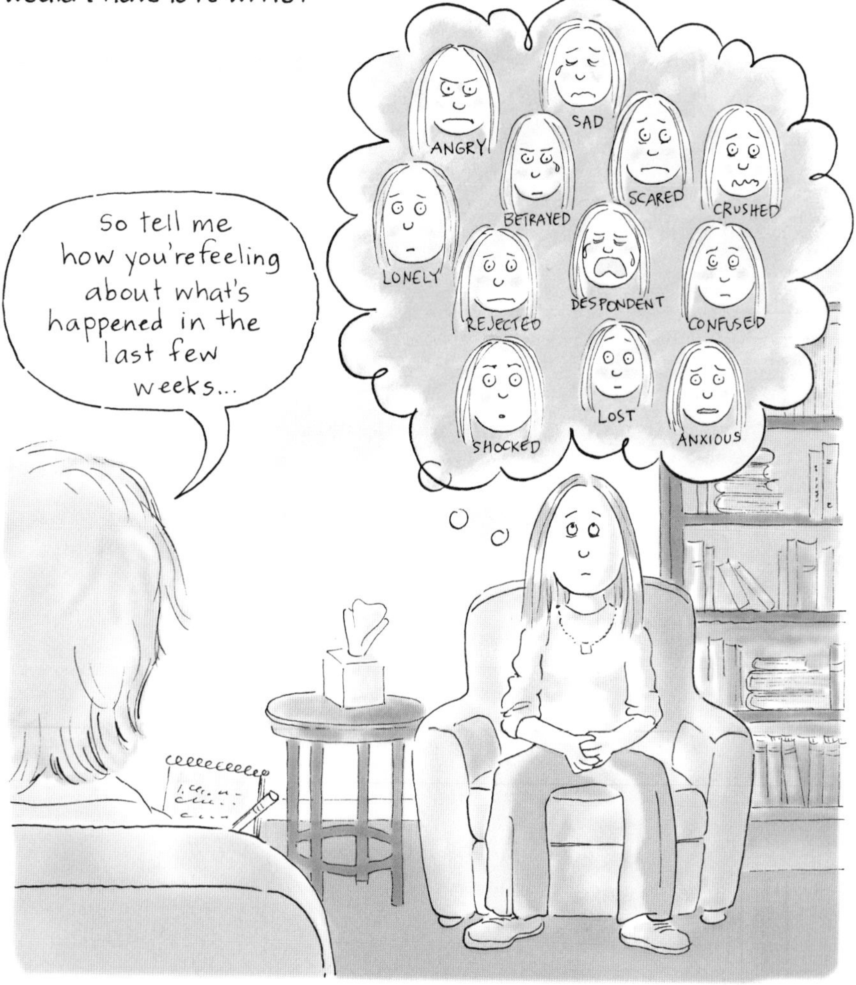
So tell me how you're feeling about what's happened in the last few weeks...
ANGRY
SAD
BETRAYED
SCARED
CRUSHED
LONELY
REJECTED
DESPONDENT
CONFUSED
SHOCKED
LOST
ANXIOUS

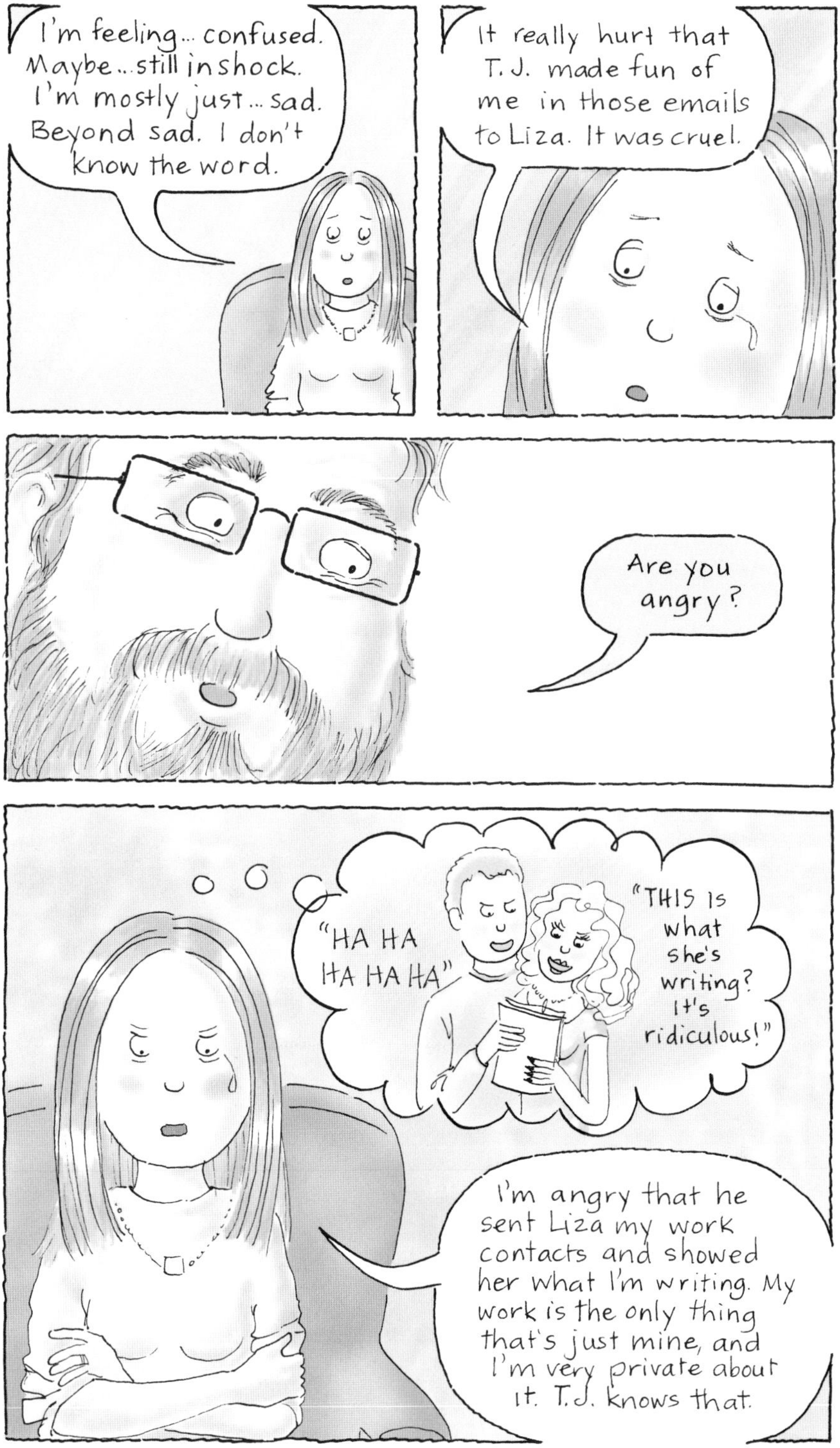
I'm feeling... confused. Maybe...still in shock. I'm mostly just... sad. Beyond sad. I don't know the word.
It really hurt that T.J. made fun of me in those emails to Liza. It was cruel.
Are you angry?
"HA HA HA HA HA"
"THIS is what she's writing? It's ridiculous!"
I'm angry that he sent Liza my work contacts and showed her what I'm writing. My work is the only thing that's just mine, and I'm very private about it. T.J. knows that.

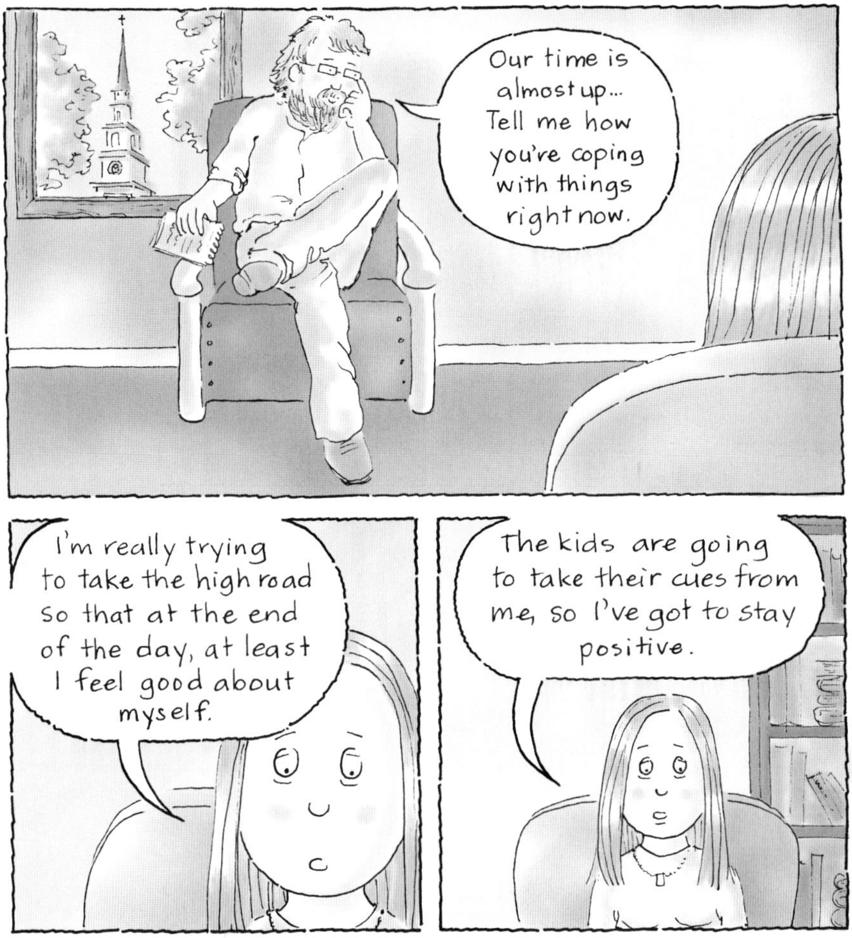
Our time is almost up... Tell me how you're coping with things right now.
I'm really trying to take the high road so that at the end of the day, at least I feel good about myself.
The kids are going to take their cues from me, so I've got to stay positive.

Gary turned out to be a kind, no-nonsense guy and a good listener. It was a relief to talk to someone who could weigh in objectively on my life.

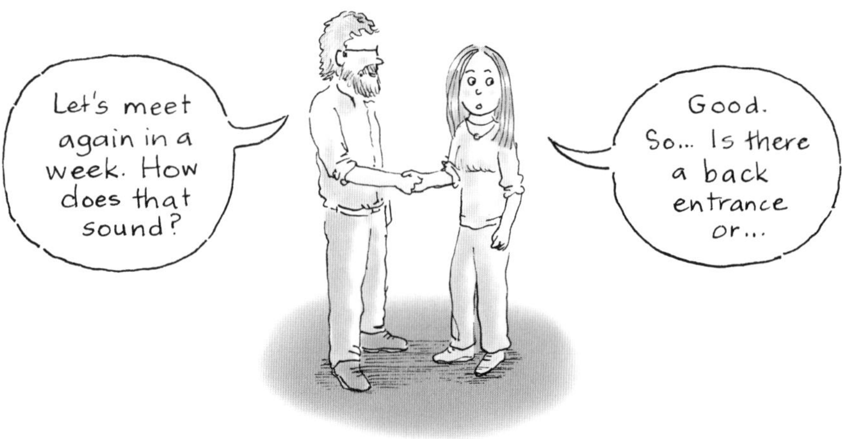
Let's meet again in a week. How does that sound?
Good. So... Is there a back entrance or...

As the weeks wore on, the kids and I settled into a rather unsettling new normal. After all, was there another option?

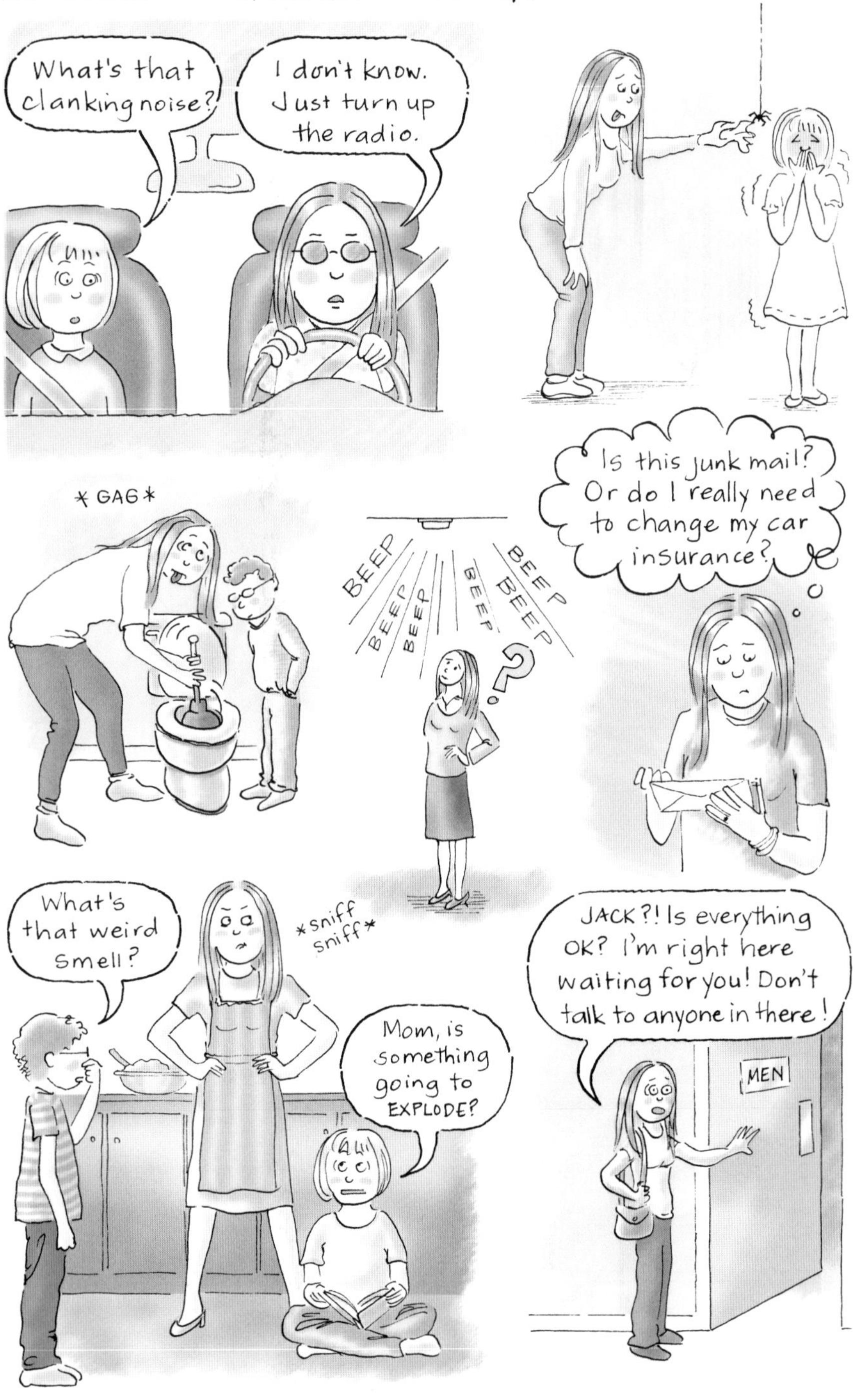
What's that clanking noise?
I don't know. Just turn up the radio.
* GAG *
BEEP
BEEP
BEEP
BEEP
BEEP
BEEP
?
Is this junk mail? Or do I really need to change my car insurance?
What's that weird smell?
sniff sniff
Mom, is something going to EXPLODE?
JACK?! Is everything OK? I'm right here waiting for you! Don't talk to anyone in there!
MEN

I tended to be more confident and capable during the day...

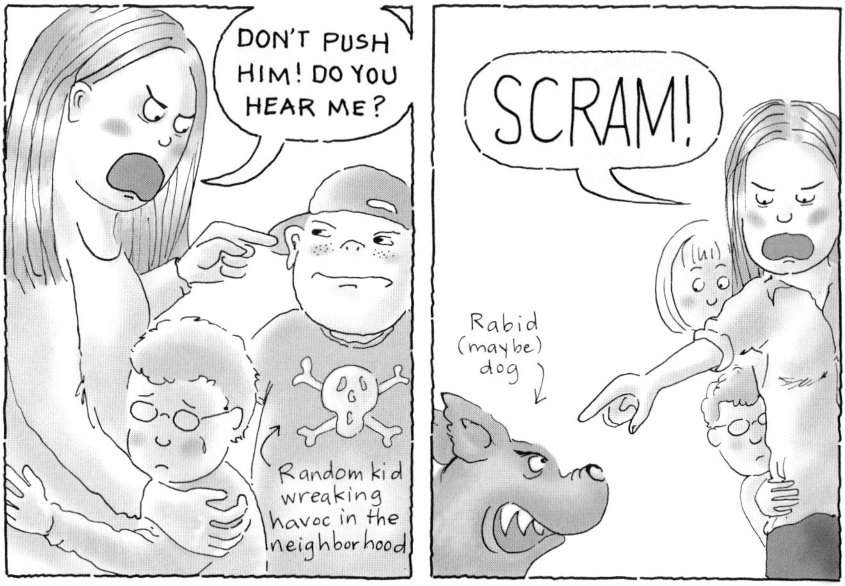
DON'T PUSH HIM! DO YOU HEAR ME?
Random kid wreaking havoc in the neighborhood
SCRAM!
Rabid (maybe) dog

...than I was at night.

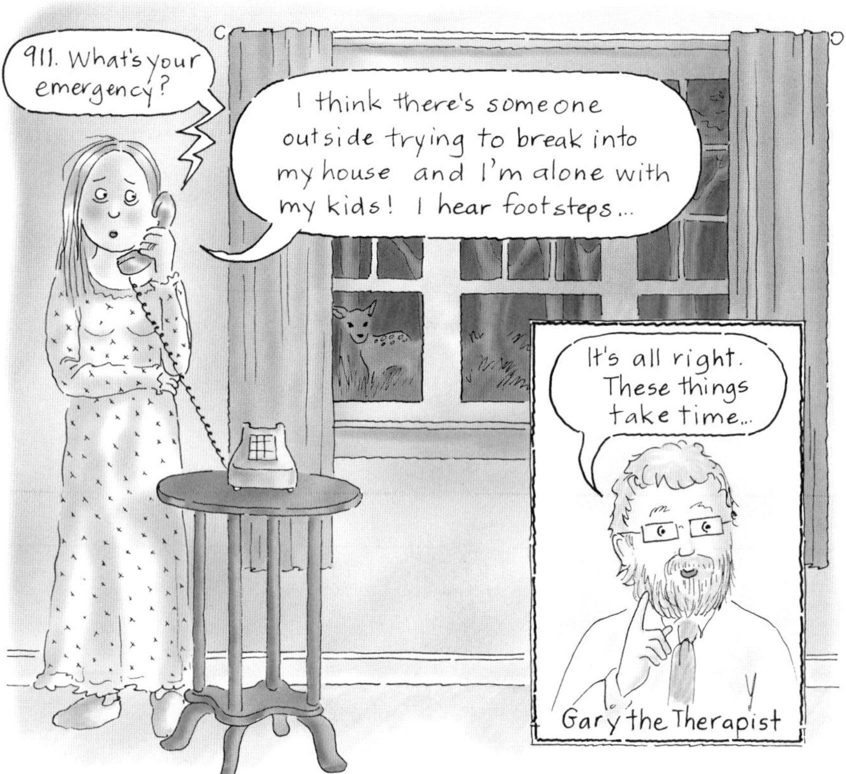
911. What's your emergency?
I think there's someone outside trying to break into my house and I'm alone with my kids! I hear footsteps...
It's all right. These things take time...
Gary the Therapist

But even though I was gradually figuring out how to manage everything, it was a lonely new life. The same events felt so different than they had a few months earlier.

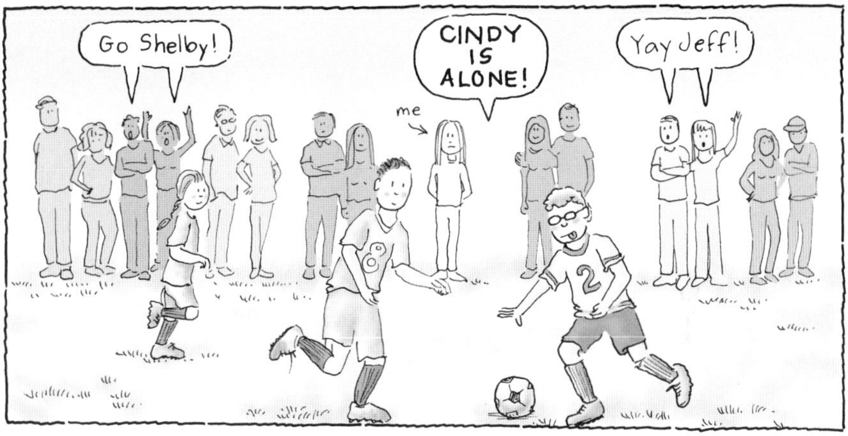
Go Shelby!
CINDY IS ALONE!
Yay Jeff!
me
8
2

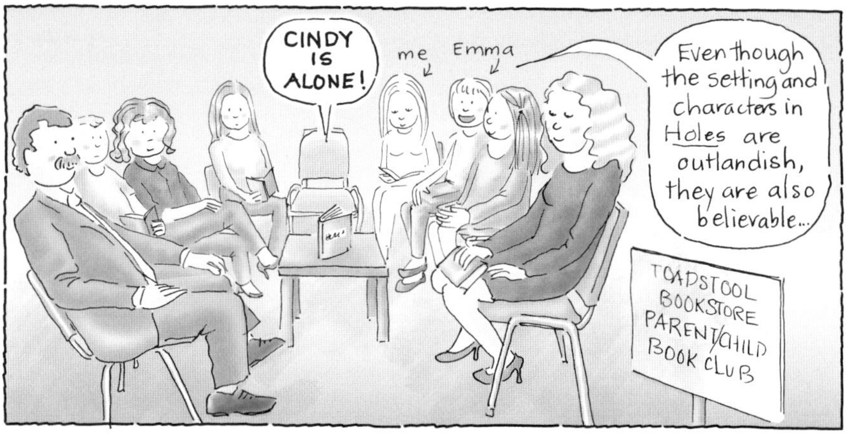
CINDY IS ALONE!
me
Emma
Even though the setting and characters in Holes are outlandish, they are also believable...
TOADSTOOL BOOKSTORE PARENT/CHILD BOOK CLUB

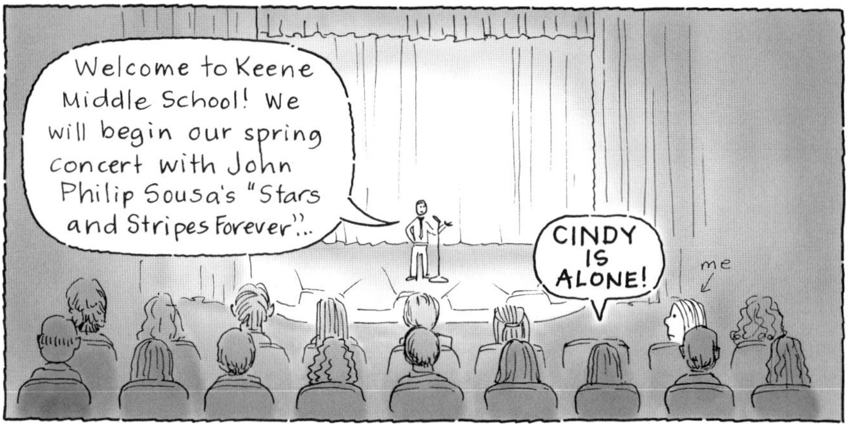
Welcome to Keene Middle School! We will begin our spring concert with John Philip Sousa's "Stars and Stripes Forever"...
CINDY IS ALONE!
me

One Saturday, I woke up feeling braver than usual. I decided to take the kids to visit my parents in Connecticut. I had never driven there on my own, but my parents had lived in the same house for 40 years and I'd been in the passenger seat dozens of times.

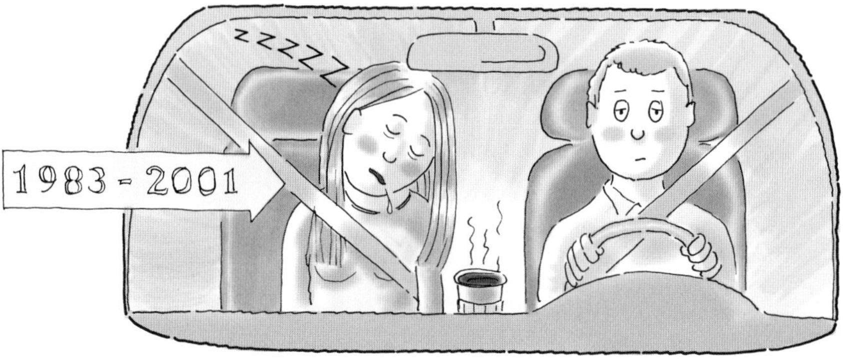
ZZZZZ
1983 - 2001

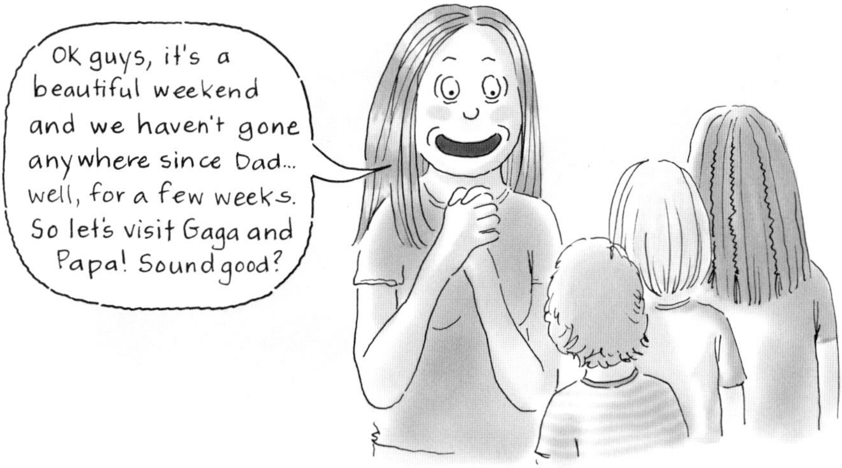
Ok guys, it's a beautiful weekend and we haven't gone anywhere since Dad... well, for a few weeks. So let's visit Gaga and Papa! Sound good?

So we packed snacks for the car and headed out.

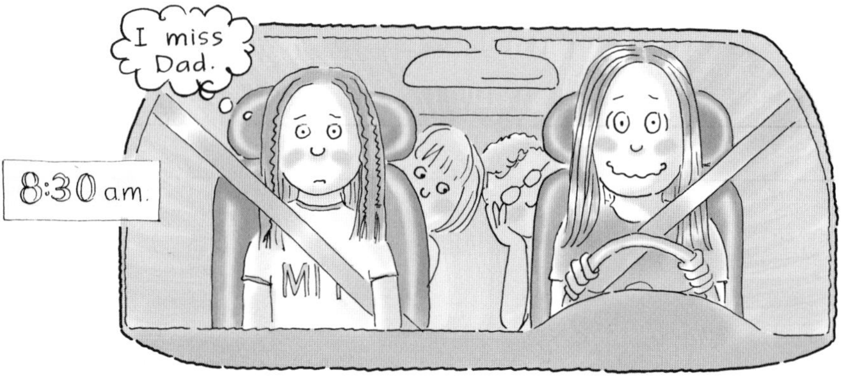
I miss Dad.
8:30 a.m.

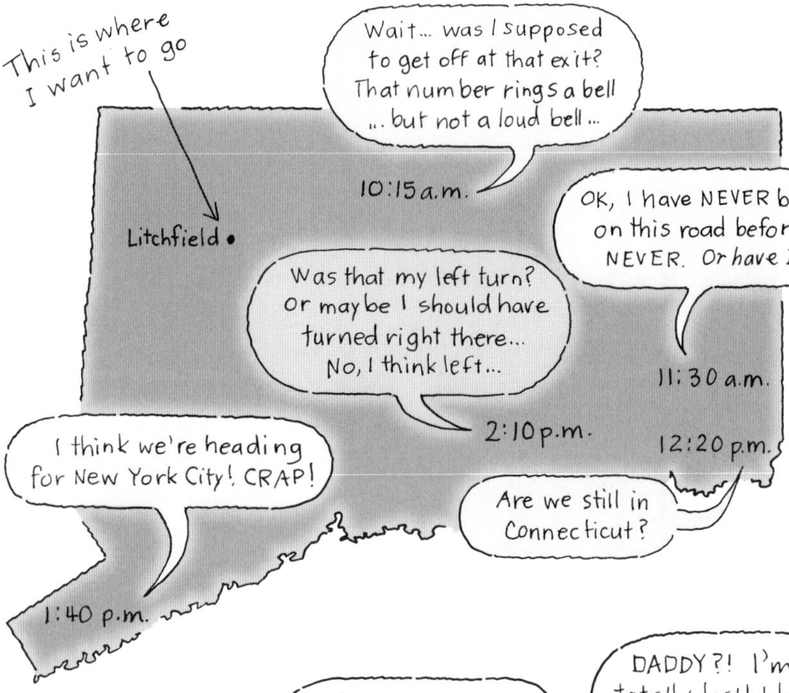
This is where I want to go
Litchfield
Wait... was I supposed to get off at that exit? That number rings a bell ... but not a loud bell...
10:15 a.m.
OK, I have NEVER been on this road before. NEVER. Or have I?
11:30 a.m.
Are we still in Connecticut?
12:20 p.m.
I think we're heading for New York City! CRAP!
1:40 p.m.
Was that my left turn? Or maybe I should have turned right there... No, I think left...
2:10 p.m.

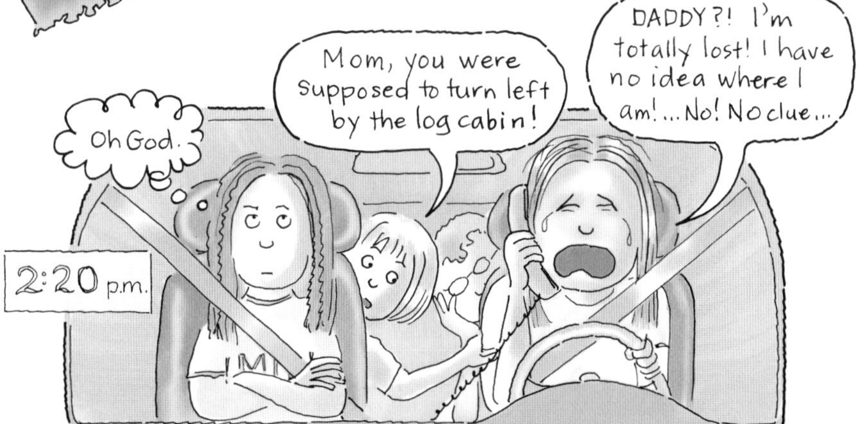
2:20 p.m.
Oh God.
Mom, you were supposed to turn left by the log cabin!
DADDY?! I'm totally lost! I have no idea where I am! ... No! No clue...

Maybe I'd made a mistake.

Maybe I couldn't do this on my own.

Not just the drive.

All of it.

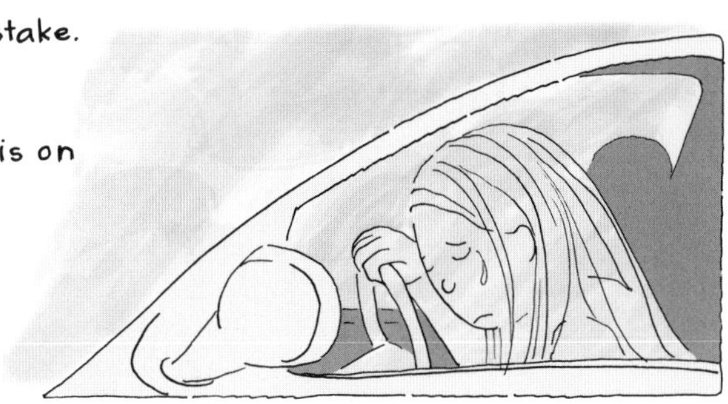

Because most of the day had been spent in the car, the visit with my parents was a short one. When we got back to New Hampshire, there was a message from T.J. on the answering machine.

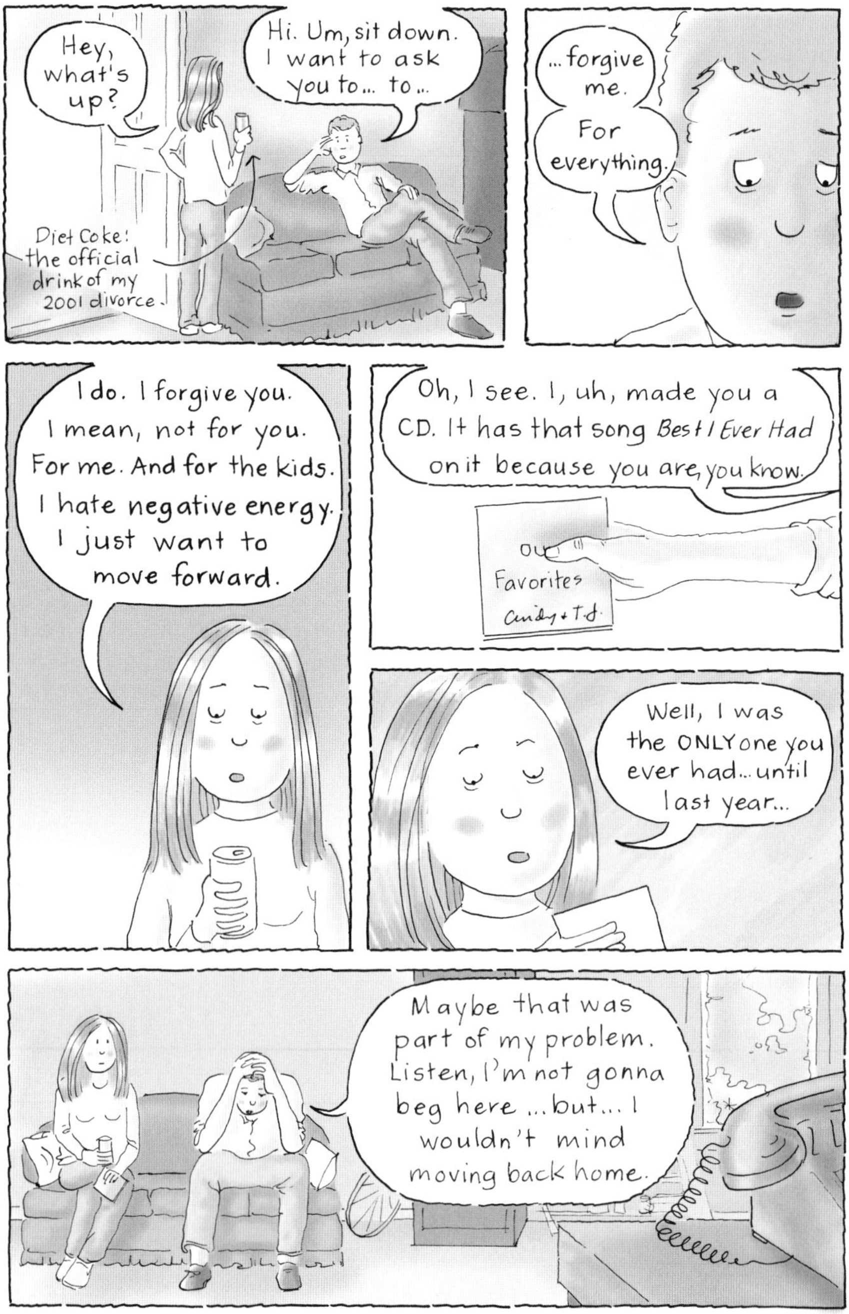
Hey, what's up?
Hi. Um, sit down. I want to ask you to... to...
Diet Coke: the official drink of my 2001 divorce.
...forgive me.
For everything.
I do. I forgive you. I mean, not for you. For me. And for the kids. I hate negative energy. I just want to move forward.
Oh, I see. I, uh, made you a CD. It has that song *Best I Ever Had* on it because you are, you know.
Favorites
Well, I was the ONLY one you ever had... until last year...
Maybe that was part of my problem. Listen, I'm not gonna beg here ...but... I wouldn't mind moving back home.

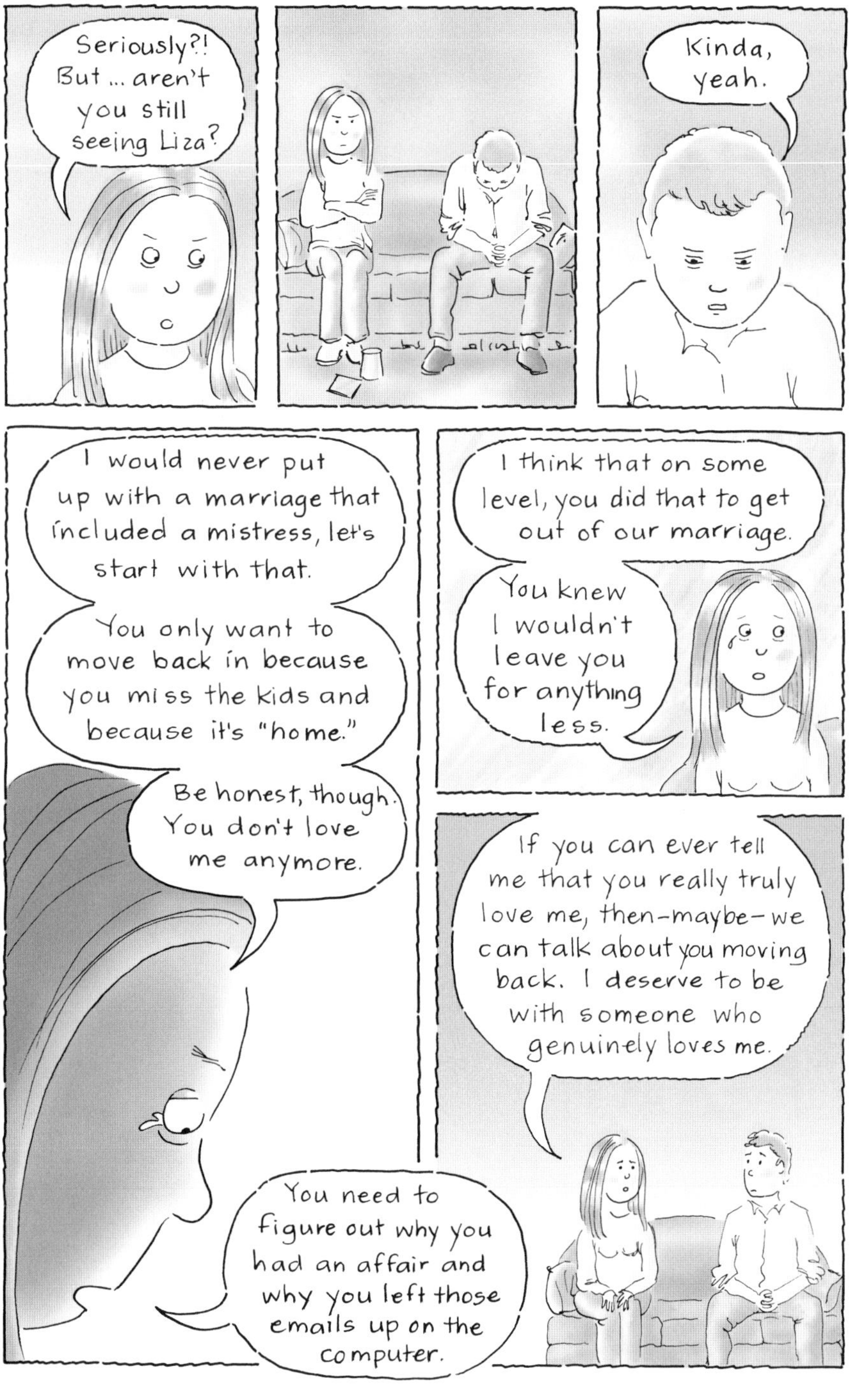
Seriously?! But ... aren't you still seeing Liza?
Kinda, yeah.
I would never put up with a marriage that included a mistress, let's start with that.
You only want to move back in because you miss the kids and because it's "home."
Be honest, though. You don't love me anymore.
You need to figure out why you had an affair and why you left those emails up on the computer.
I think that on some level, you did that to get out of our marriage.
You knew I wouldn't leave you for anything less.
If you can ever tell me that you really truly love me, then—maybe—we can talk about you moving back. I deserve to be with someone who genuinely loves me.

That was the last time we ever talked about getting back together. T.J. never told me that he really truly loved me, and he never came back home.

Summer

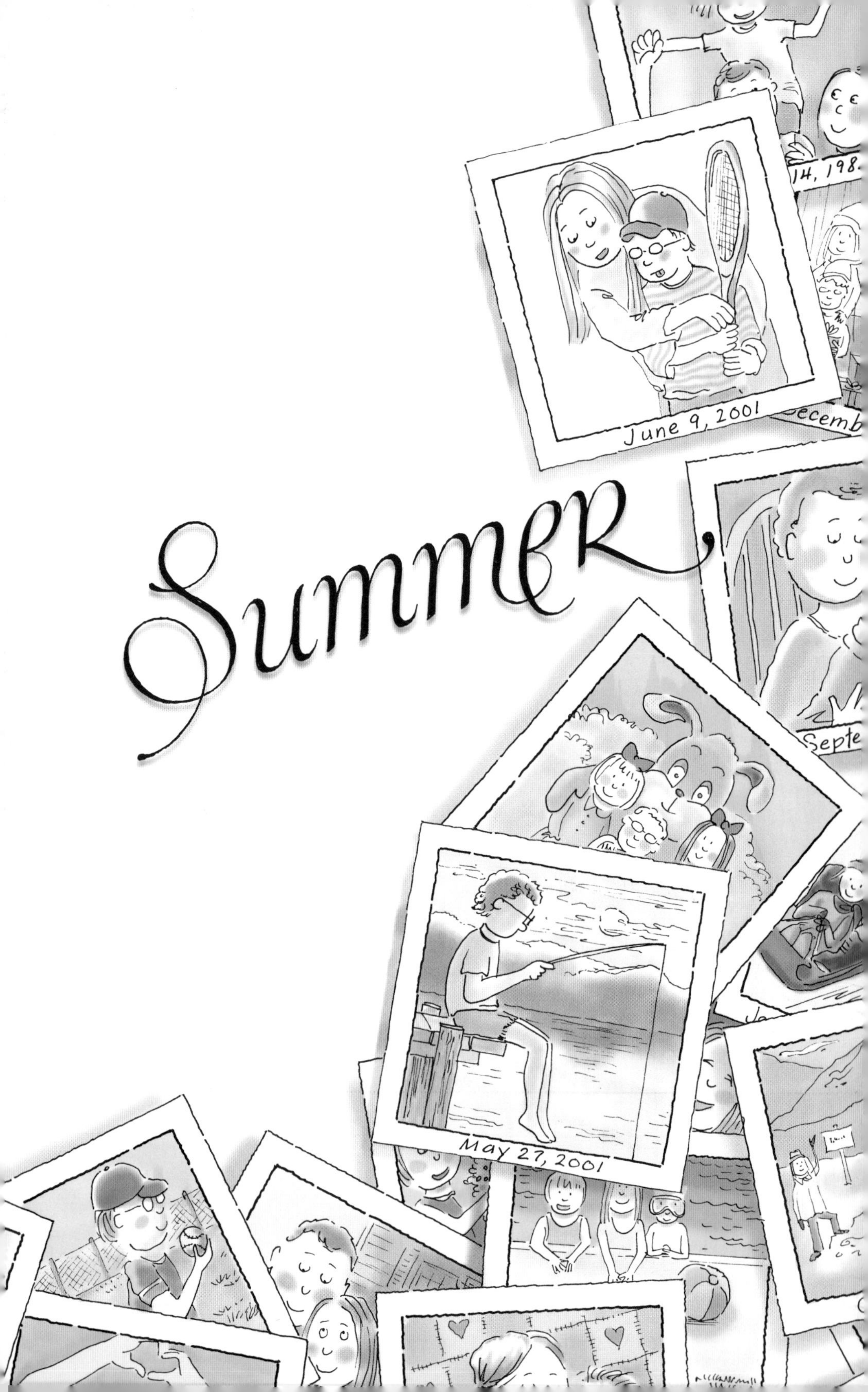
June 9, 2001
May 27, 2001

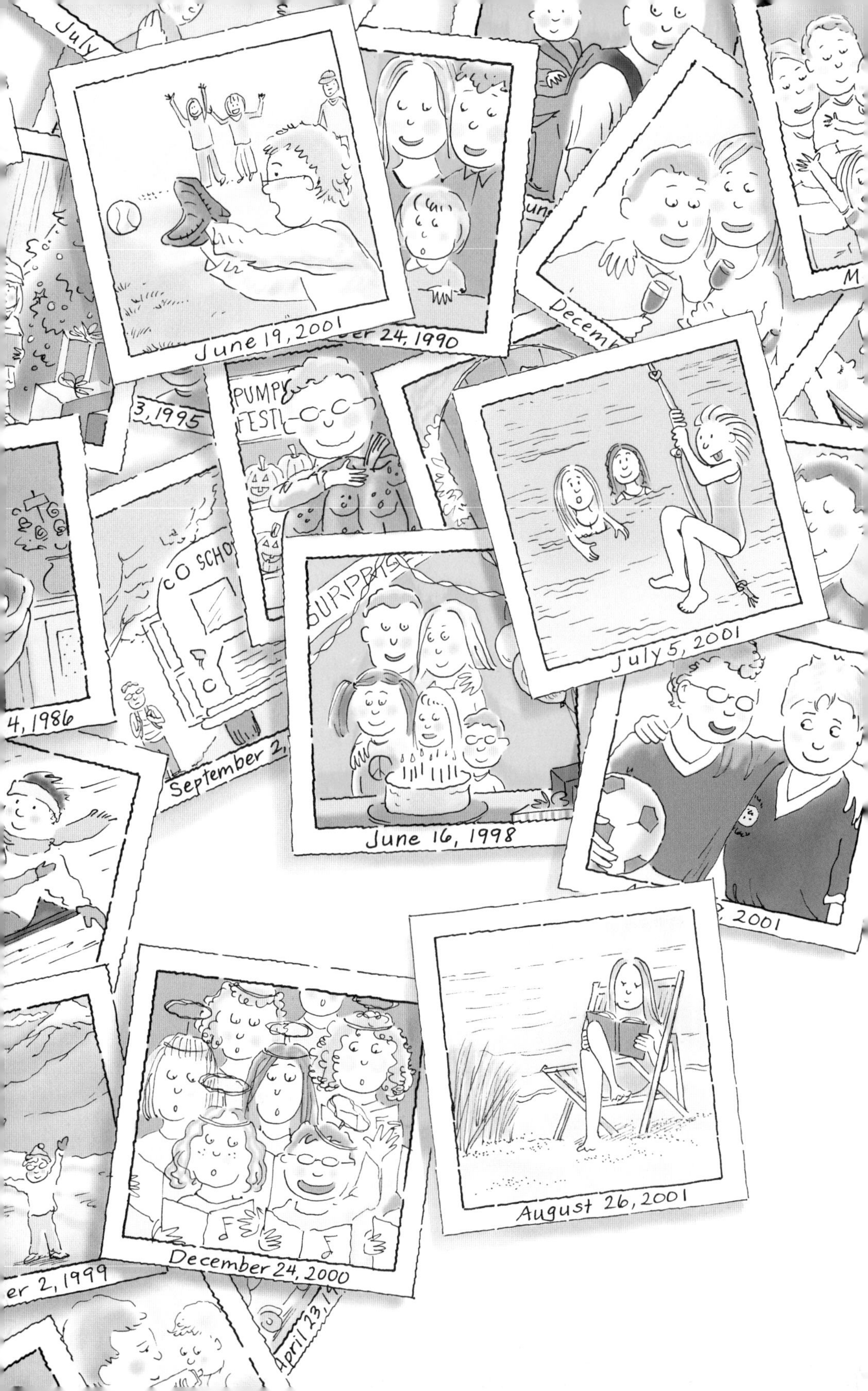
July
June 19, 2001
er 24, 1990
3, 1995
July 5, 2001
4, 1986
September 2,
June 16, 1998
2001
August 26, 2001
December 24, 2000
er 2, 1999

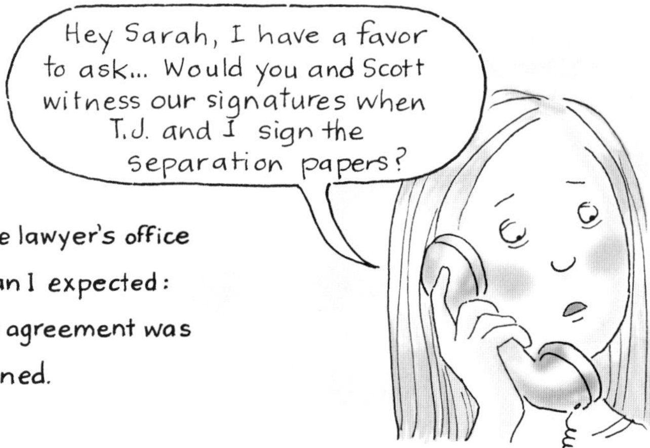
Hey Sarah, I have a favor to ask... Would you and Scott witness our signatures when T.J. and I sign the separation papers?

The call from the lawyer's office came sooner than I expected: The separation agreement was ready to be signed.

Most of our friends had taken sides as soon as they'd heard we'd split up.

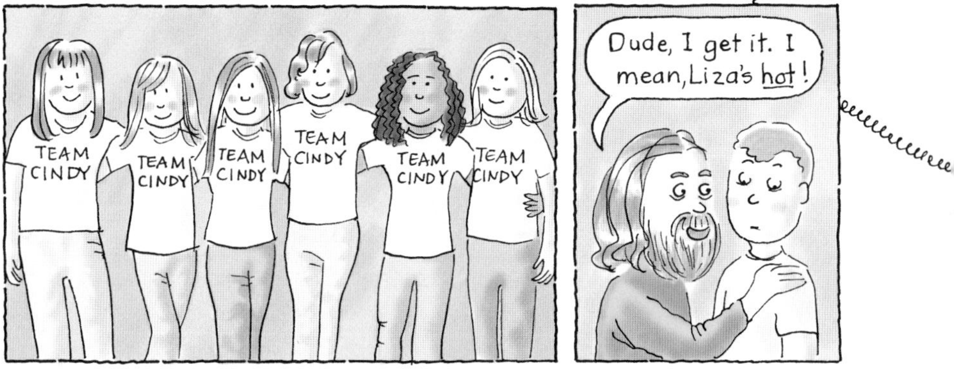
TEAM CINDY
TEAM CINDY
TEAM CINDY
TEAM CINDY
TEAM CINDY
TEAM CINDY
Dude, I get it. I mean, Liza's hot!

The ones who were on the fence we had divvied up.

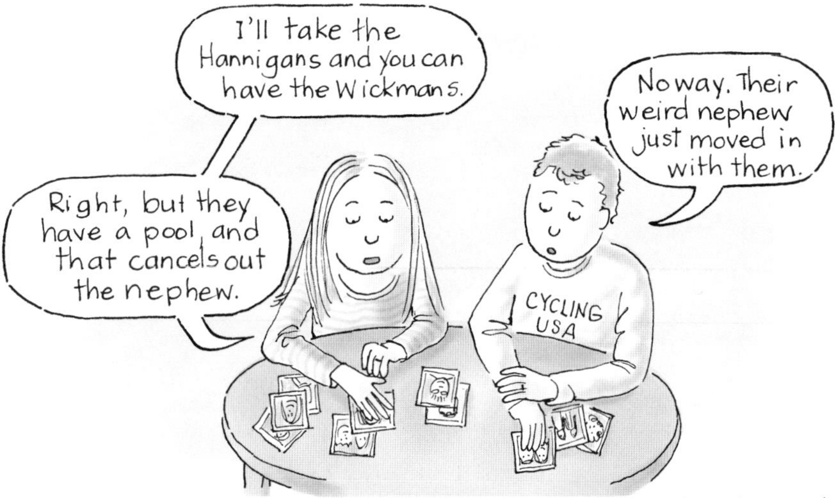
I'll take the Hannigans and you can have the Wickmans.
No way. Their weird nephew just moved in with them.
Right, but they have a pool, and that cancels out the nephew.
CYCLING USA

But Sarah and Scott were the friends neither of us wanted to relinquish.

After all, our families had been best friends for years.

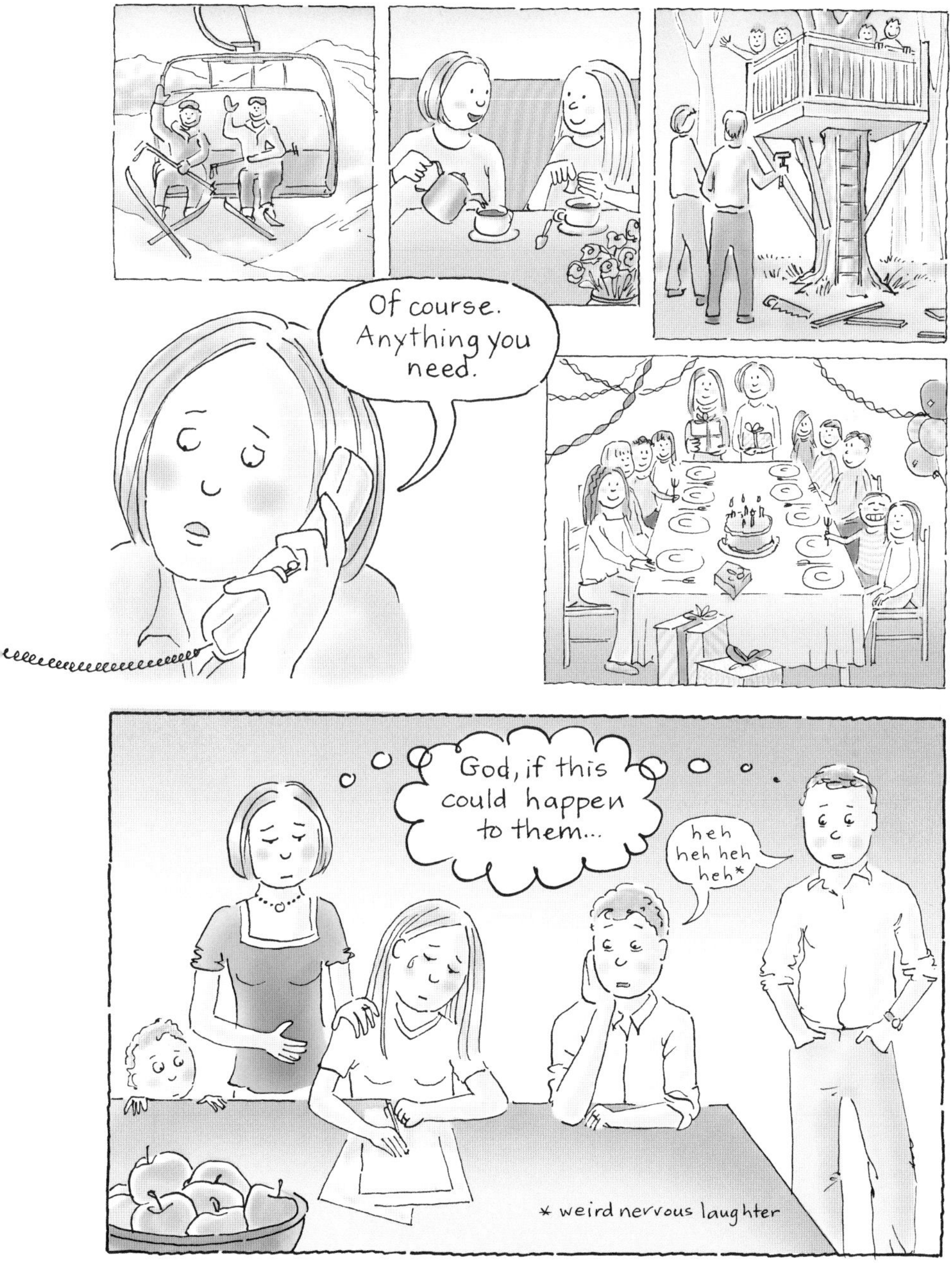
Of course. Anything you need.
God, if this could happen to them...
heh heh heh heh*
* weird nervous laughter

The whole mess was draining and inconceivable to all of us. I wasn't sure what would happen to our friendship now—I only knew it would never be the same.

As painful as it was to lose friends because of the separation, I feared it would be exponentially harder when it came to relatives. Even though they had come in "his" and "hers" sets, I considered T.J.'s extended family to be my own.

Hi! Come in! T.J.'s... um...out, but he'll be here soon!

His parents deserved to know what was happening and T.J. was stalling, so I invited them to come over after lunch one Sunday. But because "Neema" and "Papa" are retired, "after lunch," meant 10 a.m.

suitcase filled with things he "rescued" from the garbage and stole from Neema, including her teeth

Papa gave me a hug, told me a story about something that happened when he was in the Merchant Marines (which pretty much came from his imagination) and then headed down to the basement to "fix" things. (Lately, Papa has become a little confused.)

Neema, whose life revolves around doing things for Papa, none of which he wants done, hurried into the kitchen to make him some tea.

Here's your cup of tea, Artie!

I never asked for tea.

Here you go!

I don't want it.

Take your tea!

No.

92

I watched the clock and silently willed T.J. to show up early. Cheerful, chatty Neema, who tends to keep a conversation going long after the topic has worn itself out, discussed the merits of dryer lint while we waited for him.

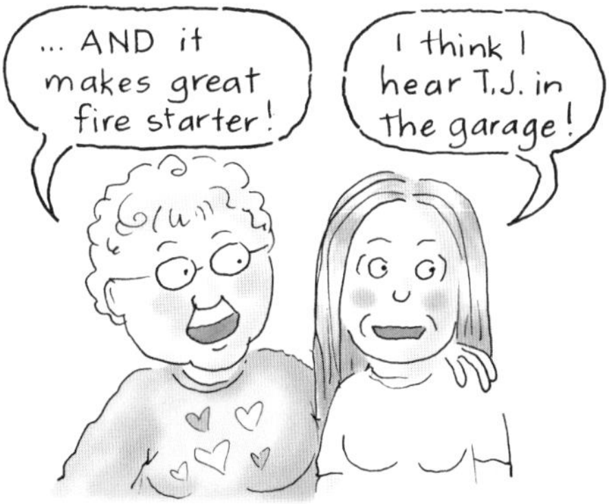
... AND it makes great fire starter!
I think I hear T.J. in the garage!

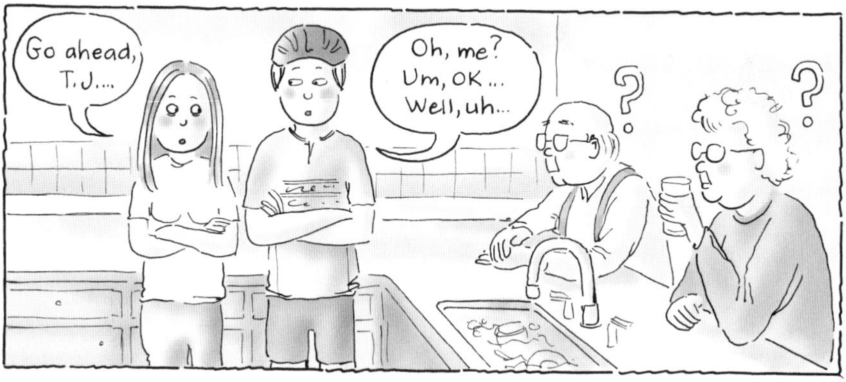
Go ahead, T.J....
Oh, me? Um, OK... Well, uh...
?
?

I guess I wasn't surprised by their reaction to T.J.'s confession, but I had hoped that they would be angrier with T.J. and sorrier for me.

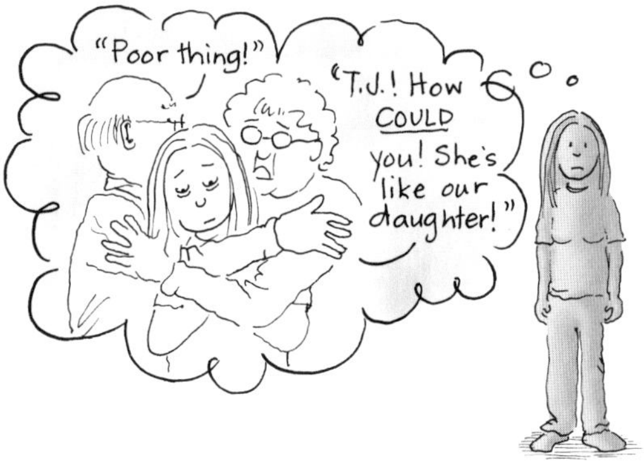
"Poor thing!"
"T.J.! How COULD you! She's like our daughter!"

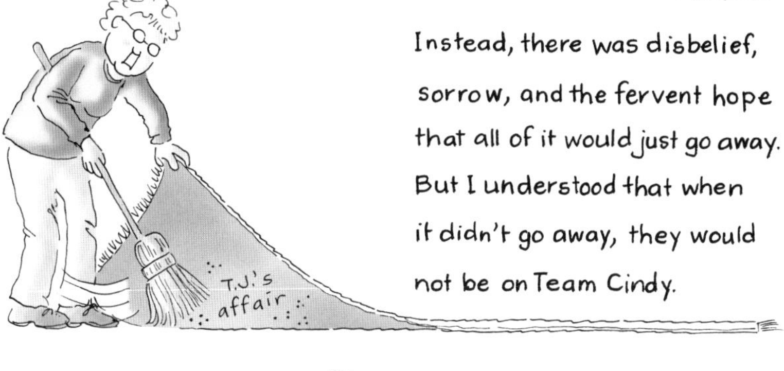
T.J.'s affair

Instead, there was disbelief, sorrow, and the fervent hope that all of it would just go away. But I understood that when it didn't go away, they would not be on Team Cindy.

My brothers, however, would. I was planning to tell them at the family's Memorial Day cookout, and I was dreading it. Every time I talked about it, I relived the whole thing. I had perfected two versions:

The Movie Trailer

He cheated, moved out, and we're movin' on.

The Director's Cut

...and we had not been paying attention to the marriage...

Although it would be emotionally draining for us all, my brothers deserved the extended version.

The kids and I left first thing on Saturday morning; three hours and only two wrong turns later, we arrived at my parents' house.

The map says to turn left here.

Yep, that's what Papa's directions say.

Good job, Mom! You didn't cry!

Hey Cin! You made it!

Where's T.J.? I've gotta ask him about my new bike!

John: Bigwig on Wall Street

Gary: Bigwig on West Street

Kids, ask Gaga if you can help with anything.

C'mere guys, I need to talk to you.

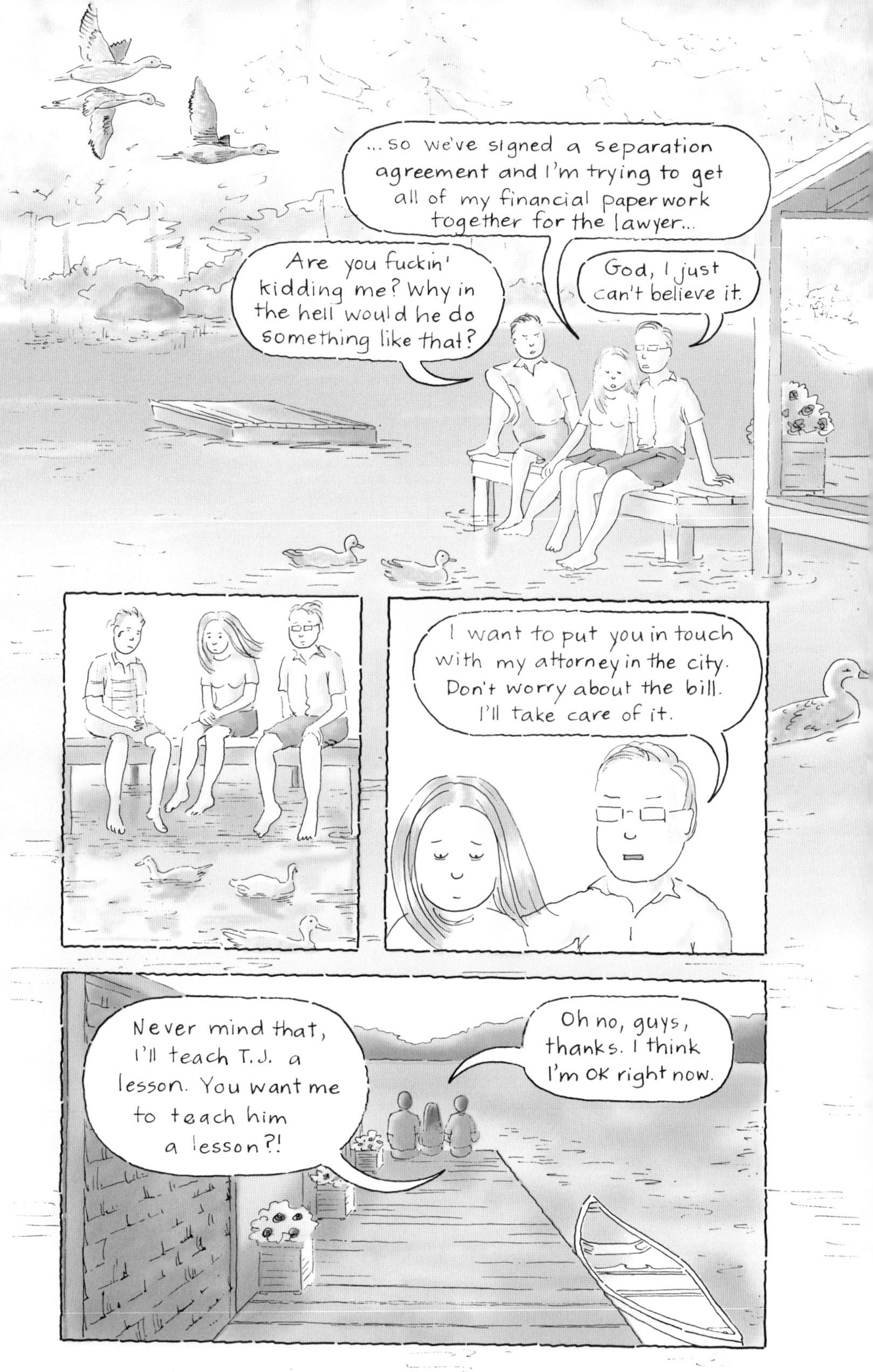
...so we've signed a separation agreement and I'm trying to get all of my financial paperwork together for the lawyer...
Are you fuckin' kidding me? Why in the hell would he do something like that?
God, I just can't believe it.
I want to put you in touch with my attorney in the city. Don't worry about the bill. I'll take care of it.
Never mind that, I'll teach T.J. a lesson. You want me to teach him a lesson?!
Oh no, guys, thanks. I think I'm OK right now.

The kids had a great time playing with their cousins and daring each other to take the first swim of the season.

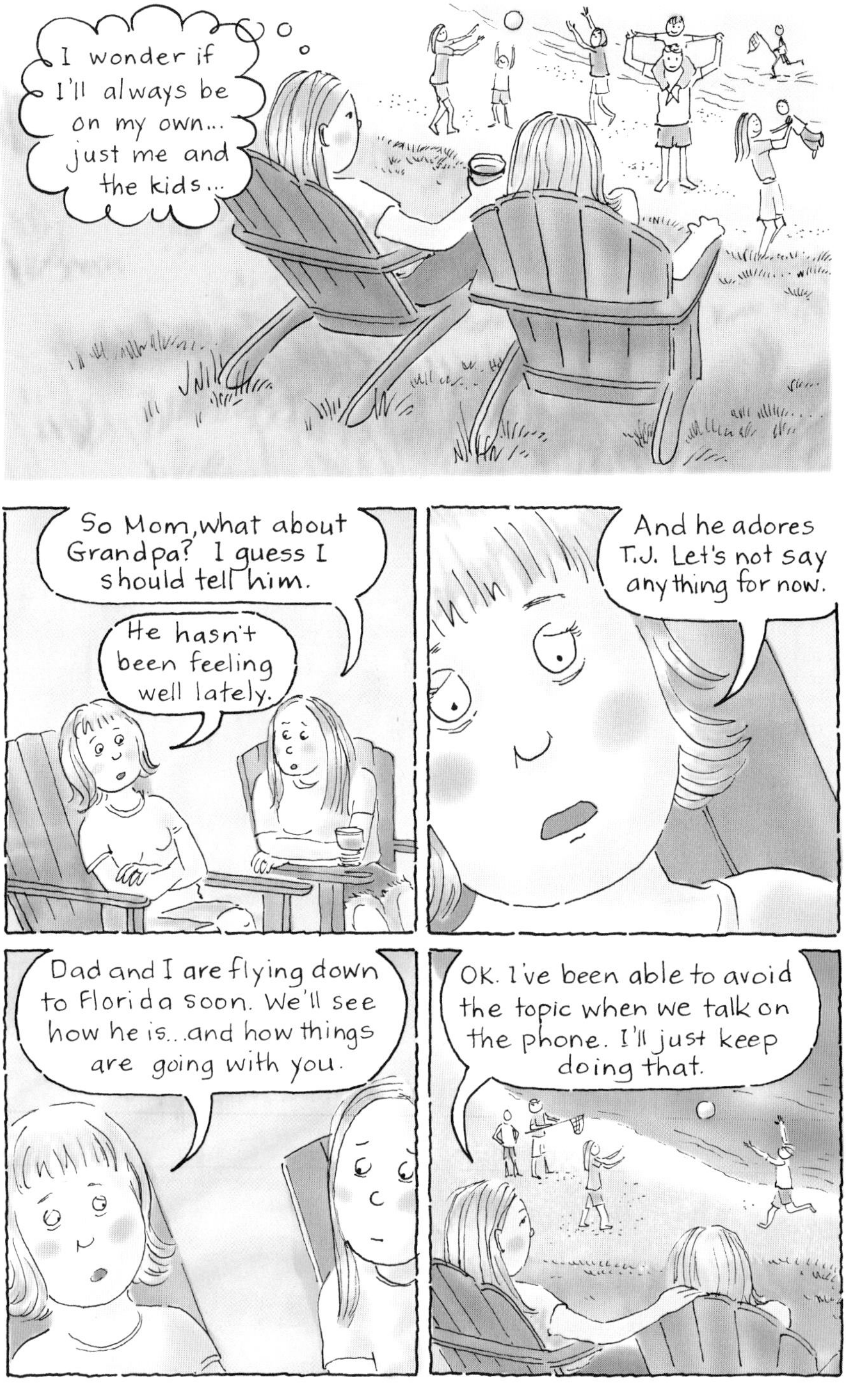
I wonder if I'll always be on my own... just me and the kids...
So Mom, what about Grandpa? I guess I should tell him.
He hasn't been feeling well lately.
And he adores T.J. Let's not say anything for now.
Dad and I are flying down to Florida soon. We'll see how he is...and how things are going with you.
OK. I've been able to avoid the topic when we talk on the phone. I'll just keep doing that.

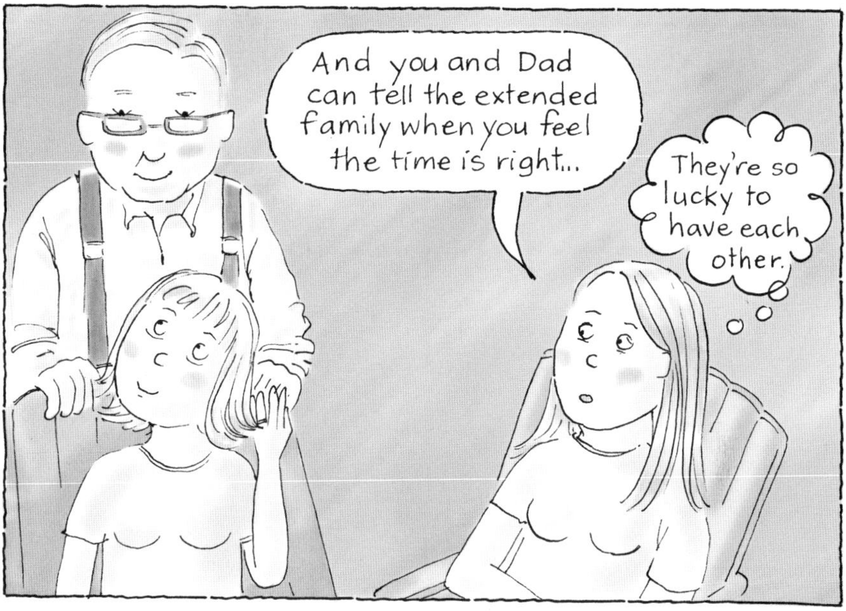
And you and Dad can tell the extended family when you feel the time is right...
They're so lucky to have each other.

...which it never quite was.

In the days before tell-all tweets and status updates on Facebook, faraway relatives could be kept out of the loop for years.

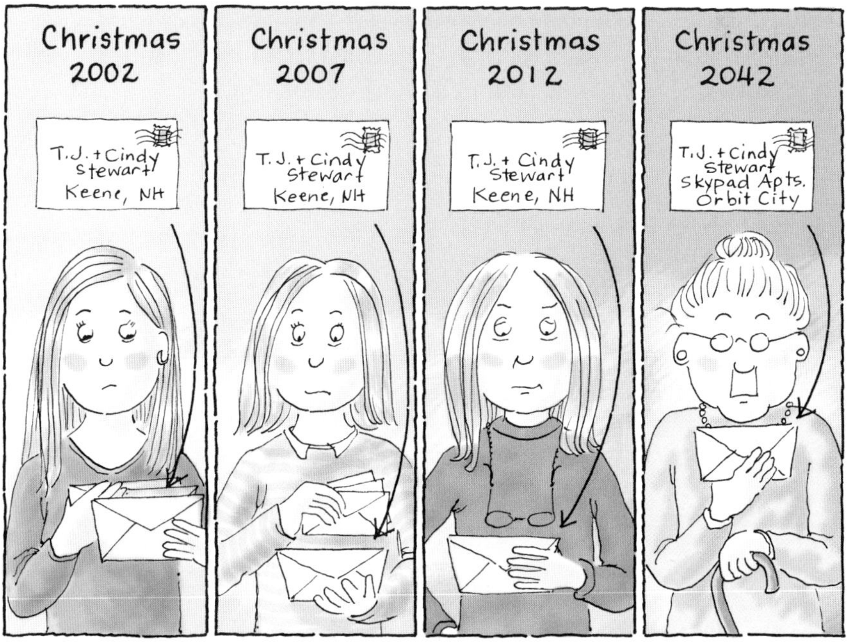
Christmas 2002
T.J. + Cindy Stewart Keene, NH
Christmas 2007
T.J. + Cindy Stewart Keene, NH
Christmas 2012
T.J. + Cindy Stewart Keene, NH
Christmas 2042
T.J. + Cindy Stewart Skypad Apts. Orbit City

School days eased into summer vacation with movie mornings, school carnival afternoons, and end-of-the-year plays and parties.

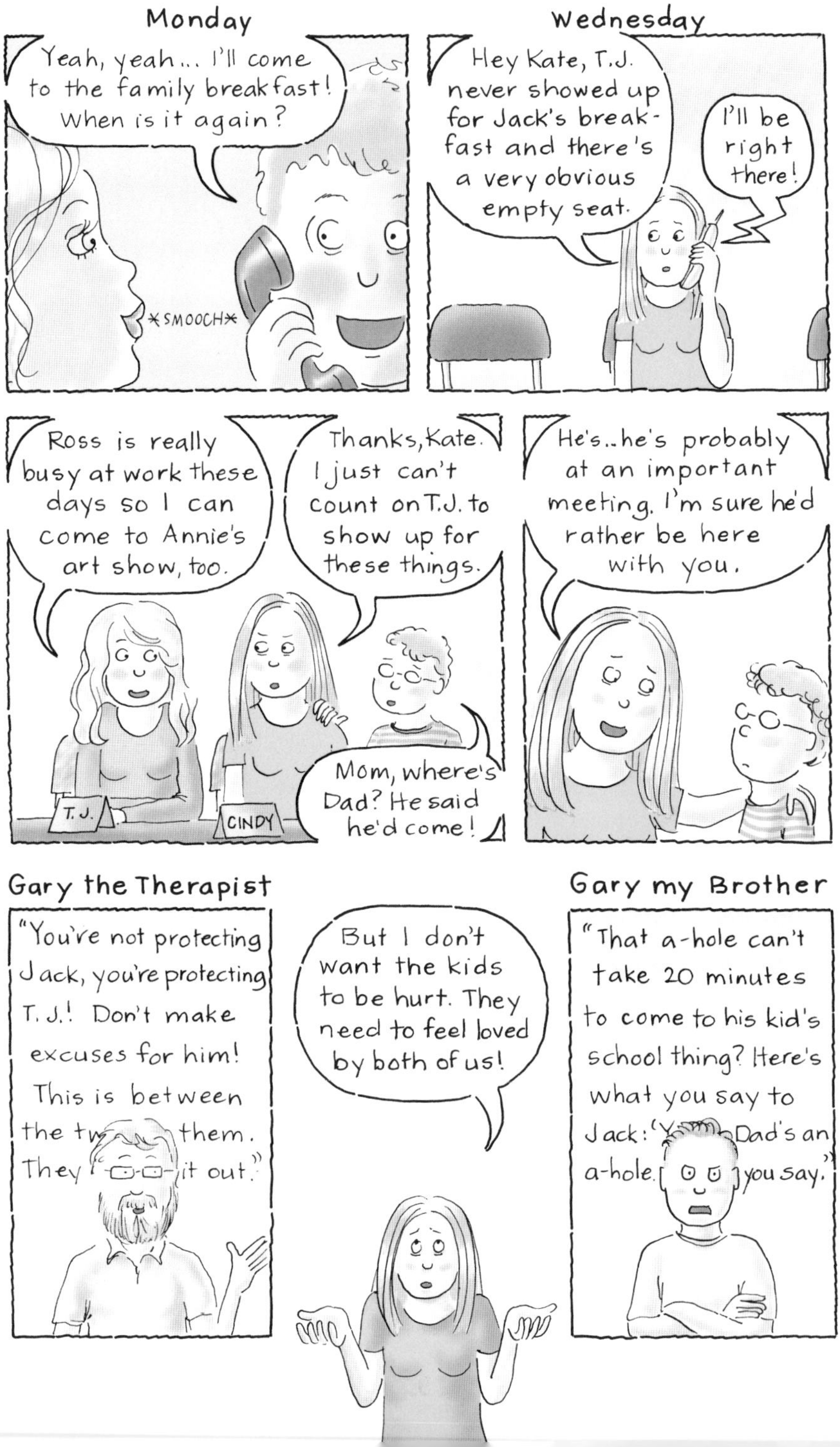
Monday
Yeah, yeah... I'll come to the family breakfast! When is it again?
SMOOCH
Wednesday
Hey Kate, T.J. never showed up for Jack's breakfast and there's a very obvious empty seat.
I'll be right there!
Ross is really busy at work these days so I can come to Annie's art show, too.
Thanks, Kate. I just can't count on T.J. to show up for these things.
T. J.
CINDY
Mom, where's Dad? He said he'd come!
He's..he's probably at an important meeting. I'm sure he'd rather be here with you.
Gary the Therapist
"You're not protecting Jack, you're protecting T. J.! Don't make excuses for him! This is between
the tw them.
They it out."
But I don't want the kids to be hurt. They need to feel loved by both of us!
Gary my Brother
"That a-hole can't take 20 minutes to come to his kid's school thing? Here's what you say to
Jack: 'Y Dad's an
a-hole. you say.'"

I had signed the kids up for their favorite day camps in the hopes that summer would feel the way it always had.

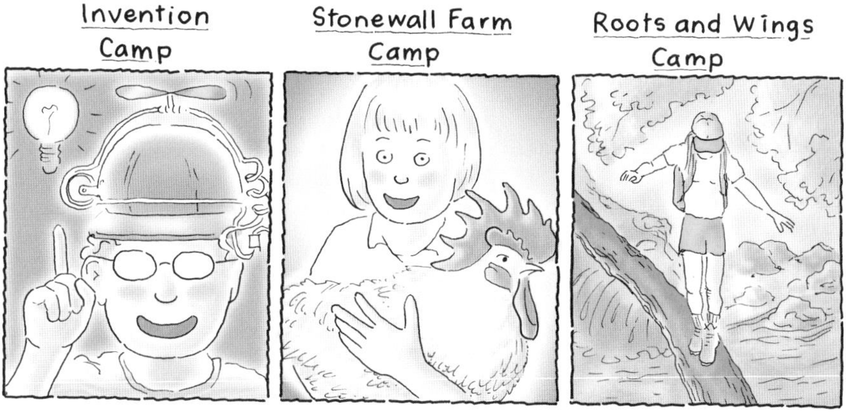
Invention Camp
Stonewall Farm Camp
Roots and Wings Camp

Cautiously, we began to explore what things were fun to do, just us four...

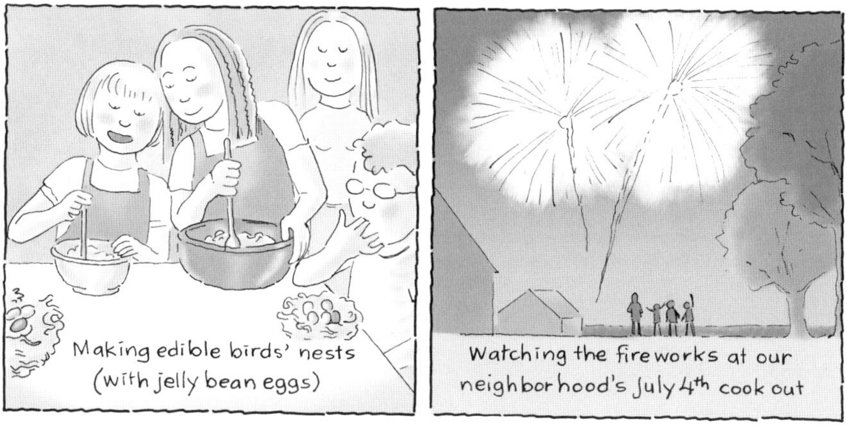
Making edible birds' nests (with jelly bean eggs)
Watching the fireworks at our neighborhood's July 4th cook out

...and what things weren't fun at all.

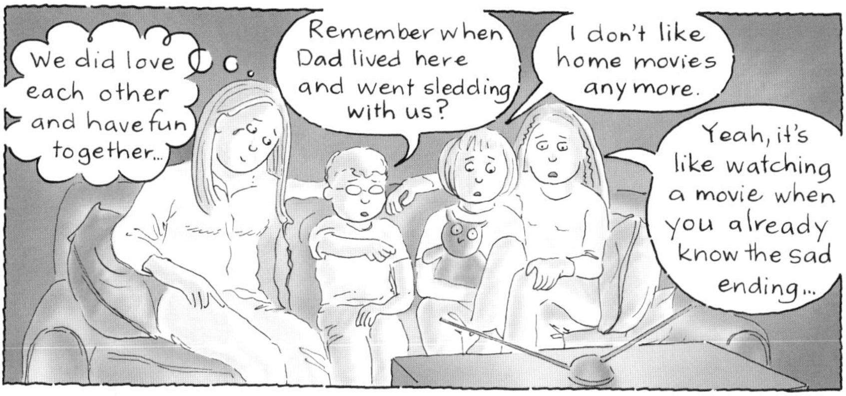
We did love each other and have fun together...
Remember when Dad lived here and went sledding with us?
I don't like home movies any more.
Yeah, it's like watching a movie when you already know the sad ending...

T.J. and I celebrated our summer birthdays together the way we always had. He bought me the new stools I'd been wanting for the kitchen counter. I enlarged and framed several photos of him with Annie, Emma, and Jack. I didn't do it for him; I did it for the kids. They wanted their dad to have a nice birthday.

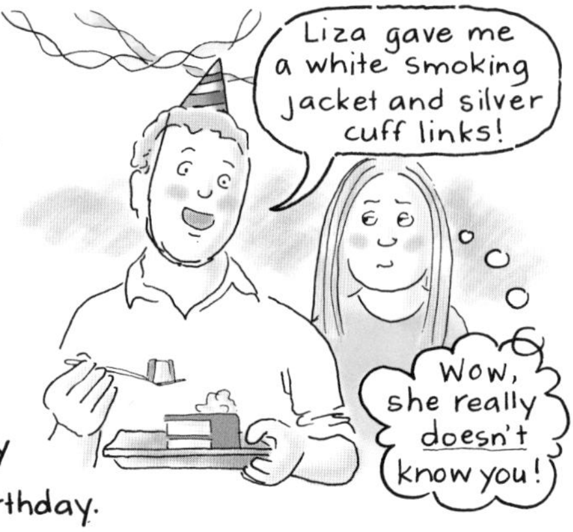
Liza gave me a white smoking jacket and silver cuff links!
Wow, she really doesn't know you!

Just as our days began to develop a tentative rhythm, my Uncle Rich called from Florida.

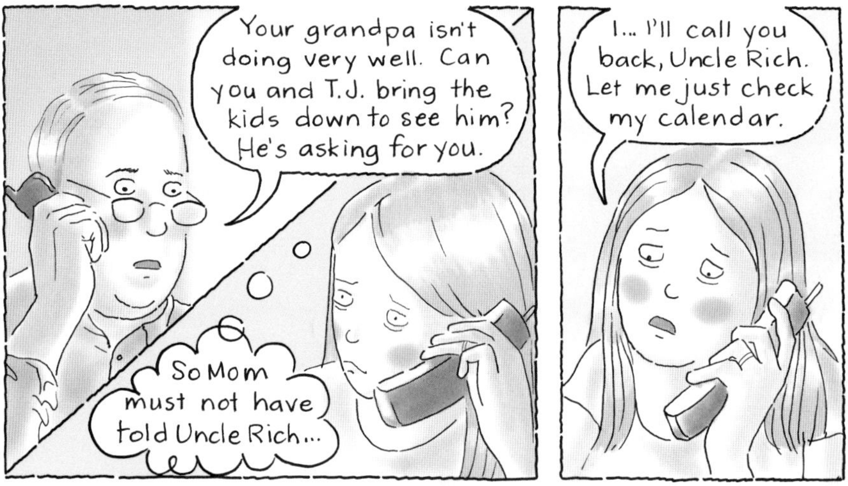
Your grandpa isn't doing very well. Can you and T.J. bring the kids down to see him? He's asking for you.
So Mom must not have told Uncle Rich...
I... I'll call you back, Uncle Rich. Let me just check my calendar.

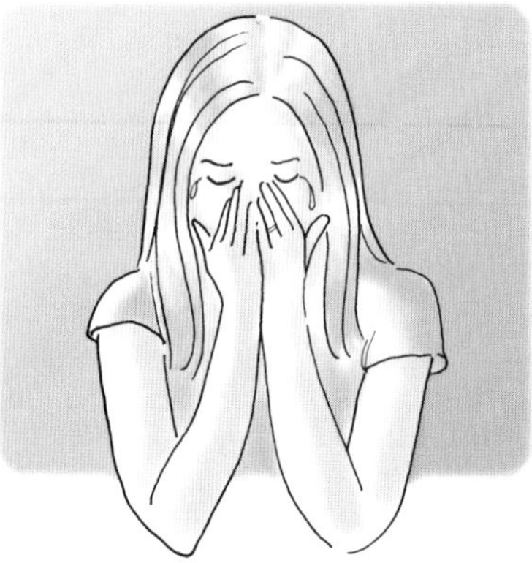

I could barely make it to my parents' house on my own. How was I going to get the kids to Florida? And how would I explain T.J.'s absence? I certainly couldn't tell the kids to lie about what had happened, but my grandfather would be devastated if he found out the truth.

I called my mom and we came up with the best plan under the circumstances.

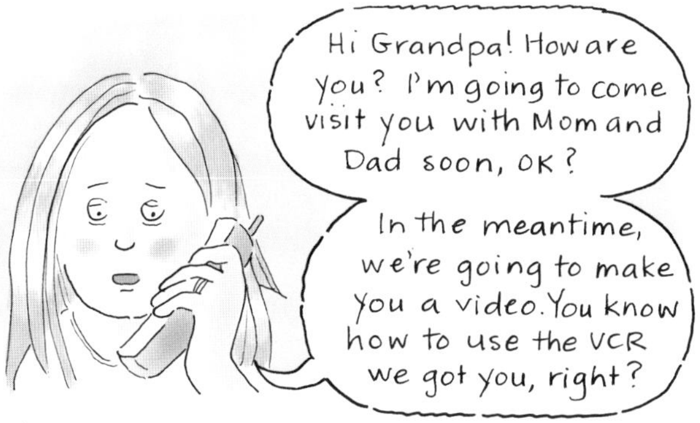
Hi Grandpa! How are you? I'm going to come visit you with Mom and Dad soon, OK?
In the meantime, we're going to make you a video. You know how to use the VCR we got you, right?

I got everyone on board with our video project—even T.J.—and we brought the camera with us everywhere for the next week.

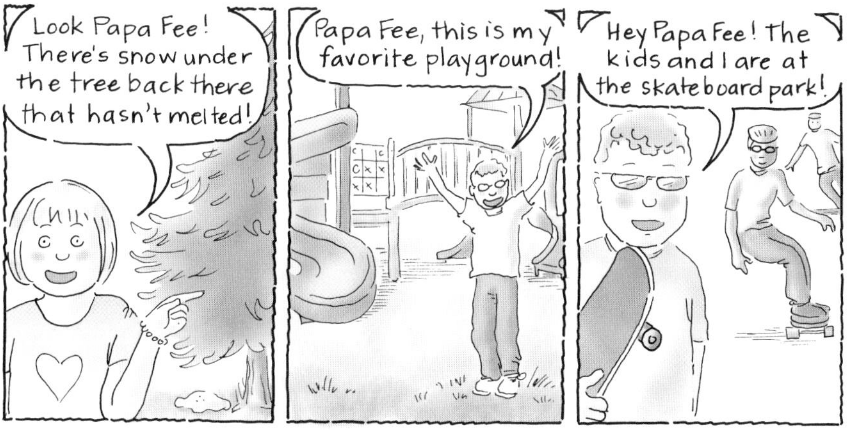
Look Papa Fee! There's snow under the tree back there that hasn't melted!
Papa Fee, this is my favorite playground!
Hey Papa Fee! The kids and I are at the skateboard park!

When we finished making the tape, I packaged it up along with a letter from each of us and then drove to the post office to mail it.

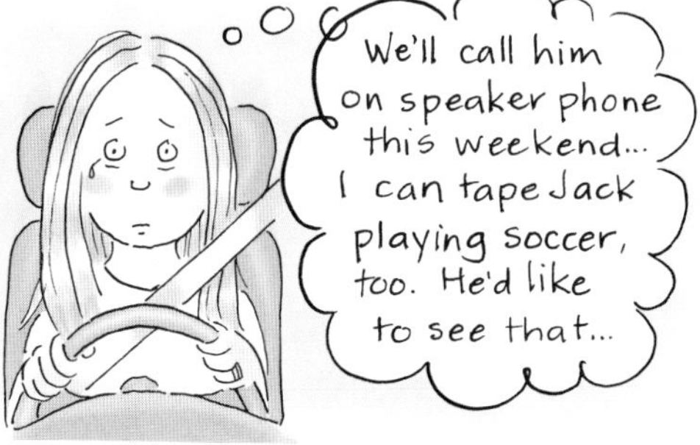
We'll call him on speaker phone this weekend... I can tape Jack playing soccer, too. He'd like to see that...

When I got back home, there was a message on the answering machine.

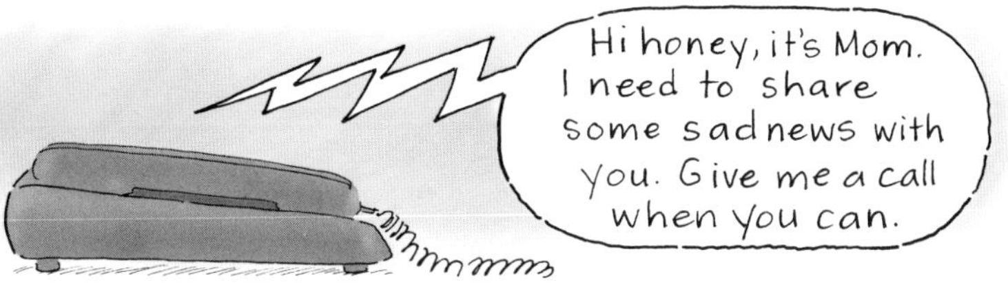
Hi honey, it's Mom. I need to share some sad news with you. Give me a call when you can.

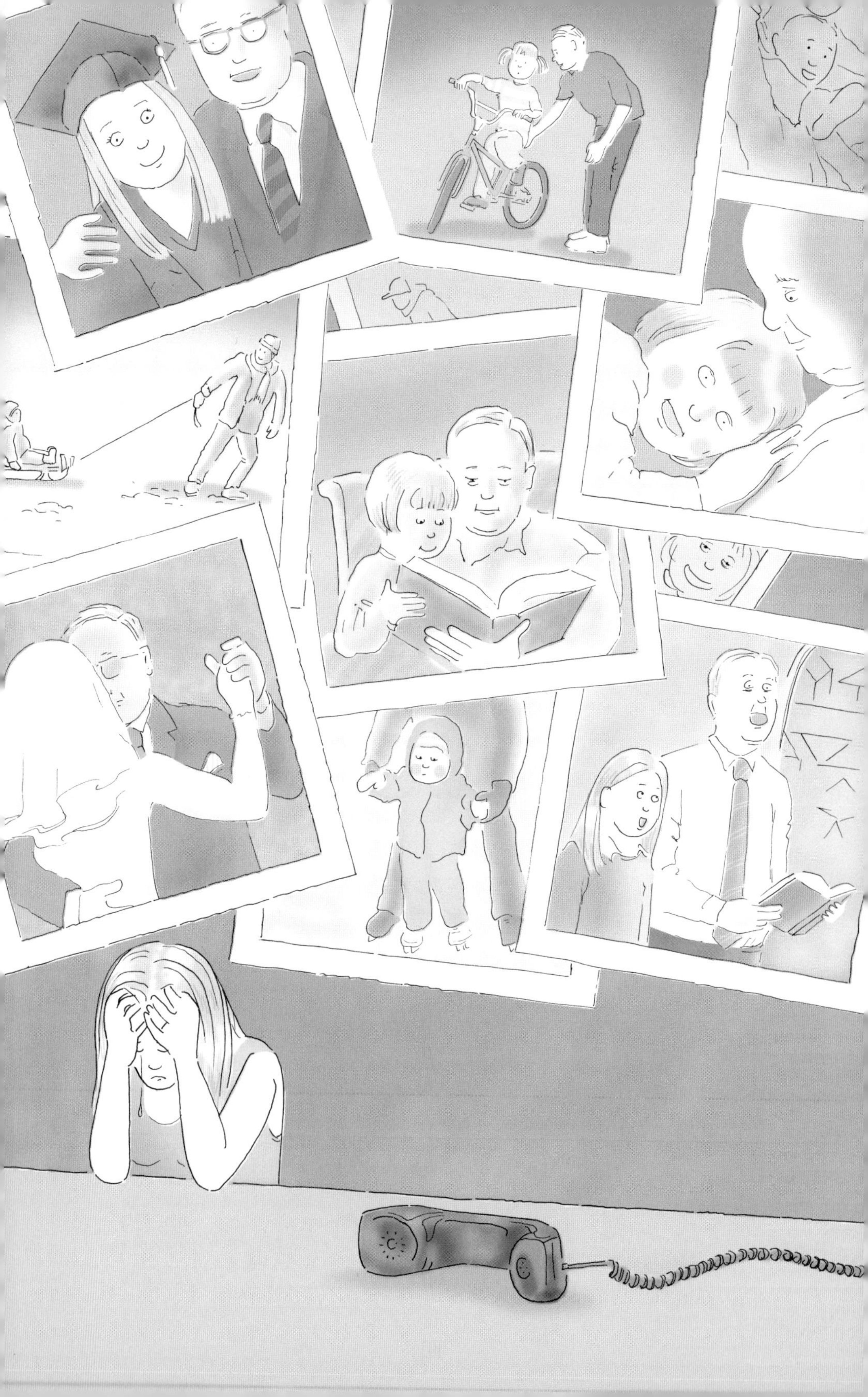

Taking it day by day, I worked hard to keep up a cheerful façade.

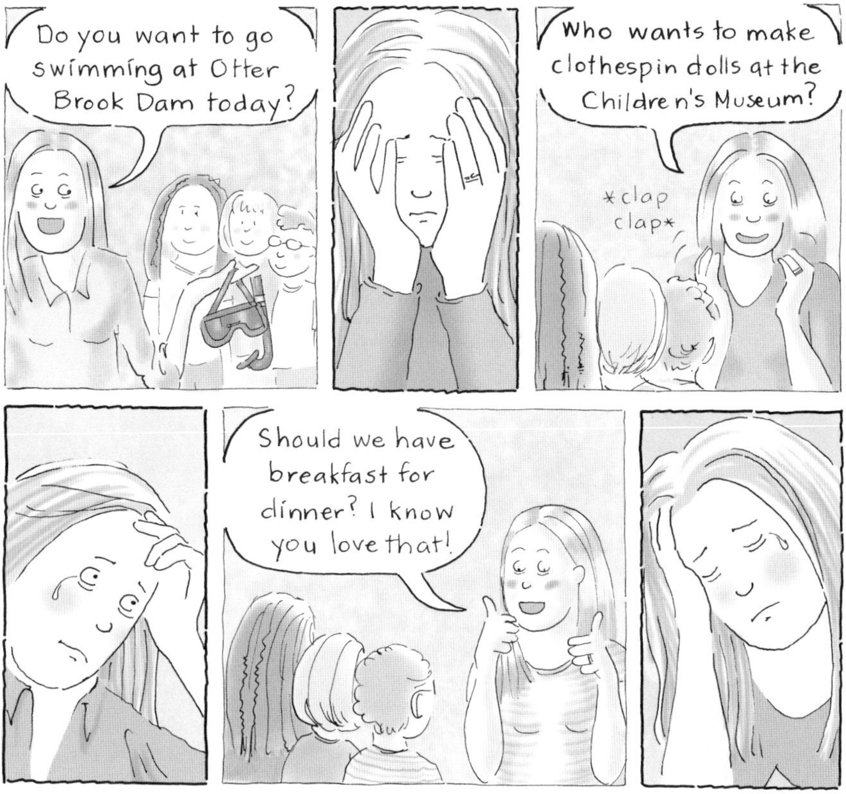
Do you want to go swimming at Otter Brook Dam today?
Who wants to make clothespin dolls at the Children's Museum?
clap clap
Should we have breakfast for dinner? I know you love that!

I was sad for me, and sad for the kids. I was a weary witness to their world collapsing. Annie, who'd always been T.J.'s sidekick, missed his daily presence more than she admitted. Emma was trying to navigate middle school while doing everything a 12-year-old can to take the place of an absent parent. And I knew that before long, Jack would scarcely remember a time when his parents were together.

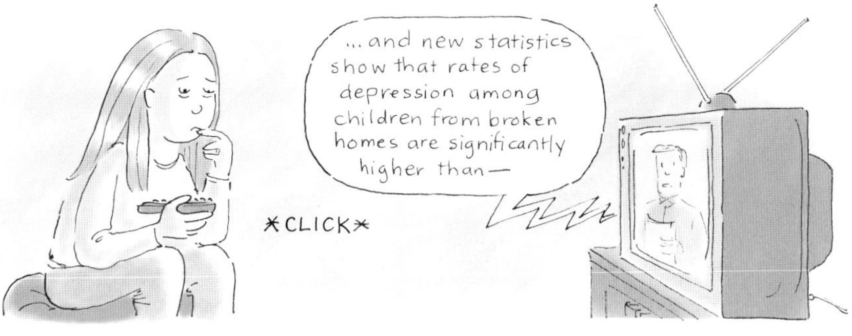
...and new statistics show that rates of depression among children from broken homes are significantly higher than—
CLICK

With guilt as my guide, and against the advice of every parenting book ever written, I was willing to do anything to make the kids feel even a little bit better.

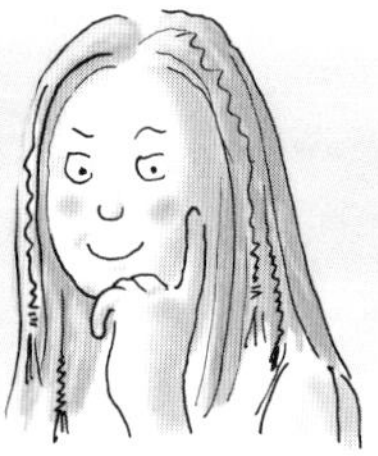

Unfortunately, children pick up on that kind of shift rather quickly.

Annie had a part-time job at a pet store, where she fell in love with a particularly cranky parrot named Henry.

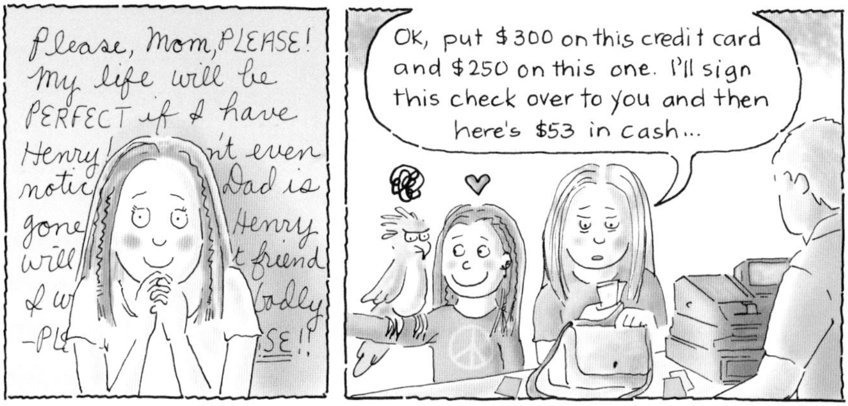
Please, Mom, PLEASE! My life will be PERFECT if I have Henry!
Dad is
Henry
OK, put $300 on this credit card and $250 on this one. I'll sign this check over to you and then here's $53 in cash...

Not only did Henry come with the expected downsides of a parrot, he had a few idiosyncrasies related to the years he'd spent squatting in the corner of the pet store.

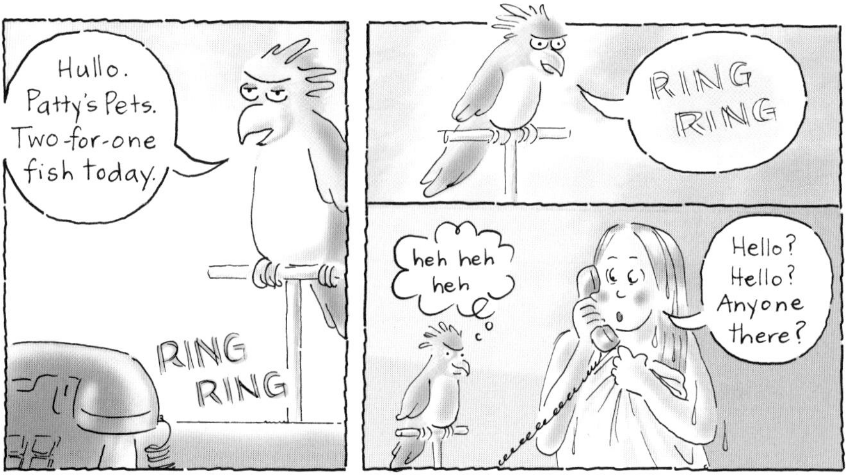
RING RING
Hullo. Patty's Pets. Two-for-one fish today.
RING RING
heh heh heh
Hello? Hello? Anyone there?

We got used to the not unpleasant sound of the cash register drawer opening after a pretend sale and the Zen-like bubbling of the non-existent fish tanks. Any movement toward the front door would inevitably lead to a bored but pleasant...

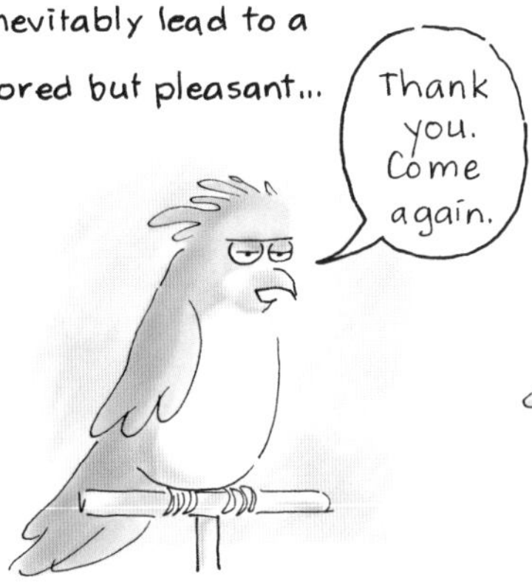
Thank you. Come again.

...or, now and then, to the more disquieting...

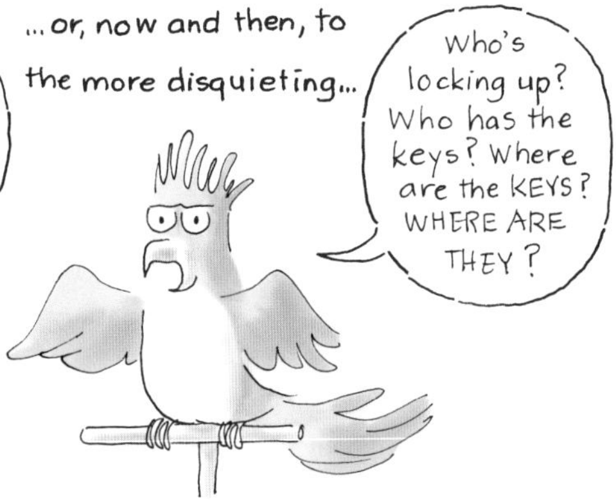
Who's locking up? Who has the keys? Where are the KEYS? WHERE ARE THEY?

But the talking wasn't the worst part. I was spending more time than I cared to scrubbing bird doo off the shoulders of every shirt Annie owned.

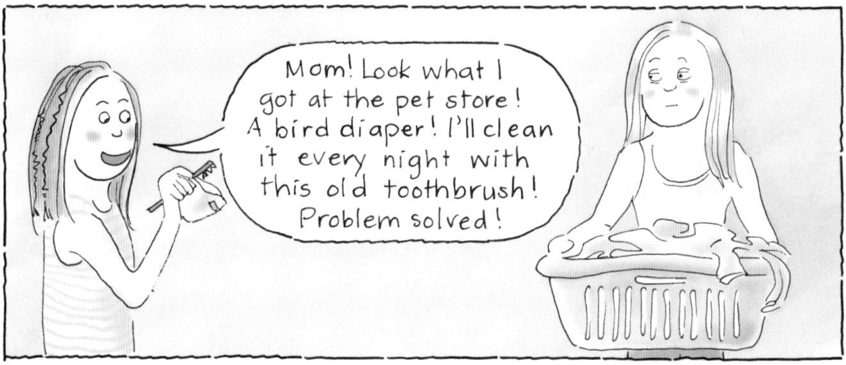
Mom! Look what I got at the pet store! A bird diaper! I'll clean it every night with this old toothbrush! Problem solved!

Problem not solved. A week later, a short but heated discussion among the children, all of whom shared a bathroom, about which toothbrush was the diaper toothbrush, resulted in the diaper going in the trash and all of the toothbrushes being replaced.

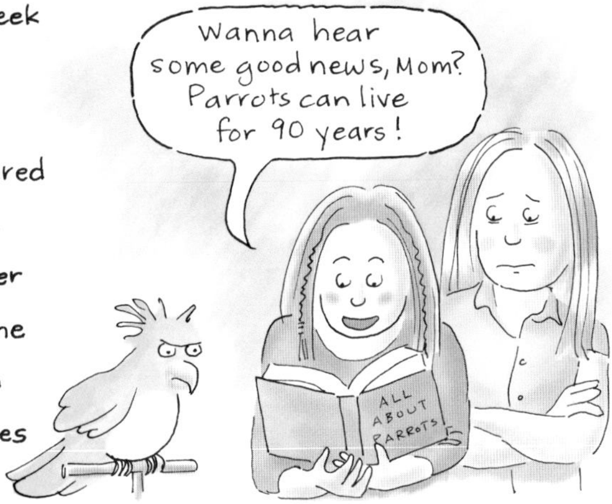
Wanna hear some good news, Mom? Parrots can live for 90 years!
ALL ABOUT PARROTS

Emma got the guilty thumbs up on Peter Pan, a cream-colored bunny she'd seen at the county fair.

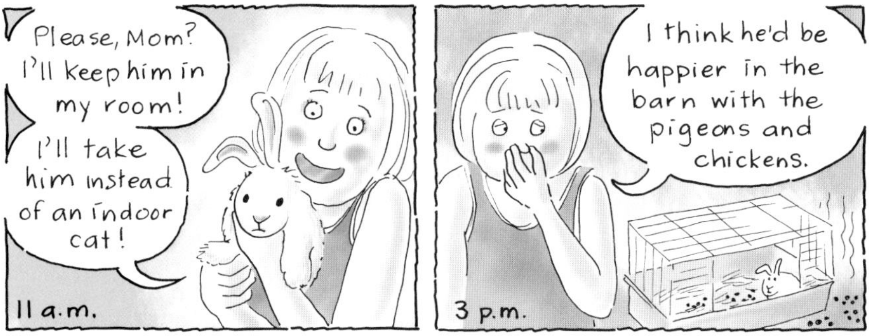
Please, Mom? I'll keep him in my room!
I'll take him instead of an indoor cat!
11 a.m.
I think he'd be happier in the barn with the pigeons and chickens.
3 p.m.

But within days of moving into the barn, Peter Pan rejected any earlier imprinting and decided that he, too, was a chicken.

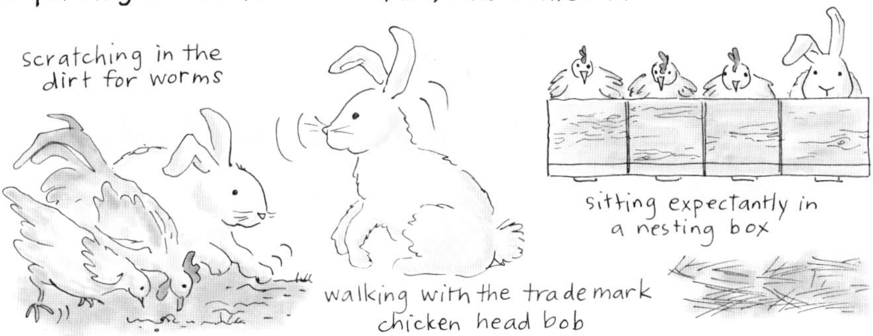
scratching in the dirt for worms
walking with the trademark chicken head bob
sitting expectantly in a nesting box

Unfortunately, as he matured, his affection for a rather peculiar hen named Peeve intensified. Peeve wasn't sure how to use her chicken language to discourage Peter. On a weirdness scale of 1 to Gary Busey, this was a solid 8.

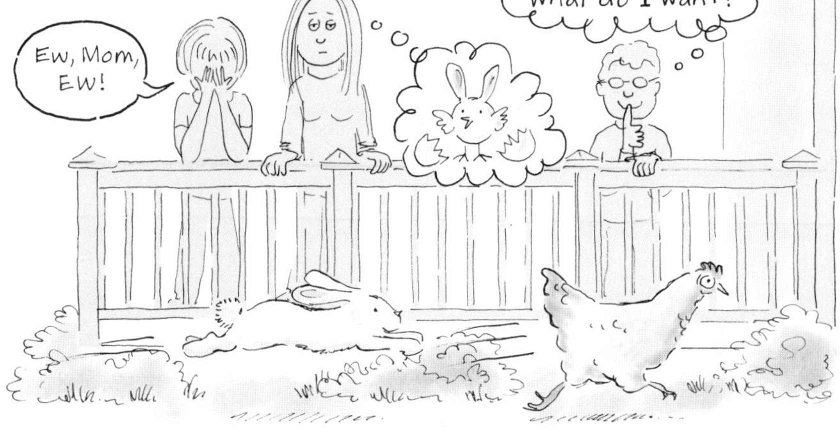
Ew, Mom, EW!
What do I want?

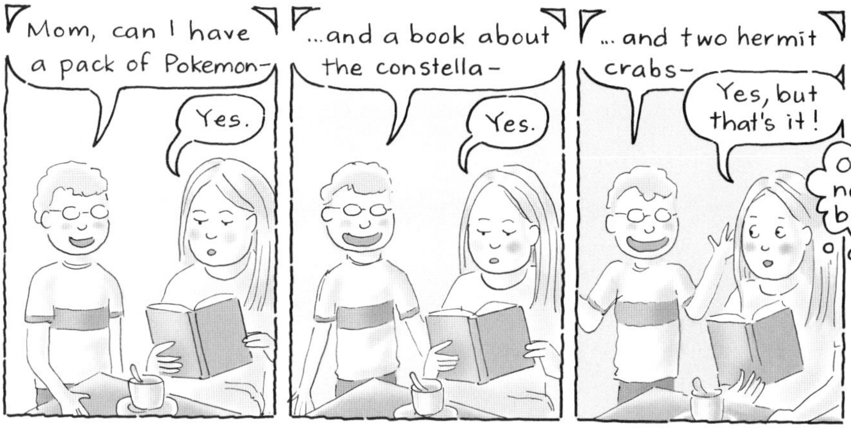
Mom, can I have a pack of Pokemon-
Yes.
...and a book about the constella-
Yes.
... and two hermit crabs-
Yes, but that's it!
Ok, not bad.

Whether hermit crabs are more work than advertised or we had a high-maintenance pair, I don't know, but they occupied a great deal more of my time than I had anticipated.

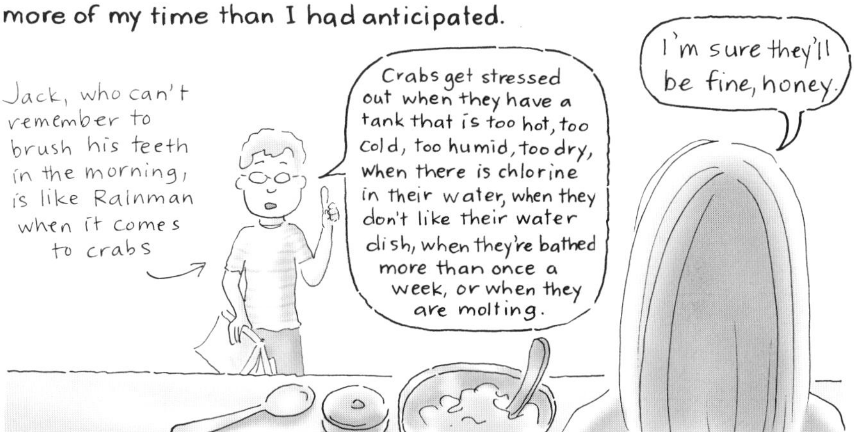
Jack, who can't remember to brush his teeth in the morning, is like Rainman when it comes to crabs
Crabs get stressed out when they have a tank that is too hot, too cold, too humid, too dry, when there is chlorine in their water, when they don't like their water dish, when they're bathed more than once a week, or when they are molting.
I'm sure they'll be fine, honey.

But crabs, it turns out, react to anxiety in a much more dramatic fashion than, say, you or I would.

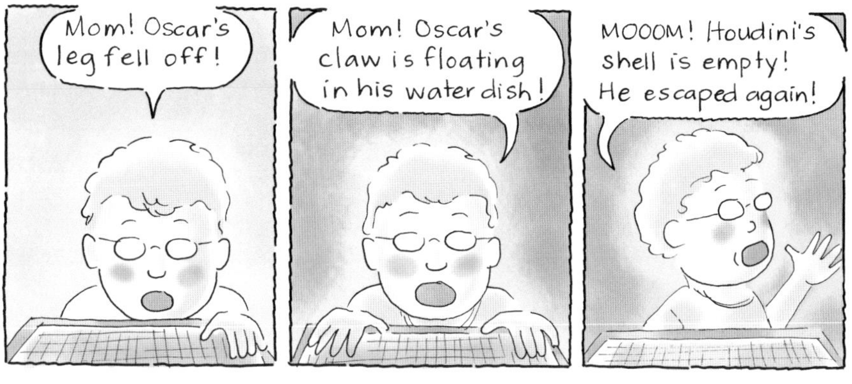
Mom! Oscar's leg fell off!
Mom! Oscar's claw is floating in his water dish!
MOOOM! Houdini's shell is empty! He escaped again!

I'll admit it: They weren't my best parenting decisions. But that summer wasn't about being a perfect mom. It was about patching up a few broken hearts.

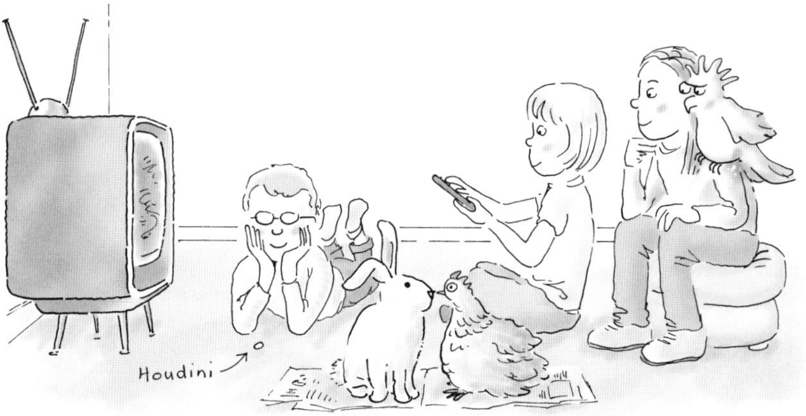
Houdini

The kids settled into a second round of day camps and a regular after-camp routine with T.J. Over ice cream sundaes, they would discuss the pros and cons of their father's latest million-dollar idea.

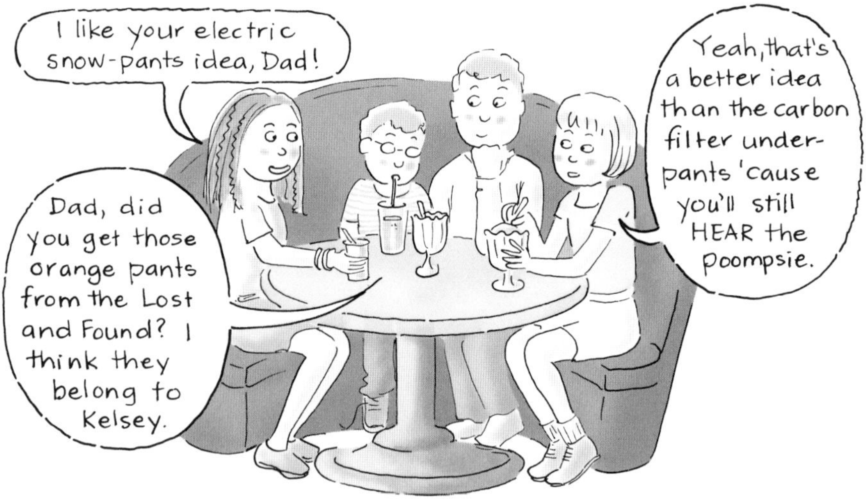
I like your electric snow-pants idea, Dad!
Dad, did you get those orange pants from the Lost and Found? I think they belong to Kelsey.
Yeah, that's a better idea than the carbon filter under-pants 'cause you'll still HEAR the poompsie.

The schedule seemed to be working for everyone. I'd been able to keep the kids' lives relatively consistent and predictable.

But divorce and upheaval go hand-in-hand, and there was a limit to what I could do to maintain equilibrium given T.J.'s distaste for it.

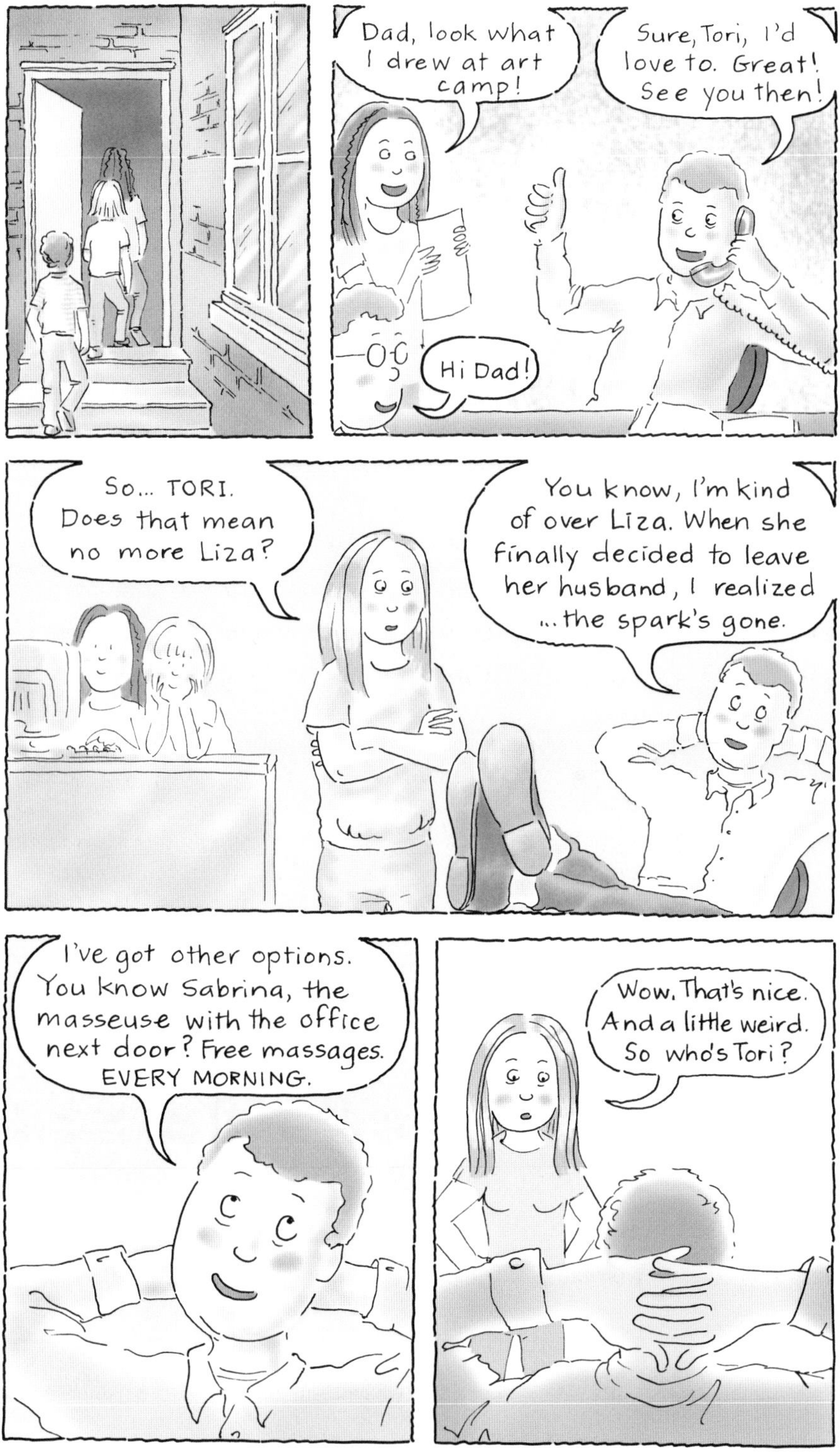
Dad, look what I drew at art camp!
Sure, Tori, I'd love to. Great! See you then!
Hi Dad!
So... TORI. Does that mean no more Liza?
You know, I'm kind of over Liza. When she finally decided to leave her husband, I realized ...the spark's gone.
I've got other options. You know Sabrina, the masseuse with the office next door? Free massages. EVERY MORNING.
Wow. That's nice. And a little weird. So who's Tori?

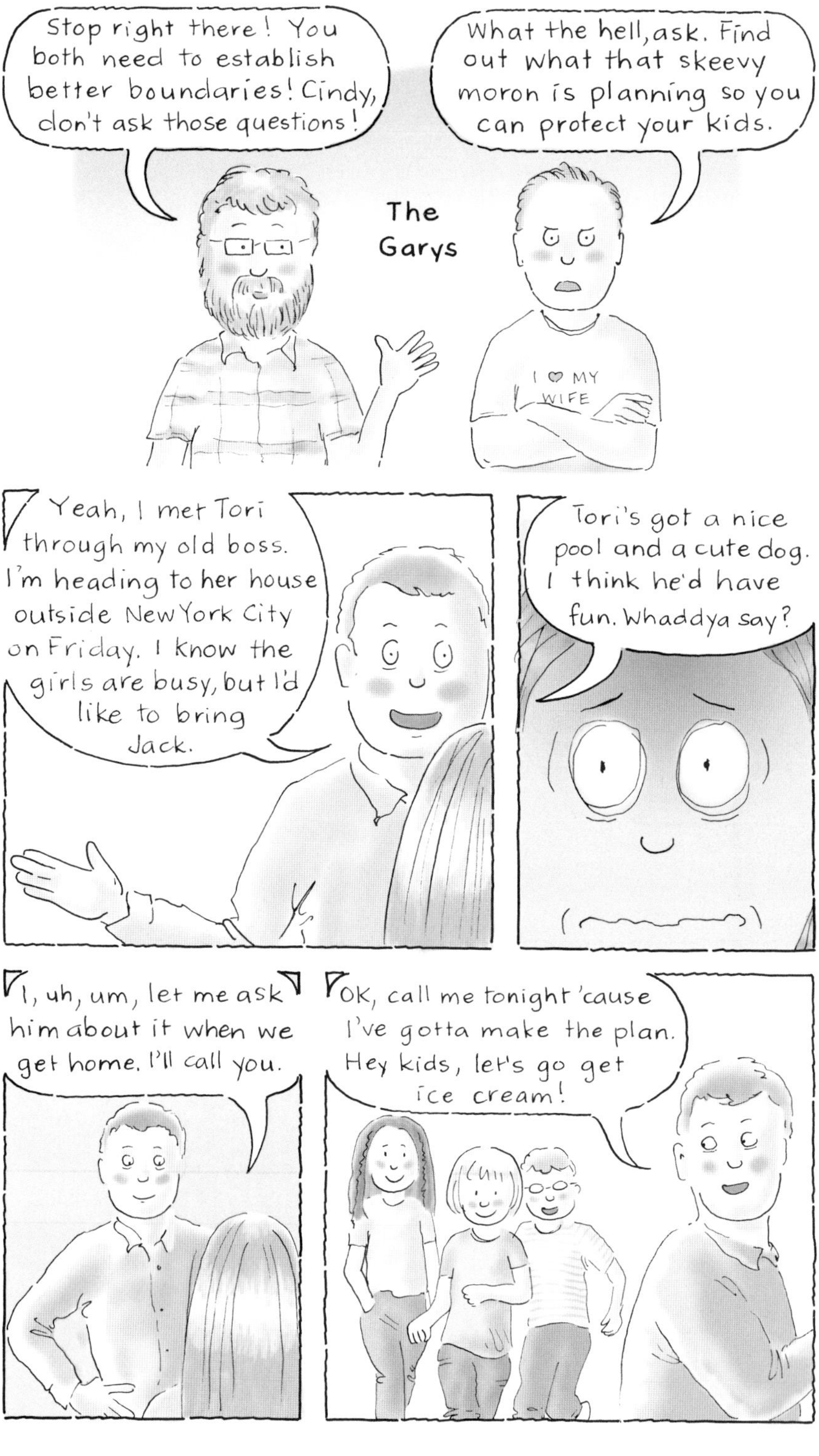
Stop right there! You both need to establish better boundaries! Cindy, don't ask those questions!
What the hell, ask. Find out what that skeevy moron is planning so you can protect your kids.
The Garys
I ♥ MY WIFE
Yeah, I met Tori through my old boss. I'm heading to her house outside New York City on Friday. I know the girls are busy, but I'd like to bring Jack.
Tori's got a nice pool and a cute dog. I think he'd have fun. Whaddya say?
I, uh, um, let me ask him about it when we get home. I'll call you.
OK, call me tonight 'cause I've gotta make the plan. Hey kids, let's go get ice cream!

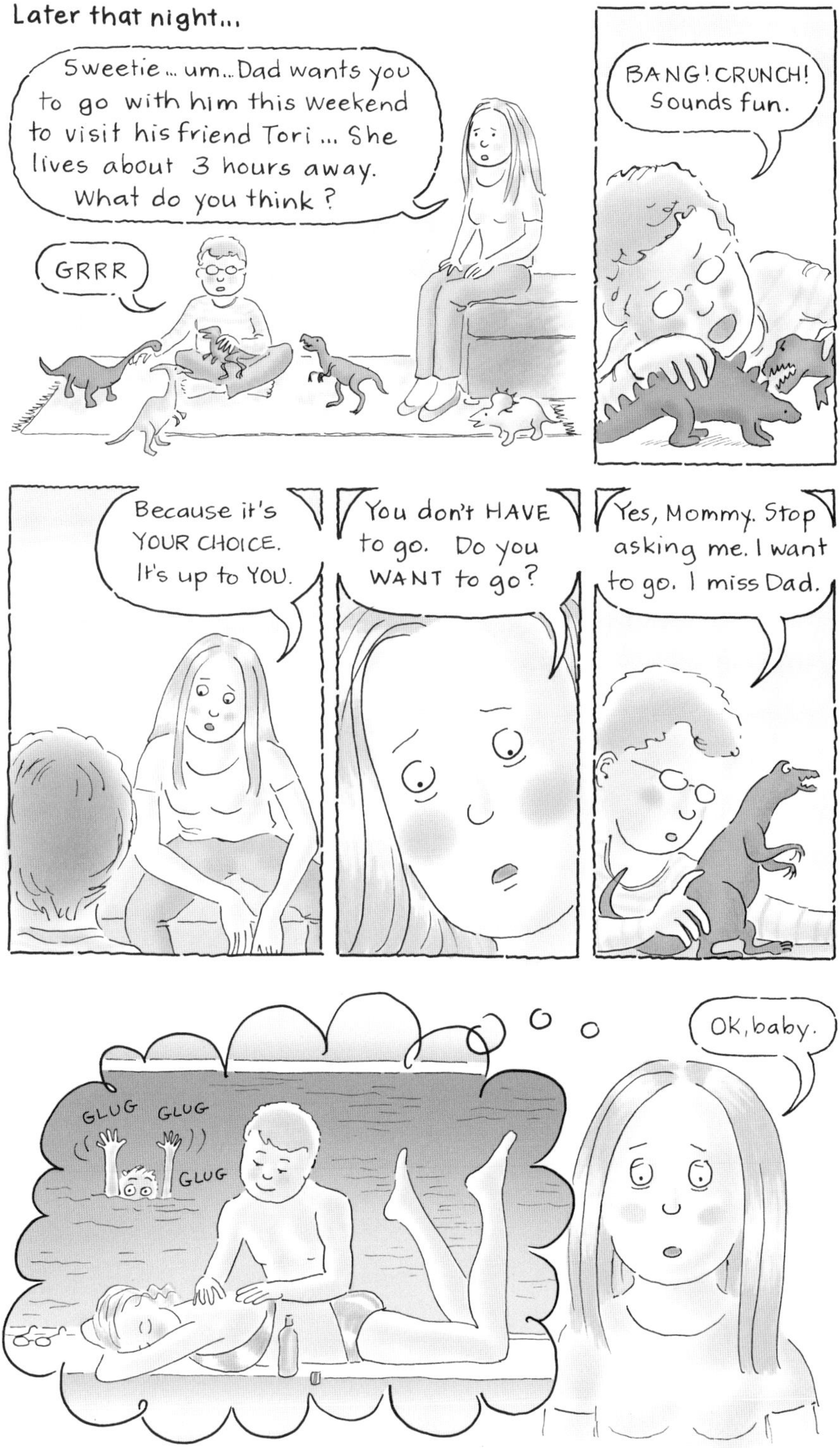
Later that night...
Sweetie... um... Dad wants you to go with him this weekend to visit his friend Tori... She lives about 3 hours away. What do you think?
GRRR
BANG! CRUNCH! Sounds fun.
Because it's YOUR CHOICE. It's up to YOU.
You don't HAVE to go. Do you WANT to go?
Yes, Mommy. Stop asking me. I want to go. I miss Dad.
GLUG GLUG GLUG
OK, baby.

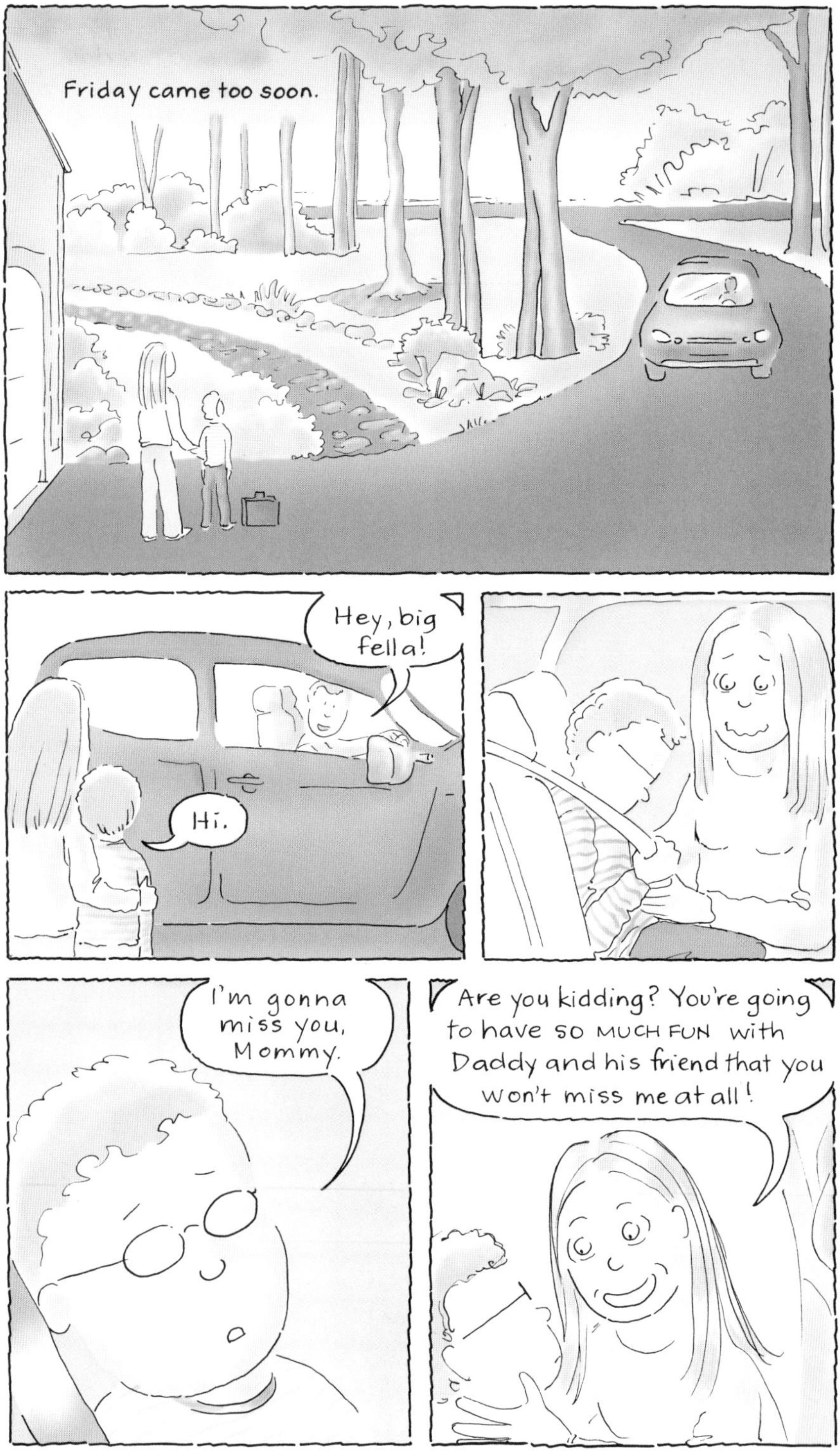
Friday came too soon.
Hey, big fella!
Hi.
I'm gonna miss you, Mommy.
Are you kidding? You're going to have SO MUCH FUN with Daddy and his friend that you won't miss me at all!

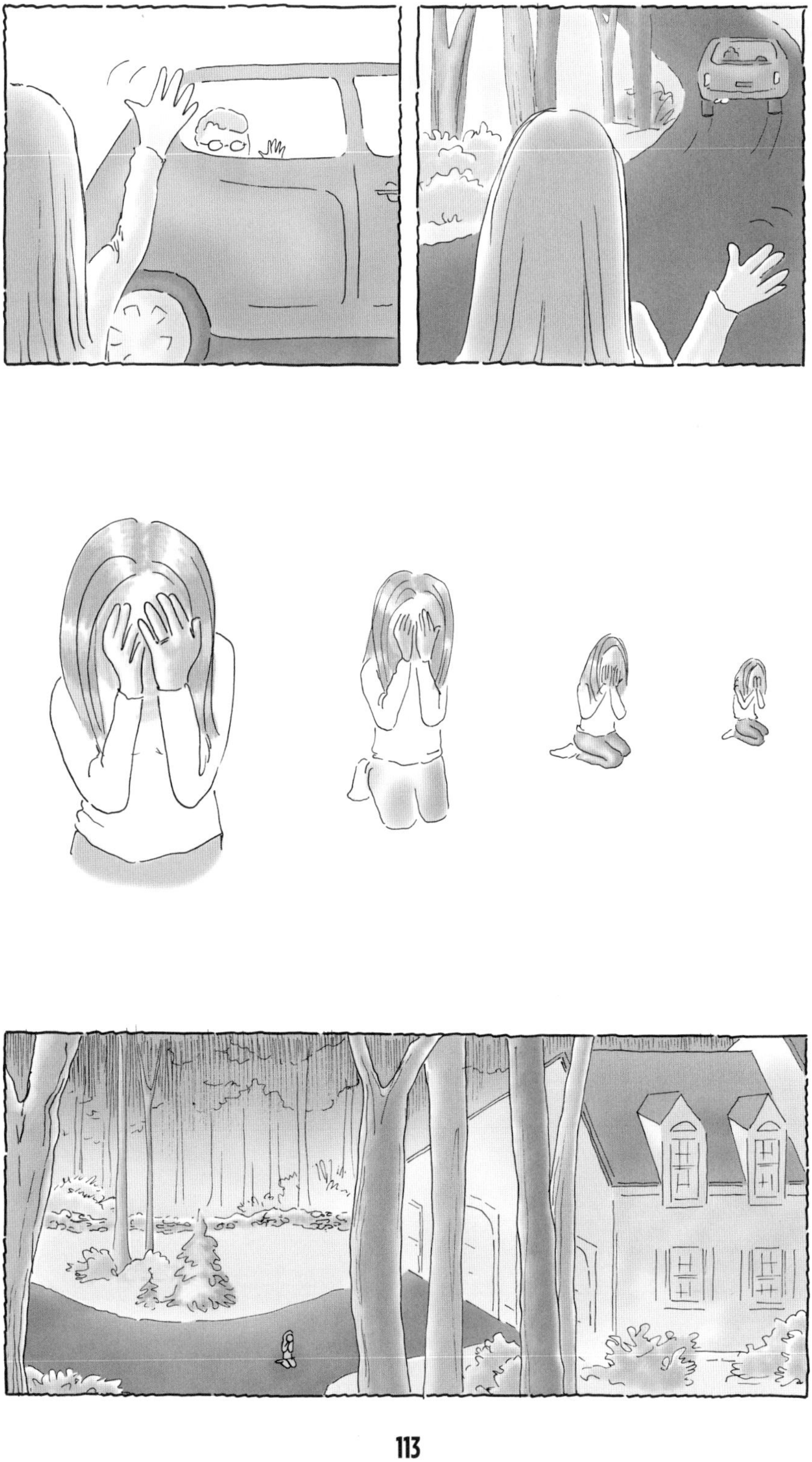

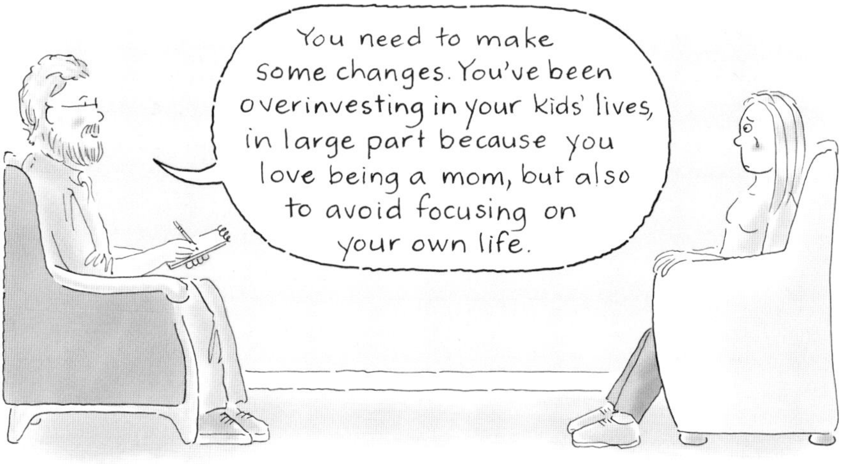
You need to make some changes. You've been overinvesting in your kids' lives, in large part because you love being a mom, but also to avoid focusing on your own life.

Gary was right. I had probably overdone it.

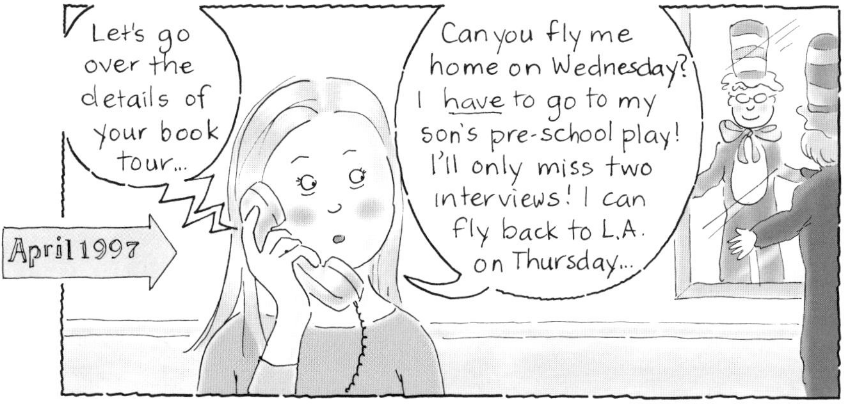
April 1997
Let's go over the details of your book tour...
Can you fly me home on Wednesday? I have to go to my son's pre-school play! I'll only miss two interviews! I can fly back to L.A. on Thursday...

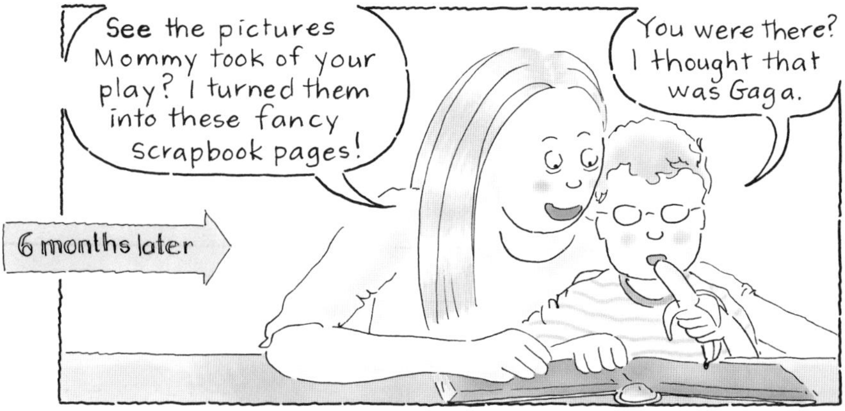
6 months later
See the pictures Mommy took of your play? I turned them into these fancy scrapbook pages!
You were there? I thought that was Gaga.

For practical reasons as well as personal ones, it was time to start paying more attention to my own health, emotional well-being, and career.

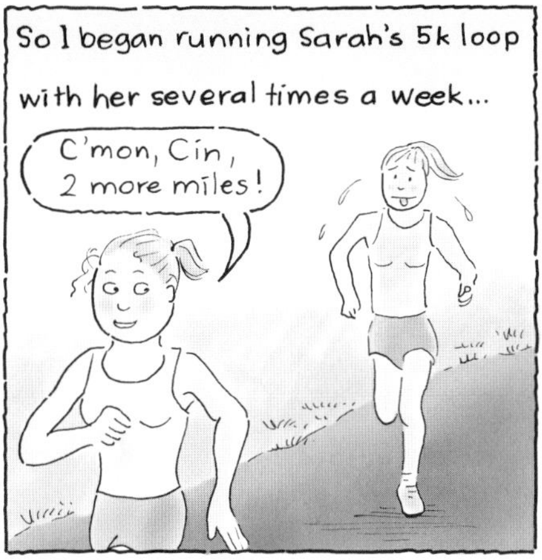
So I began running Sarah's 5k loop with her several times a week...
C'mon, Cin, 2 more miles!

...though I tried to eliminate a k or two whenever possible.

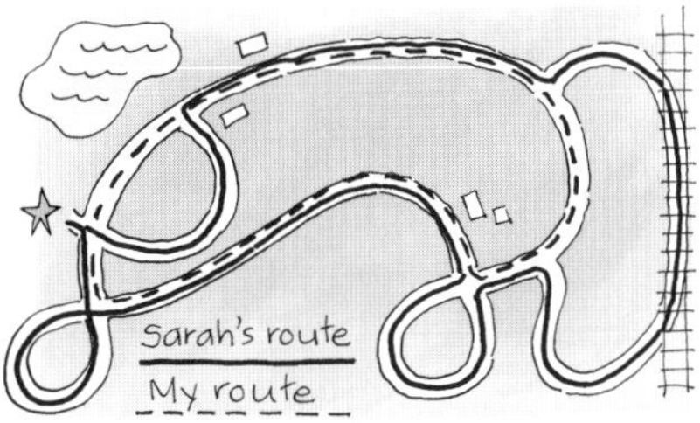
Sarah's route
My route

I signed up for weekend computer classes at the local college to learn how to use Adobe Illustrator.

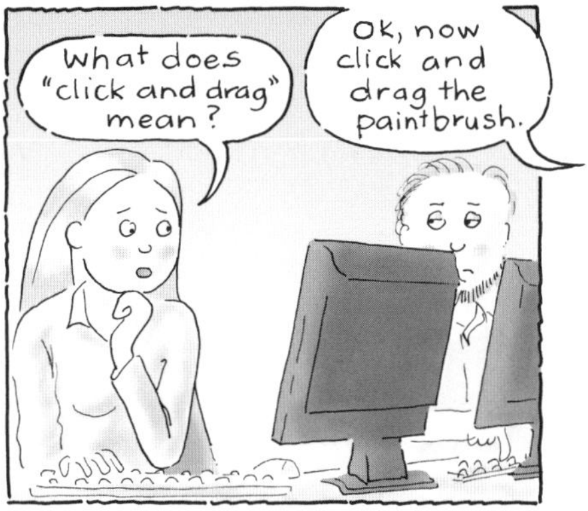
What does "click and drag" mean?
Ok, now click and drag the paintbrush.

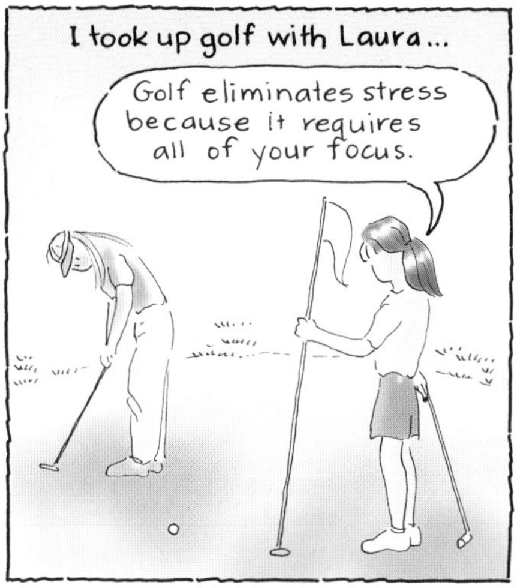
I took up golf with Laura...
Golf eliminates stress because it requires all of your focus.

...which at first was more like an incredibly long, tedious game of croquet.

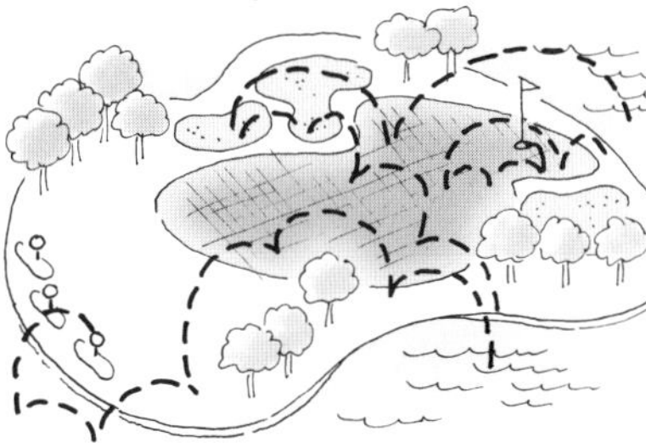

And I spent a lot of time promoting my recent books and working on new ones.

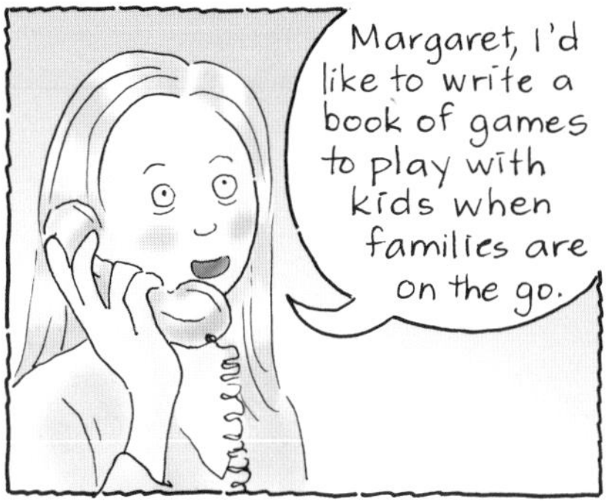
Margaret, I'd like to write a book of games to play with kids when families are on the go.

Sometimes all the possibilities and my new independence were exciting and empowering...

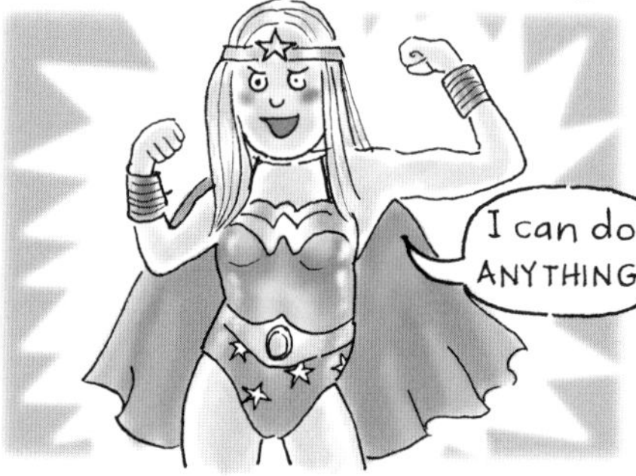
I can do ANYTHING!

(5 MINUTES LATER)

...and sometimes not so much.

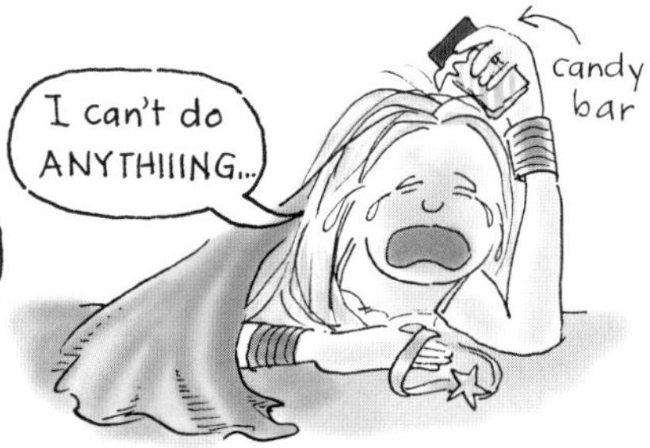
I can't do ANYTHIIING...
candy bar

Propelled by gut instinct rather than calculation and craving certainty over limbo, I forged ahead with the divorce. I had no idea what lay ahead, but I didn't see another alternative.

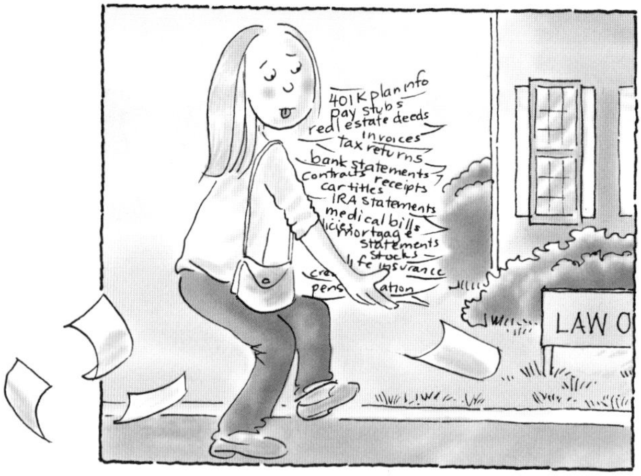
401K plan info
pay stubs
real estate deeds
invoices
tax returns
bank statements
contracts
receipts
car titles
IRA statements
medical bills
mortgage statements
stocks
life insurance
LAW O

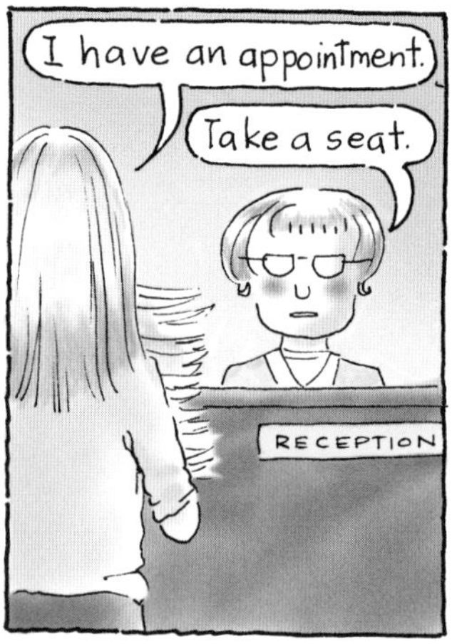
I have an appointment.
Take a seat.
RECEPTION

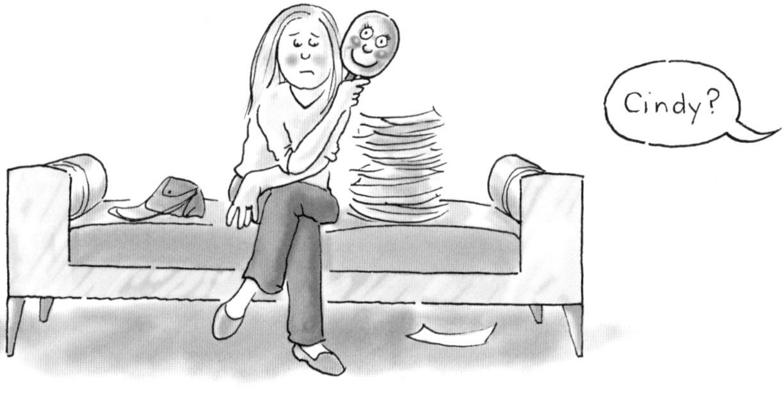
Cindy?

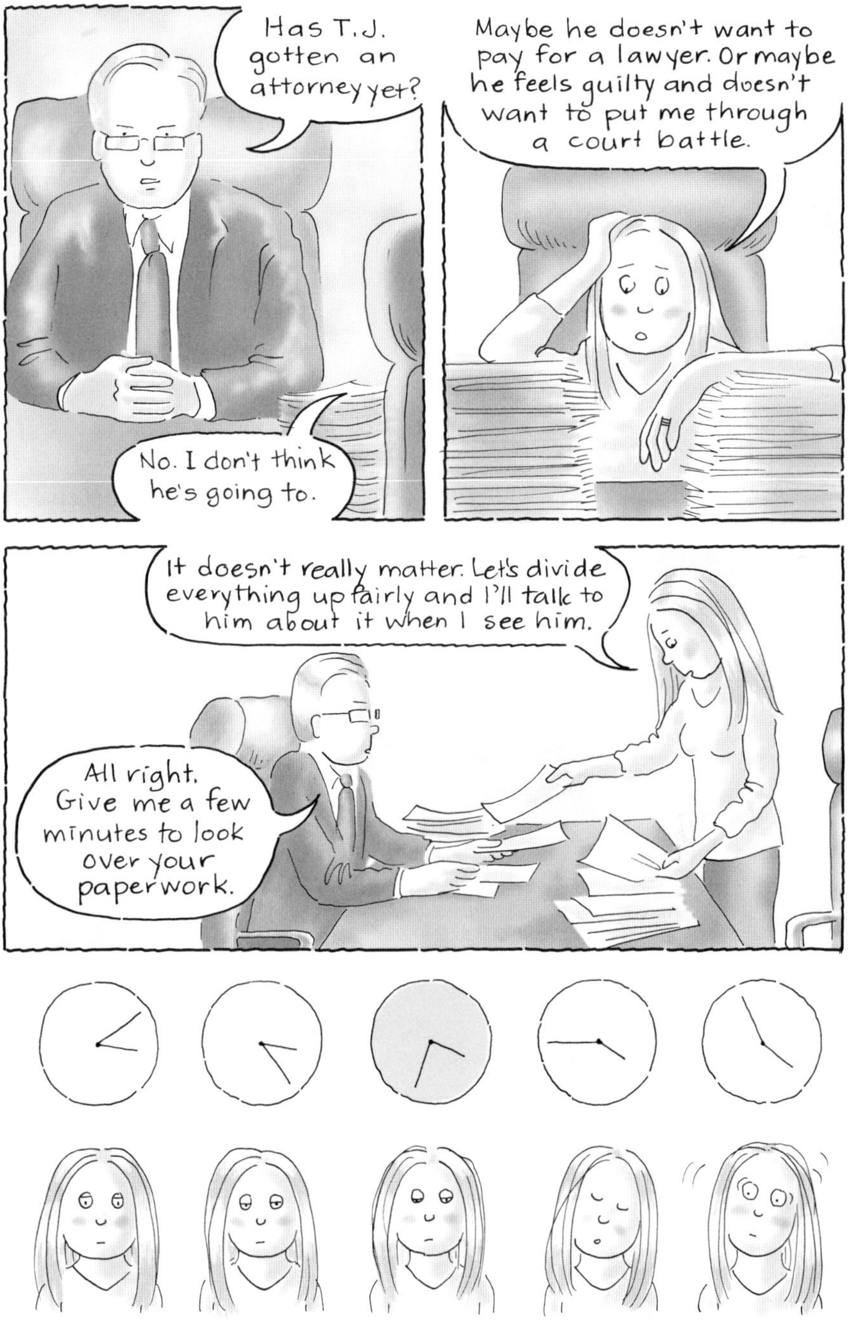
Has T.J. gotten an attorney yet?
No. I don't think he's going to.
Maybe he doesn't want to pay for a lawyer. Or maybe he feels guilty and doesn't want to put me through a court battle.
It doesn't really matter. Let's divide everything up fairly and I'll talk to him about it when I see him.
All right. Give me a few minutes to look over your paperwork.

Our finances were thoroughly intertwined. T.J. and I had set up our lives together never intending to separate them. It wasn't until I tried to unravel everything that I fully understood just how connected we were.

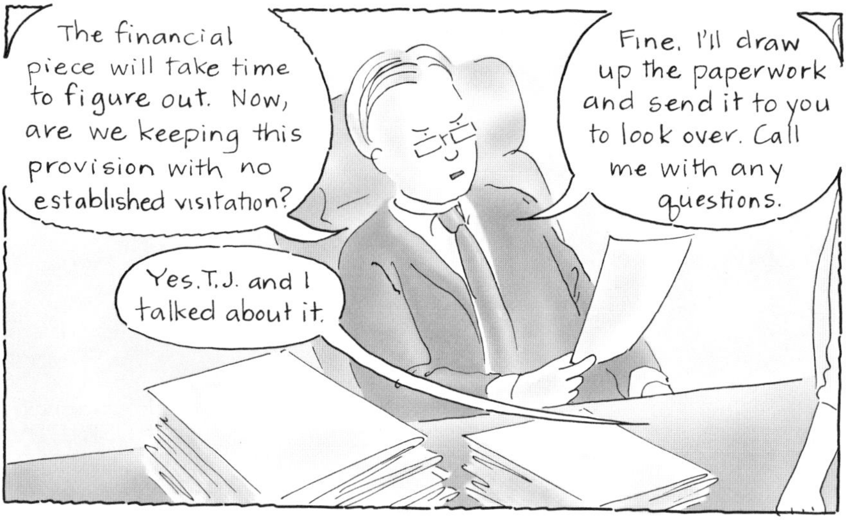
The financial piece will take time to figure out. Now, are we keeping this provision with no established visitation?
Yes. T.J. and I talked about it.
Fine. I'll draw up the paperwork and send it to you to look over. Call me with any questions.

I walked out of the lawyer's office one step closer to resolving everything and moving forward with my life. I assumed that once the divorce papers had been signed and stamped and filed, and everything was official, it would be over. At the time, I didn't realize that these agreements could be challenged and changed, and that closure was really an illusion.

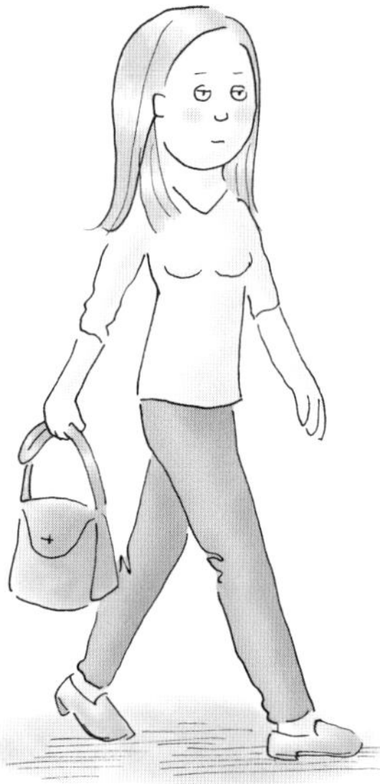

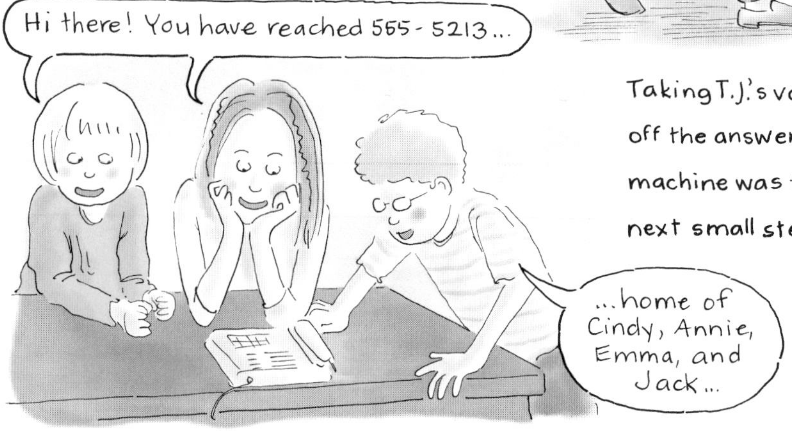
Hi there! You have reached 555-5213...
...home of Cindy, Annie, Emma, and Jack...

Taking T.J.'s voice off the answering machine was the next small step.

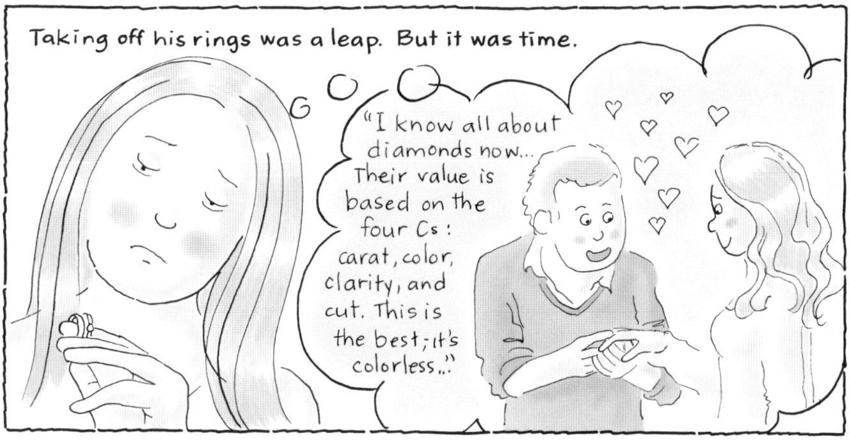
Taking off his rings was a leap. But it was time.
"I know all about diamonds now... Their value is based on the four Cs: carat, color, clarity, and cut. This is the best; it's colorless..."

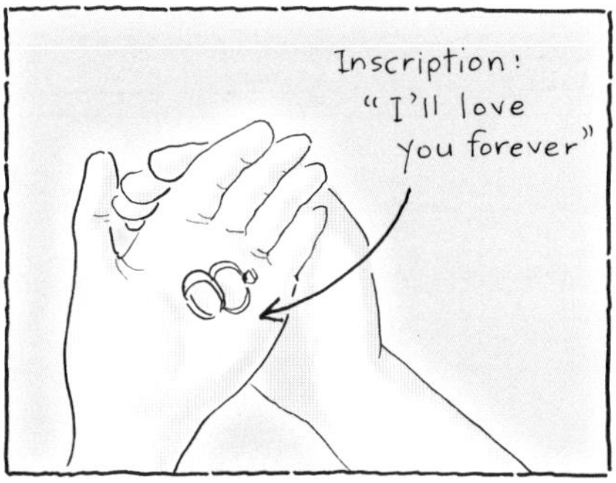
Inscription: "I'll love you forever"

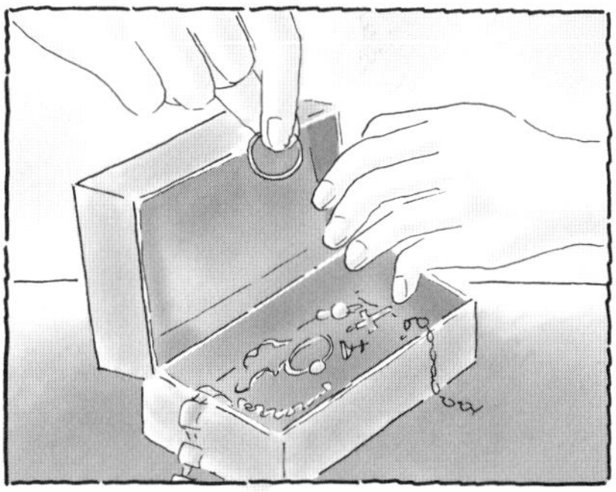

These rings had been chosen with care, in the spirit of true and lasting love, and someday I would pass them along to one of my children. They represented the best part of my relationship with T. J.

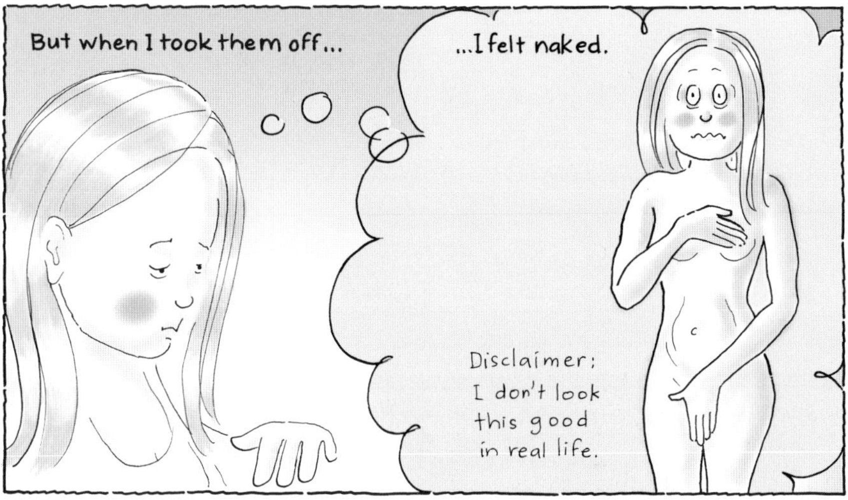
But when I took them off...
...I felt naked.
Disclaimer: I don't look this good in real life.

From what I could tell, everyone was staring at my ring-less ring finger.

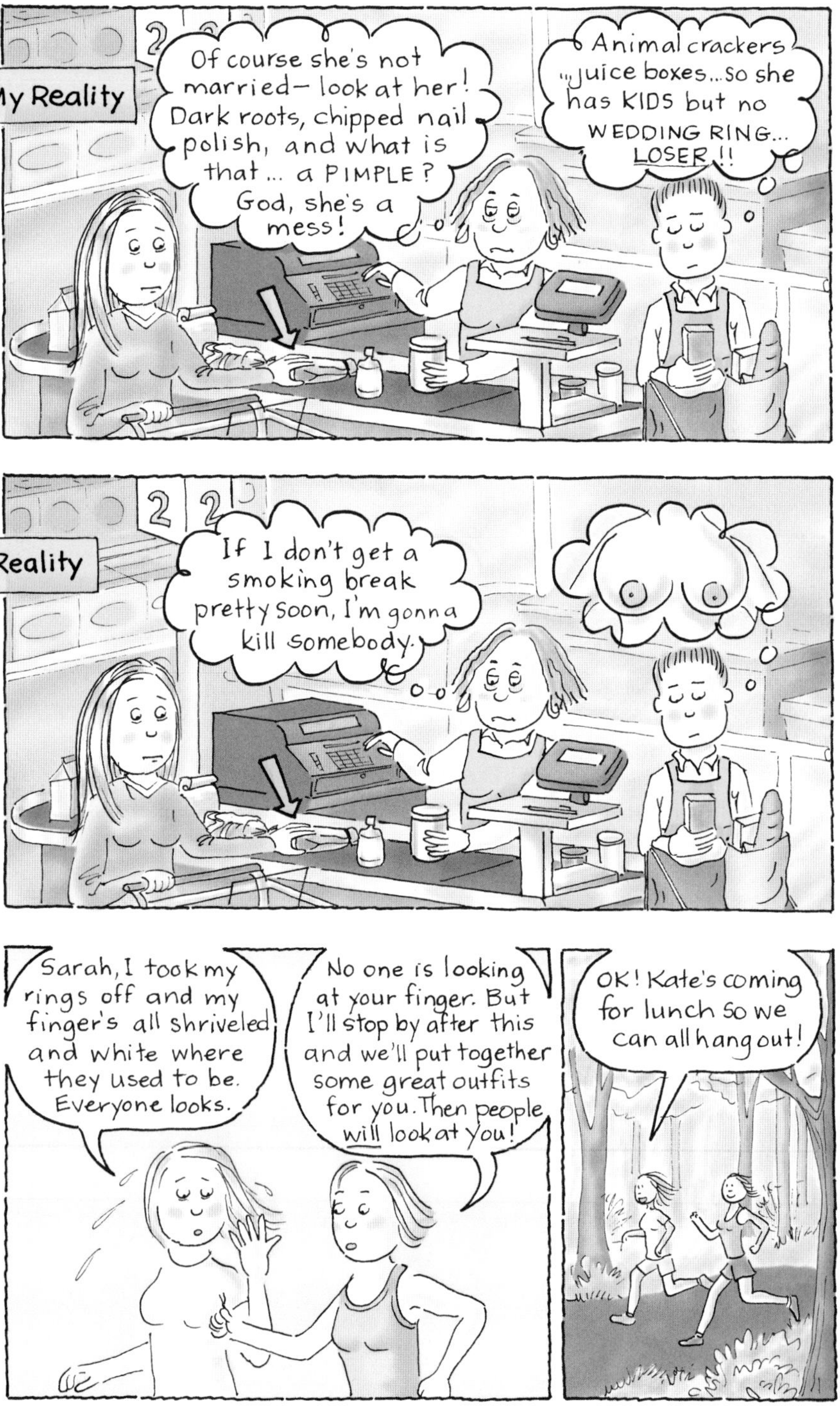
My Reality
Of course she's not married— look at her! Dark roots, chipped nail polish, and what is that ... a PIMPLE? God, she's a mess!
Animal crackers ... juice boxes... so she has KIDS but no WEDDING RING... LOSER!!
Reality
If I don't get a smoking break pretty soon, I'm gonna kill somebody.
Sarah, I took my rings off and my finger's all shriveled and white where they used to be. Everyone looks.
No one is looking at your finger. But I'll stop by after this and we'll put together some great outfits for you. Then people will look at you!
OK! Kate's coming for lunch so we can all hang out!

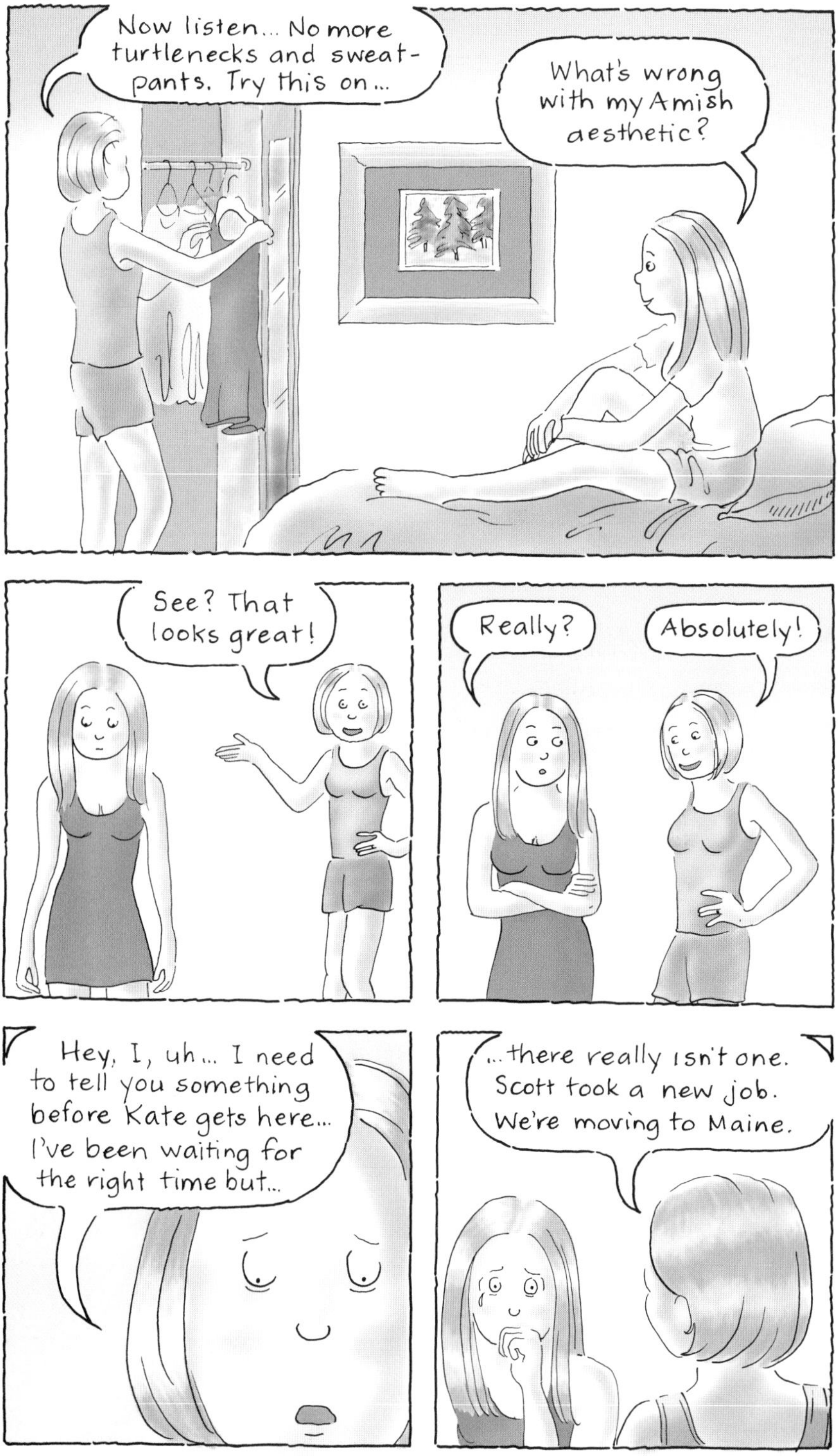
Now listen... No more turtlenecks and sweatpants. Try this on...
What's wrong with my Amish aesthetic?
See? That looks great!
Really?
Absolutely!
Hey, I, uh... I need to tell you something before Kate gets here... I've been waiting for the right time but...
...there really isn't one. Scott took a new job. We're moving to Maine.

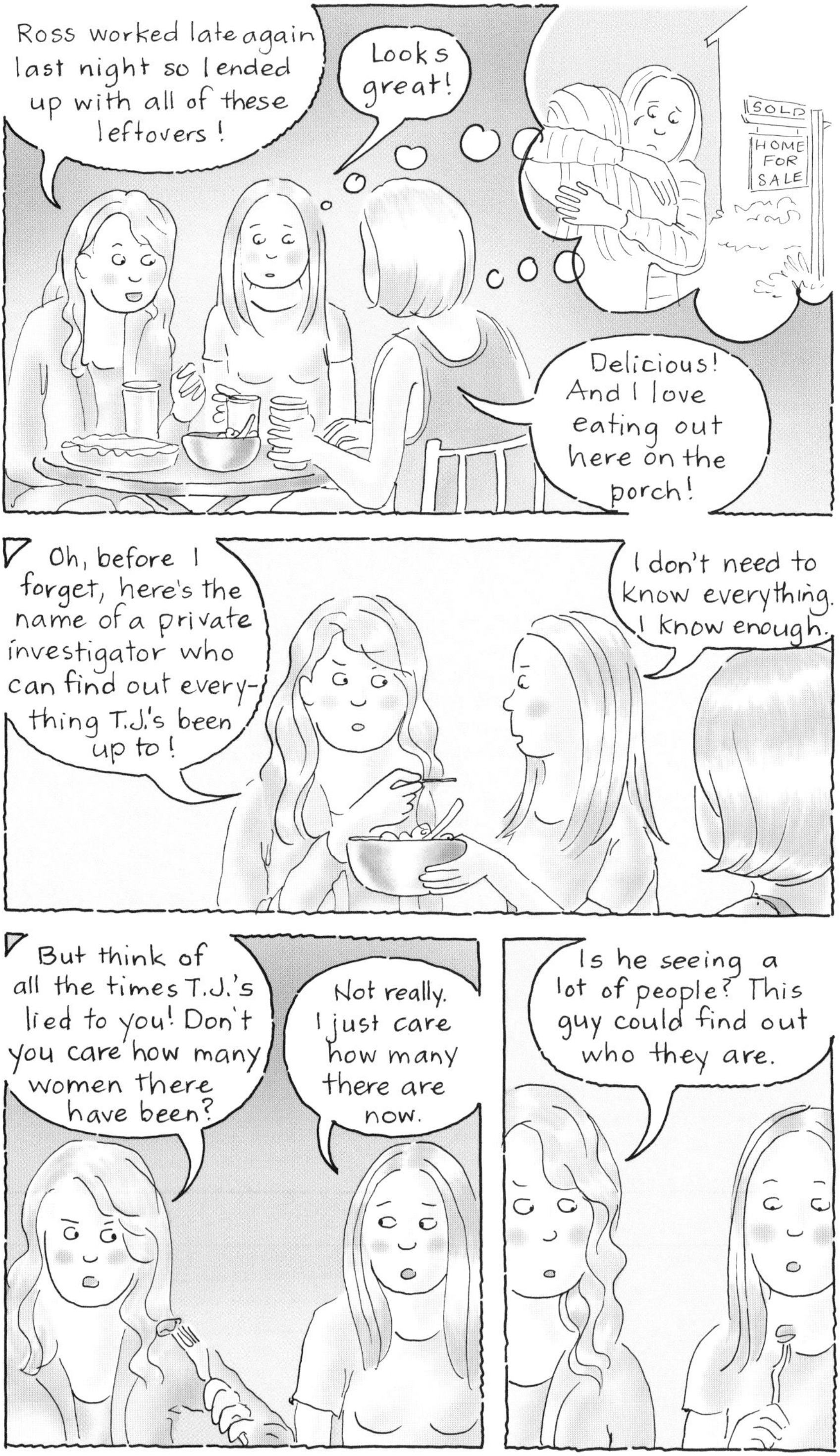
Ross worked late again last night so I ended up with all of these leftovers!
Looks great!
SOLD
HOME FOR SALE
Delicious! And I love eating out here on the porch!
Oh, before I forget, here's the name of a private investigator who can find out everything T.J.'s been up to!
I don't need to know everything. I know enough.
But think of all the times T.J.'s lied to you! Don't you care how many women there have been?
Not really. I just care how many there are now.
Is he seeing a lot of people? This guy could find out who they are.

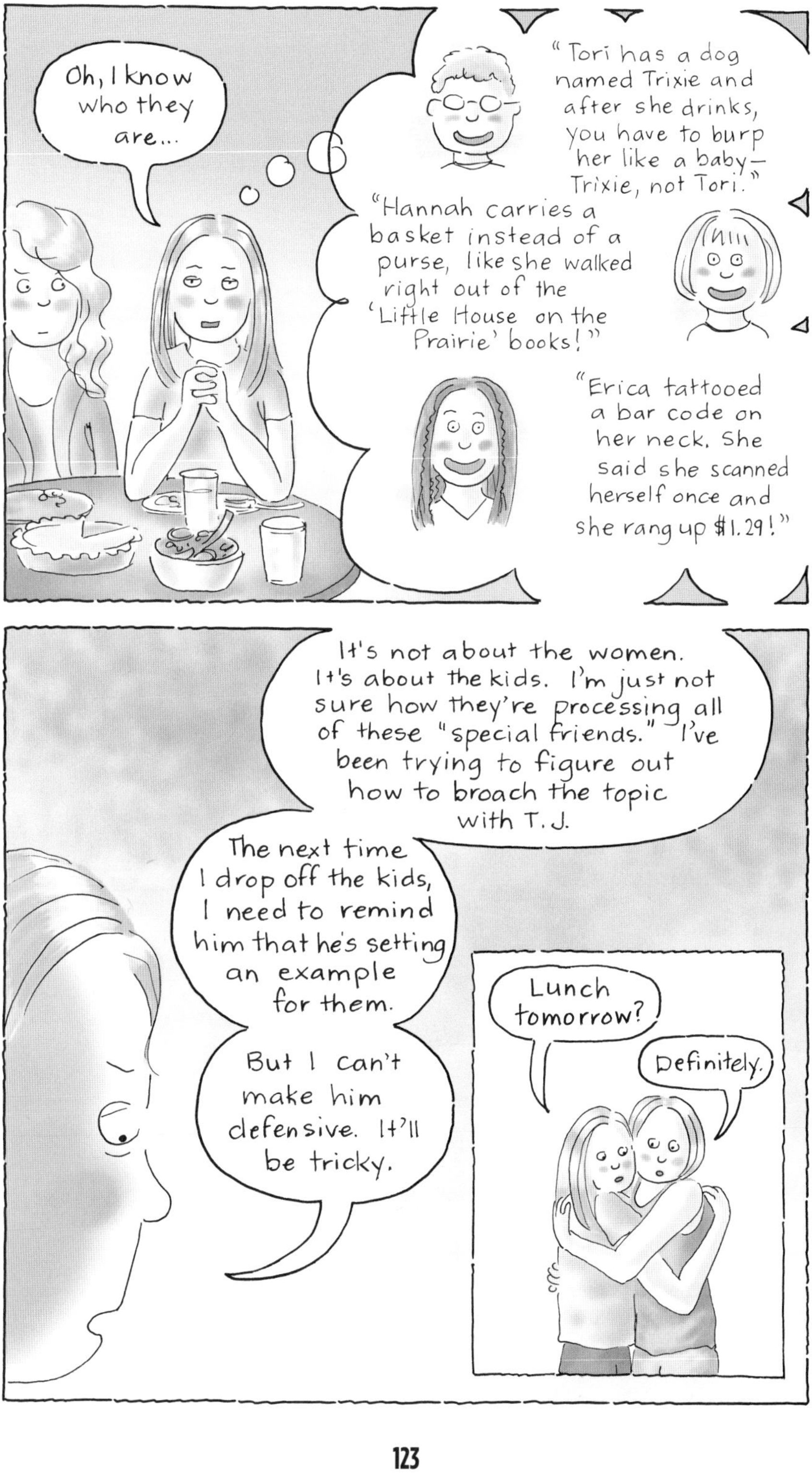
Oh, I know who they are...
"Tori has a dog named Trixie and after she drinks, you have to burp her like a baby— Trixie, not Tori."
"Hannah carries a basket instead of a purse, like she walked right out of the 'Little House on the Prairie' books!"
"Erica tattooed a bar code on her neck. She said she scanned herself once and she rang up $1.29!"
It's not about the women. It's about the kids. I'm just not sure how they're processing all of these "special friends." I've been trying to figure out how to broach the topic with T.J.
The next time I drop off the kids, I need to remind him that he's setting an example for them.
But I can't make him defensive. It'll be tricky.
Lunch tomorrow?
Definitely.

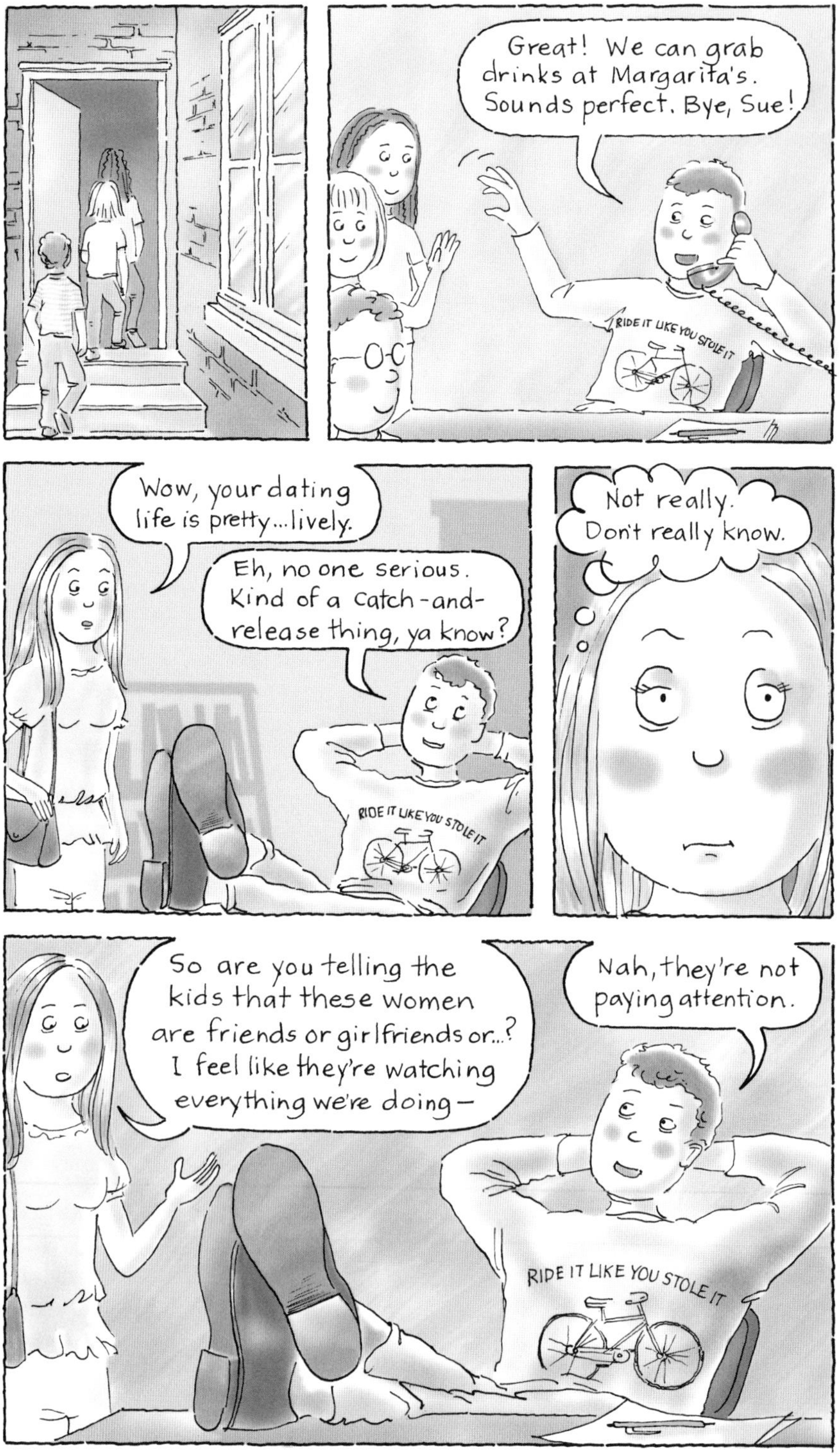
Great! We can grab drinks at Margarita's. Sounds perfect. Bye, Sue!
RIDE IT LIKE YOU STOLE IT
Wow, your dating life is pretty...lively.
Eh, no one serious. Kind of a catch-and-release thing, ya know?
RIDE IT LIKE YOU STOLE IT
Not really. Don't really know.
So are you telling the kids that these women are friends or girlfriends or...? I feel like they're watching everything we're doing—
Nah, they're not paying attention.
RIDE IT LIKE YOU STOLE IT

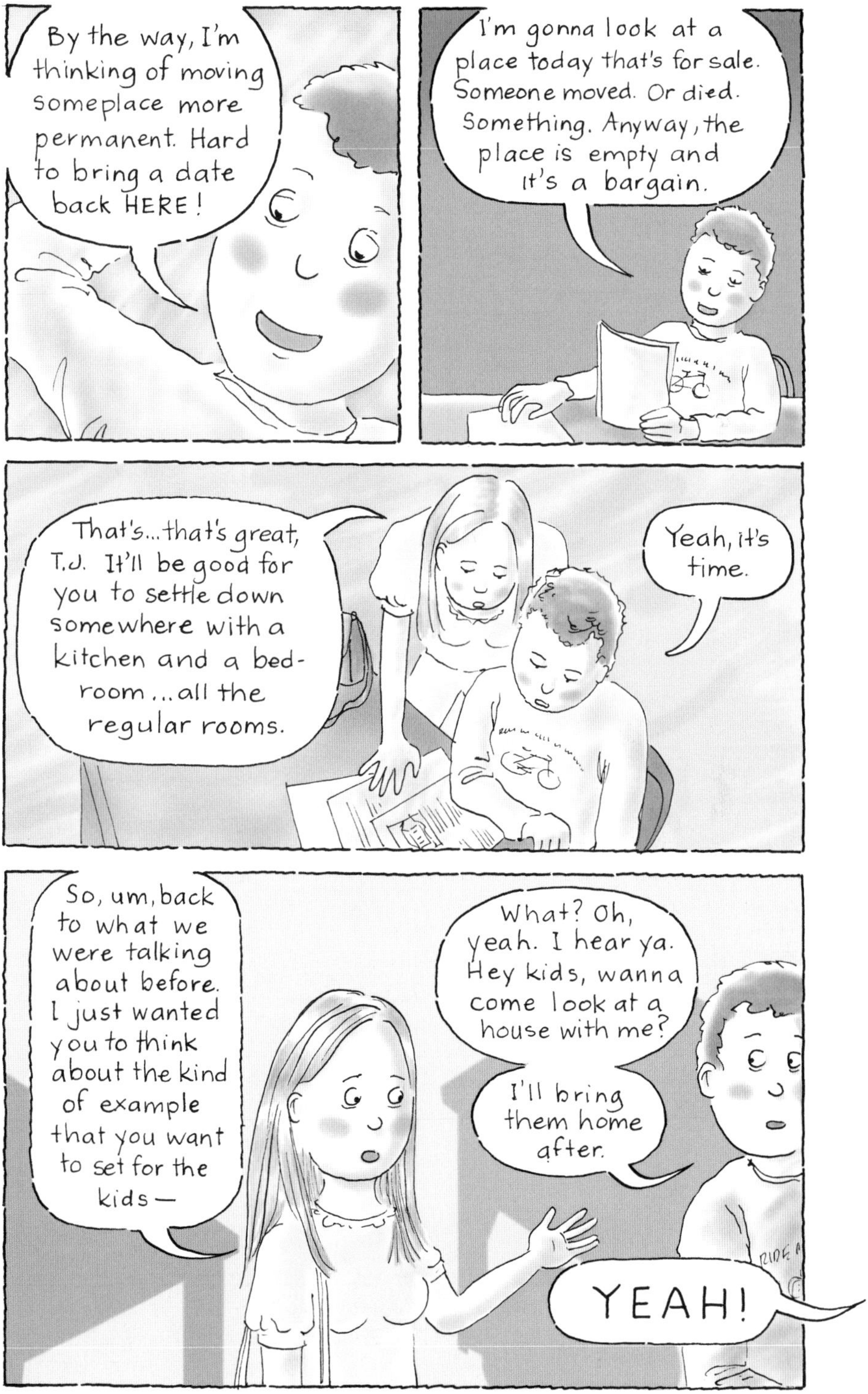
By the way, I'm thinking of moving someplace more permanent. Hard to bring a date back HERE!
I'm gonna look at a place today that's for sale. Someone moved. Or died. Something. Anyway, the place is empty and it's a bargain.
That's... that's great, T.J. It'll be good for you to settle down somewhere with a kitchen and a bed-room ... all the regular rooms.
Yeah, it's time.
So, um, back to what we were talking about before. I just wanted you to think about the kind of example that you want to set for the kids—
What? Oh, yeah. I hear ya. Hey kids, wanna come look at a house with me?
I'll bring them home after.
YEAH!

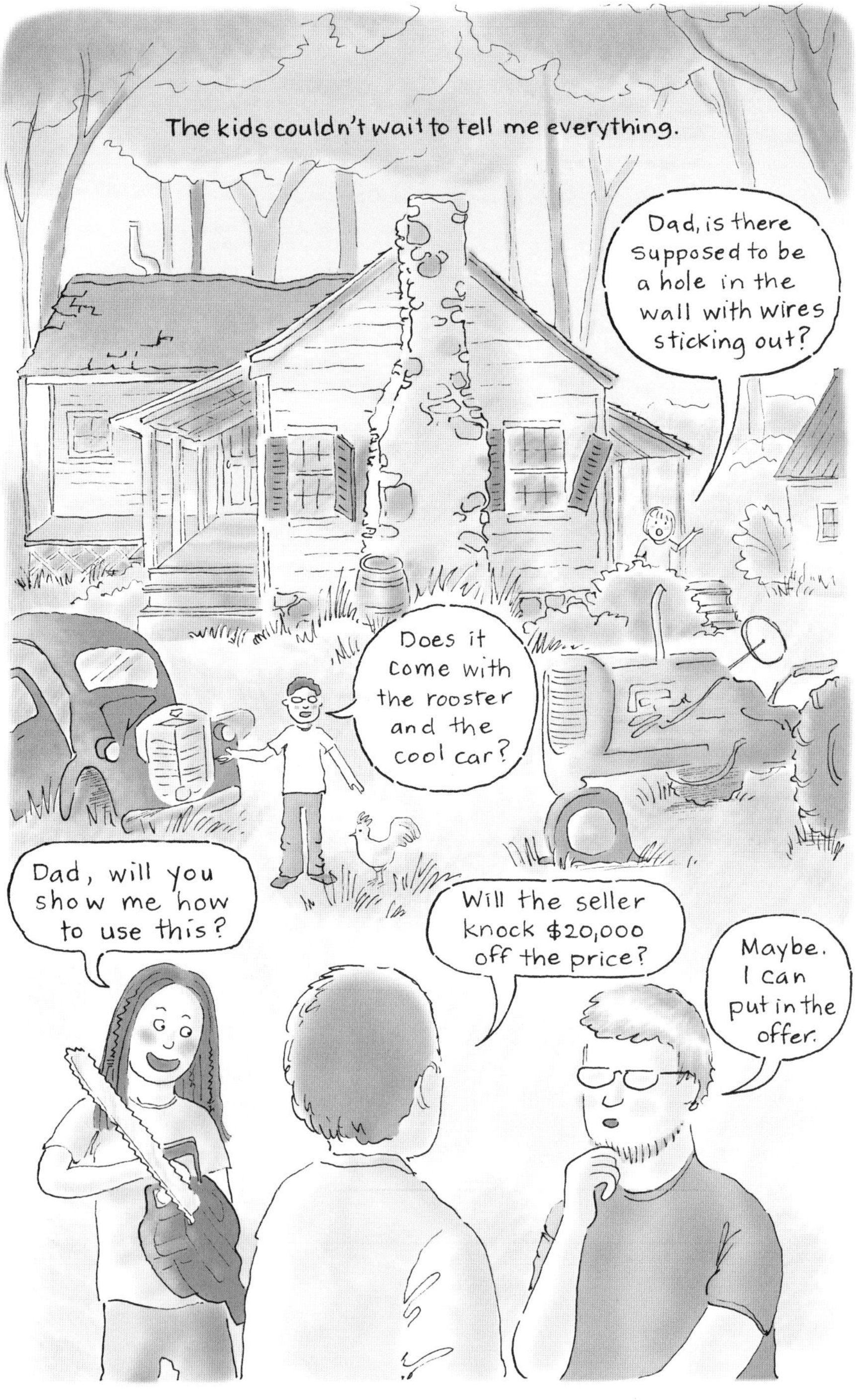
The kids couldn't wait to tell me everything.
Dad, is there supposed to be a hole in the wall with wires sticking out?
Does it come with the rooster and the cool car?
Dad, will you show me how to use this?
Will the seller knock $20,000 off the price?
Maybe. I can put in the offer.

T.J. closed on the house soon after he saw it.

And shortly after that...

Wow... You guys are taking some of your favorite things to Dad's...

Is that ok, Mom?

Oh, sure.

NO, NO, NO! NOT OK!

Dad's here!

Hi T.J. Uh, here's this.* And I packed lunches for the kids for tomorrow. I also bought you smoke detectors.

Great!

*bag of antidotes for child who might be hungry or thirsty or bored or cold or sick or sleepy

"Tomorrow morning, Emma can show you where to drop her off for Shakespeare camp. That's at 9. Then you can take Annie to the college: She needs to remember her art supplies and her... Jack gets dropp... college, too. He pl... in the field nex... to th... rt. Not the on... ne a... lun... at's the... look... the... blue and un... ll have to r... nin... is water bot... You... mma at 2, Ann... at 3... d Jack at 3:30."

Uh huh, uh huh

So do you kids have anything going on tomorrow? Wanna help clean my office?

Bye, Mom!

Thank God my mom is visiting me...

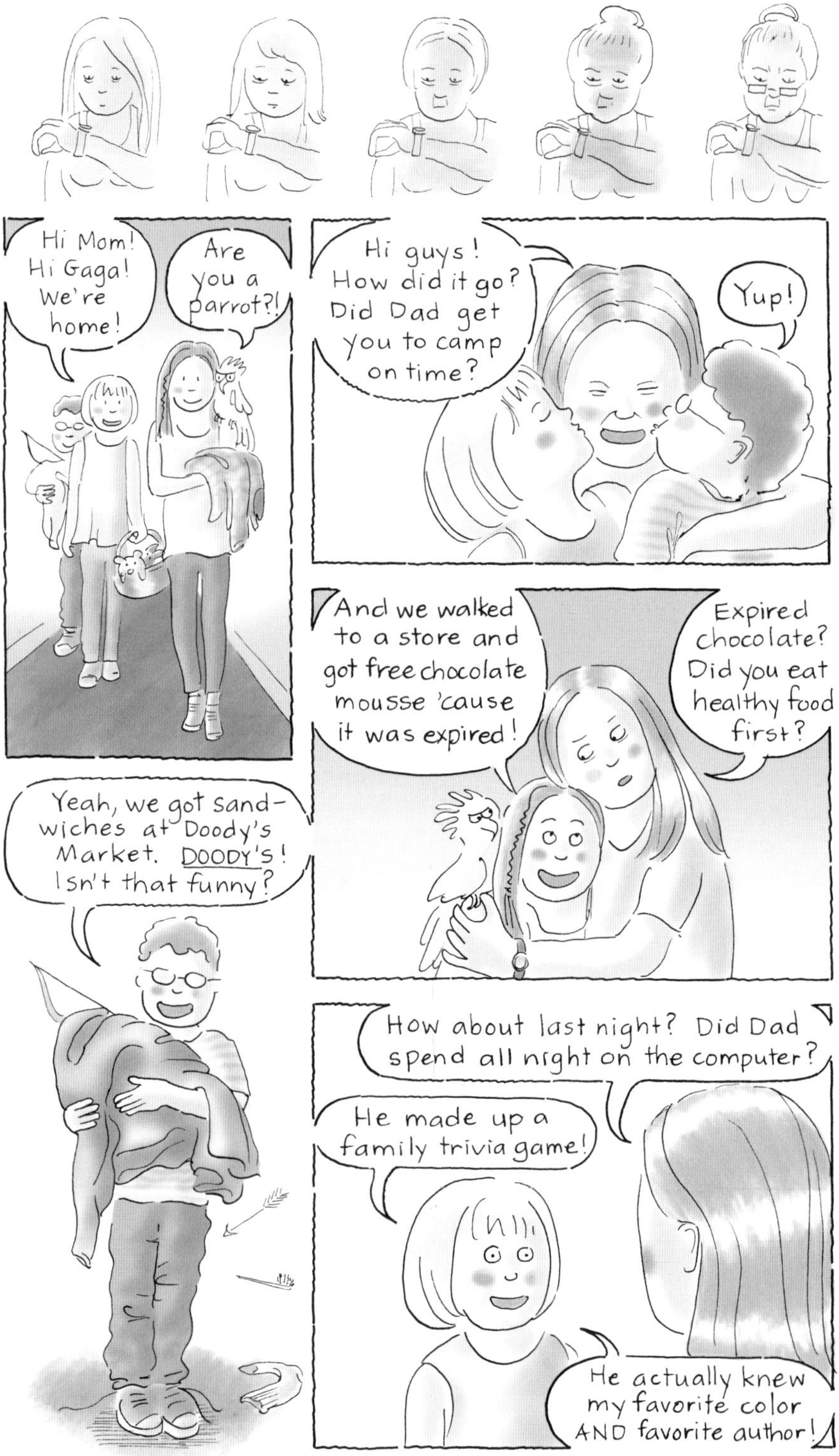
Hi Mom! Hi Gaga! We're home!
Are you a parrot?!
Hi guys! How did it go? Did Dad get you to camp on time?
Yup!
And we walked to a store and got free chocolate mousse 'cause it was expired!
Expired chocolate? Did you eat healthy food first?
Yeah, we got sandwiches at Doody's Market. DOODY's! Isn't that funny?
How about last night? Did Dad spend all night on the computer?
He made up a family trivia game!
He actually knew my favorite color AND favorite author!

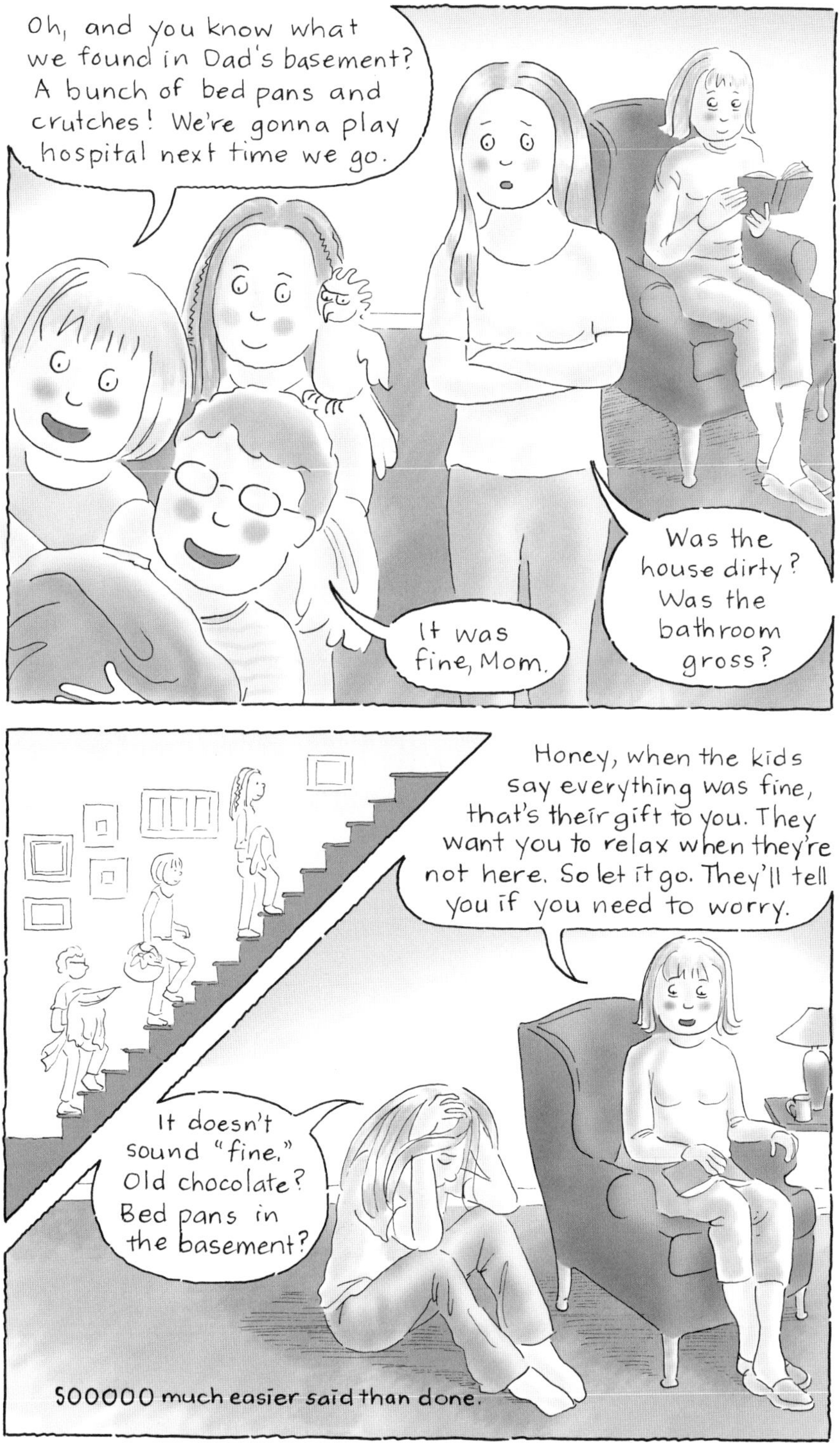
Oh, and you know what we found in Dad's basement? A bunch of bed pans and crutches! We're gonna play hospital next time we go.
Was the house dirty? Was the bathroom gross?
It was fine, Mom.
Honey, when the kids say everything was fine, that's their gift to you. They want you to relax when they're not here. So let it go. They'll tell you if you need to worry.
It doesn't sound "fine." Old chocolate? Bed pans in the basement?
SOOOOO much easier said than done.

Without me to help filter his ideas, T.J. immediately began transforming his 25 acres into a weird and wacky playground. Within two weeks, the property was like Neverland Ranch, if Neverland had been built by Evel Knievel using stuff he found at the dump.

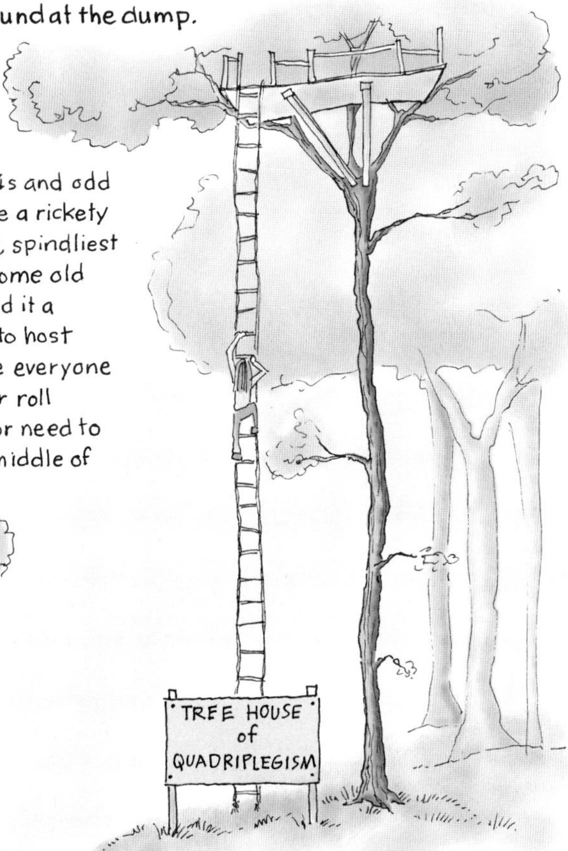
TREE HOUSE
of
QUADRIPLEGISM

T.J. hoisted up enough 2x4s and odd pieces of plywood to make a rickety tree house atop his tallest, spindliest tree. He then hauled up some old sleeping bags and declared it a terrific place for the kids to host friends overnight because everyone knows that children never roll around when they sleep or need to use the bathroom in the middle of the night.

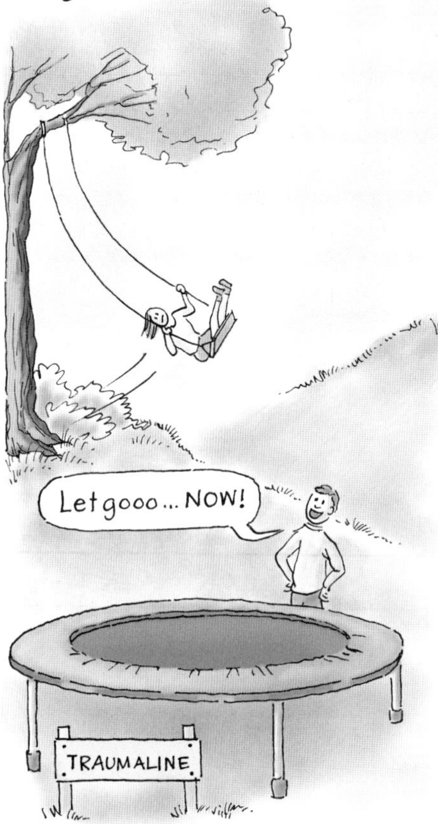
Let gooo... NOW!
TRAUMALINE

When a friend disassembled his trampoline, T.J. claimed it, bragging about his plans to make a "jumping room" in his house. Perhaps because his ceilings were your typical 7½ footers, he abandoned that idea and pieced it back together outdoors. But then he attached a swing to an overhanging tree branch so that at the end of its arc it dangled over the surface of the trampoline.

T.J. dismantled an old car and mounted the wheel axle on a motor he anchored to the top of a sheared-off tree. Then he hung knotted ropes on opposite sides so that the kids would swing around in a circle when he flipped a switch. Unfortunately, he never figured out how to control the motor's speed...

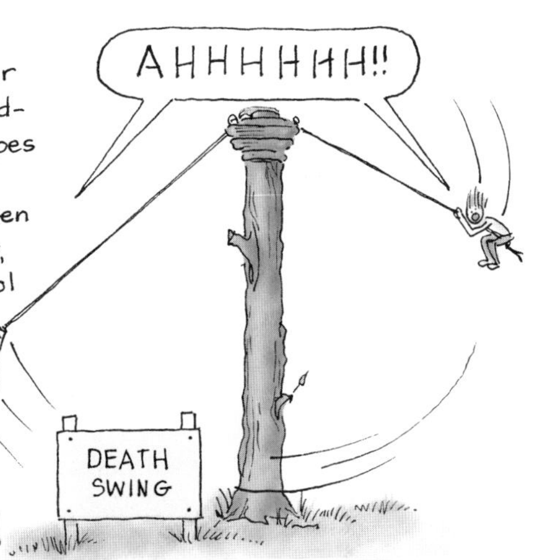
AHHHHHH!!
DEATH SWING

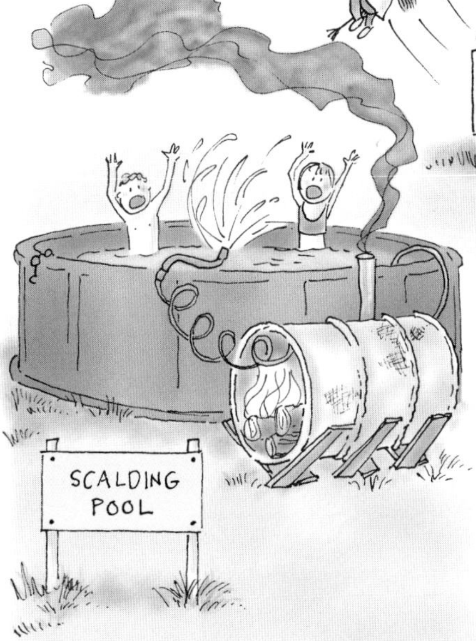
SCALDING POOL

He sprang for a pool on clearance at Walmart, the kind where four or five people have to hold up the plastic sides for about 35 hours while water dribbles from a hose to fill it. Then he hauled a rusted oil drum out of the woods and rigged up a system of copper tubing so that when he set a fire in the drum, it heated up the water. Drawback: The hose that re-circulated the heated water regularly popped up and spewed hot water on everyone.

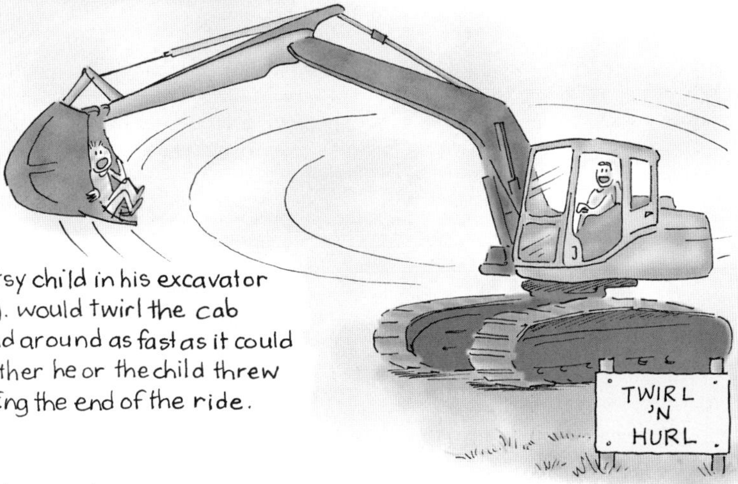
TWIRL 'N HURL

With a gutsy child in his excavator bucket, T.J. would twirl the cab around and around as fast as it could go until either he or the child threw up, signaling the end of the ride.

I prayed that the hospital paraphernalia in his basement would only be needed for some gross, fun game.

I was a nervous wreck when the kids were at T.J.'s house. My apprehension peaked at night when I tried to fall asleep and there were no distractions to push aside my fears.

The T.J.'s House Game
Did it really happen or was it just a bad dream?

1. Jack sliced his finger open and T.J. didn't have a Band-Aid so he used Super Glue to stick the two pieces of skin back together.
   (It really happened.)
2. T.J. drove all over his property with Jack inside the car's roof box.
   (It really happened.)
3. T.J. coated an old slide with Teflon powder and the kids jettisoned off the end like clowns shot out of a cannon. *(It really happened.)*
4. Hamish the rooster joined the family for dinner, pecking away at tidbits on everyone's plate as he strutted across the dining room table.
   (It really happened.)
5. Using old waterskiing ropes tied to his roof rack, T.J. towed the kids on their sleds (or skateboards) behind his old Subaru and deposited them at the top of his sledding/skateboarding hill.
   (It really happened, many times.)

When panic compelled me to sneak over and peek into T.J.'s window, I looked in on a rollicking, unfettered family tableau. The kids might be...

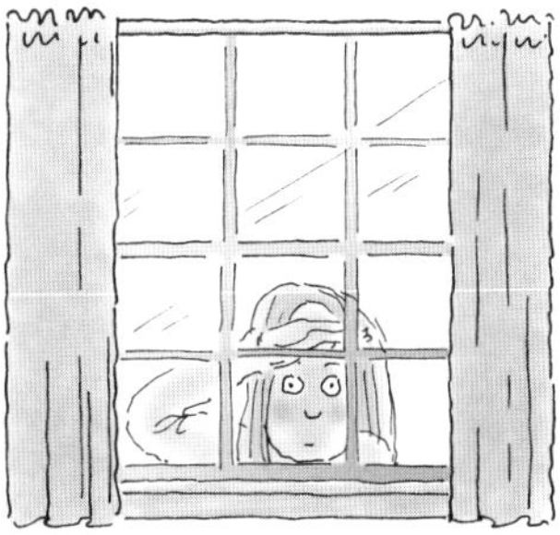

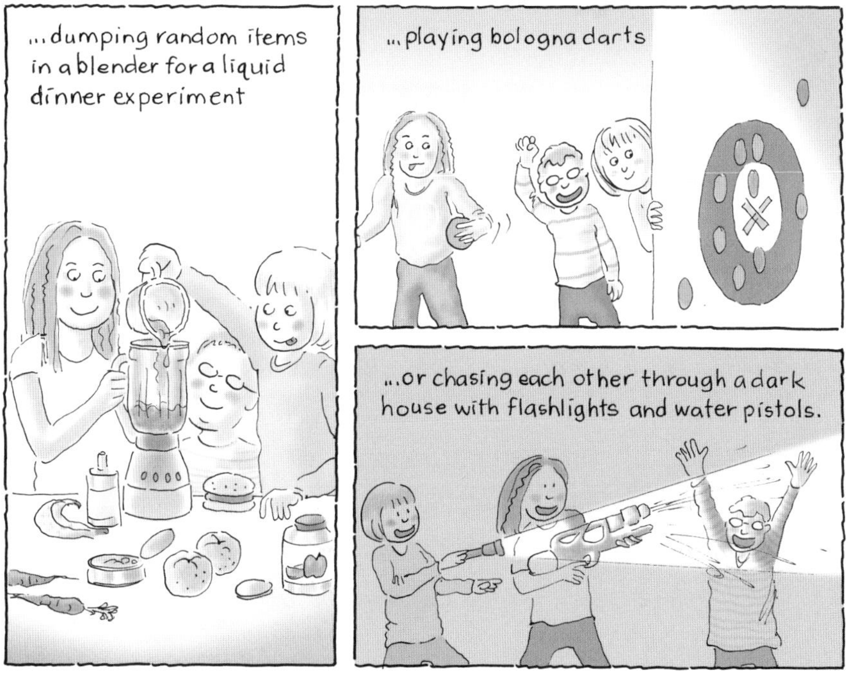
...dumping random items in a blender for a liquid dinner experiment
...playing bologna darts
...or chasing each other through a dark house with flashlights and water pistols.

I never saw anything that would prompt a call to 911. Or even to my mother. But I dropped them off every time with the same mantra:

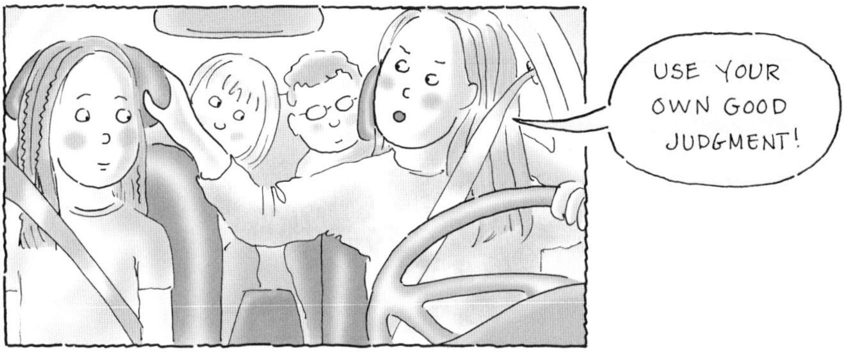
USE YOUR OWN GOOD JUDGMENT!

Because visitation was up to them and because they were drawn to T.J.'s like bugs to a zapper, I was repeating my mantra frequently. I resisted the urge to discuss more mundane matters like teeth brushing because I wanted that <u>one</u> message to resonate.

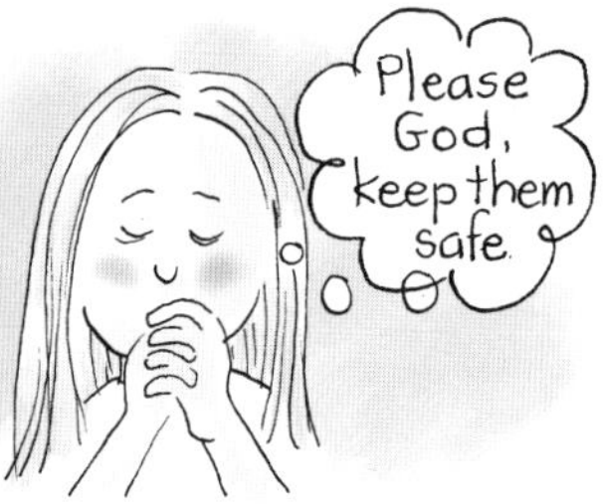
Please God, keep them safe.

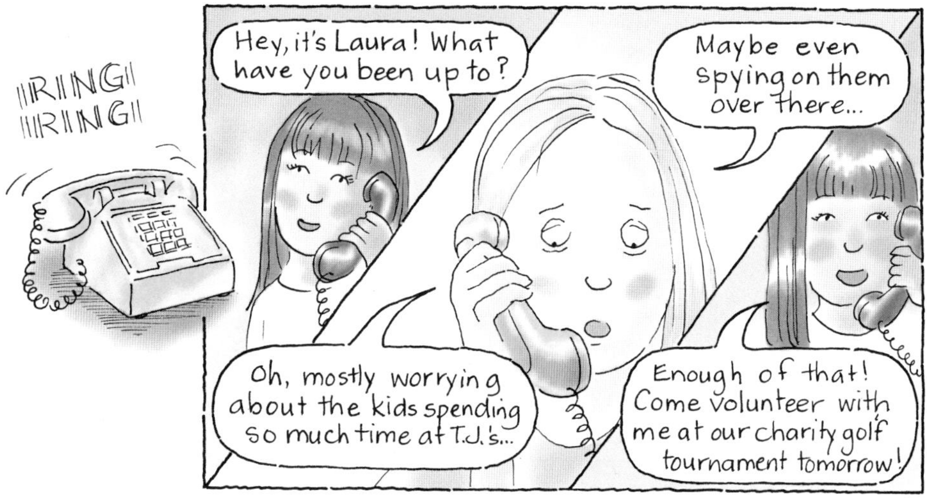
RING RING
Hey, it's Laura! What have you been up to?
Oh, mostly worrying about the kids spending so much time at T.J.'s...
Maybe even spying on them over there...
Enough of that! Come volunteer with me at our charity golf tournament tomorrow!

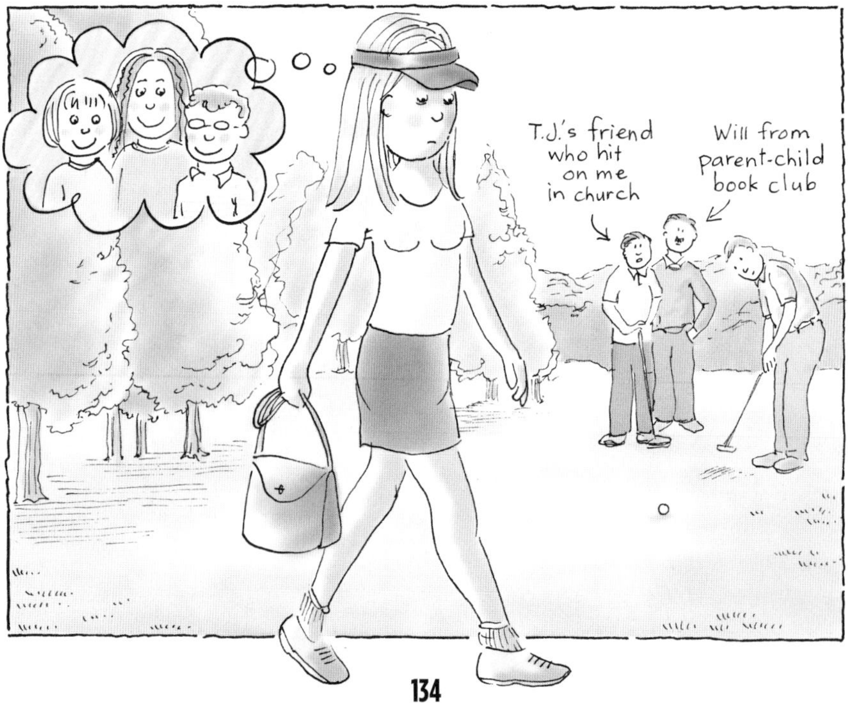
T.J.'s friend who hit on me in church
Will from parent-child book club

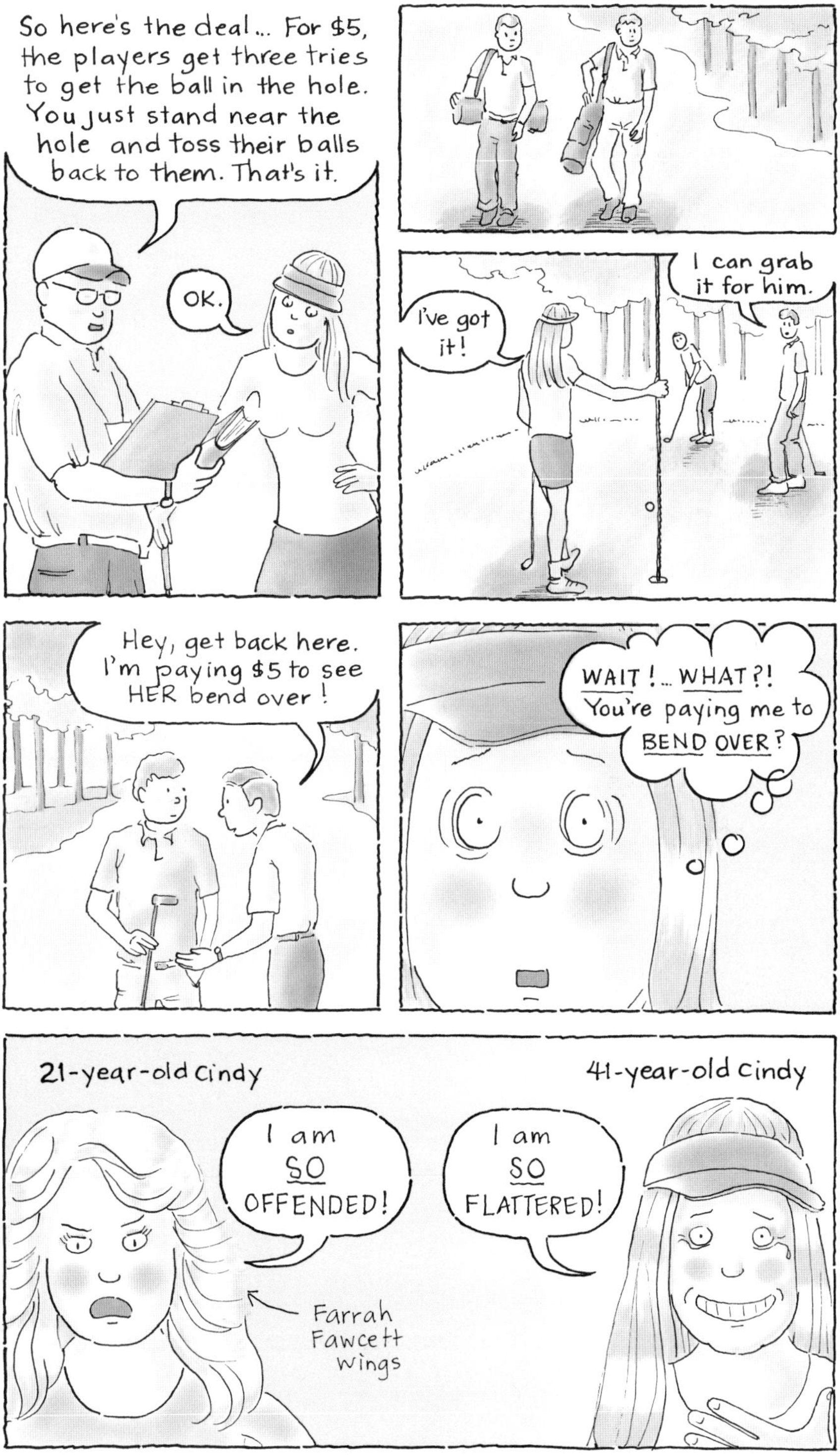
So here's the deal... For $5, the players get three tries to get the ball in the hole. You just stand near the hole and toss their balls back to them. That's it.
OK.
I've got it!
I can grab it for him.
Hey, get back here. I'm paying $5 to see HER bend over!
WAIT!... WHAT?! You're paying me to BEND OVER?
21-year-old Cindy
41-year-old Cindy
I am SO OFFENDED!
I am SO FLATTERED!
Farrah Fawcett wings

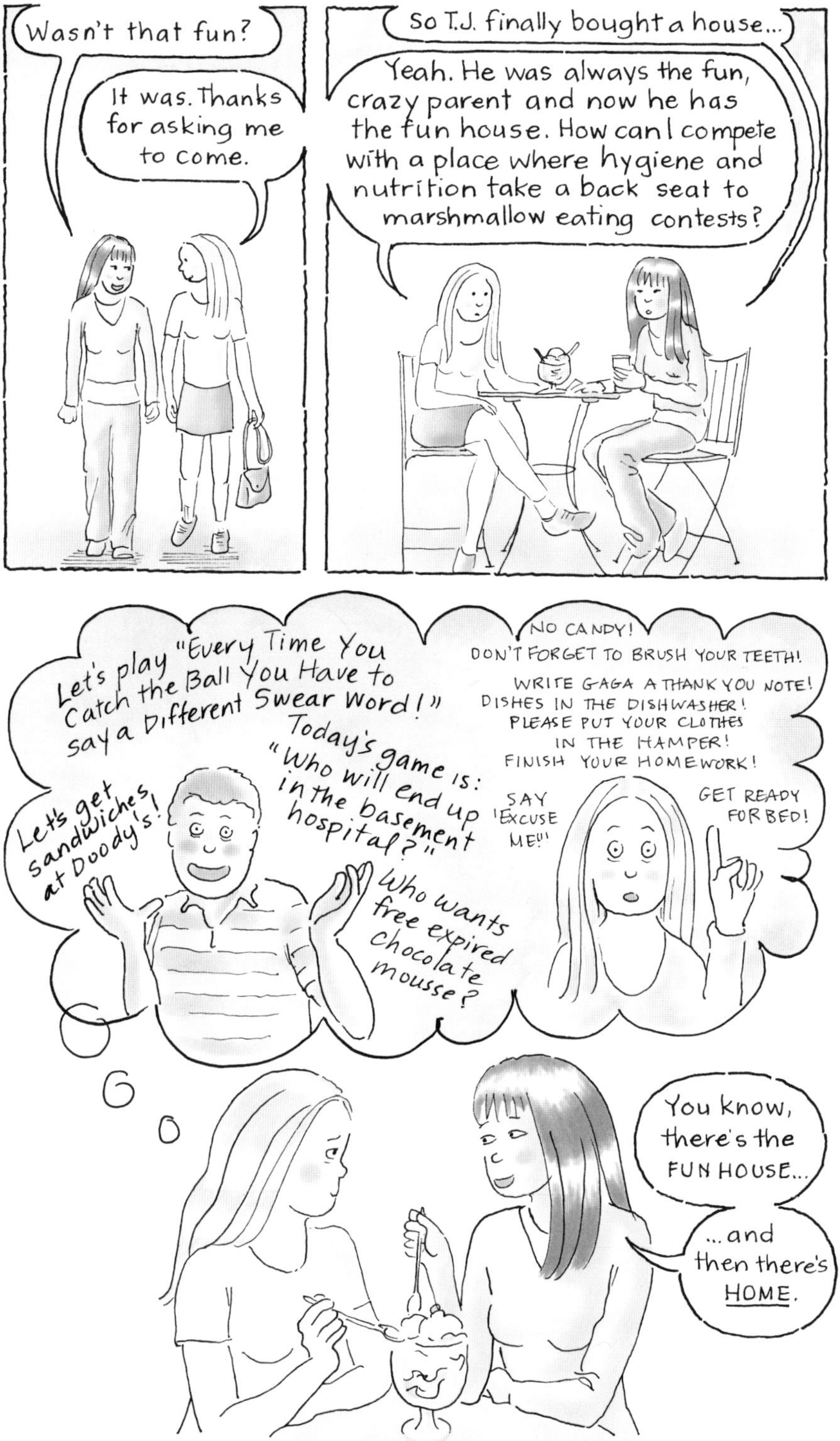
Wasn't that fun?
It was. Thanks for asking me to come.
So T.J. finally bought a house...
Yeah. He was always the fun, crazy parent and now he has the fun house. How can I compete with a place where hygiene and nutrition take a back seat to marshmallow eating contests?
Let's play "Every Time You Catch the Ball You Have to say a Different Swear Word!"
Today's game is: "Who will end up in the basement hospital?"
Let's get sandwiches at Doody's!
Who wants free expired chocolate mousse?
NO CANDY!
DON'T FORGET TO BRUSH YOUR TEETH!
WRITE GAGA A THANK YOU NOTE!
DISHES IN THE DISHWASHER!
PLEASE PUT YOUR CLOTHES IN THE HAMPER!
FINISH YOUR HOMEWORK!
SAY 'EXCUSE ME!'
GET READY FOR BED!
You know, there's the FUN HOUSE...
...and then there's HOME.

Laura was right. In fact, the novelty of Fun Dad and his Fun House began to wear off more quickly than I would have guessed.

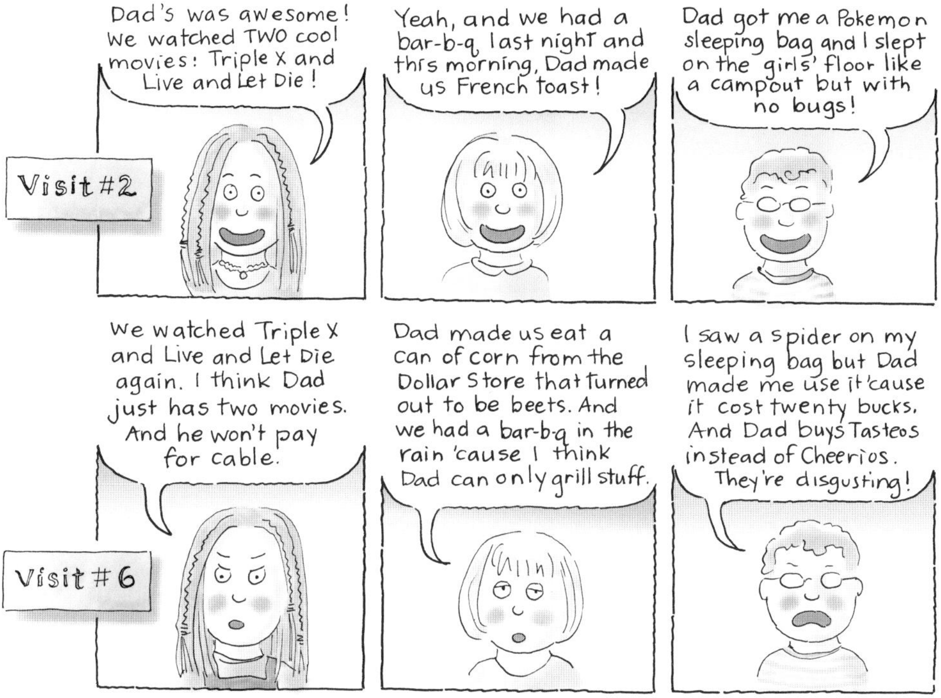
Visit #2
Dad's was awesome! We watched TWO cool movies: Triple X and Live and Let Die!
Yeah, and we had a bar-b-q last night and this morning, Dad made us French toast!
Dad got me a Pokemon sleeping bag and I slept on the girls' floor like a campout but with no bugs!
Visit #6
We watched Triple X and Live and Let Die again. I think Dad just has two movies. And he won't pay for cable.
Dad made us eat a can of corn from the Dollar Store that turned out to be beets. And we had a bar-b-q in the rain 'cause I think Dad can only grill stuff.
I saw a spider on my sleeping bag but Dad made me use it 'cause it cost twenty bucks. And Dad buys Tasteos instead of Cheerios. They're disgusting!

The kids still spent a lot of time at T.J.'s, but I stopped worrying about losing them forever. And I began to worry a little less about their safety and well-being, too, because I noticed that they were taking my mantra to heart. Without me running interference, they were developing an admirable resistance to "peer" pressure.

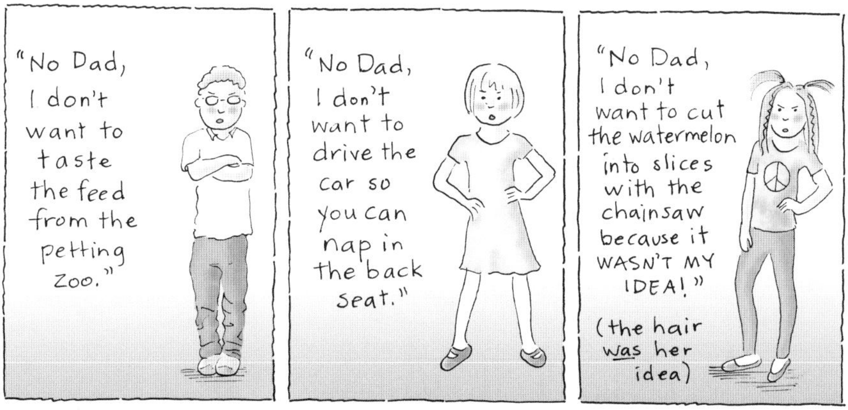
"No Dad, I don't want to taste the feed from the petting zoo."
"No Dad, I don't want to drive the car so you can nap in the back seat."
"No Dad, I don't want to cut the watermelon into slices with the chainsaw because it WASN'T MY IDEA!"
(the hair was her idea)

Because they were required to do more for themselves at T.J.'s, they began to help me out more, too. Together, we were figuring it out, a little at a time.

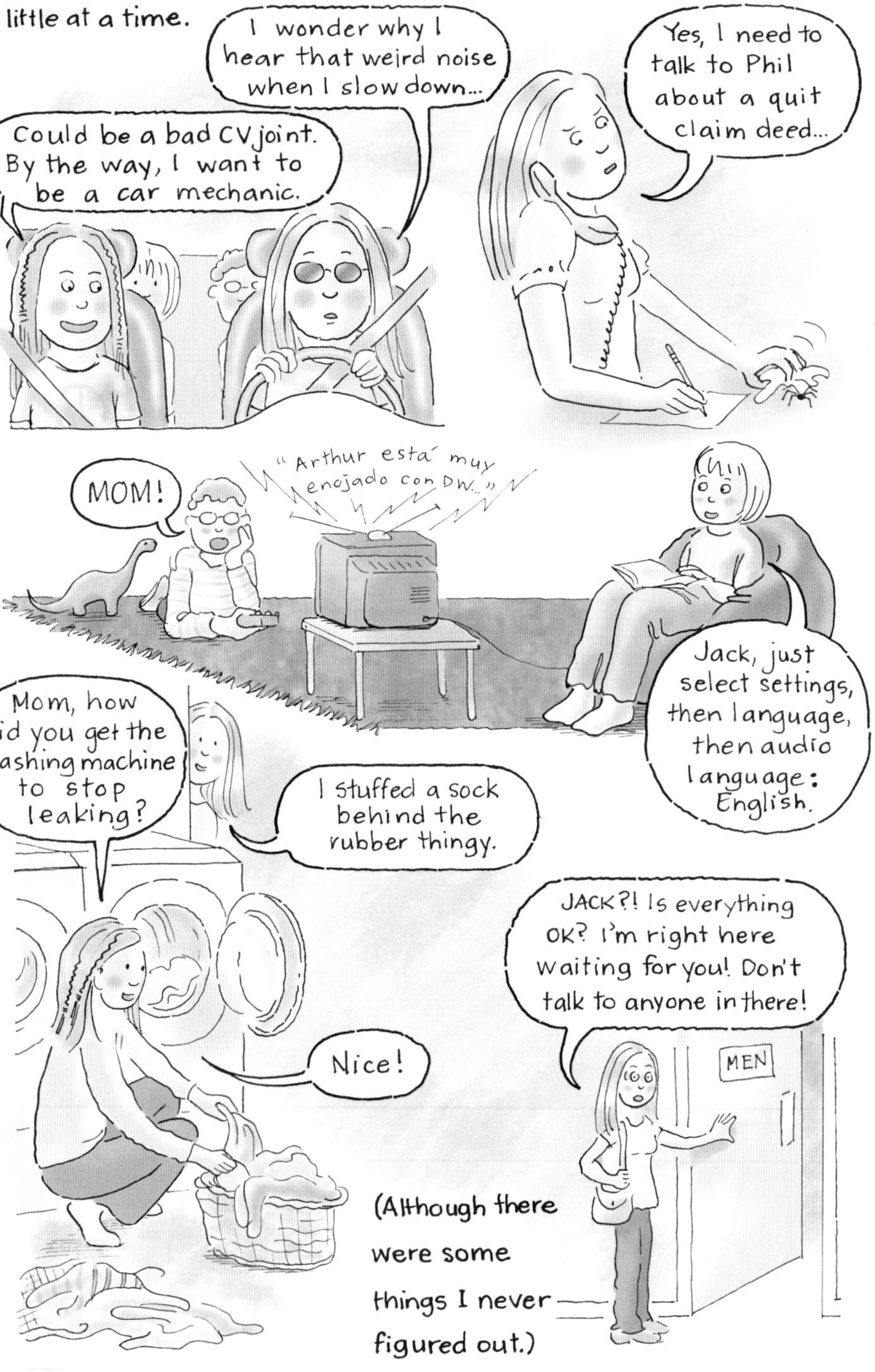
I wonder why I hear that weird noise when I slow down...
Could be a bad CV joint. By the way, I want to be a car mechanic.
Yes, I need to talk to Phil about a quit claim deed...
MOM!
"Arthur está muy enojado con DW..."
Jack, just select settings, then language, then audio language: English.
Mom, how did you get the washing machine to stop leaking?
I stuffed a sock behind the rubber thingy.
Nice!
JACK?! Is everything OK? I'm right here waiting for you! Don't talk to anyone in there!
MEN
(Although there were some things I never figured out.)

Summer slipped into fall; each morning, the sun felt a bit weaker as it pushed away the longer, crisper night. We were counting down our final vacation activities.

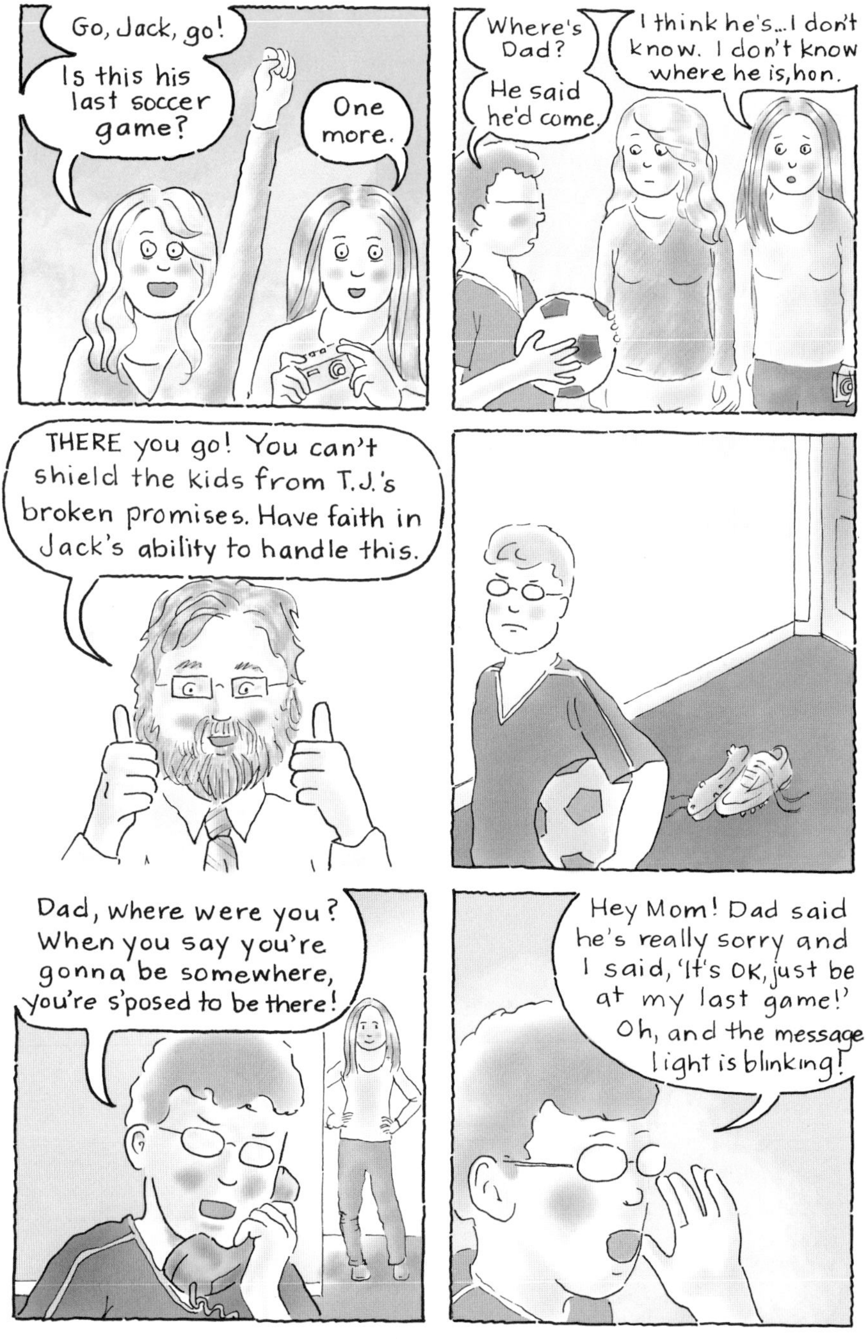
Go, Jack, go!
Is this his last soccer game?
One more.
Where's Dad?
He said he'd come.
I think he's...I don't know. I don't know where he is, hon.
THERE you go! You can't shield the kids from T.J.'s broken promises. Have faith in Jack's ability to handle this.
Dad, where were you? When you say you're gonna be somewhere, you're s'posed to be there!
Hey Mom! Dad said he's really sorry and I said, 'It's OK, just be at my last game!'
Oh, and the message light is blinking!

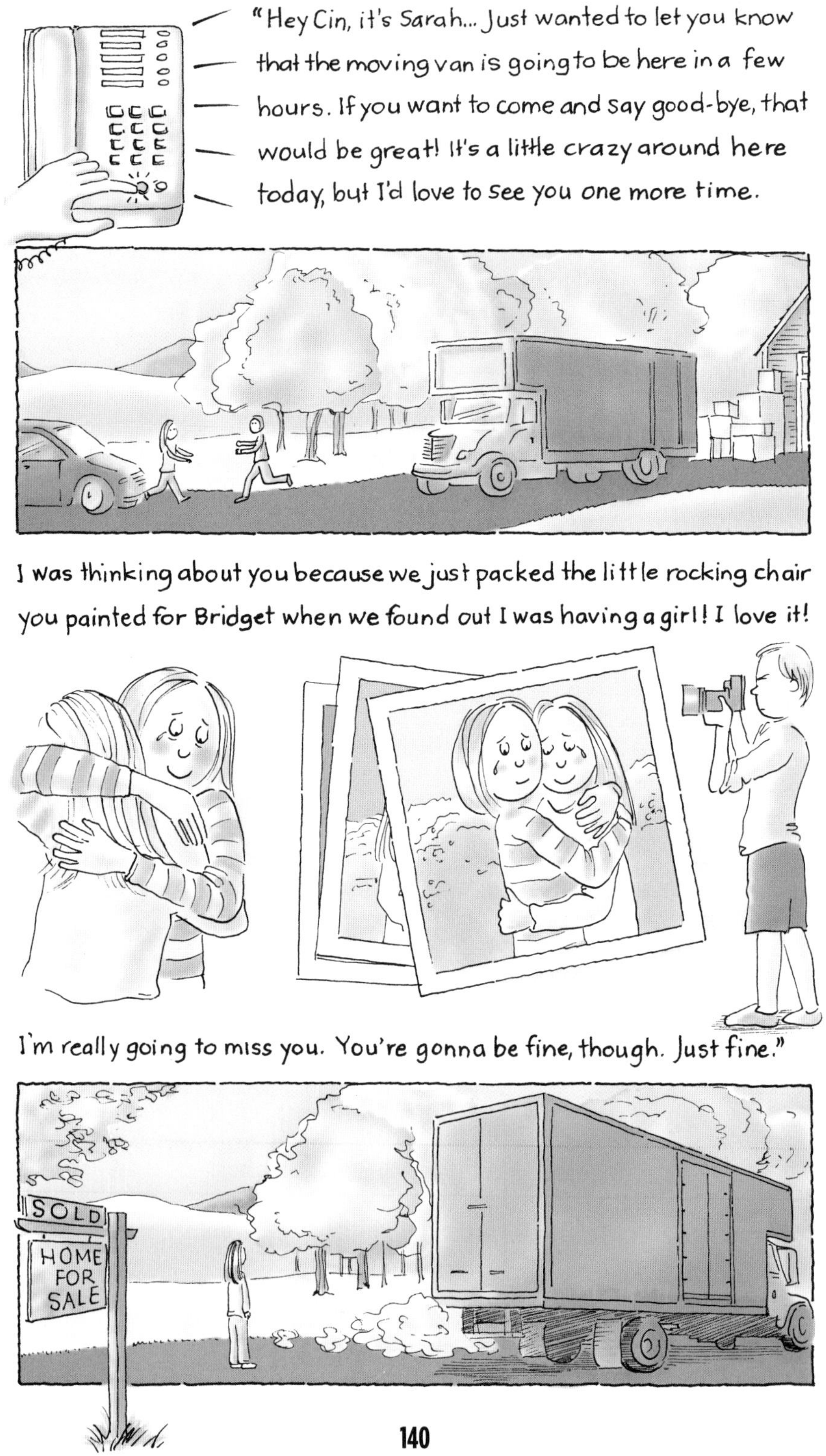
"Hey Cin, it's Sarah... Just wanted to let you know that the moving van is going to be here in a few hours. If you want to come and say good-bye, that would be great! It's a little crazy around here today, but I'd love to see you one more time.
I was thinking about you because we just packed the little rocking chair you painted for Bridget when we found out I was having a girl! I love it!
I'm really going to miss you. You're gonna be fine, though. Just fine."
SOLD
HOME FOR SALE

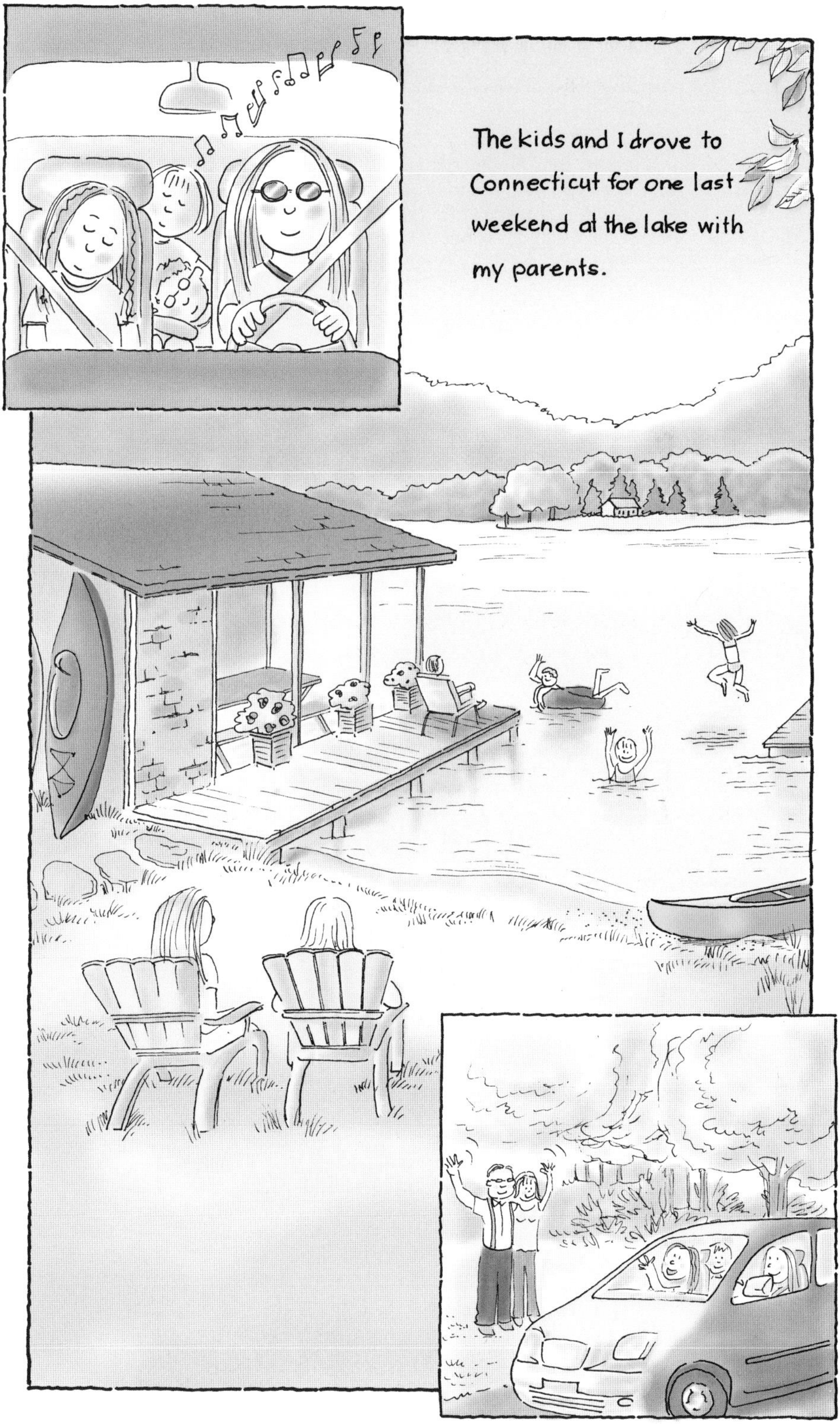
The kids and I drove to Connecticut for one last weekend at the lake with my parents.

And T.J. not only came to Jack's final soccer game...

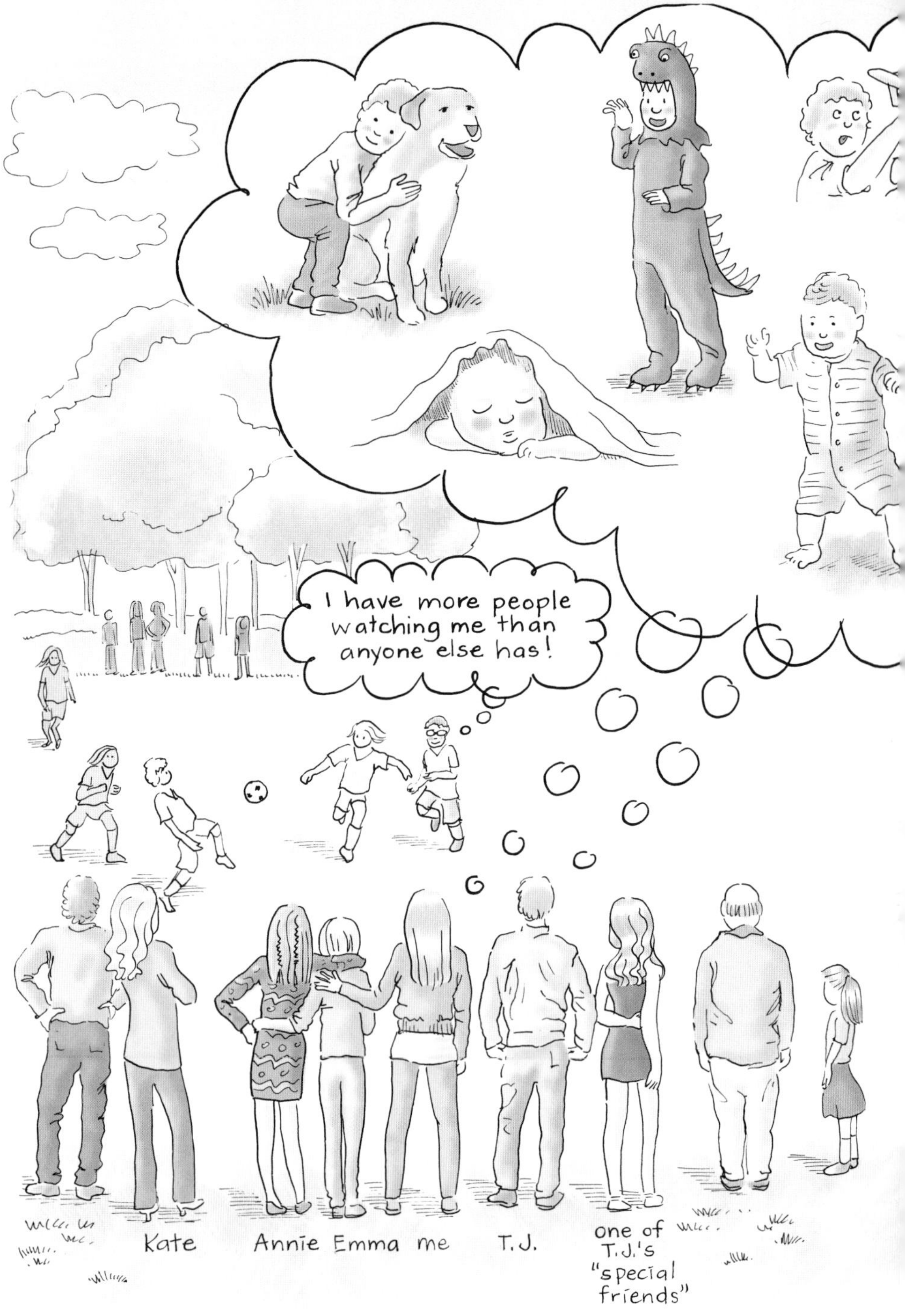
I have more people watching me than anyone else has!
Kate
Annie
Emma
me
T.J.
one of T.J.'s "special friends"

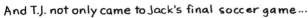

...he also met Jack and me at the playground on the first day of school.

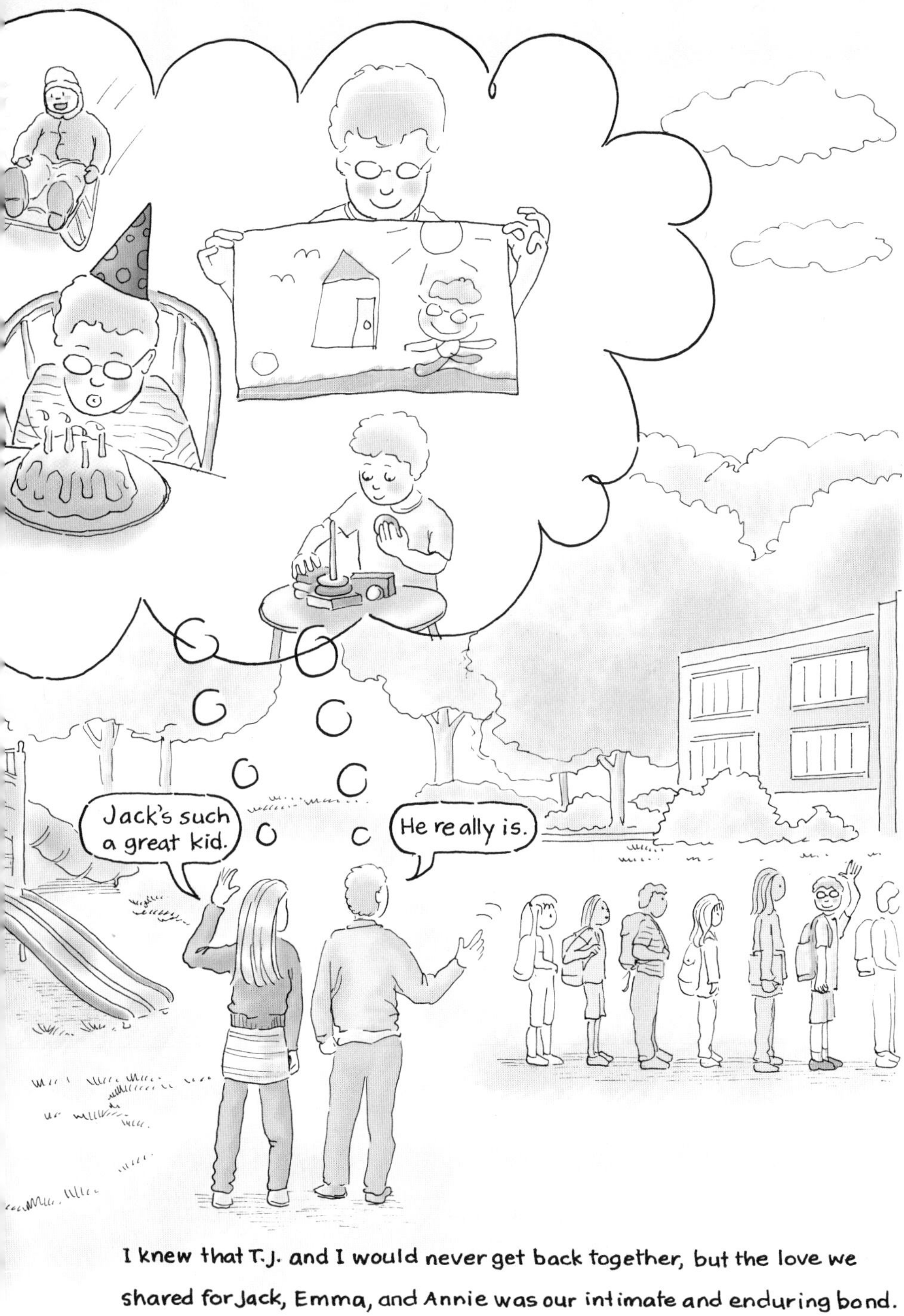
Jack's such a great kid.
He really is.

I knew that T.J. and I would never get back together, but the love we shared for Jack, Emma, and Annie was our intimate and enduring bond.

Fall

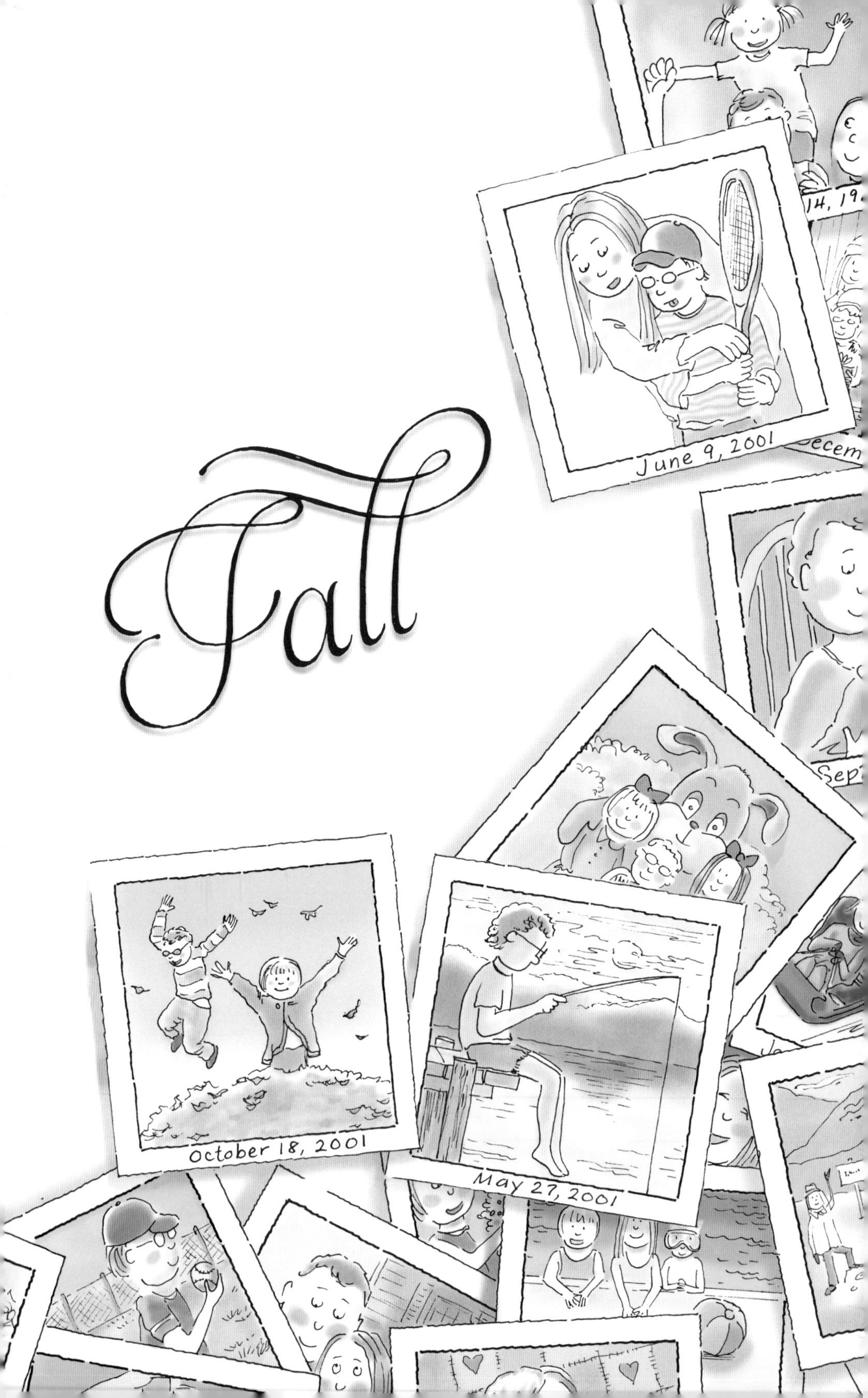
June 9, 2001
October 18, 2001
May 27, 2001

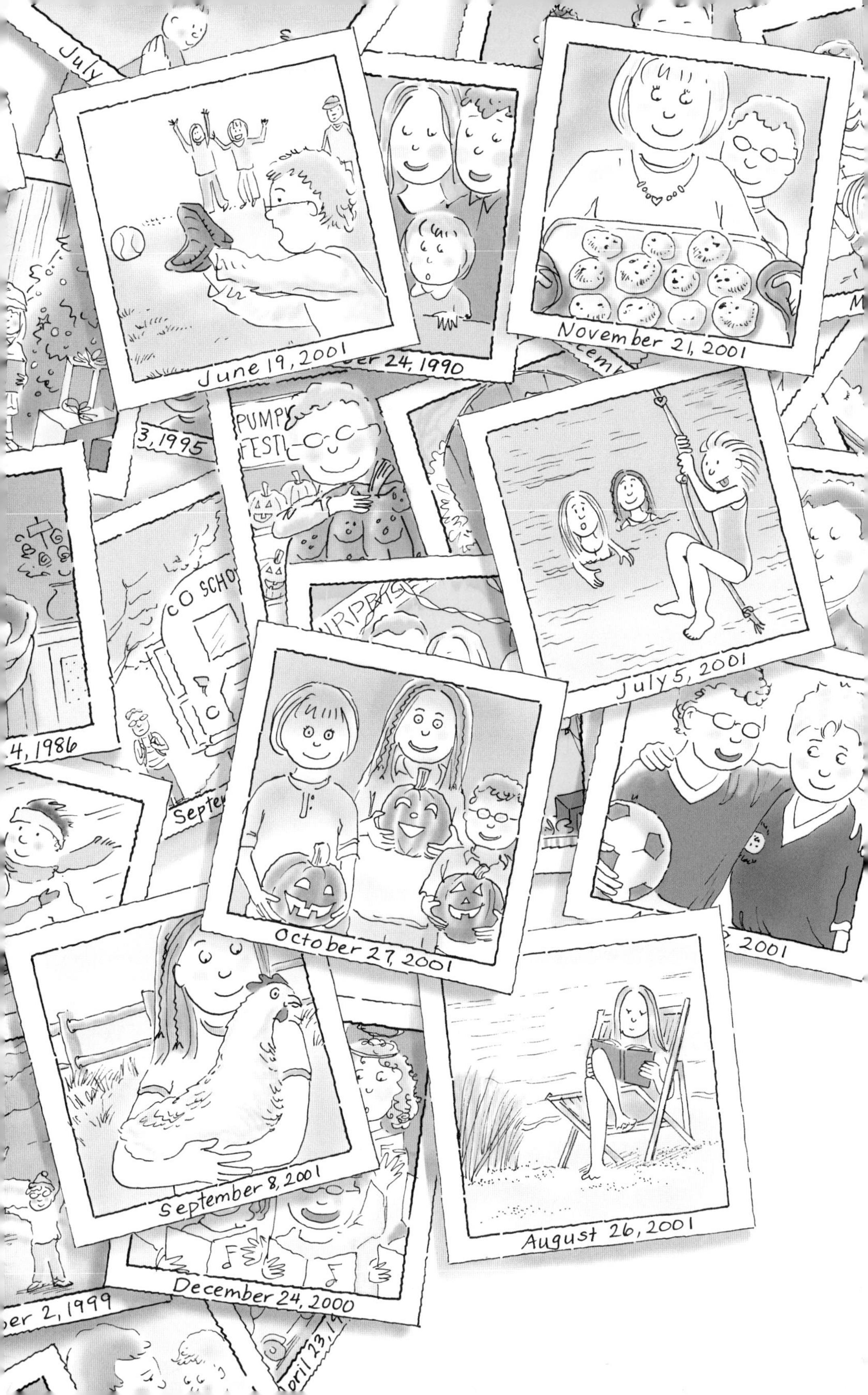
June 19, 2001
er 24, 1990
November 21, 2001
3, 1995
PUMPK
FESTI
July 5, 2001
4, 1986
Septem
October 27, 2001
2001
September 8, 2001
August 26, 2001
December 24, 2000
ber 2, 1999
July

As the kids settled into their new classes, we all took comfort in the familiar school routine.

Starting second grade made Jack feel like a big boy, so he dragged his blanket and pillow back to his own room.

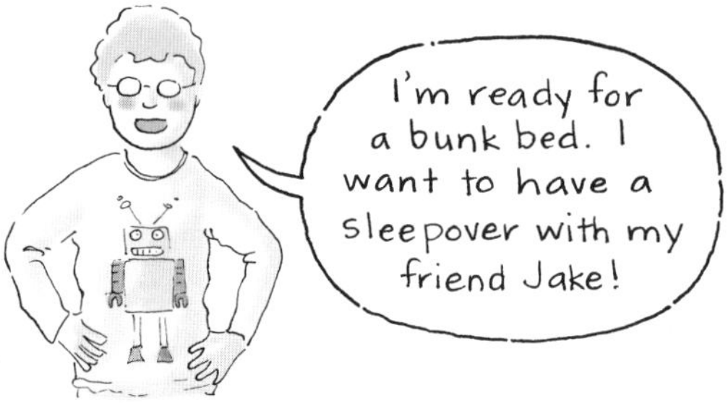
I'm ready for a bunk bed. I want to have a sleepover with my friend Jake!

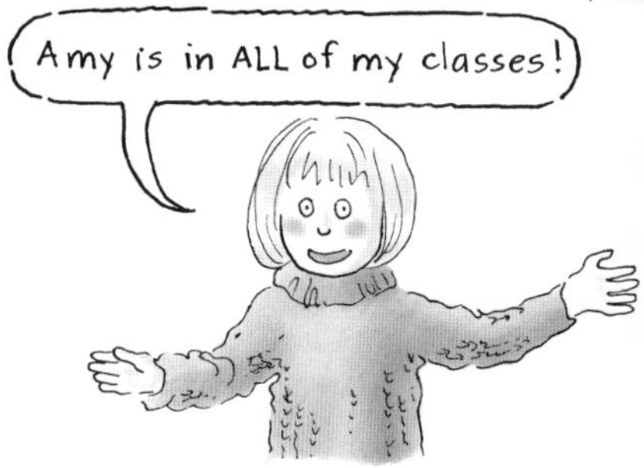
Amy is in ALL of my classes!

Emma returned to middle school with a new backpack and red and black rubber bands on her braces (the school colors).

Annie decided that she would ride her bike to school so that she could go directly to the pet store afterward, and to help her train for the annual bicycle race up Mt. Washington she was planning to enter with T.J.

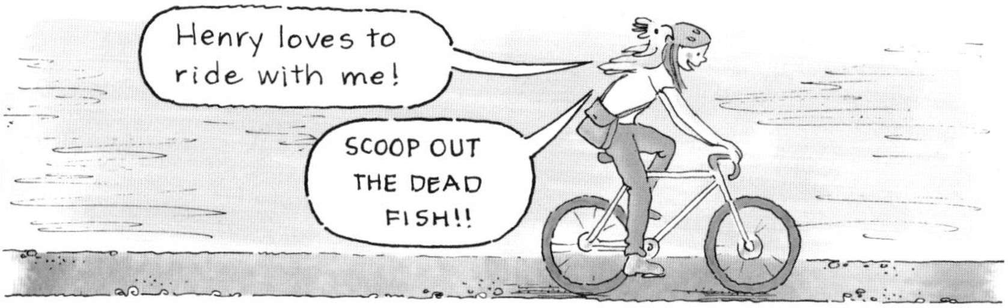
Henry loves to ride with me!
SCOOP OUT THE DEAD FISH!!

Fingers crossed, I eased us into fall.

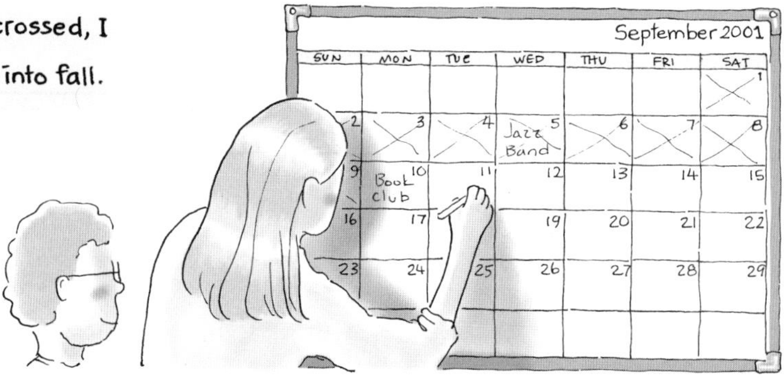
September 2001
SUN
MON
TUE
WED
THU
FRI
SAT
Jazz Band
Book Club

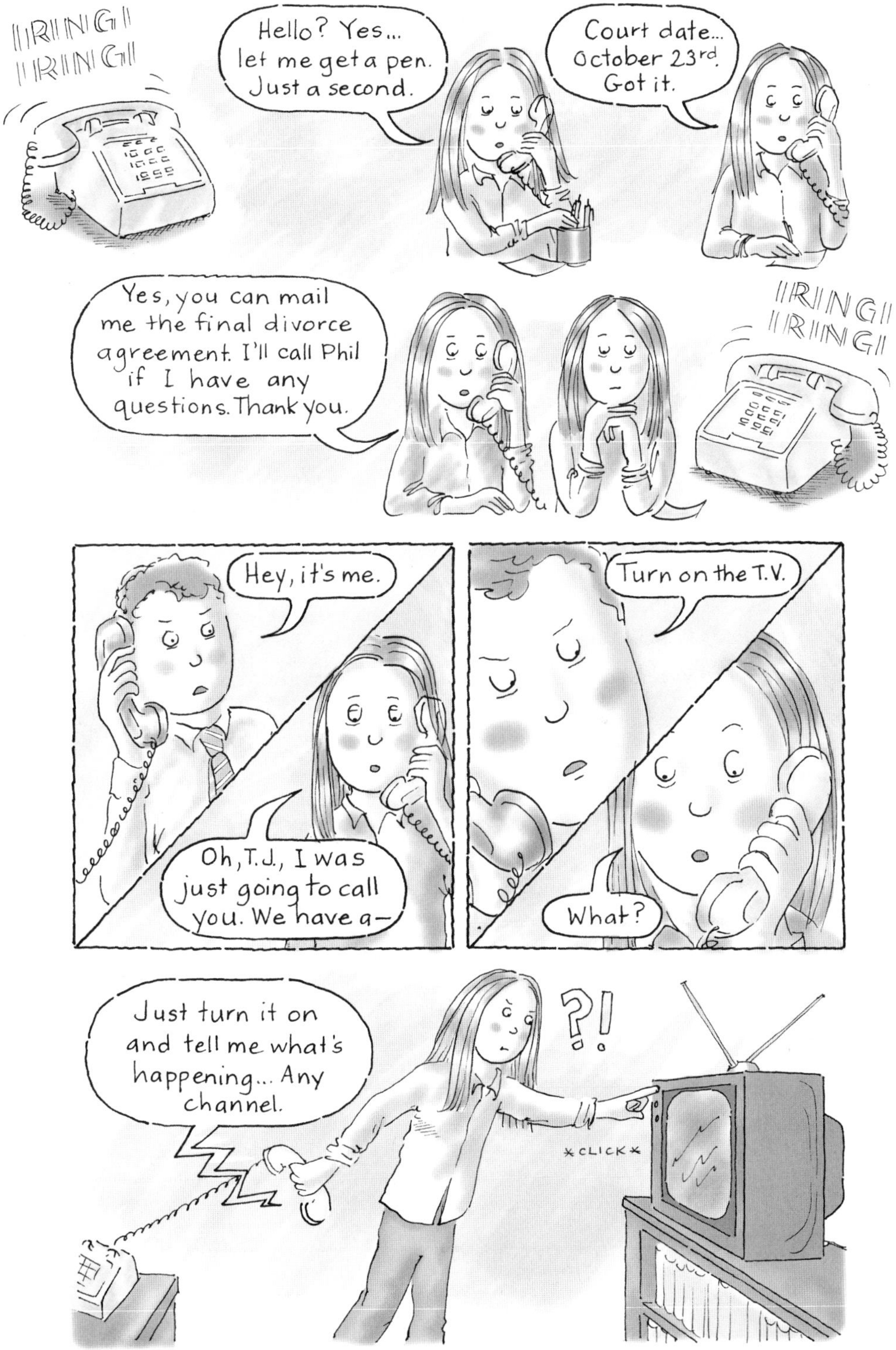
RING! RING!
Hello? Yes... let me get a pen. Just a second.
Court date... October 23rd. Got it.
Yes, you can mail me the final divorce agreement. I'll call Phil if I have any questions. Thank you.
RING! RING!
Hey, it's me.
Oh, T.J., I was just going to call you. We have a—
Turn on the T.V.
What?
Just turn it on and tell me what's happening... Any channel.
?!
CLICK

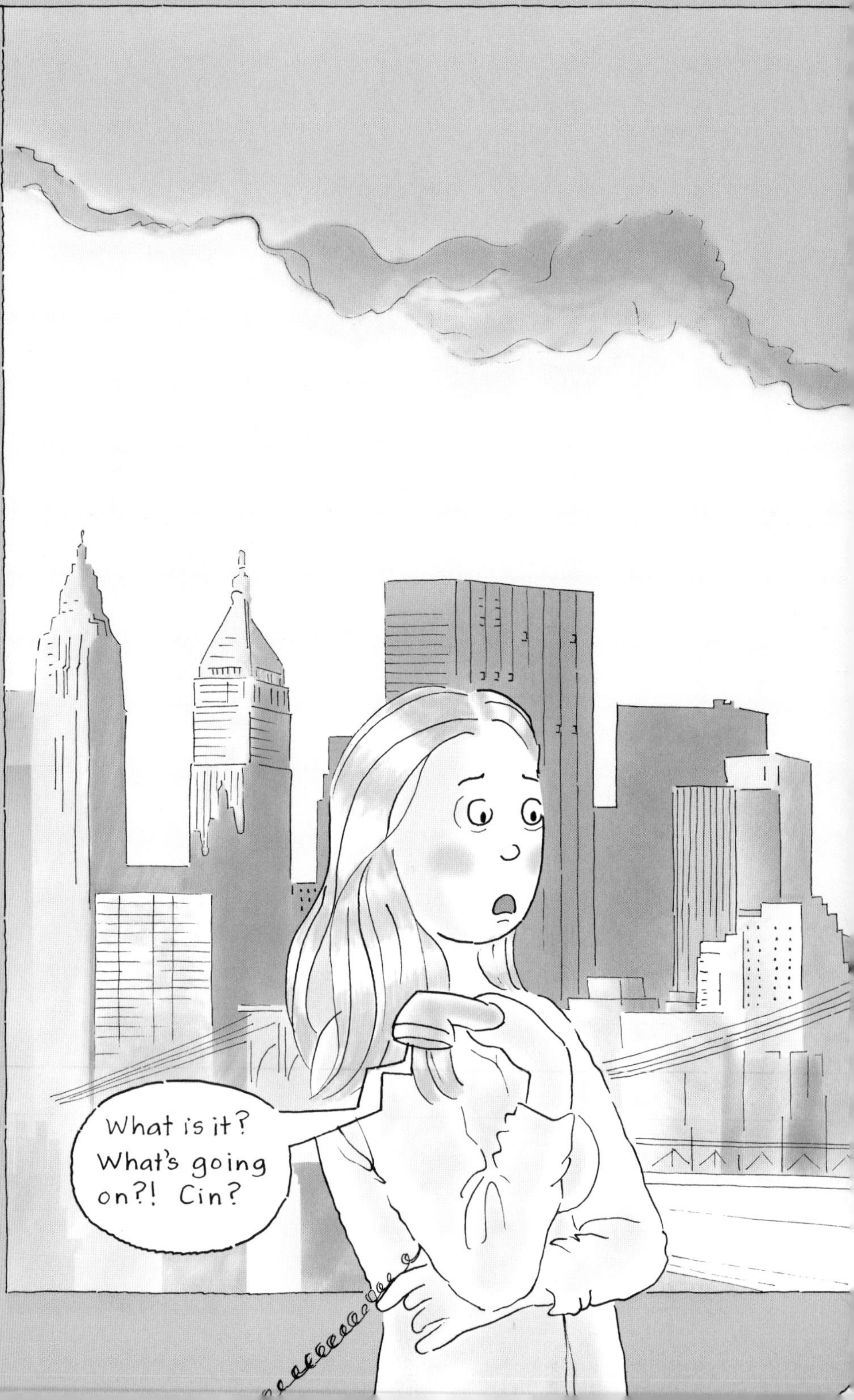
What is it? What's going on?! Cin?

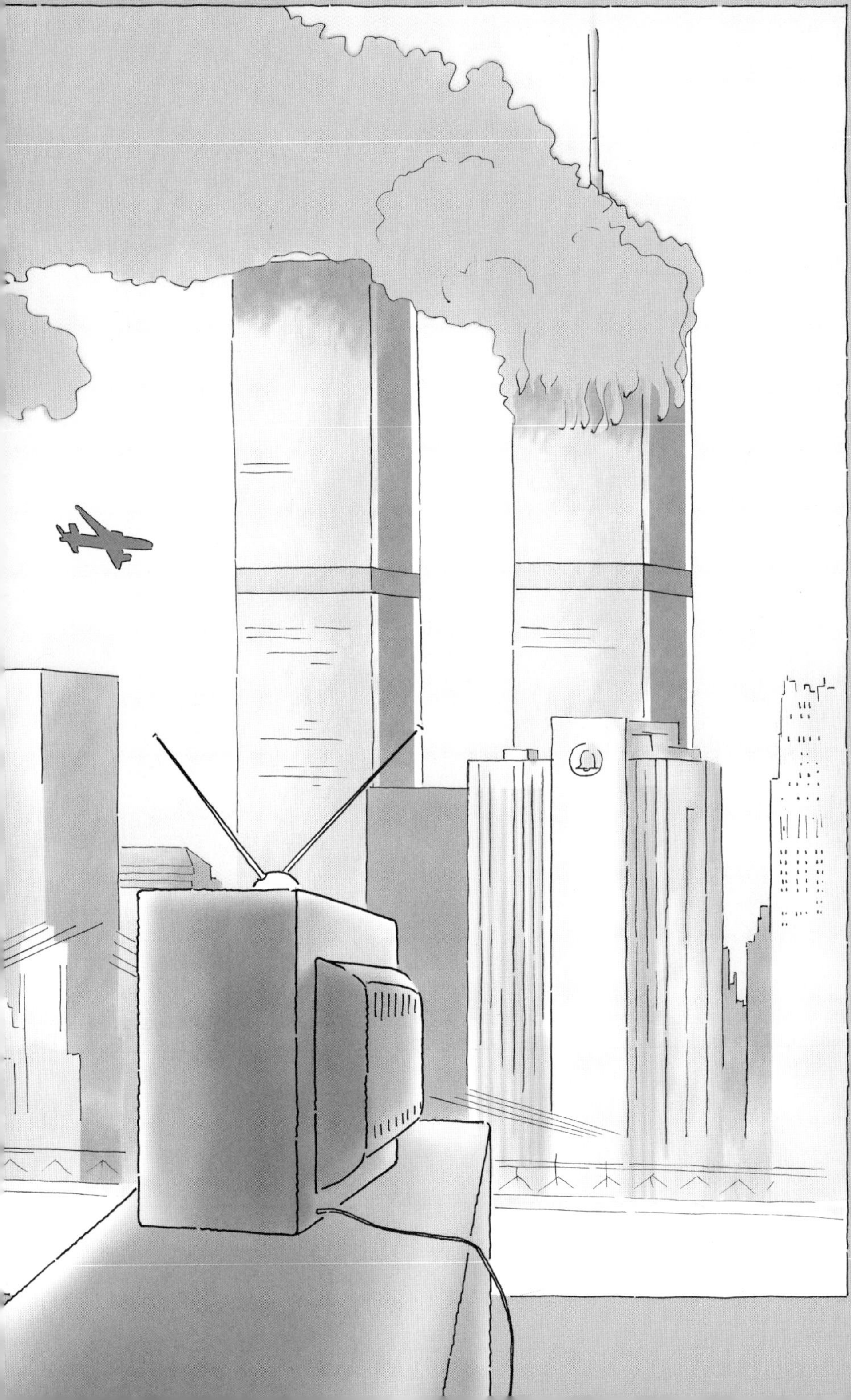

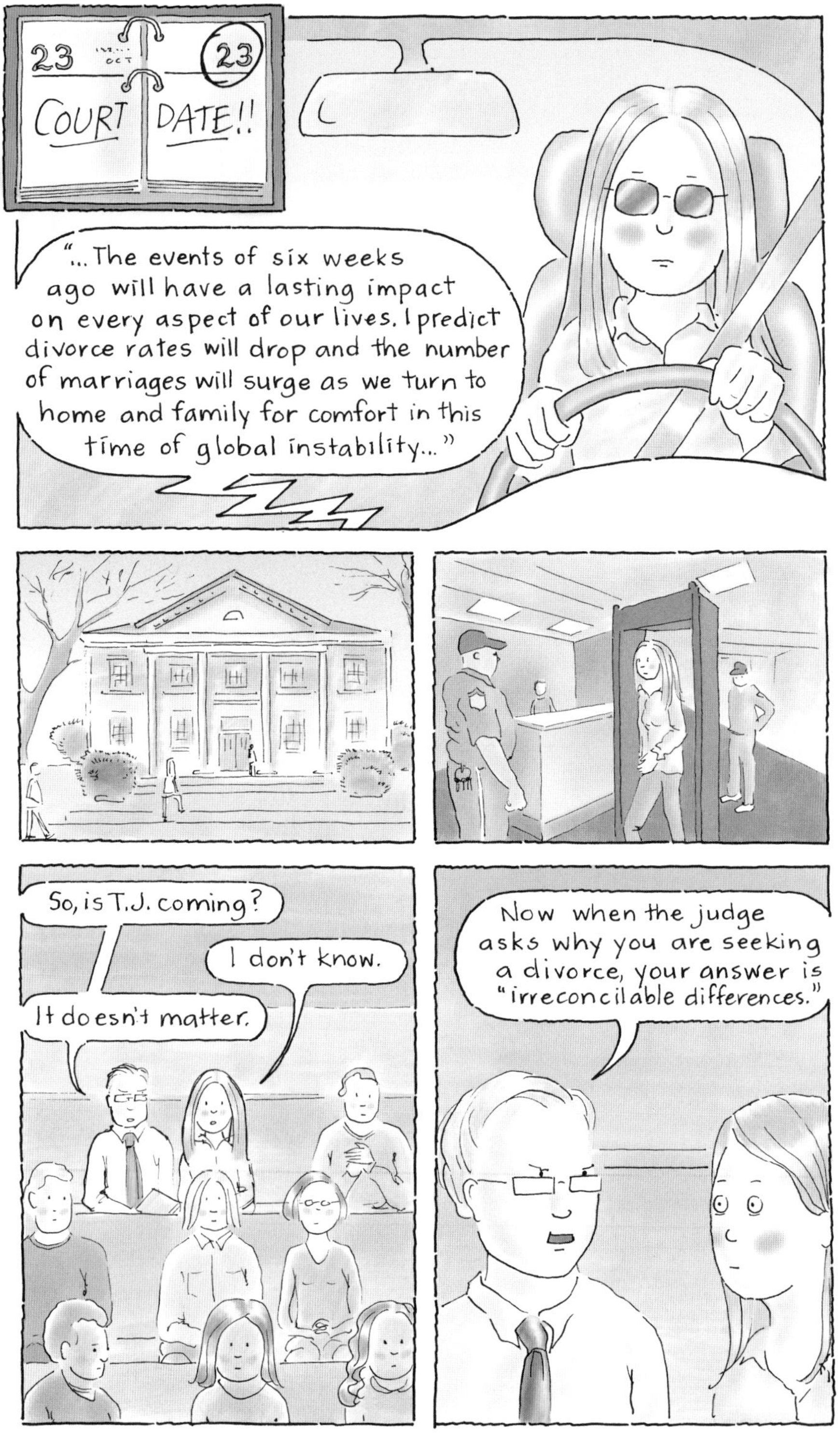
23
OCT
23
COURT DATE!!
"...The events of six weeks ago will have a lasting impact on every aspect of our lives. I predict divorce rates will drop and the number of marriages will surge as we turn to home and family for comfort in this time of global instability..."
So, is T.J. coming?
I don't know.
It doesn't matter.
Now when the judge asks why you are seeking a divorce, your answer is "irreconcilable differences."

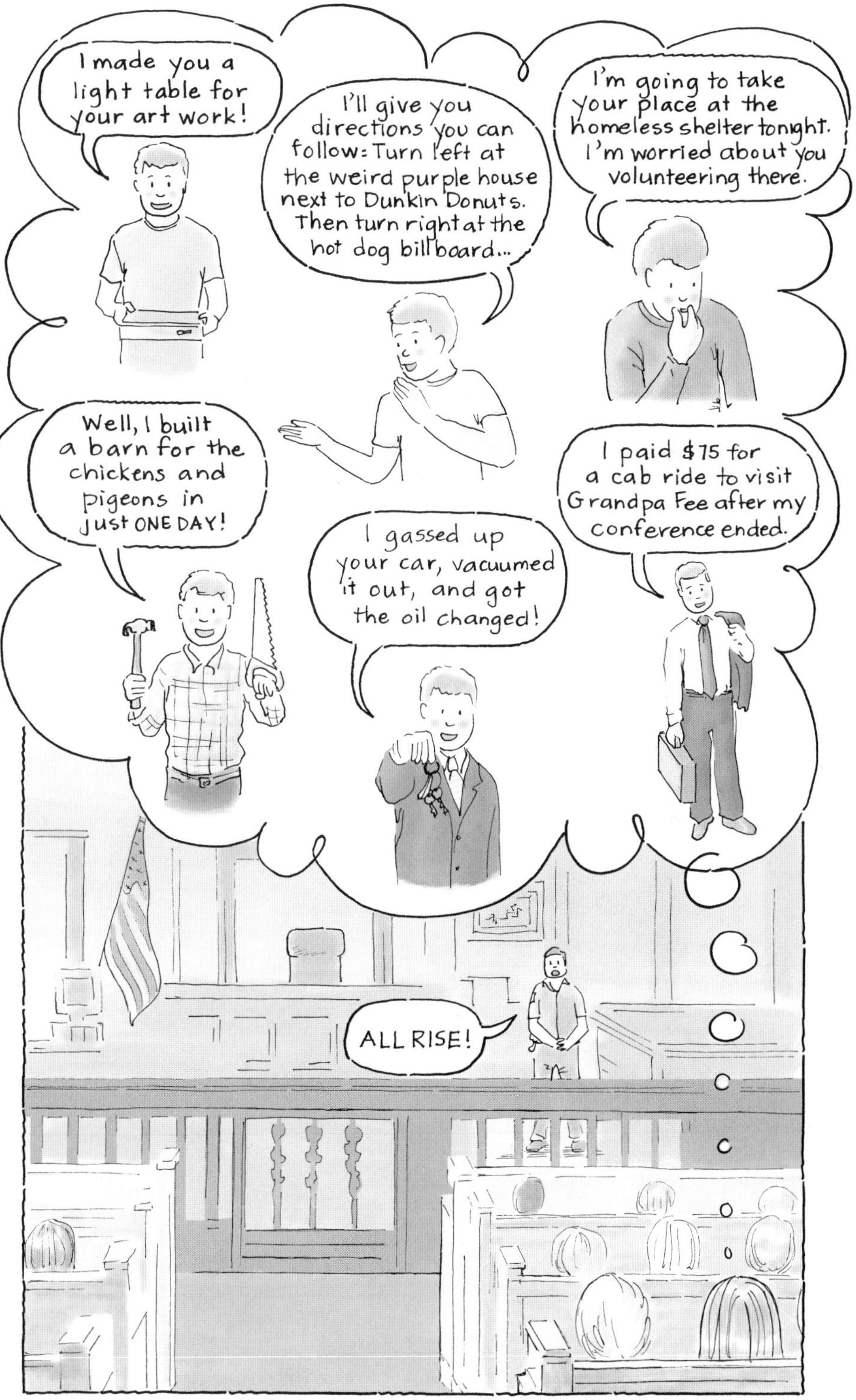
I made you a light table for your art work!
I'll give you directions you can follow: Turn left at the weird purple house next to Dunkin Donuts. Then turn right at the hot dog billboard...
I'm going to take your place at the homeless shelter tonight. I'm worried about you volunteering there.
Well, I built a barn for the chickens and pigeons in JUST ONE DAY!
I gassed up your car, vacuumed it out, and got the oil changed!
I paid $75 for a cab ride to visit Grandpa Fee after my conference ended.
ALL RISE!

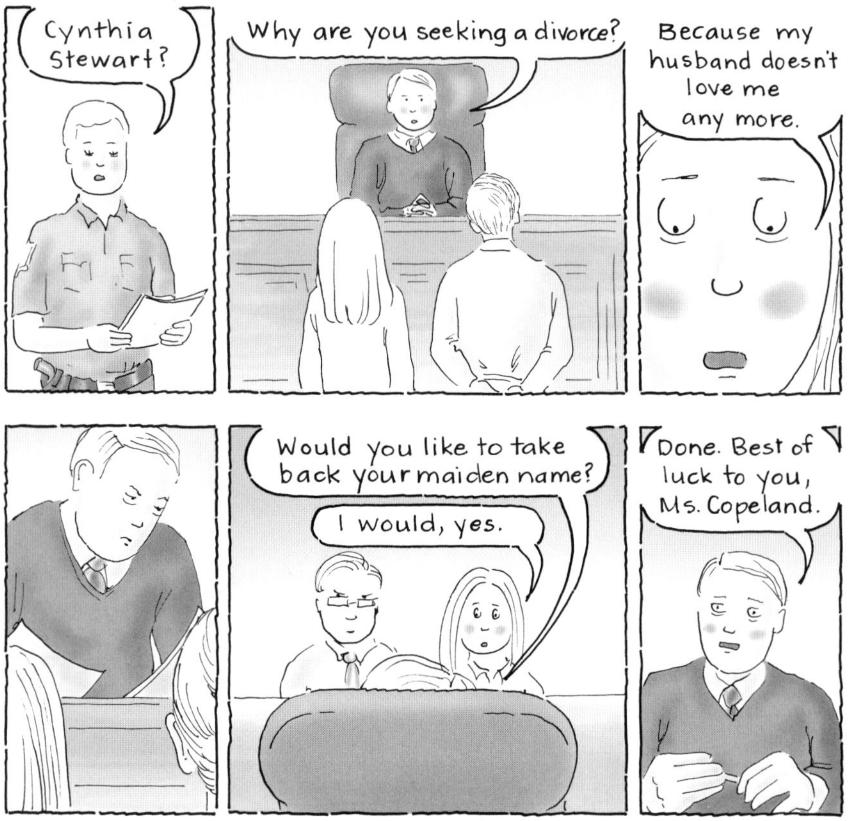
Cynthia Stewart?
Why are you seeking a divorce?
Because my husband doesn't love me any more.
Would you like to take back your maiden name?
I would, yes.
Done. Best of luck to you, Ms. Copeland.

I'd missed my name. That part was, strangely, a comfort. Like going home. I'd had a good run as Cindy Copeland.

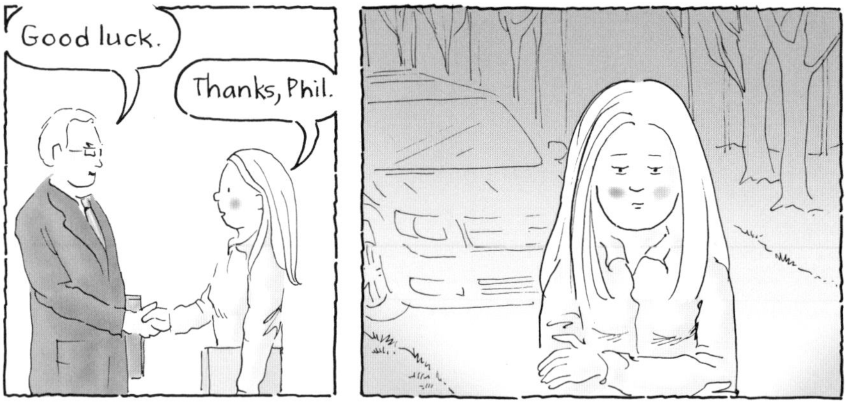
Good luck.
Thanks, Phil.

Getting the court date had taken only seven months. The process of unloving T.J., however, would take much longer.

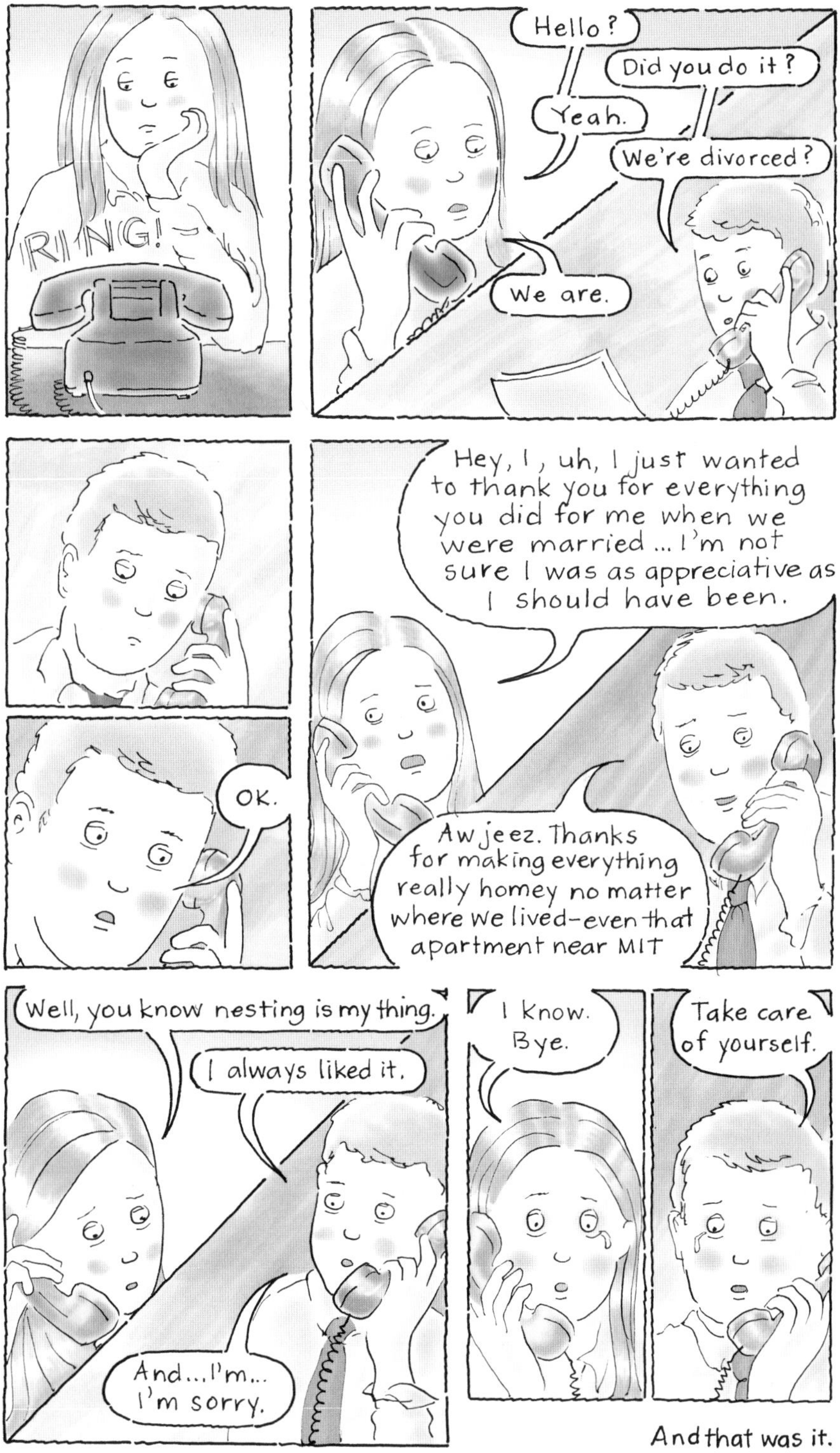
RING!
Hello?
Did you do it?
Yeah.
We're divorced?
We are.
Hey, I, uh, I just wanted to thank you for everything you did for me when we were married ... I'm not sure I was as appreciative as I should have been.
OK.
Aw jeez. Thanks for making everything really homey no matter where we lived–even that apartment near MIT
Well, you know nesting is my thing.
I always liked it.
And... I'm... I'm sorry.
I know. Bye.
Take care of yourself.
And that was it.

Now that he had a wacky bachelor pad and was officially divorced, T.J. pursued women in earnest. I genuinely wanted him to be happy and to find someone special (and by "special" I mean someone who was not as smart as me or as good a cook).

BUT. There were things about the whole dating process that irked me. These new girlfriends were reaping the benefits of decades of my delicate yet persistent husband tweaking.

T.J. no longer blew his nose in his undershirt...

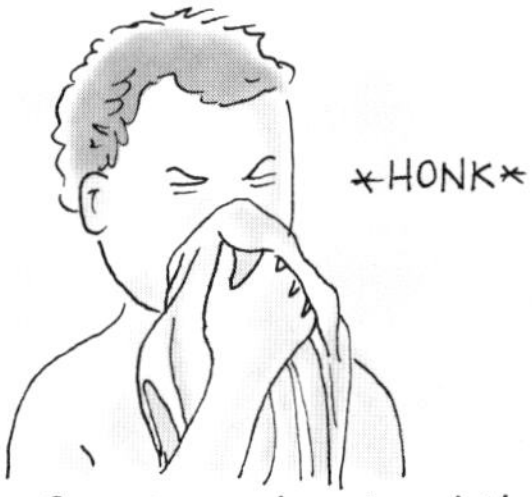
HONK

or left his hockey equipment strewn across the dining room table to "air out."

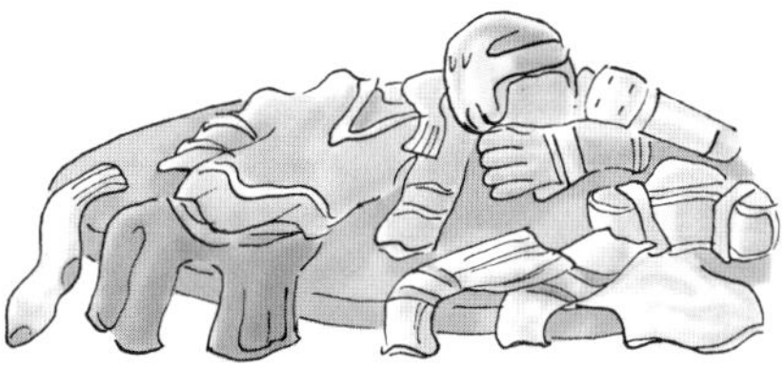

He finally understood that sex isn't all that sexy when he pretends to be one of the Three Stooges, especially Curly.

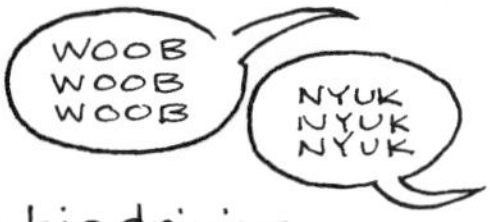
WOOB WOOB WOOB
NYUK NYUK NYUK

And recently, I had made tangible headway on his driving.

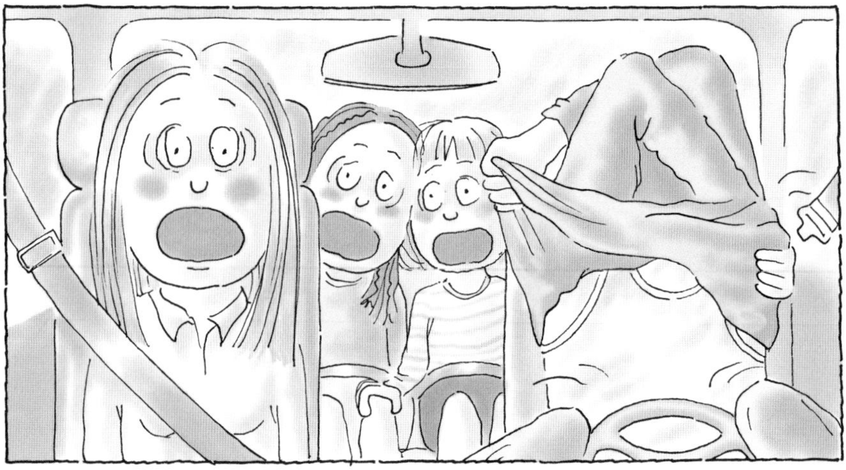

I felt like I was giving away a puppy right after it learned to go outside.

Even more frustrating, the things I'd given up on for lack of progress, T.J. would change in a weekend for the girlfriend who requested it!

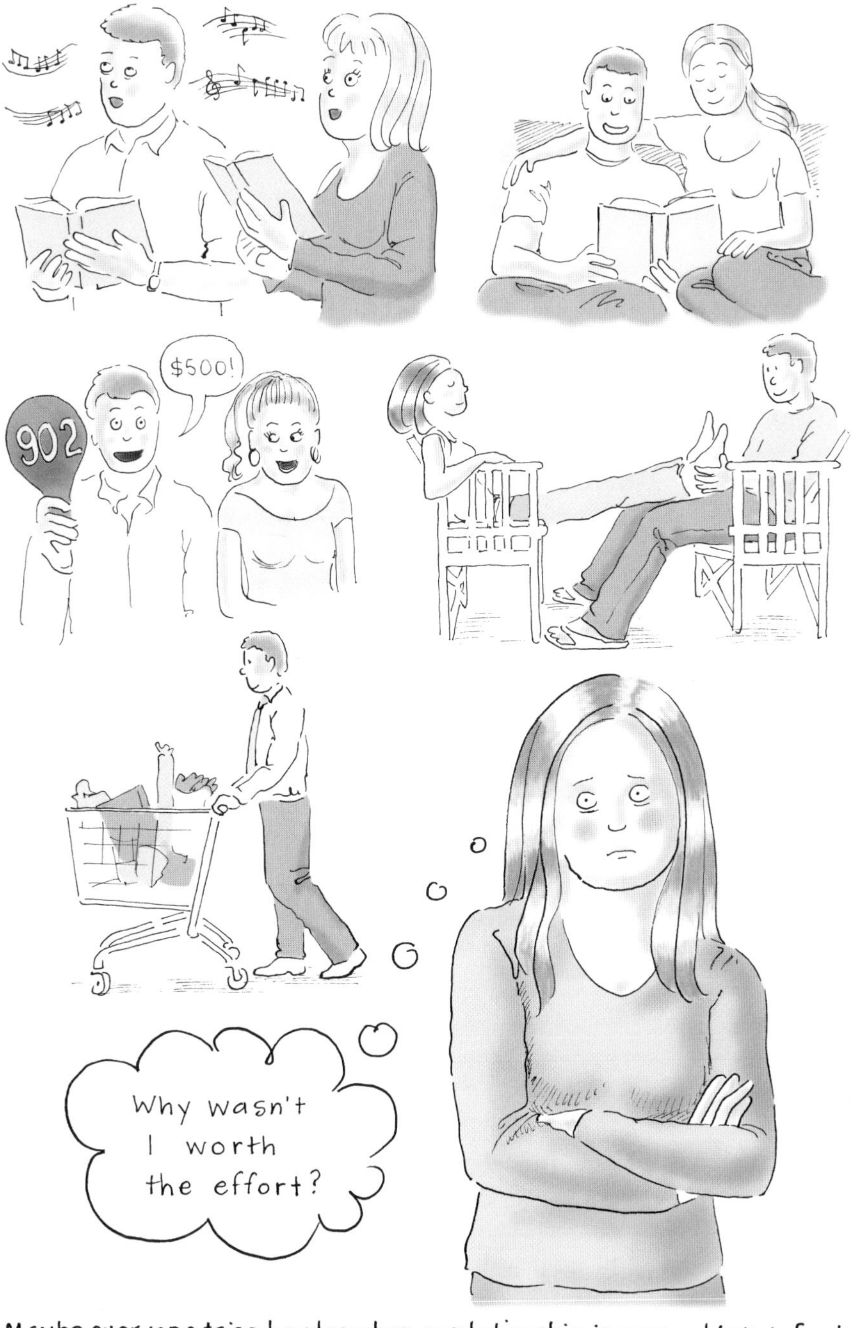
902
$500!
Why wasn't I worth the effort?

Maybe everyone tries harder when a relationship is new and love is fresh.

I explained T.J.'s frenzied social life to the kids as best I could, but I worried about how the frequent turnover of girlfriends was affecting them. As with most things maternal, I probably worried more than I needed to.

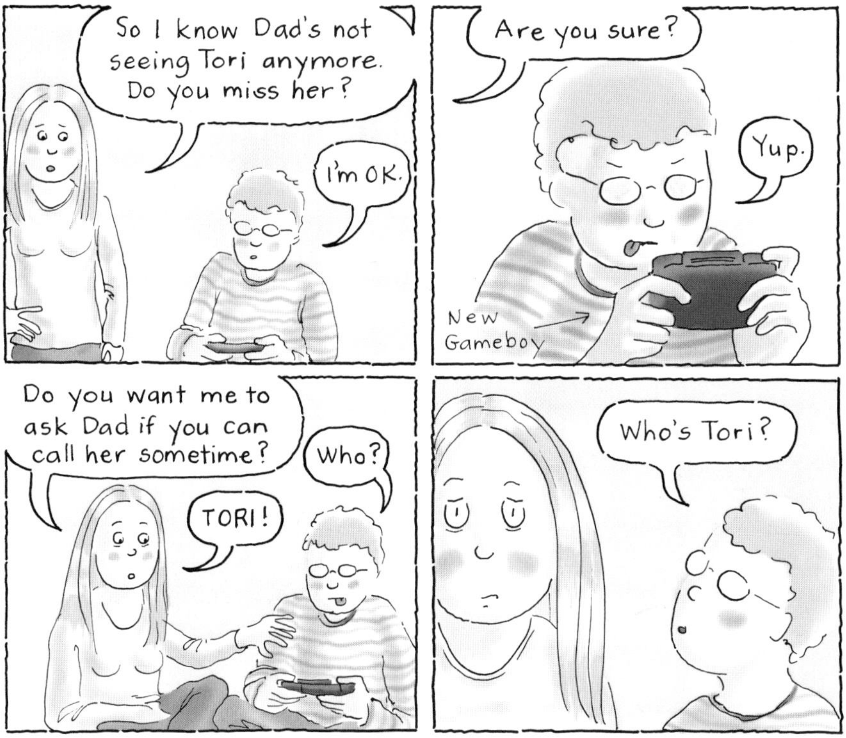
So I know Dad's not seeing Tori anymore. Do you miss her?
I'm OK.
Are you sure?
Yup.
New Gameboy
Do you want me to ask Dad if you can call her sometime?
Who?
TORI!
Who's Tori?

The only time I wasn't worrying about the kids was when I was running. Even though I'd lost my running partner when Sarah moved, I continued to make our 5k loop four or five times a week. It was a temporary, albeit miserable, escape.

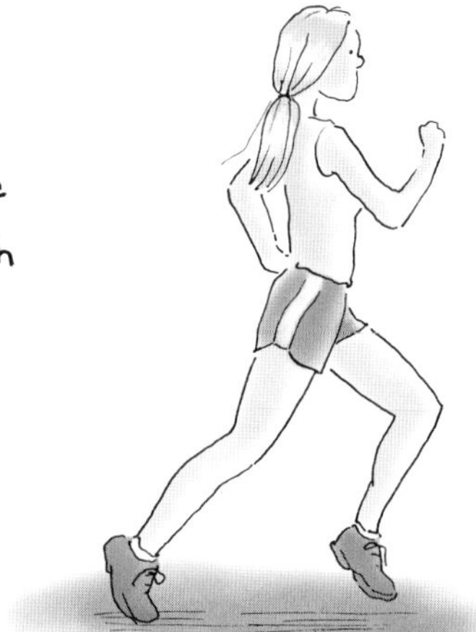

My confidence grew with every run. I decided to enter the Cranberry Race on Thanksgiving. Sarah had promised that she would stop in Keene on her way to visit Scott's family and run with me.

I woke up that morning feeling ready. And proud of myself. A year earlier, I didn't own a pair of running shoes and now I was about to run in an actual race!

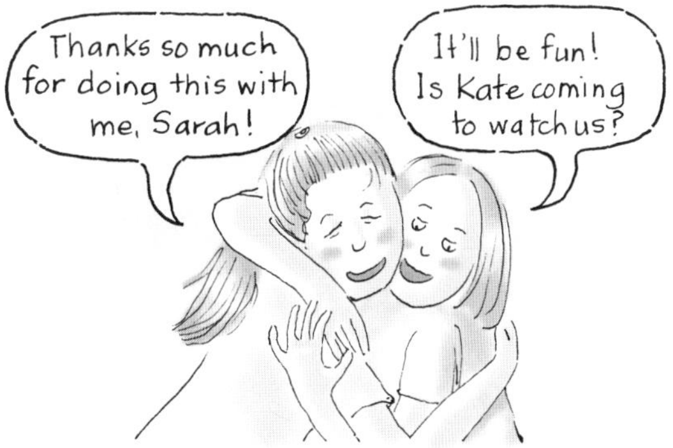
Thanks so much for doing this with me, Sarah!
It'll be fun! Is Kate coming to watch us?

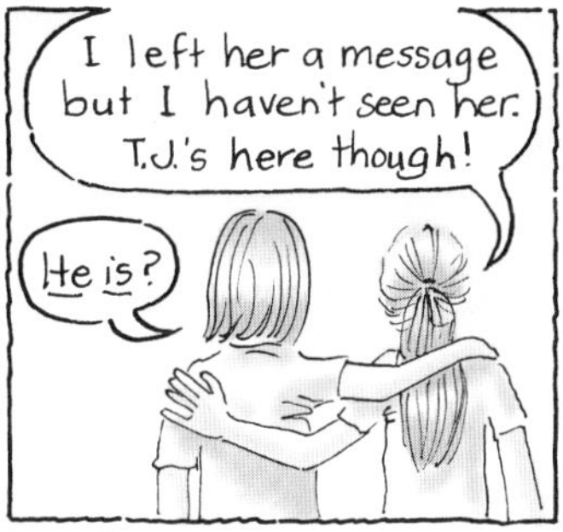
I left her a message but I haven't seen her. T.J.'s here though!
He is?

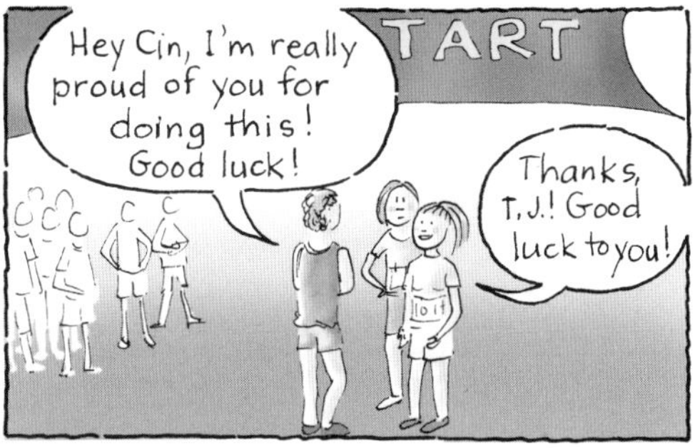
TART
Hey Cin, I'm really proud of you for doing this! Good luck!
Thanks, T.J.! Good luck to you!
101

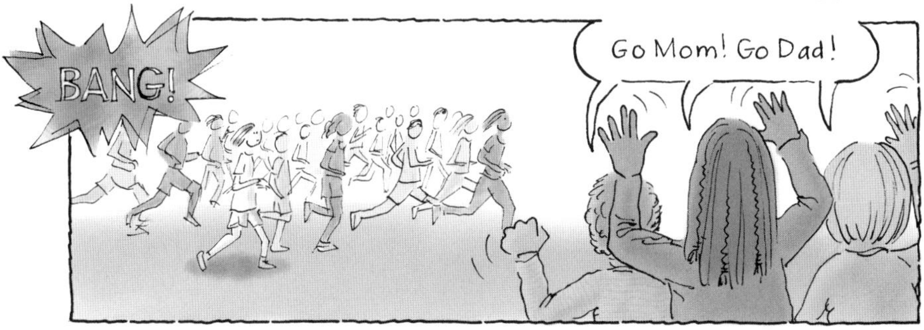
BANG!
Go Mom! Go Dad!

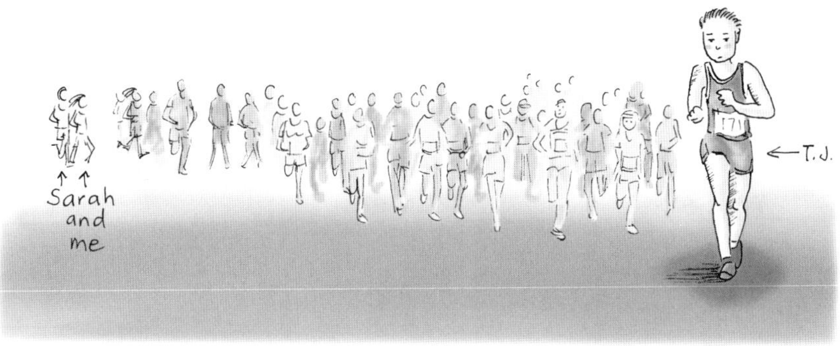
171
← T.J.
↑ ↑ Sarah and me

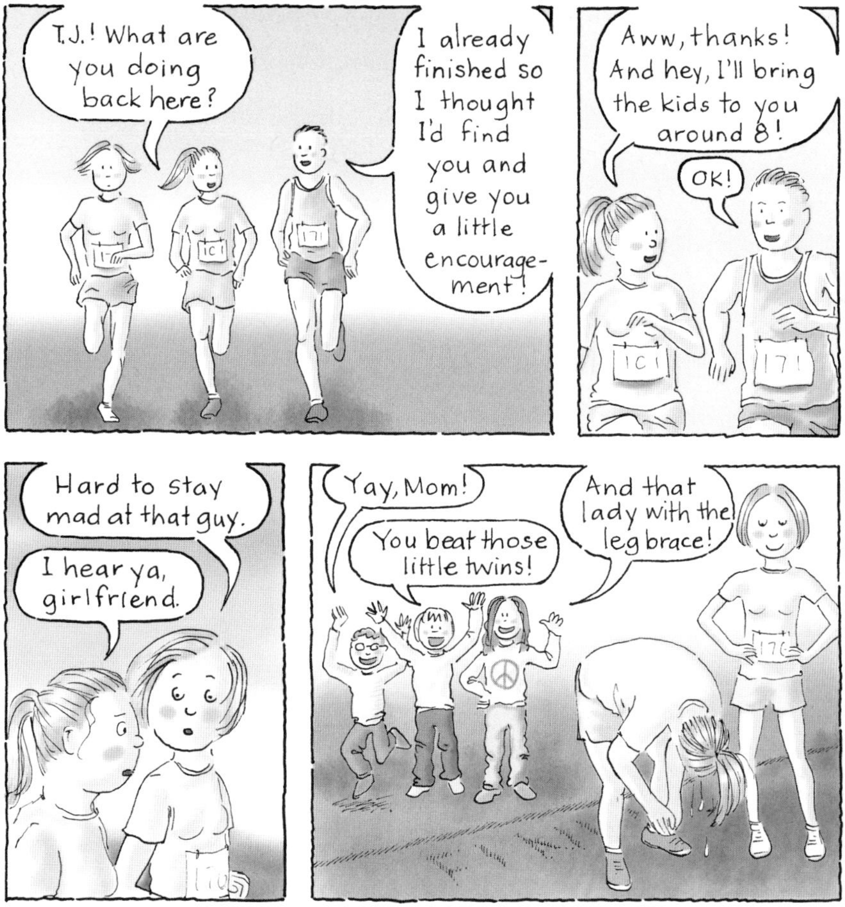
T.J.! What are you doing back here?
I already finished so I thought I'd find you and give you a little encouragement!
Aww, thanks! And hey, I'll bring the kids to you around 8!
OK!
Hard to stay mad at that guy.
I hear ya, girlfriend.
Yay, Mom!
You beat those little twins!
And that lady with the leg brace!

It was no Chariots of Fire ending, but I was satisfied: I hadn't tripped, thrown up, or passed out. And I had run across the finish line.

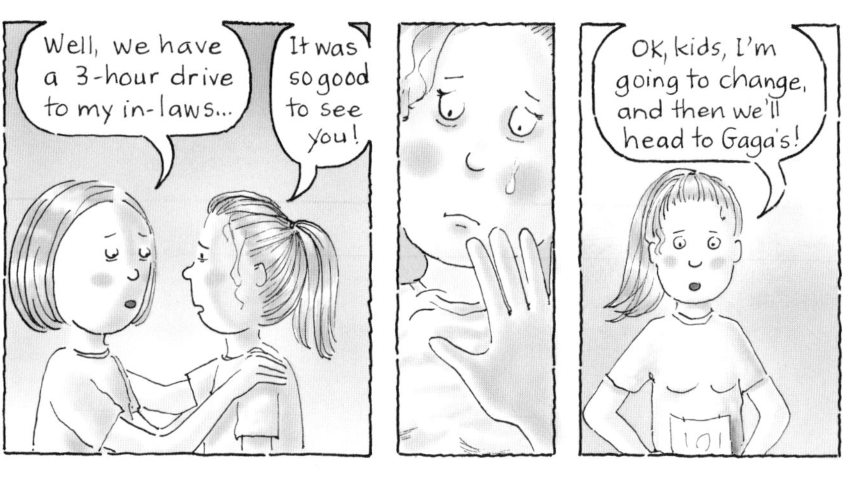
Well, we have a 3-hour drive to my in-laws...
It was so good to see you!
OK, kids, I'm going to change, and then we'll head to Gaga's!

At the family Thanksgiving table, T. J.'s absence was more noticeable than anyone's presence. I sensed the communal strain as everyone tiptoed around topics that might prompt thoughts of him. I didn't know how to diffuse the tension.

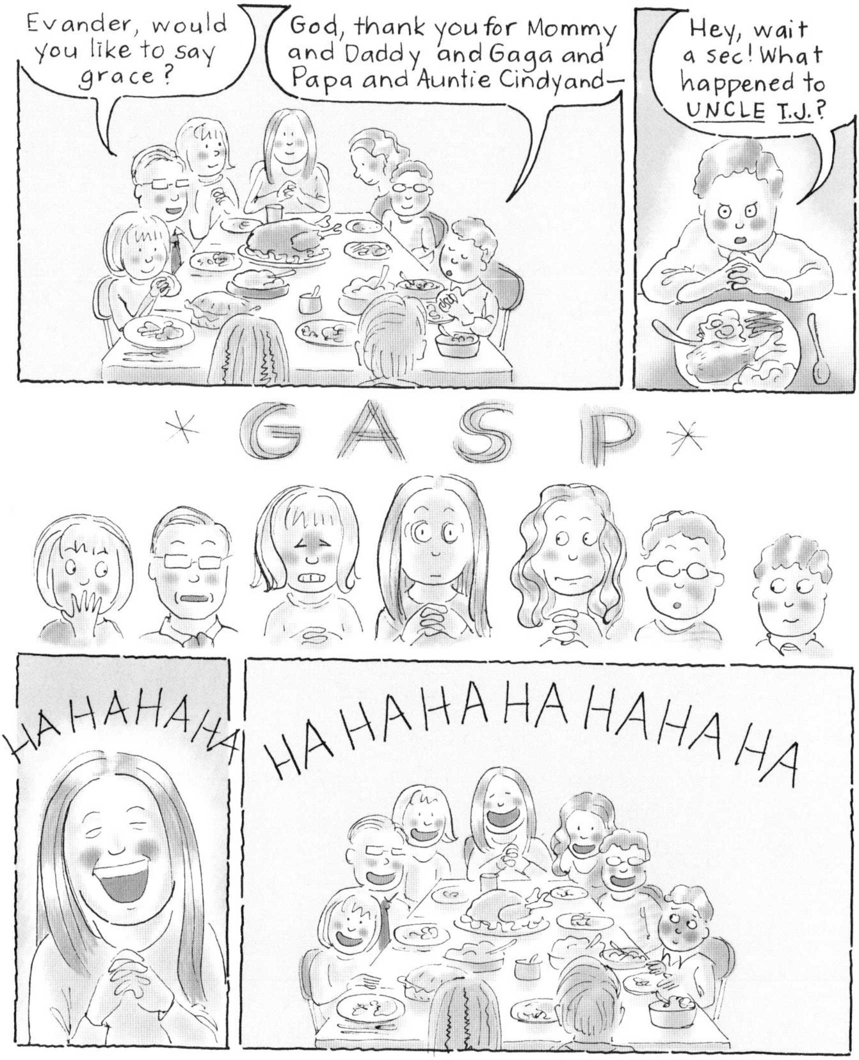
Evander, would you like to say grace?
God, thank you for Mommy and Daddy and Gaga and Papa and Auntie Cindy and—
Hey, wait a sec! What happened to UNCLE T.J.?
GASP
HAHAHAHA
HAHAHAHAHAHAHAHA

I had so many things to be thankful for, not the least of which was that I had burned enough calories in the race to help myself to seconds (guilt-free).

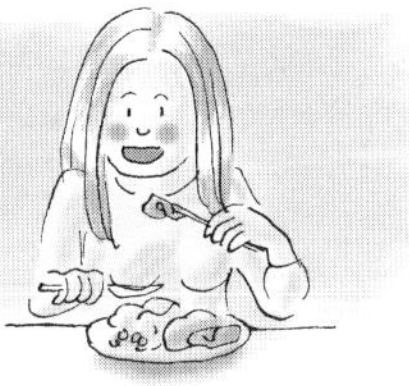

Winter

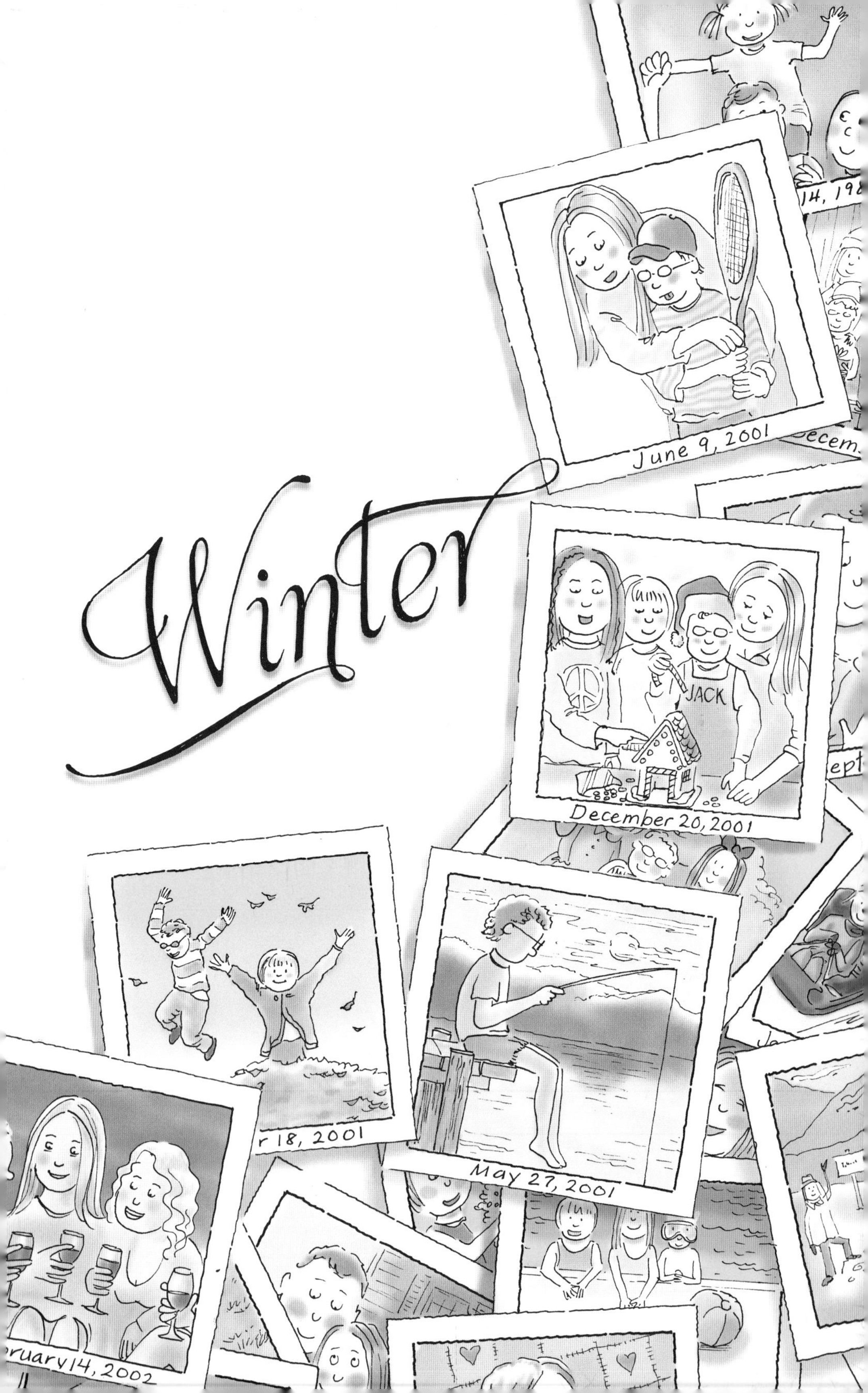
June 9, 2001
JACK
December 20, 2001
May 27, 2001

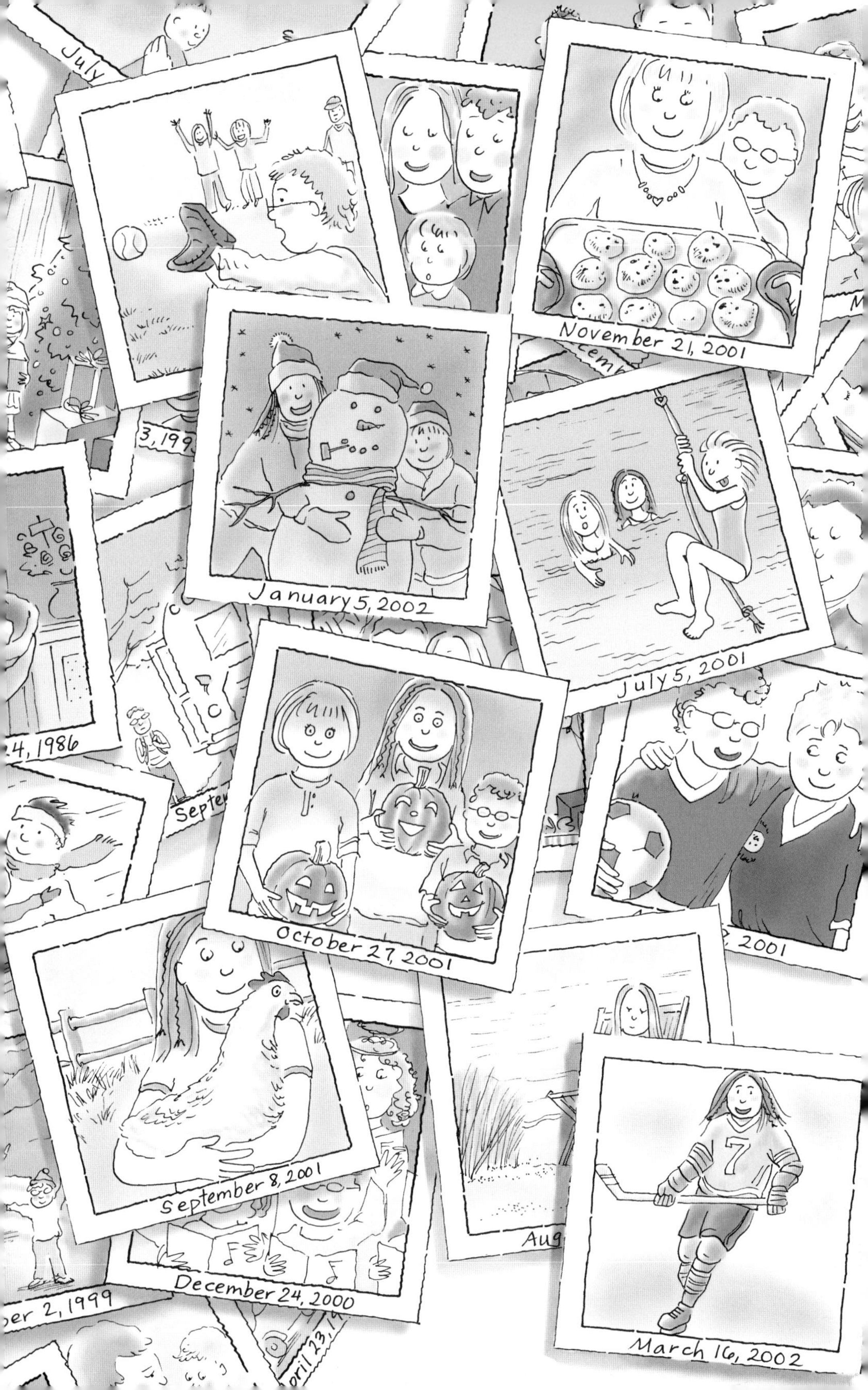

November 21, 2001
January 5, 2002
July 5, 2001
October 27, 2001
September 8, 2001
December 24, 2000
March 16, 2002

The holiday season was soon in full swing, with the world decked out in red and green. I couldn't escape the ubiquitous images of happy two-parent households bustling with Christmas  activity. Under the best of circumstances, it was a challenge to live up to the hype, to be the flawless family featured in holiday ads and on cards.

Like most other families, we had taken comfort in re-enacting our carefully orchestrated holiday traditions year after year.

Christmas 2000

Can't we just BUY a tree like everyone else?

We live in New Hampshire! We should get a tree from the woods!

But these aren't even OUR woods...

On the Saturday after Thanksgiving, the kids and T.J. picked out a tree.

How about this one?

Fine.

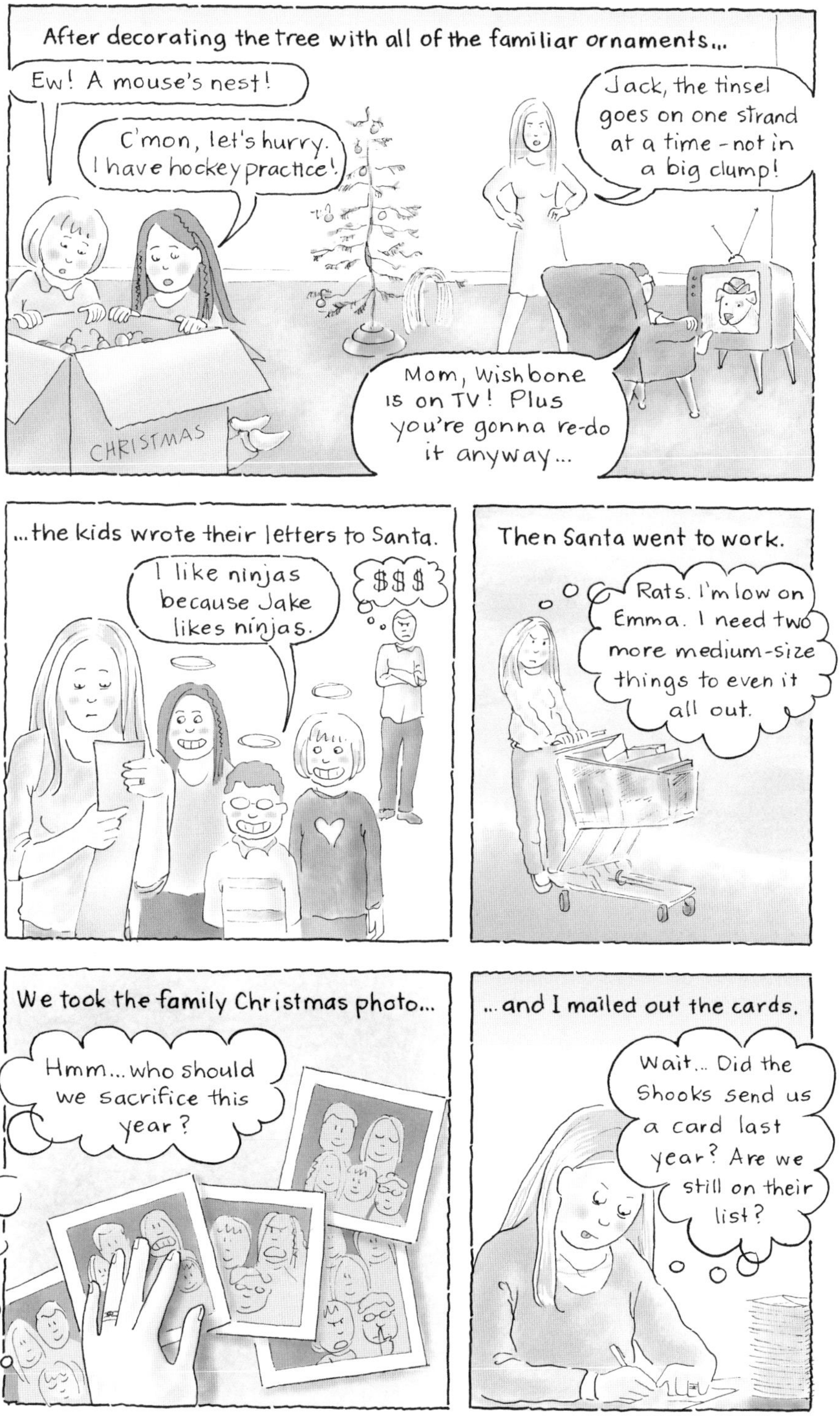
After decorating the tree with all of the familiar ornaments...
Ew! A mouse's nest!
C'mon, let's hurry. I have hockey practice!
Jack, the tinsel goes on one strand at a time - not in a big clump!
Mom, Wishbone is on TV! Plus you're gonna re-do it anyway...
CHRISTMAS
...the kids wrote their letters to Santa.
I like ninjas because Jake likes ninjas.
$$$
Then Santa went to work.
Rats. I'm low on Emma. I need two more medium-size things to even it all out.
We took the family Christmas photo...
Hmm... who should we sacrifice this year?
...and I mailed out the cards.
Wait... Did the Shooks send us a card last year? Are we still on their list?

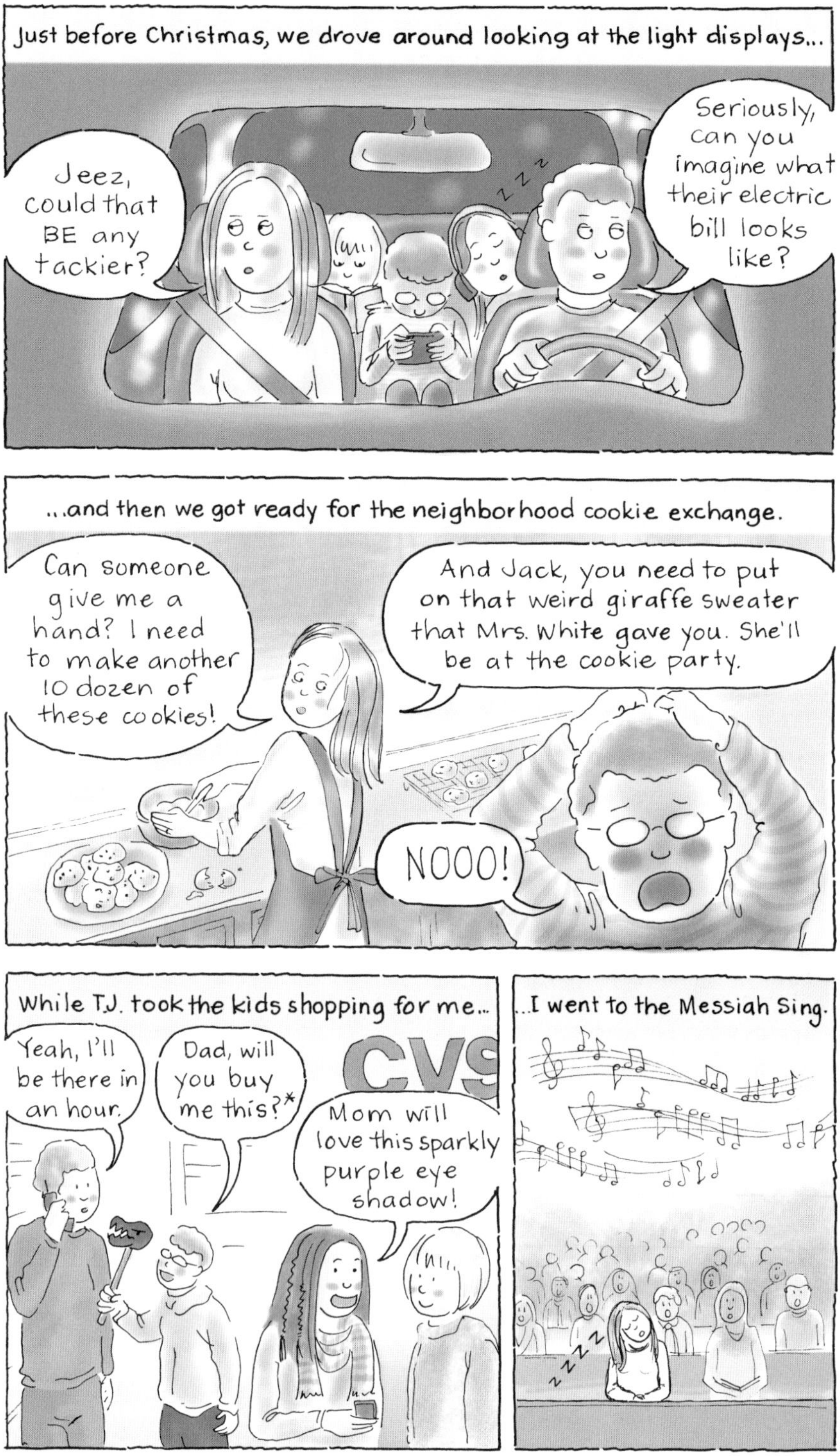
Just before Christmas, we drove around looking at the light displays...
Jeez, could that BE any tackier?
Seriously, can you imagine what their electric bill looks like?
...and then we got ready for the neighborhood cookie exchange.
Can someone give me a hand? I need to make another 10 dozen of these cookies!
And Jack, you need to put on that weird giraffe sweater that Mrs. White gave you. She'll be at the cookie party.
NOOO!
While T.J. took the kids shopping for me...
Yeah, I'll be there in an hour.
Dad, will you buy me this?*
Mom will love this sparkly purple eye shadow!
CVS
...I went to the Messiah Sing.

* Santa already bought it for him.

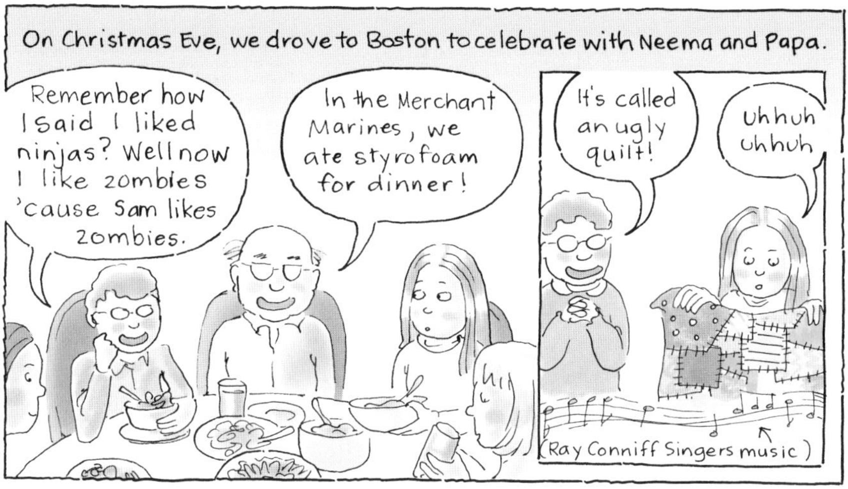
On Christmas Eve, we drove to Boston to celebrate with Neema and Papa.
Remember how I said I liked ninjas? Well now I like zombies 'cause Sam likes zombies.
In the Merchant Marines, we ate styrofoam for dinner!
It's called an ugly quilt!
Uhhuh uhhuh
(Ray Conniff Singers music)

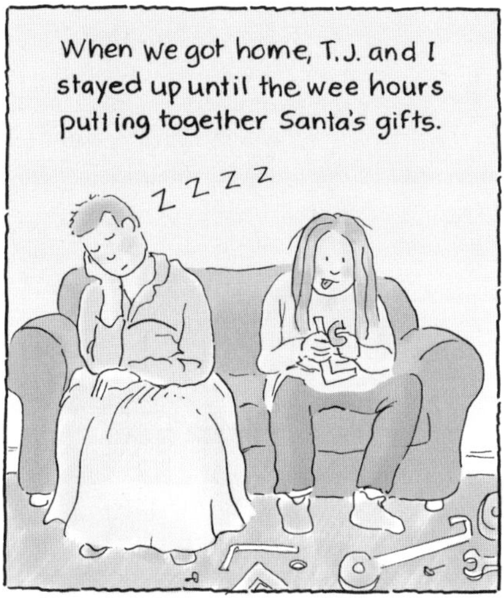
When we got home, T.J. and I stayed up until the wee hours putting together Santa's gifts.
Z Z Z Z

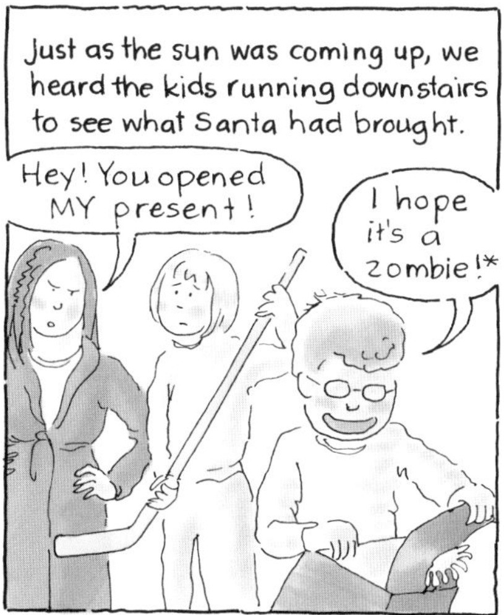
Just as the sun was coming up, we heard the kids running downstairs to see what Santa had brought.
Hey! You opened MY present!
I hope it's a zombie!*

*It's a ninja.

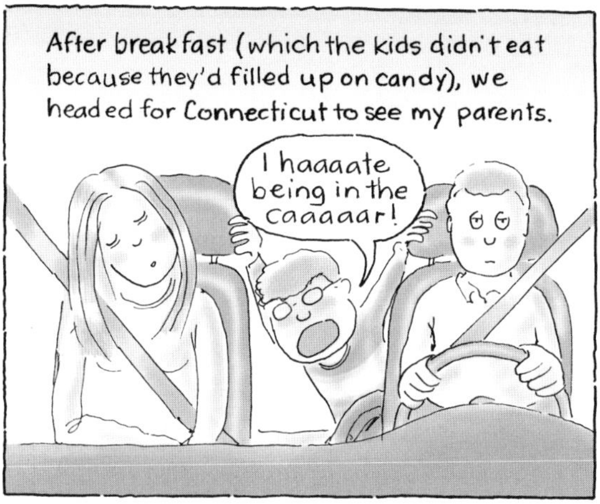
After breakfast (which the kids didn't eat because they'd filled up on candy), we headed for Connecticut to see my parents.
I haaaate being in the caaaaar!

It was magical.

And by magical,

I mean perfectly

acceptable.

This year, the Perfect Family Christmas was unattainable. With the pressure off, maybe I could relax and simplify. Maybe the divorce was going to provide the excuse we needed for a Christmas makeover.

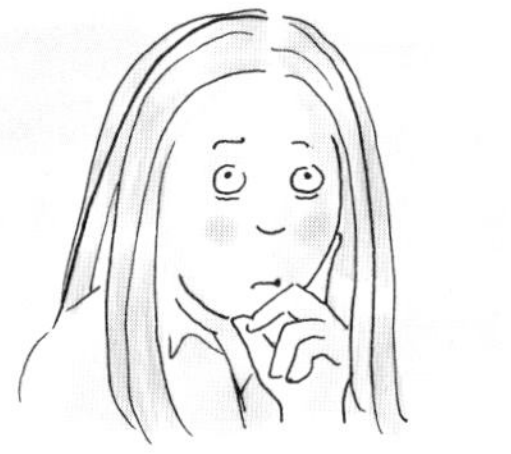

I called a family meeting so that the kids and I could figure out what traditions we should keep, which ones we should tweak, and which ones we should replace outright.

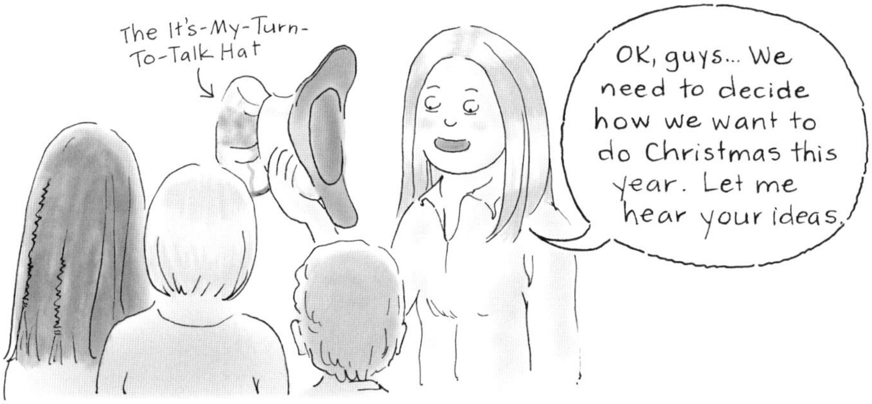
The It's-My-Turn-To-Talk Hat
OK, guys... We need to decide how we want to do Christmas this year. Let me hear your ideas.

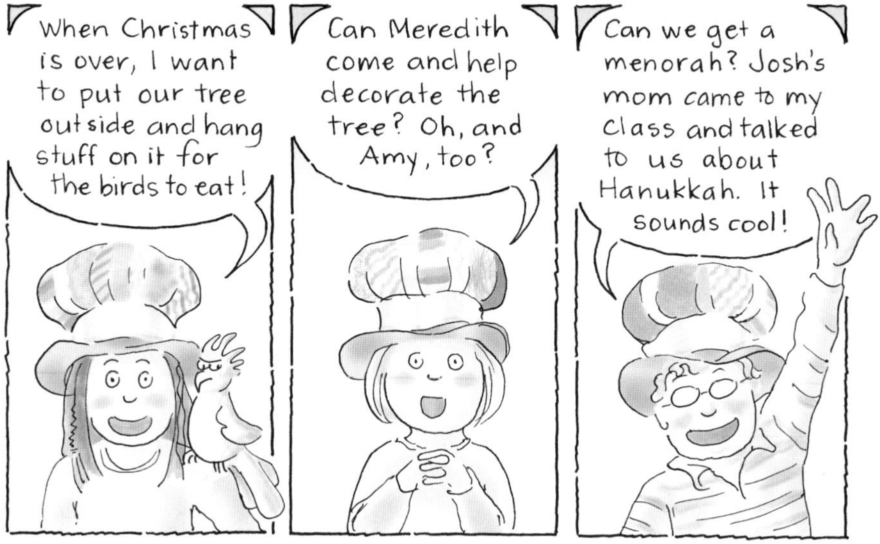
When Christmas is over, I want to put our tree outside and hang stuff on it for the birds to eat!
Can Meredith come and help decorate the tree? Oh, and Amy, too?
Can we get a menorah? Josh's mom came to my class and talked to us about Hanukkah. It sounds cool!

I hadn't given the kids nearly enough credit: They were flexible and resilient and had loads of suggestions for our new Christmas.

Christmas P.D. (post-divorce)

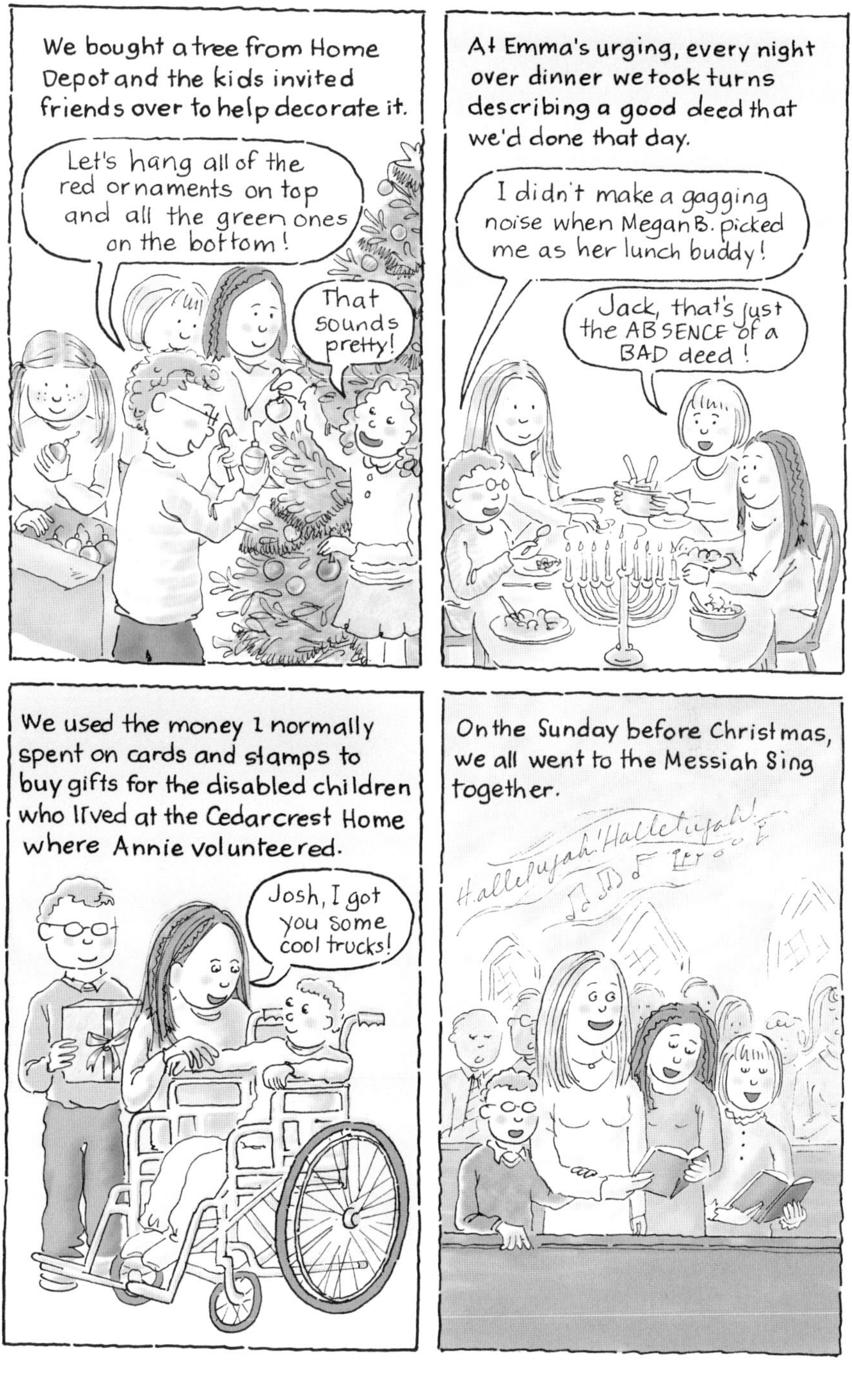
We bought a tree from Home Depot and the kids invited friends over to help decorate it.
Let's hang all of the red ornaments on top and all the green ones on the bottom!
That sounds pretty!
At Emma's urging, every night over dinner we took turns describing a good deed that we'd done that day.
I didn't make a gagging noise when Megan B. picked me as her lunch buddy!
Jack, that's just the ABSENCE of a BAD deed!
We used the money I normally spent on cards and stamps to buy gifts for the disabled children who lived at the Cedarcrest Home where Annie volunteered.
Josh, I got you some cool trucks!
On the Sunday before Christmas, we all went to the Messiah Sing together.
Hallelujah! Hallelujah!

The kids had suggested that they go to T.J.'s two days before Christmas and then come back to my house late on Christmas Eve. They'd asked T.J. to invite Neema and Papa to come to his house so that Annie could cook a vegetarian holiday meal for everyone. As I dropped them off in his driveway, T.J. appeared with an armload of firewood.

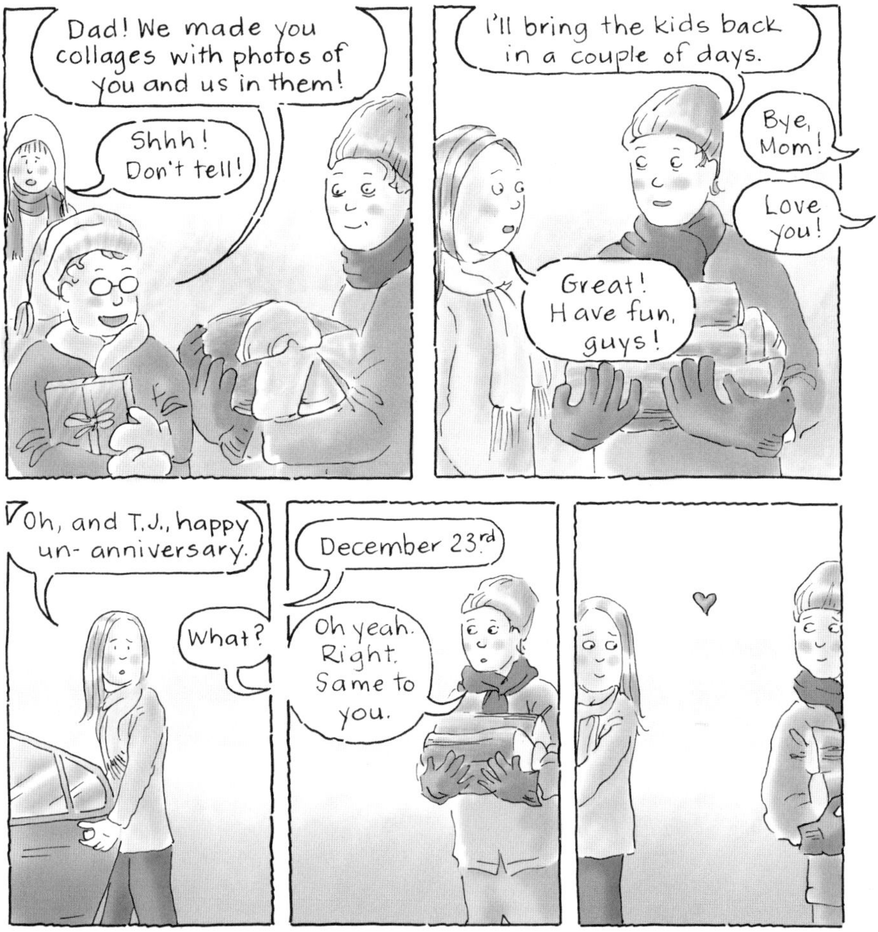
Dad! We made you collages with photos of you and us in them!
Shhh! Don't tell!
I'll bring the kids back in a couple of days.
Bye, Mom!
Love you!
Great! Have fun, guys!
Oh, and T.J., happy un-anniversary.
What?
December 23rd
Oh yeah. Right. Same to you.

When I saw him, I still saw the past. I saw all of our years together. One laugh took me back decades. One weird joke reminded me of a thousand others. I wondered if he saw the same in me.

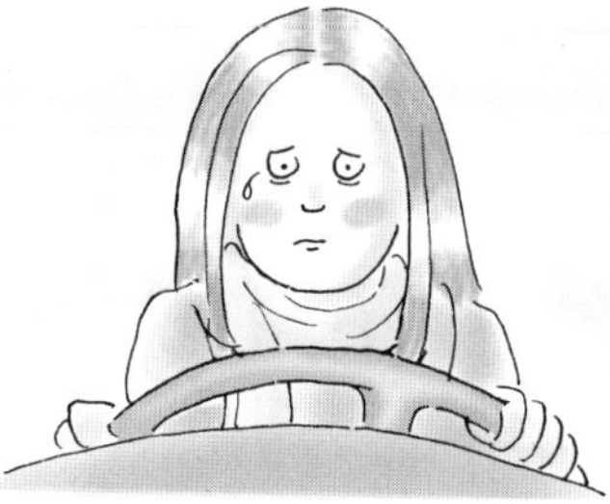

When I got back home, I plugged in the Christmas lights, put on my favorite holiday CD, and lit a fire in the fireplace. I spent the rest of the night wrapping and labeling presents. It wasn't at all lonely or sad; it was a pleasant pause in the middle of a busy holiday season.

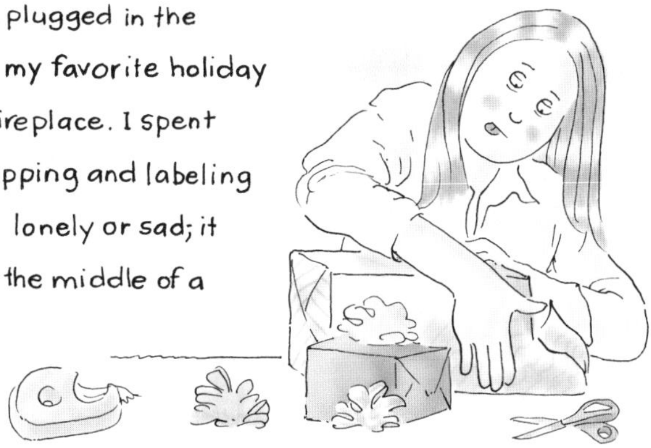

The next morning, after a leisurely and luxurious hour spent sipping coffee and reading the newspaper, I loaded the car with gifts I'd bought for neighbors and friends and headed off to make my deliveries.

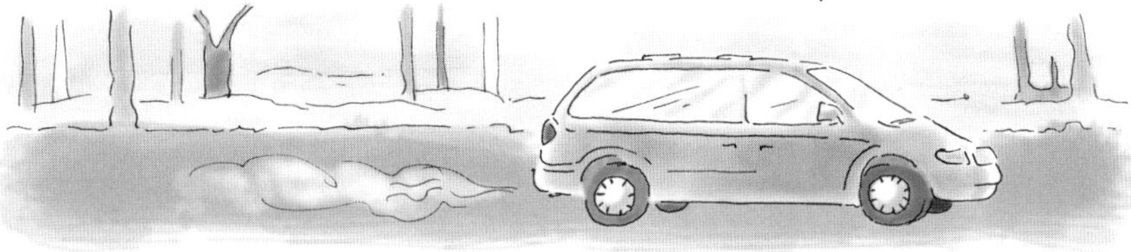

I saved Kate for last. She hadn't returned my phone calls recently and I wondered if she might be upset because I'd been too busy to make any plans with her for several weeks. Maybe we could go out for lunch at Luca's, her favorite restaurant. That would smooth things over.

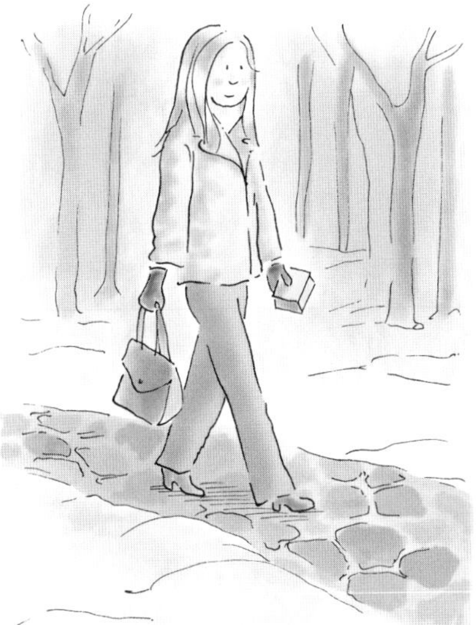

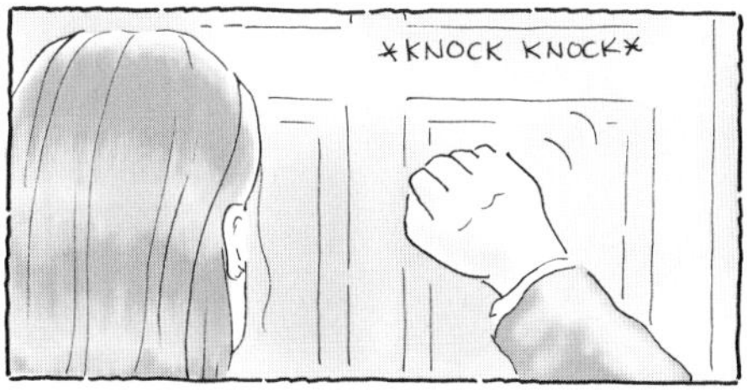
KNOCK KNOCK

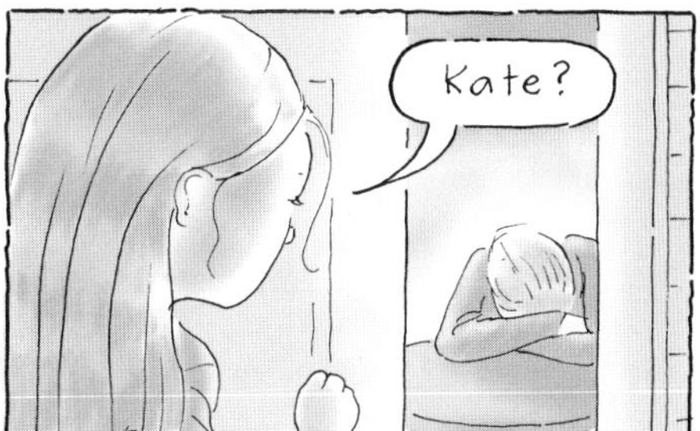
Kate?

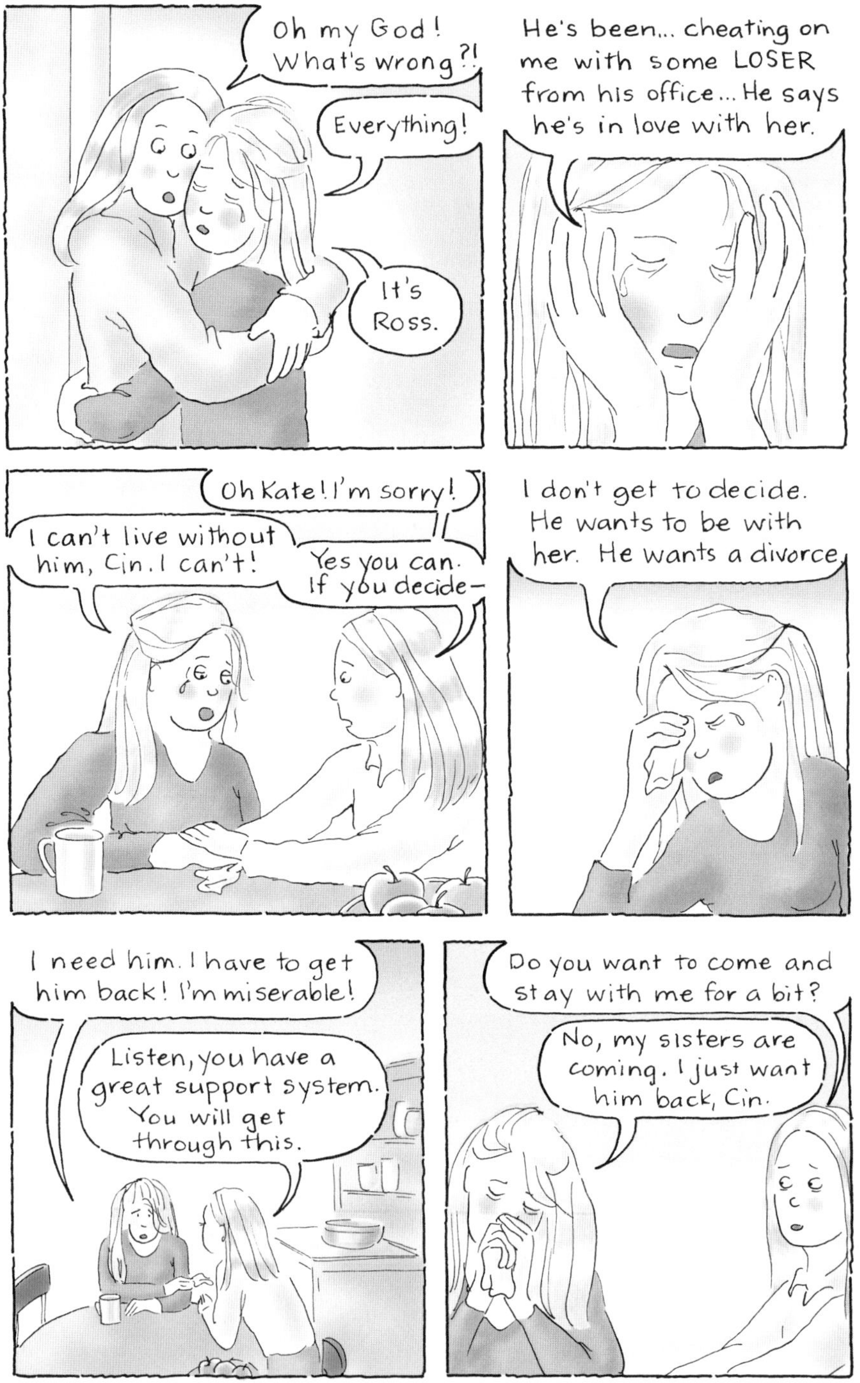
Oh my God! What's wrong?!
Everything!
It's Ross.
He's been... cheating on me with some LOSER from his office... He says he's in love with her.
Oh Kate! I'm sorry!
I can't live without him, Cin. I can't!
Yes you can. If you decide–
I don't get to decide. He wants to be with her. He wants a divorce.
I need him. I have to get him back! I'm miserable!
Listen, you have a great support system. You will get through this.
Do you want to come and stay with me for a bit?
No, my sisters are coming. I just want him back, Cin.

It's so different when it's your own husband's infidelity.

My head was still full of Kate's troubling news that evening when I slid into one of the back pews in church. I'd decided to attend the candlelight service, which was more subdued than the earlier family service. As I reached for the hymnal, the organist began to play Silent Night. I sat back and closed my eyes, drawing strength and comfort from the familiar song. I felt a fleeting sadness: I'd never been to church alone on Christmas Eve. But as the music swelled and the congregation stood in unison, I was reminded that I wasn't alone at all.

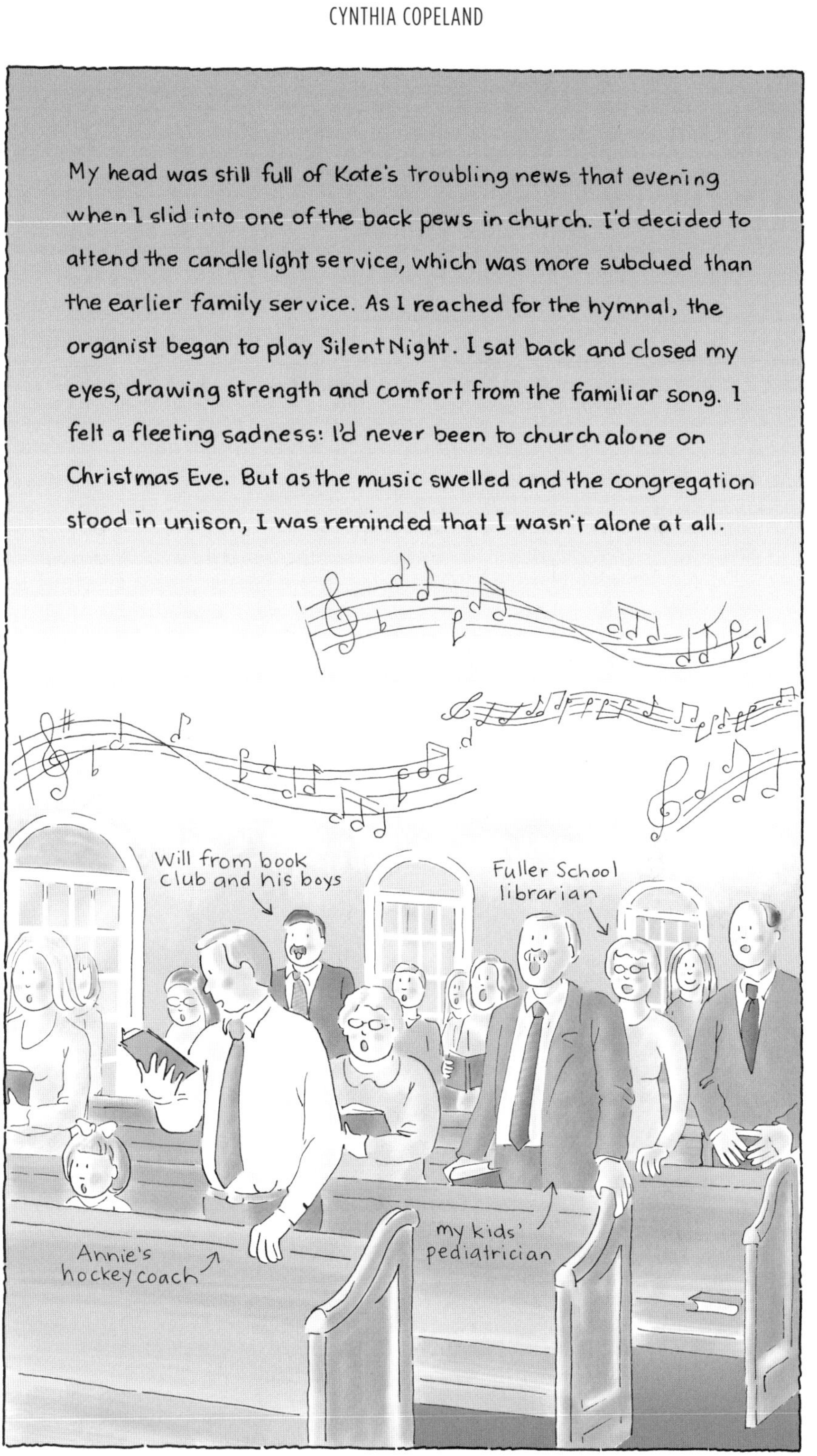
Will from book club and his boys
Fuller School librarian
Annie's hockey coach
my kids' pediatrician

Later that evening, T.J. dropped the kids off. I had hot chocolate and cookies waiting for them.

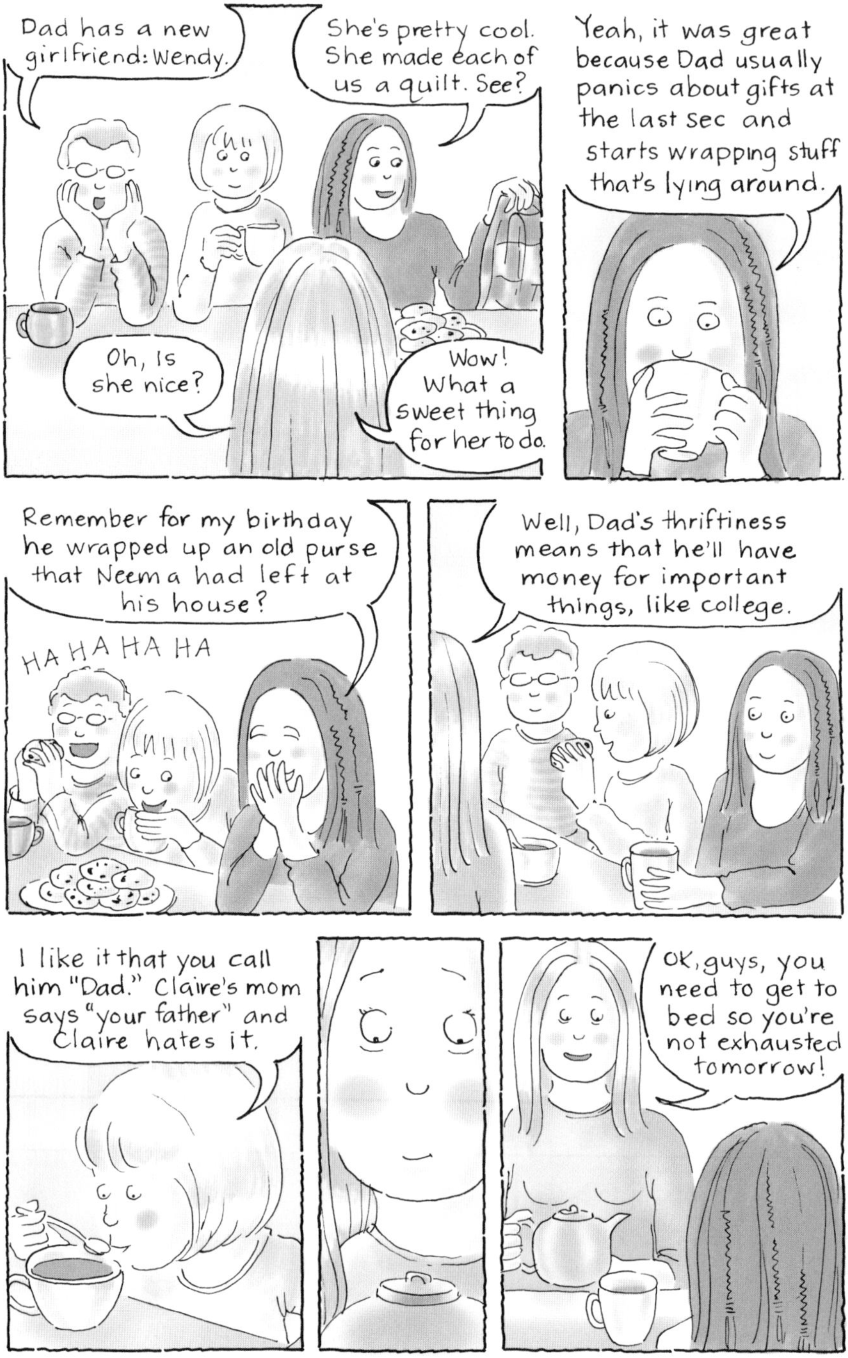
Dad has a new girlfriend: Wendy.
She's pretty cool. She made each of us a quilt. See?
Oh, is she nice?
Wow! What a sweet thing for her to do.
Yeah, it was great because Dad usually panics about gifts at the last sec and starts wrapping stuff that's lying around.
Remember for my birthday he wrapped up an old purse that Neema had left at his house?
HA HA HA HA
Well, Dad's thriftiness means that he'll have money for important things, like college.
I like it that you call him "Dad." Claire's mom says "your father" and Claire hates it.
OK, guys, you need to get to bed so you're not exhausted tomorrow!

We had told my parents we'd visit them the following weekend. The kids didn't want to travel on Christmas Day. They just wanted to hang out at home.

And so did I.

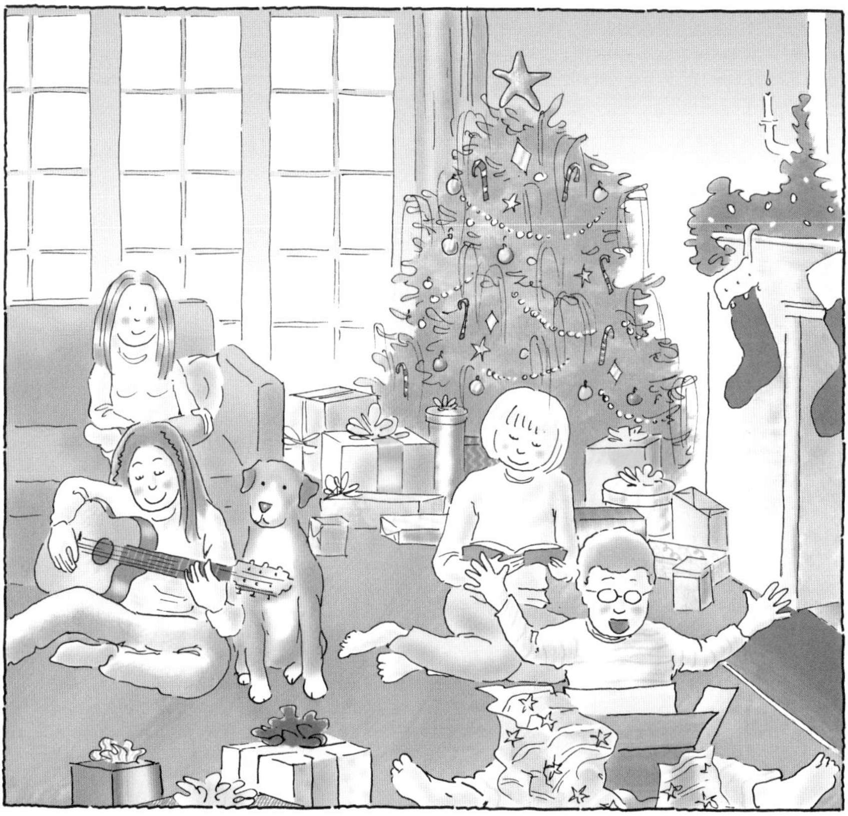

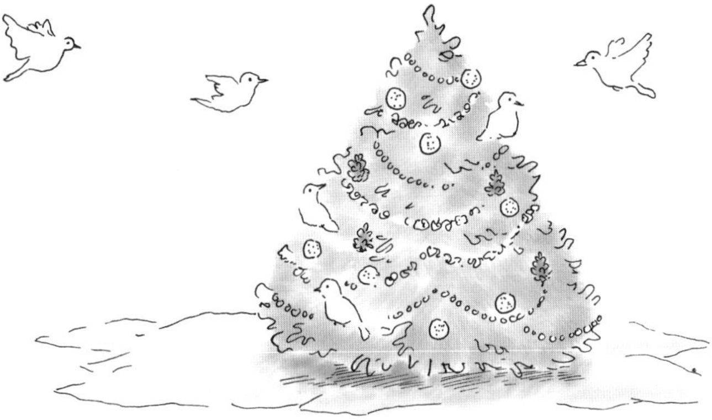

The customary post-Christmas crash was especially hard for Kate. I included her in my plans whenever I could.

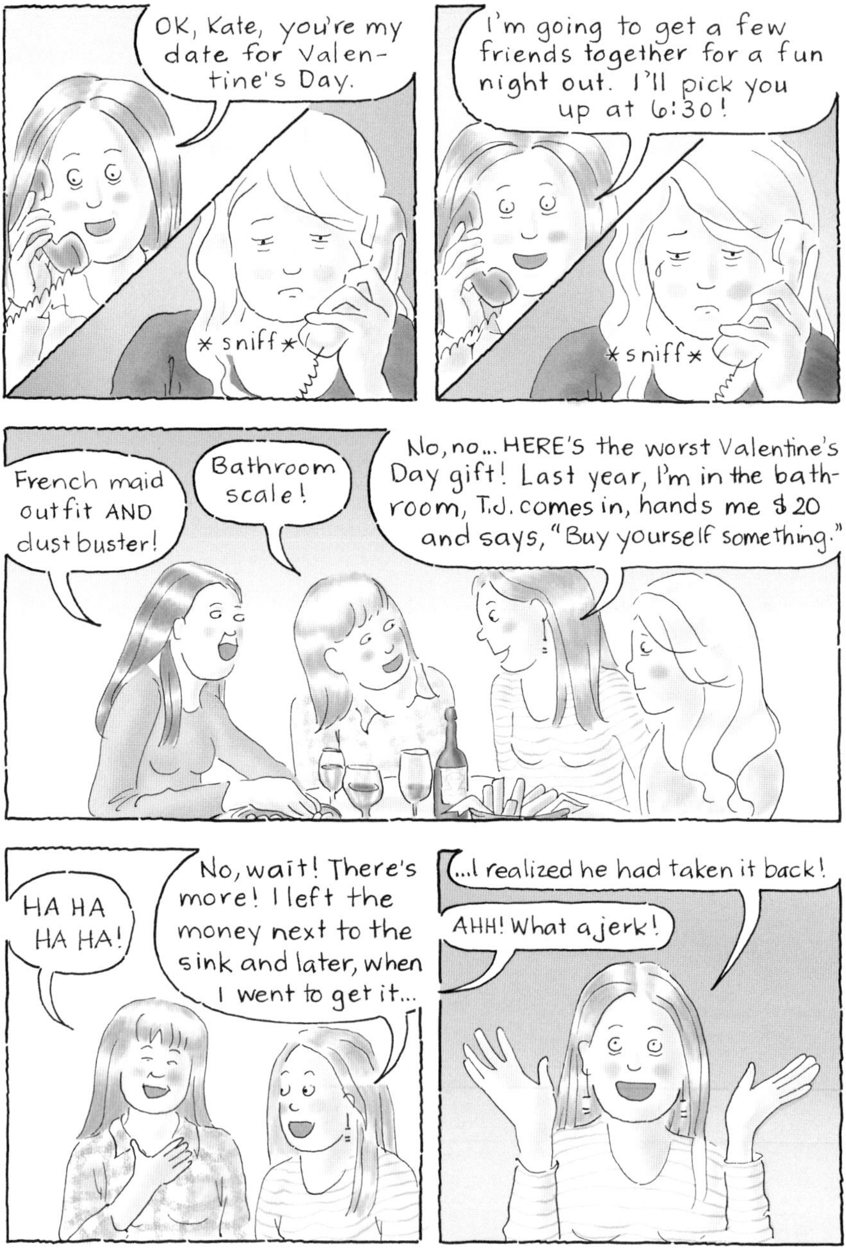
OK, Kate, you're my date for Valen-tine's Day.
sniff
I'm going to get a few friends together for a fun night out. I'll pick you up at 6:30!
sniff
French maid outfit AND dust buster!
Bathroom scale!
No, no... HERE'S the worst Valentine's Day gift! Last year, I'm in the bath-room, T.J. comes in, hands me $20 and says, "Buy yourself something."
HA HA HA HA!
No, wait! There's more! I left the money next to the sink and later, when I went to get it...
...I realized he had taken it back!
AHH! What a jerk!

Despite the fun we were having at our ladies-only table, it was impossible to ignore the smitten couples around us.

I couldn't help contemplating my own romantic future. I had been getting by recently as the third wheel, joining my married friends on their date nights. As grateful as I was for the mercy invites, I knew this wasn't a permanent solution to lonely weekends.

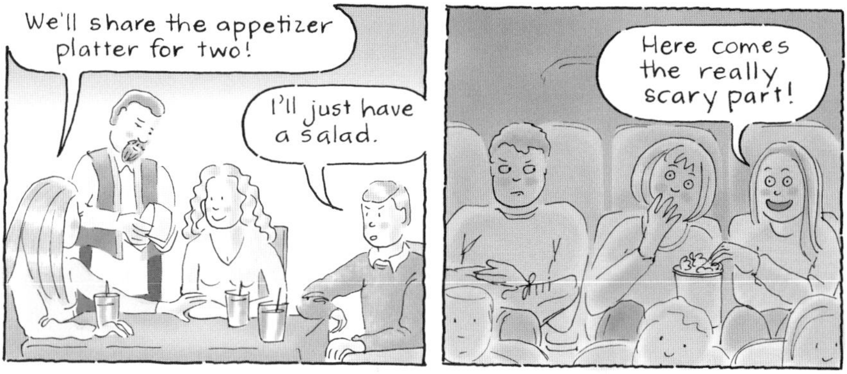
We'll share the appetizer platter for two!
I'll just have a salad.
Here comes the really scary part!

But was I ready to dip a toe in the dating pool? Maybe in a wet suit. I felt like I was... well, past my prime. And I'd never really had one.

One Saturday, however, I got an ego boost from an unlikely source: T.J.

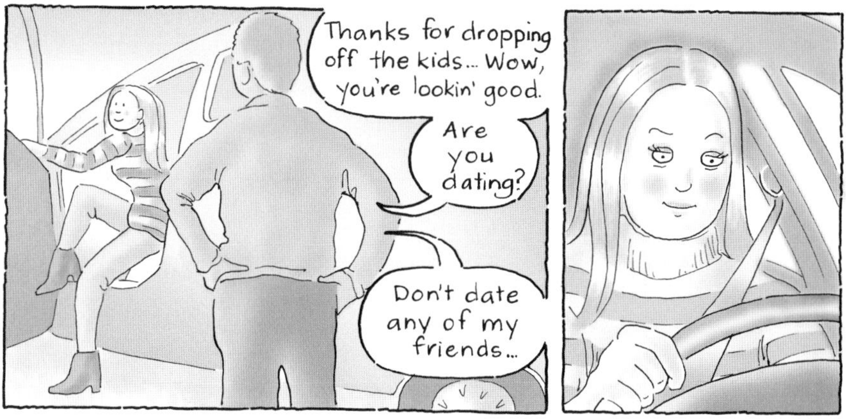
Thanks for dropping off the kids... Wow, you're lookin' good.
Are you dating?
Don't date any of my friends...

Ironically, I was probably more like the person T.J. was looking for when he fell for Liza. I was in better shape physically and I felt like a more interesting and well-rounded person. But part of that personal evolution involved the realization that I wouldn't want someone like T.J. I deserved someone who would love me enough to work through challenging times in the relationship rather than look for a replacement.

I didn't want T.J. (or his friends) but I did want one special person in my life. Someone kind. And funny. Someone who would squeeze my hand at the end of a rough day and tell me everything was going to be OK.

The challenge was going to be finding that special person. I desperately wanted to skip over the lingerie/bikini wax/Spanx dating phase and get right to the cotton undies/pimple cream/pajama pants relationship phase. But no can do.

Before you get to this... ...you have to suffer through this...

teeth picking,
comfortable silence
So... do you like movies?
popcorn kernel suctioned to the back of your molar,
awkward small talk

And before you can suffer through that, you have to suffer through this:

Biore stripping
eyebrow and chin hair plucking
ear re-piercing
mustache bleaching

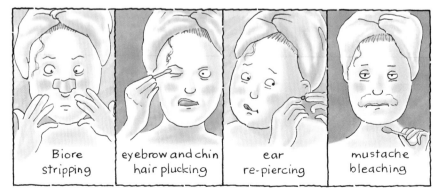

Dating, The Prequel

I'd had some close calls, but no actual dates.
While volunteering at the Community Kitchen, I was chatted up by a friendly fellow who winked at me at least once.

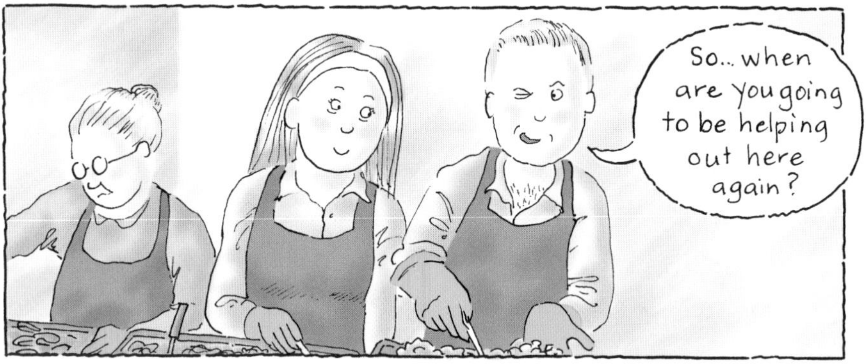
So... when are you going to be helping out here again?

I was ridiculously flattered by the attention... until I read in the newspaper that he had been arrested for groping patients in the nursing home where he also volunteered. NURSING HOME.

Not long after that, I was flying to a writers' conference when my bawdy yet entertaining seatmate handed me his card.

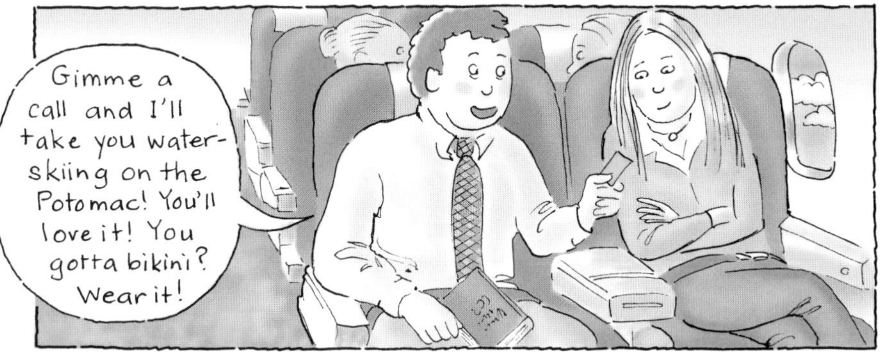
Gimme a call and I'll take you water-skiing on the Potomac! You'll love it! You gotta bikini? Wear it!

I realized after we landed, however, that he really only appealed to me during the flight, like the stuff in the Sky Mall catalog.

It was clear that if I really wanted to find a special guy, I needed a plan.

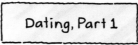

Dating, Part 1

I began perusing the personal ads in the newspaper. It didn't take long for me to realize that the folks who advertised there tended to be "active seniors" and/or pretty high on the quirk meter.

JUST A SIMPLE GUY SWM, 52, 5'1", chubby, bald, looking for a very simple person, 21-60, for LTR. I love the simple things like beaches and the rain, ETC.
Maybe the men who aren't as "simple" are advertising online...

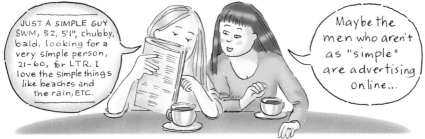

Even though online dating was relatively new at the time and still a little creepy, I was willing to consider it. I imagined the profile I might write...

Country mouse. Nester. Prefer reading books about travels to exotic places to actually going there.
Hate the gym but love doin thing outdoors: hiking, snowshoeing, stacking firewood, gardening... anything that to Little House on the Prairie (also something I like: the books, not the TV show).
Can draw anything but h e an
Sold as is. Not lookin projec take on a project.
Looking for someon ds, and who will go to church with me without p
Funny a plus.

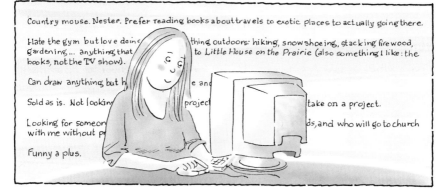

It was a good exercise in determining my priorities, but I decided against putting my information online. Instead, I answered a handful of ads using an alias and arranged meetings in public places. It was a bit like my life would have been if I'd accepted that job offer from the CIA in 1982 (but that's a story for another time).

insert perfect husband and stepdad here

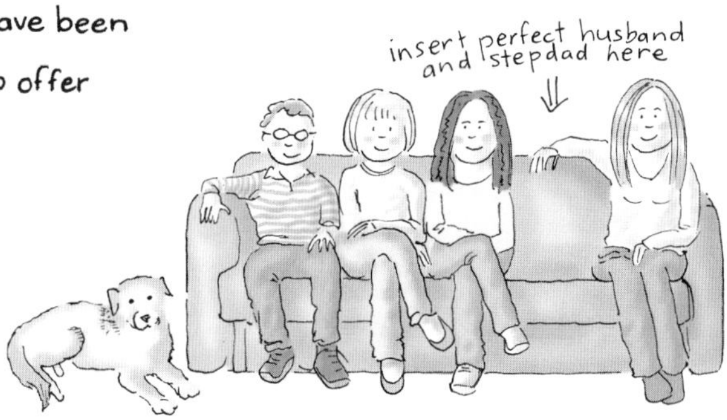

Let me say this. Dating is nothing like *Sex and the City.* It's more like a drive I took one time from Las Vegas to Sedona, Arizona. After cruising miles and miles of brown, barren desert, I began craving a milkshake.

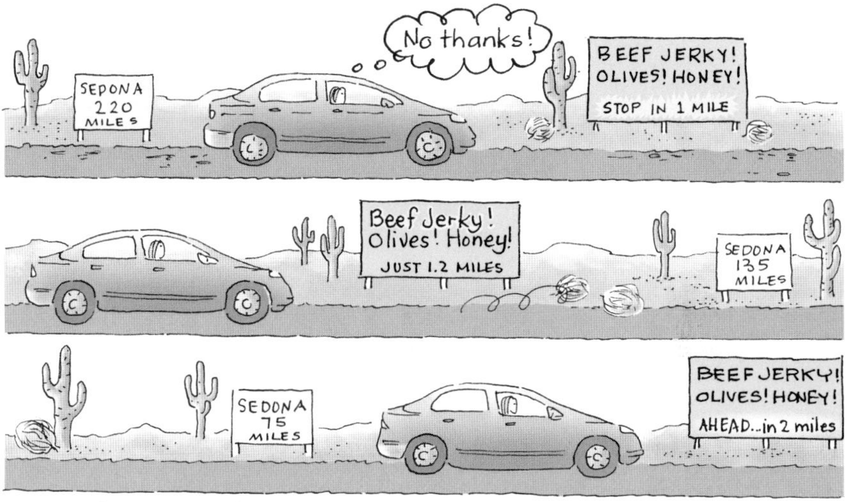
SEDONA 220 MILES
No thanks!
BEEF JERKY! OLIVES! HONEY! STOP IN 1 MILE
Beef Jerky! Olives! Honey! JUST 1.2 MILES
SEDONA 135 MILES
SEDONA 75 MILES
BEEF JERKY! OLIVES! HONEY! AHEAD...in 2 miles

But by the time I drove by the third enthusiastic advertisement for the same three items, beef jerky was starting to sound rather appealing. That's what happens when you begin dating after a divorce. You start out wanting a milkshake; you settle for beef jerky.

Beef jerky with baggage.

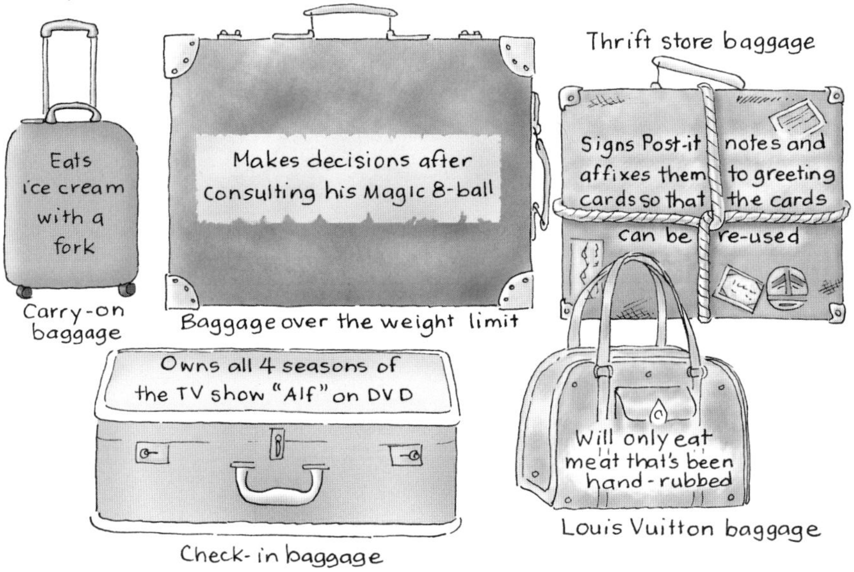
Eats ice cream with a fork
Carry-on baggage
Makes decisions after consulting his Magic 8-ball
Baggage over the weight limit
Thrift store baggage
Signs Post-it notes and affixes them to greeting cards so that the cards can be re-used
Owns all 4 seasons of the TV show "Alf" on DVD
Check-in baggage
Will only eat meat that's been hand-rubbed
Louis Vuitton baggage

Dating, Part 2

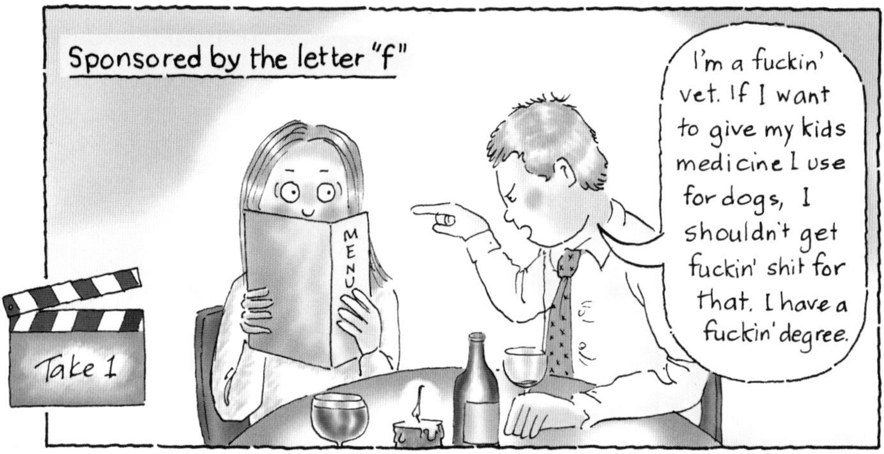
Sponsored by the letter "f"
MENU
I'm a fuckin' vet. If I want to give my kids medicine I use for dogs, I shouldn't get fuckin' shit for that. I have a fuckin' degree.
Take 1

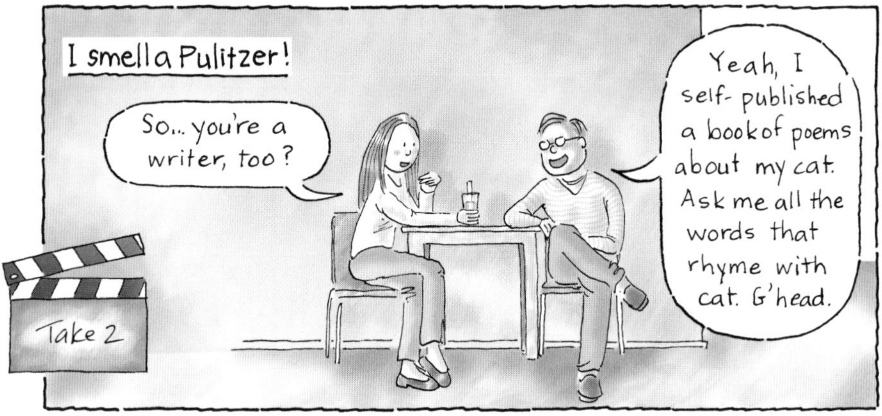
I smell a Pulitzer!
So... you're a writer, too?
Yeah, I self-published a book of poems about my cat. Ask me all the words that rhyme with cat. G'head.
Take 2

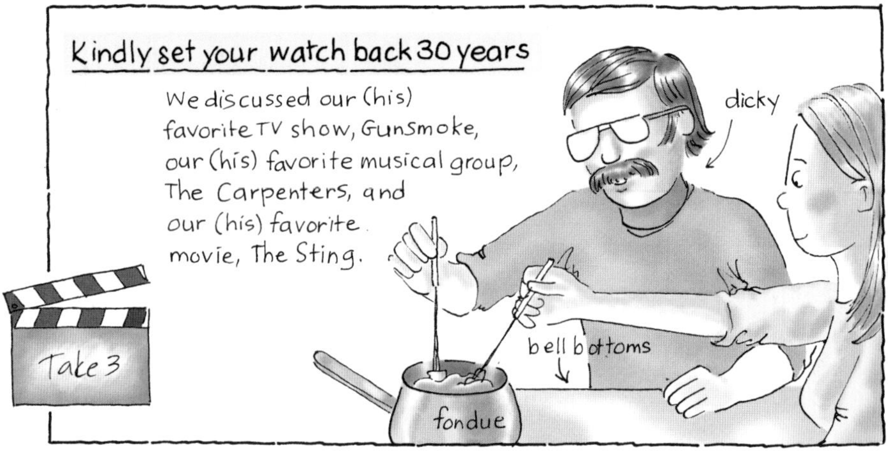
Kindly set your watch back 30 years
We discussed our (his) favorite TV show, Gunsmoke, our (his) favorite musical group, The Carpenters, and our (his) favorite movie, The Sting.
dicky
bell bottoms
fondue
Take 3

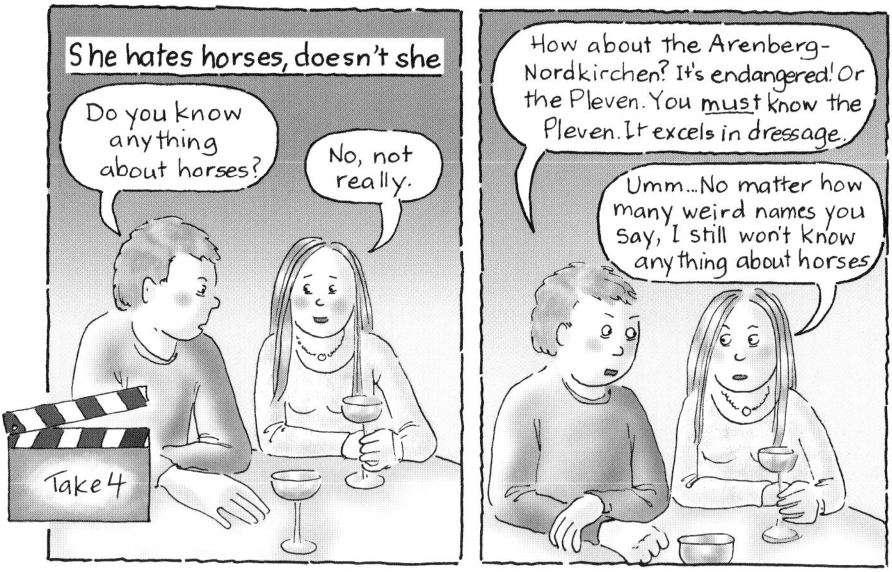
She hates horses, doesn't she
Do you know anything about horses?
No, not really.
Take 4
How about the Arenberg-Nordkirchen? It's endangered! Or the Pleven. You must know the Pleven. It excels in dressage.
Umm...No matter how many weird names you say, I still won't know anything about horses

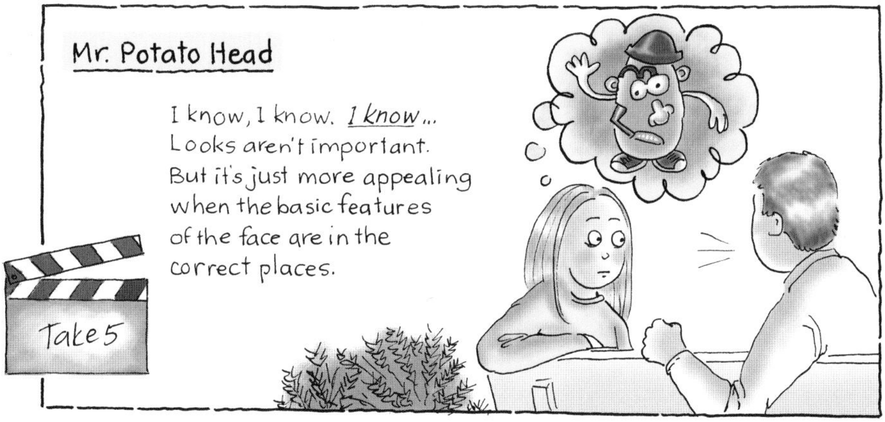
Mr. Potato Head
I know, I know. I know... Looks aren't important. But it's just more appealing when the basic features of the face are in the correct places.
Take 5

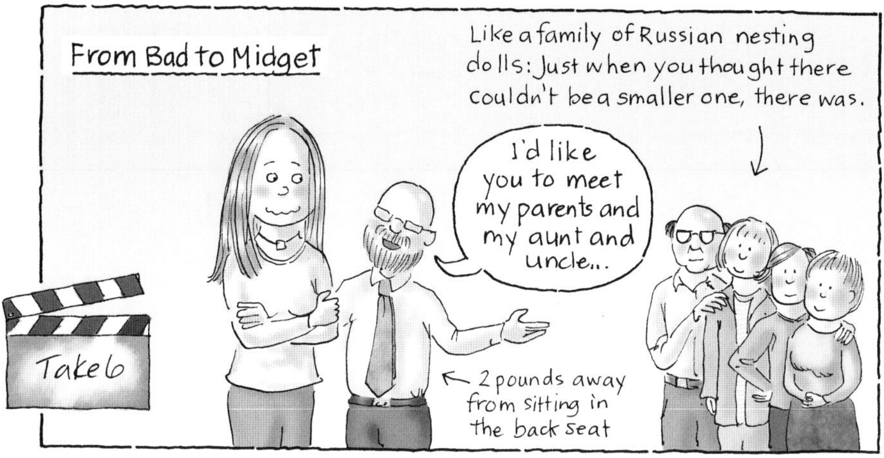
From Bad to Midget
Like a family of Russian nesting dolls: Just when you thought there couldn't be a smaller one, there was.
I'd like you to meet my parents and my aunt and uncle...
2 pounds away from sitting in the back seat
Take 6

It wasn't just about the quality of single men who were available. The very idea of bringing a stranger into our lives was alarming. I couldn't help assessing every guy in terms of how he'd fit into our family and be received by my kids. Not many passed the initial screening.

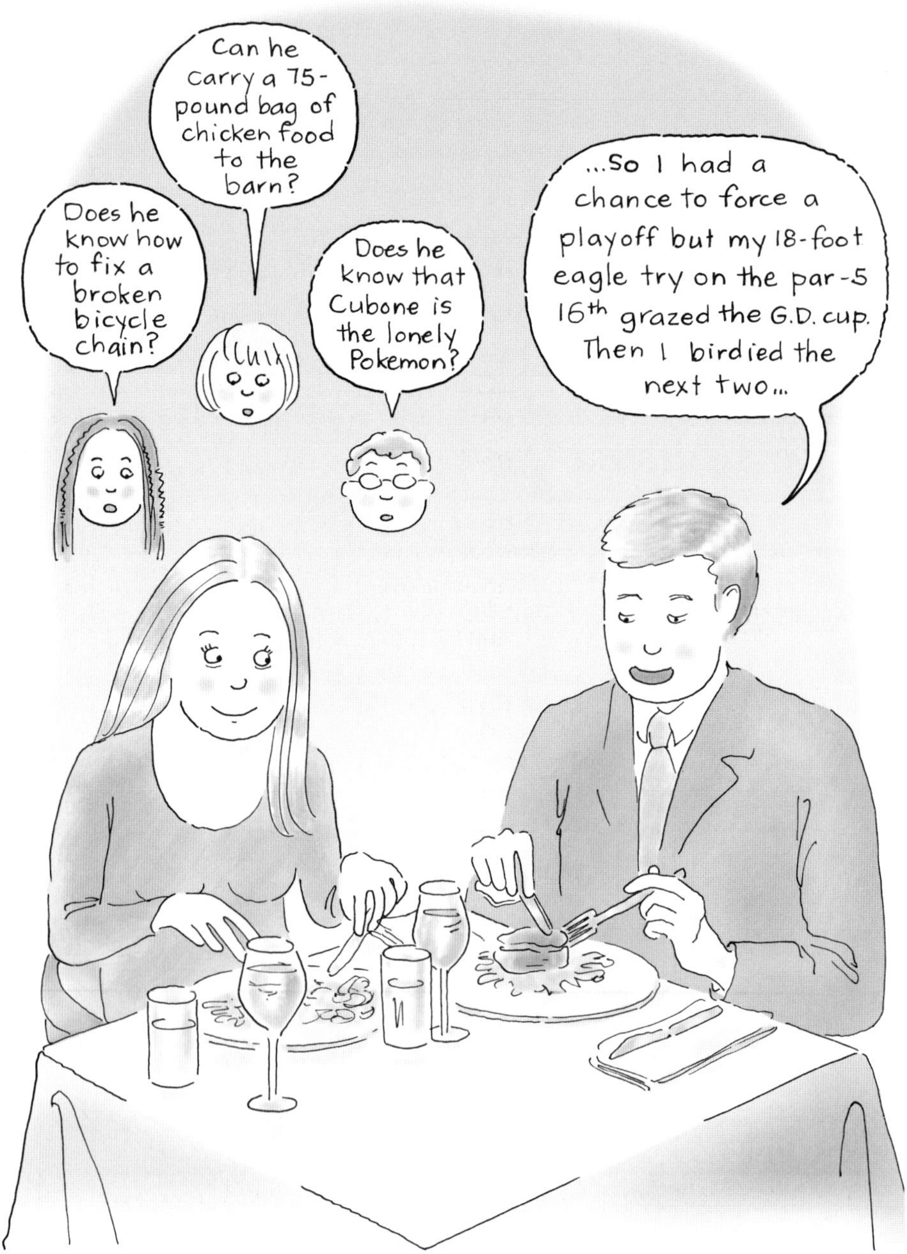
Does he know how to fix a broken bicycle chain?
Can he carry a 75-pound bag of chicken food to the barn?
Does he know that Cubone is the lonely Pokemon?
...So I had a chance to force a playoff but my 18-foot eagle try on the par-5 16th grazed the G.D. cup. Then I birdied the next two...

But the kids weren't as anxious about it as I was. In fact, they weren't anxious at all. They may even have been relieved by the idea that someone else in my life might take a little pressure off of them.

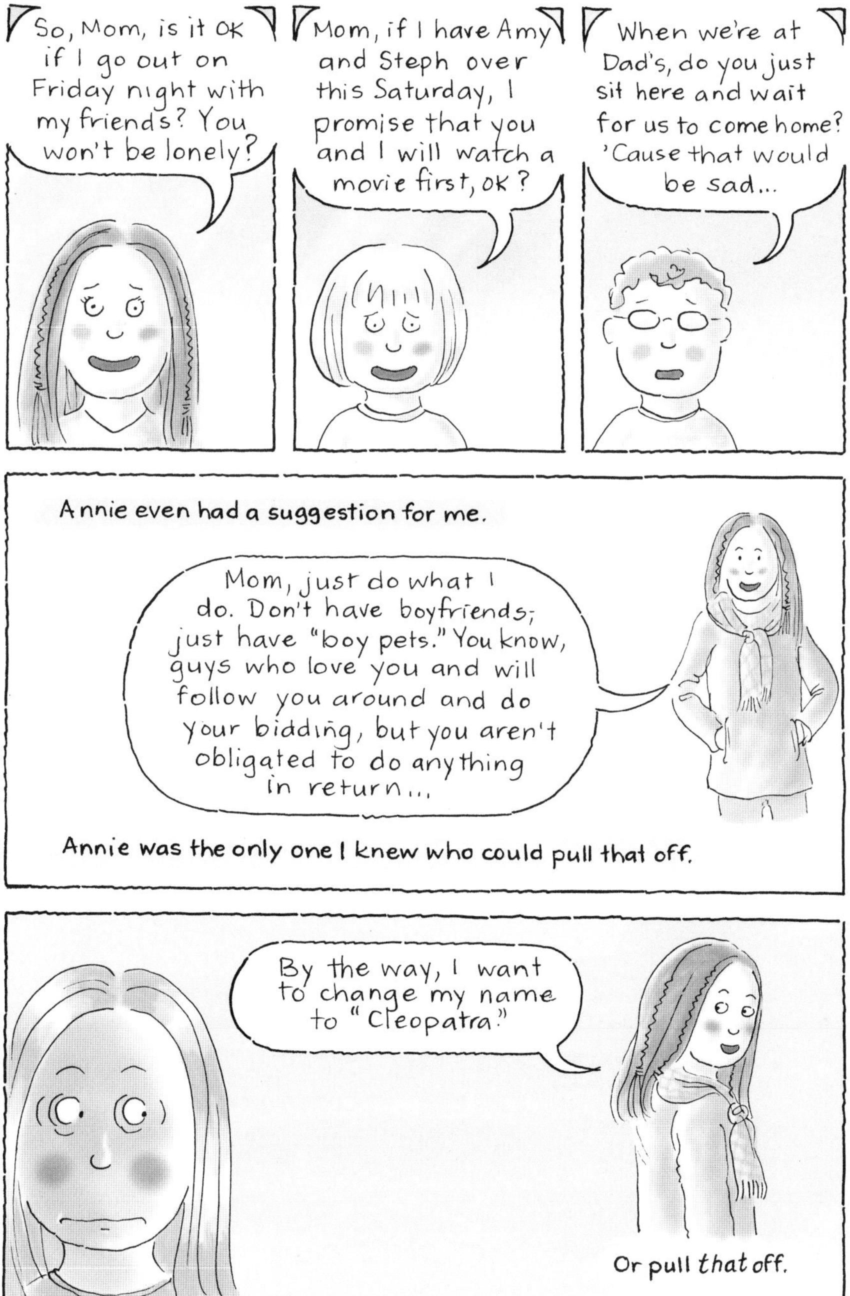
So, Mom, is it OK if I go out on Friday night with my friends? You won't be lonely?
Mom, if I have Amy and Steph over this Saturday, I promise that you and I will watch a movie first, OK?
When we're at Dad's, do you just sit here and wait for us to come home? 'Cause that would be sad...
Annie even had a suggestion for me.
Mom, just do what I do. Don't have boyfriends; just have "boy pets." You know, guys who love you and will follow you around and do your bidding, but you aren't obligated to do anything in return...
Annie was the only one I knew who could pull that off.
By the way, I want to change my name to "Cleopatra."
Or pull *that* off.

The next time I dragged Kate along on a girls' night out, I polled the group.

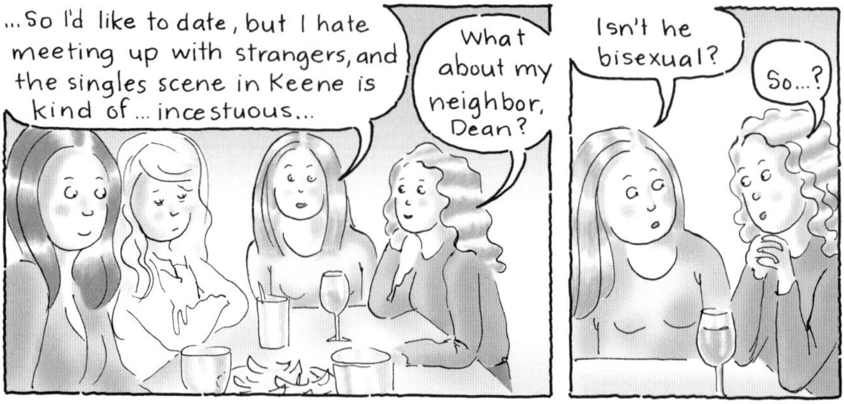
...So I'd like to date, but I hate meeting up with strangers, and the singles scene in Keene is kind of... incestuous...
What about my neighbor, Dean?
Isn't he bisexual?
So...?

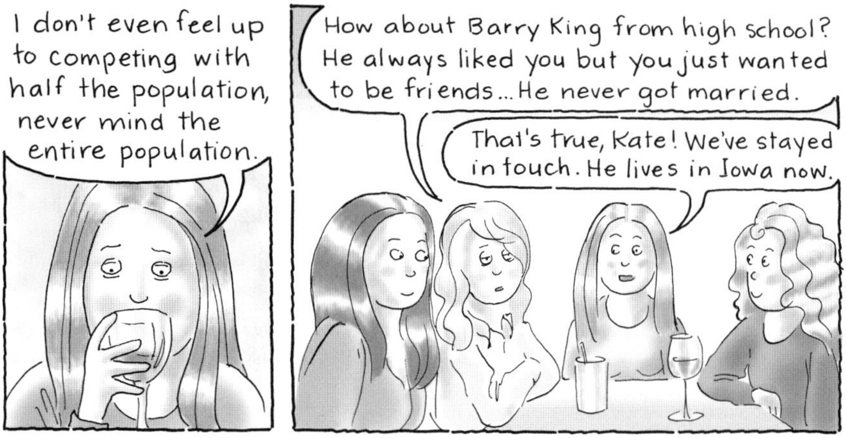
I don't even feel up to competing with half the population, never mind the entire population.
How about Barry King from high school? He always liked you but you just wanted to be friends... He never got married.
That's true, Kate! We've stayed in touch. He lives in Iowa now.

Nostalgia has a way of distorting the past. Why hadn't I liked Barry in *that* way? Had I been too choosy back then? He *was* a nice guy. Maybe not Mr. Excitement, but excitement is overrated. I had been married to it.

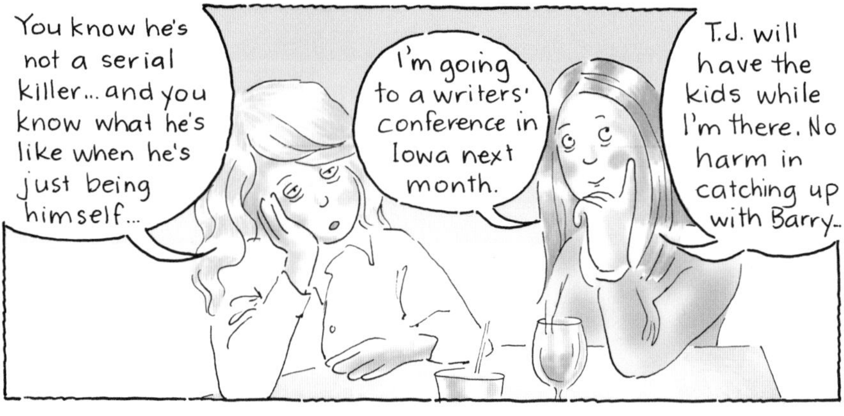
You know he's not a serial killer... and you know what he's like when he's just being himself...
I'm going to a writers' conference in Iowa next month.
T.J. will have the kids while I'm there. No harm in catching up with Barry...

Two decades had passed since I'd seen Barry, so familiarity was more illusion than reality. But when we had dinner that night, I felt a little like I was back in high school, with all of my options open, my life still in front of me. It was an escape from the anxieties and regrets of my real life.

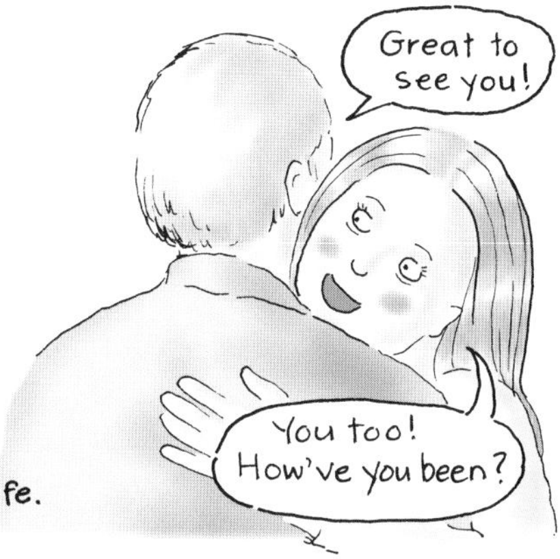
Great to see you!
You too! How've you been?

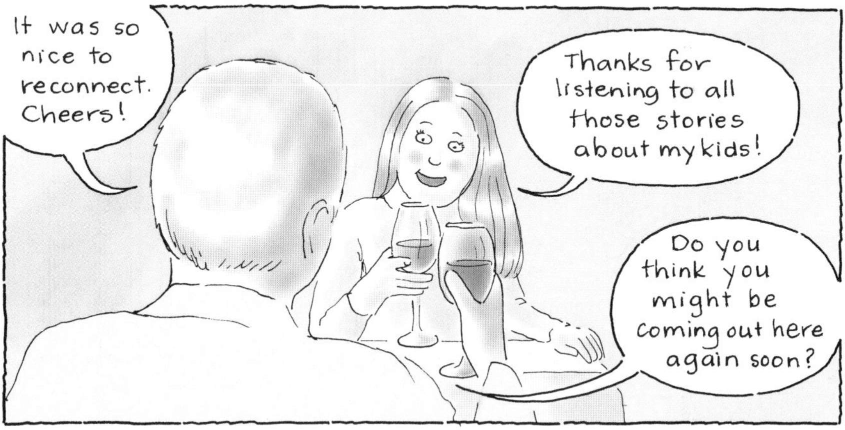
It was so nice to reconnect. Cheers!
Thanks for listening to all those stories about my kids!
Do you think you might be coming out here again soon?

A month later, when T.J. had the kids for another long weekend, I flew out to Iowa again. As we drove to Barry's house from the airport, we talked about old times, then newer ones.

He didn't have too many newer times.

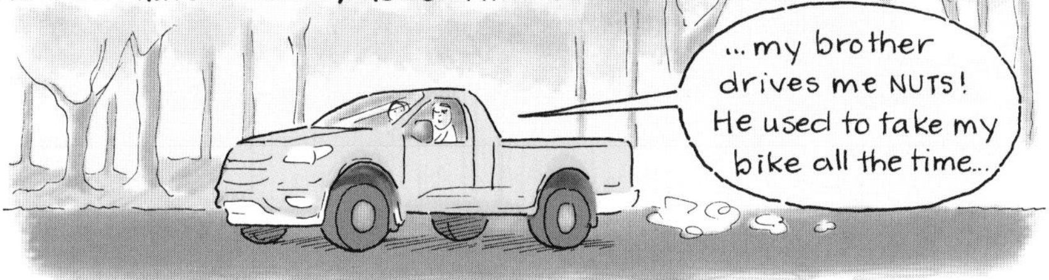
...my brother drives me NUTS! He used to take my bike all the time...

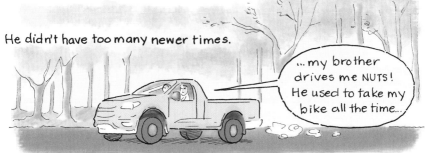

Because he'd never gotten married and had kids, or embarked on adventures or been consumed by passion projects, the years after college appeared to have run together. He had the same engineering job that he'd landed right after graduation.

Barry's scrapbooks — even his mental ones — stopped in about 1981, save for a few photos from vacations with his mother.

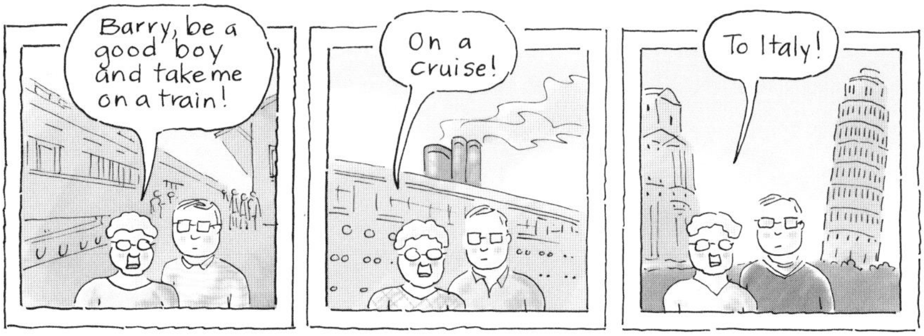
Barry, be a good boy and take me on a train!
On a cruise!
To Italy!

But he was a very sweet person, steady and predictable. He didn't embrace life, he just limply held its hand. If life were a Merry-Go-Round, he would be sitting on one of those benches between the horses that doesn't go up and down. He was everything T.J. wasn't.

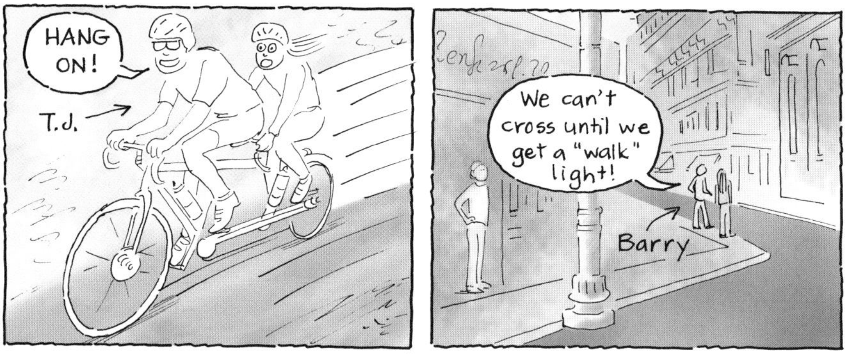
HANG ON!
T.J.
We can't cross until we get a "walk" light!
Barry

So every other month, when the kids were with T.J. for a few days, I would visit him.

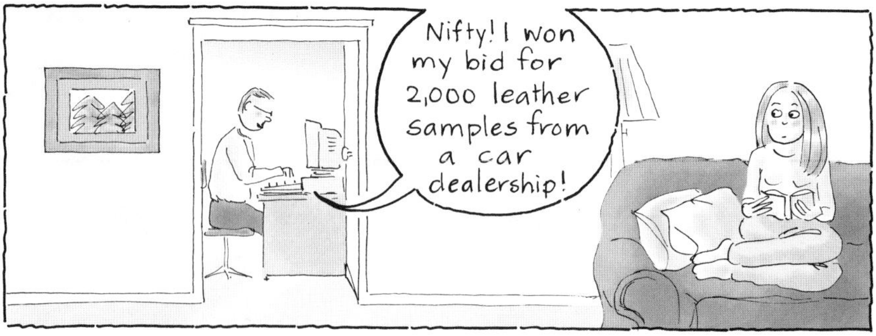
Nifty! I won my bid for 2,000 leather samples from a car dealership!

He took me out to eat at places that served boar and buffalo. He ordered stuff on eBay and played war games on the computer while I read.

After an emotionally exhausting year, I was content with this old person version of our relationship from high school.

But sometimes his place was so quiet and calm that I wanted to shoot myself. I played a mental game of Barry Bingo for my own amusement.

Phone call from his mother asking if I'm "still there"	Reference to something that happened in high school	One-sided conversation about why Medieval: Total War is the best computer game ever	Advice about raising kids, circa 1972	
Awkward silence following phone call from his mother		Going-out-to-dinner plans morph into me going out and getting him a Double Whopper	Phone call to his mother reassuring her that I'm not after his money	Lesson on proper placement of utensils in kitchen drawer
Critical sporting event on TV, likely involving cheerleaders	Comment about hrs girlfriend from high school and how big her chest was	FREE SPACE	Civil War factoid	Email from his mother reminding him how much he likes his freedom and independence
Weather prediction based on frequent visits to the Weather Channel rather than time spent outside		Merits of firearms discussion	Complaint about the humidity or the Democrats	Fried spam for lunch
Oddly timed nap ZZZ	Recollection of summers spent at his grandfather's farm in Georgia	Faith Hill or Shania Twain debate	Explanation of how he likes his grocery bags organized	

After I'd been out to see him a few times, Barry flew to New Hampshire; he wanted to meet the kids. Despite the fact that we struggled to be on our best behavior, Barry seemed overwhelmed by the four of us. Watching him maneuver awkwardly in my world was eye opening.

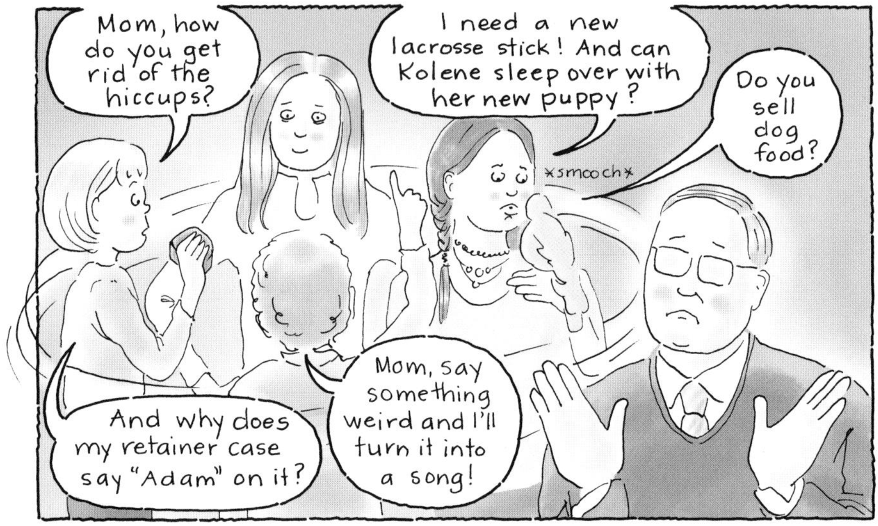
Mom, how do you get rid of the hiccups?
I need a new lacrosse stick! And can Kolene sleep over with her new puppy?
smooch
Do you sell dog food?
And why does my retainer case say "Adam" on it?
Mom, say something weird and I'll turn it into a song!

After he headed back to Iowa, I casually tried to gauge the kids' reactions.

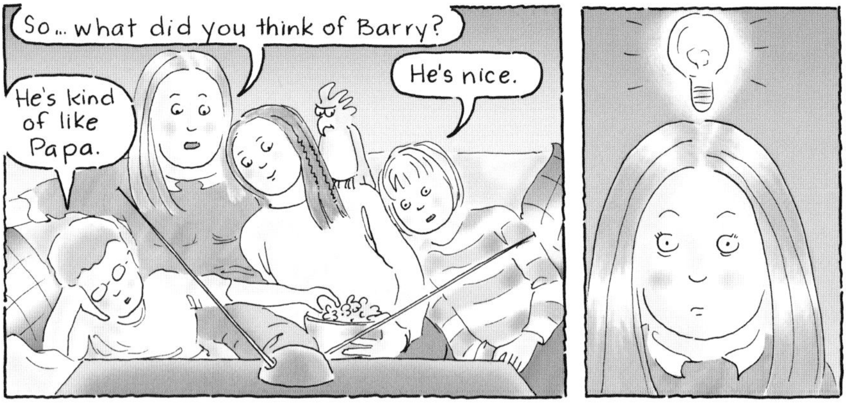
So... what did you think of Barry?
He's nice.
He's kind of like Papa.

And as soon as he said it, I realized that Jack was right. The kind, even-tempered, dependable guy who was always sitting by the phone waiting for my call reminded me of my dad—without the unconditional love and funny stories about my childhood. When I was with Barry, I felt safe. But comfort isn't any basis for a permanent relationship.

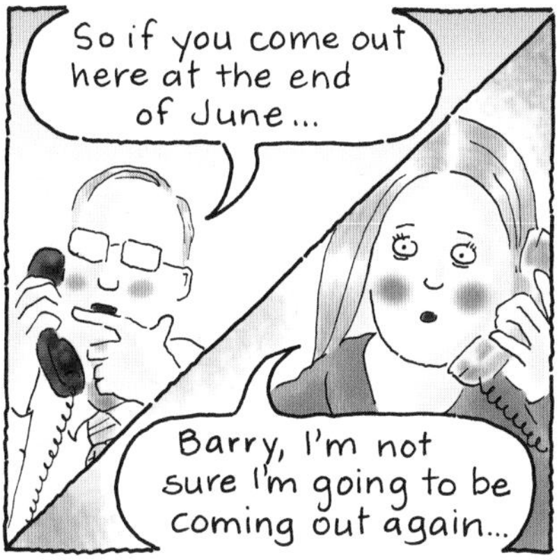
So if you come out here at the end of June...
Barry, I'm not sure I'm going to be coming out again...

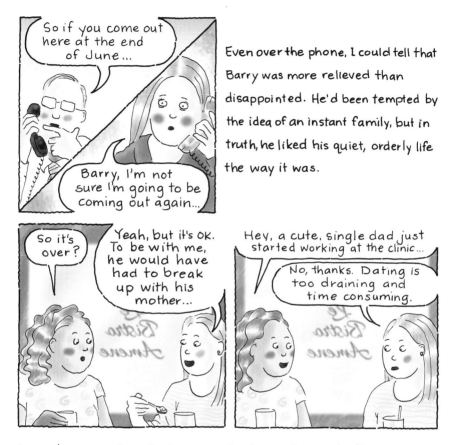

Even over the phone, I could tell that Barry was more relieved than disappointed. He'd been tempted by the idea of an instant family, but in truth, he liked his quiet, orderly life the way it was.

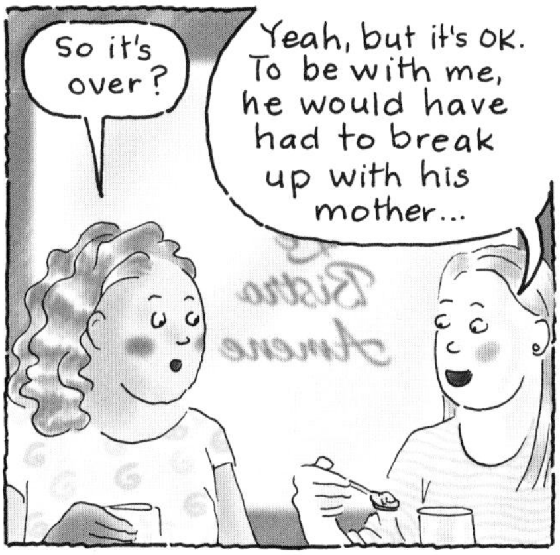
So it's over?
Yeah, but it's OK. To be with me, he would have had to break up with his mother...

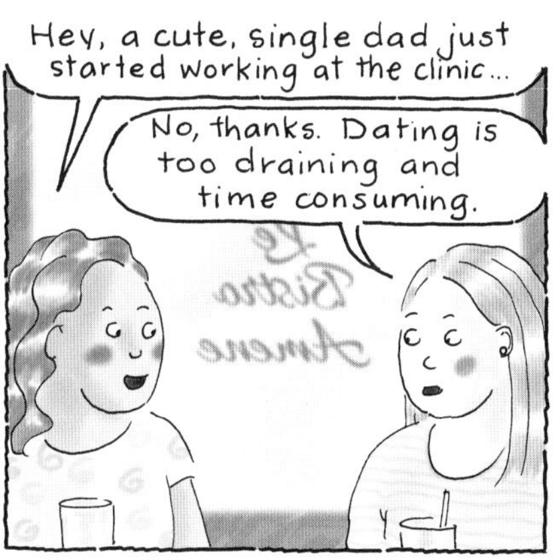
Hey, a cute, single dad just started working at the clinic...
No, thanks. Dating is too draining and time consuming.

I was done searching for the prince holding that second glass slipper. It didn't feel like a productive use of my time. If the perfect guy happened to cross my path, that was one thing. But I wasn't going to go out of my way to cross someone else's path.

Just as I gave up, Ross gave in.

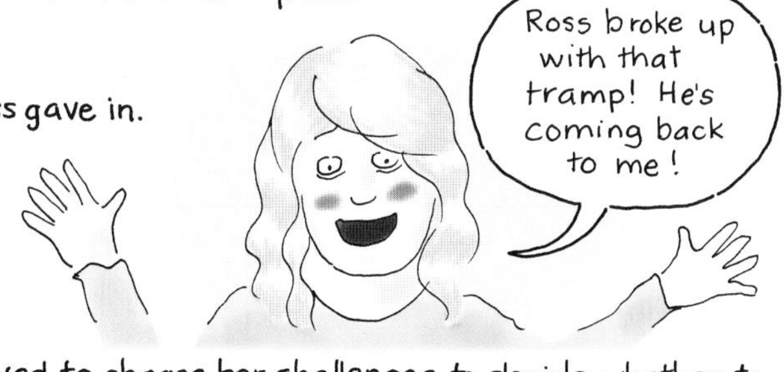
Ross broke up with that tramp! He's coming back to me!

Every woman is allowed to choose her challenges, to decide whether to stay and fight for the relationship or to leave and make a fresh start. Where some see grounds for divorce, others see grounds for working harder to stay married.

A New Year

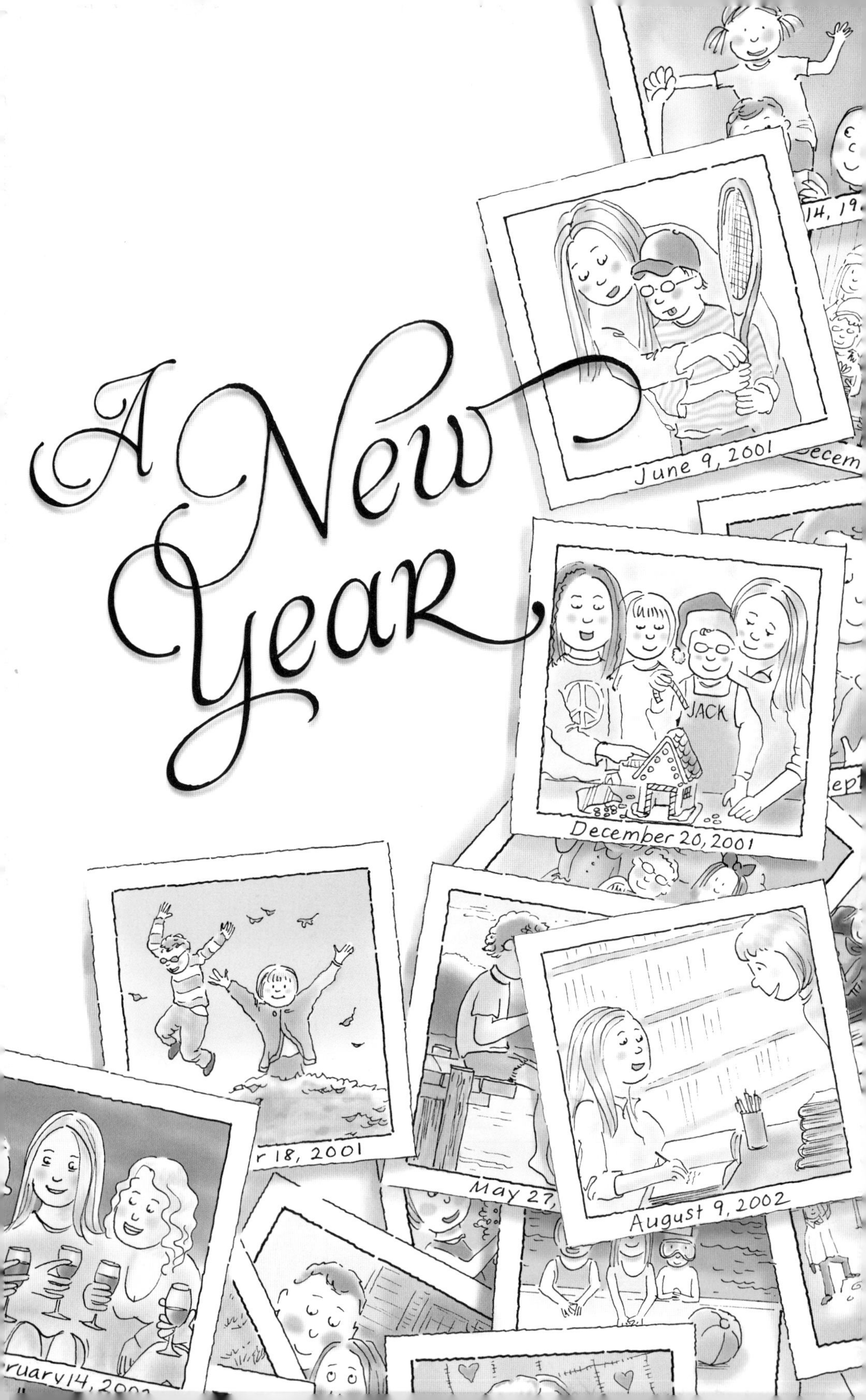

June 9, 2001
JACK
December 20, 2001
August 9, 2002

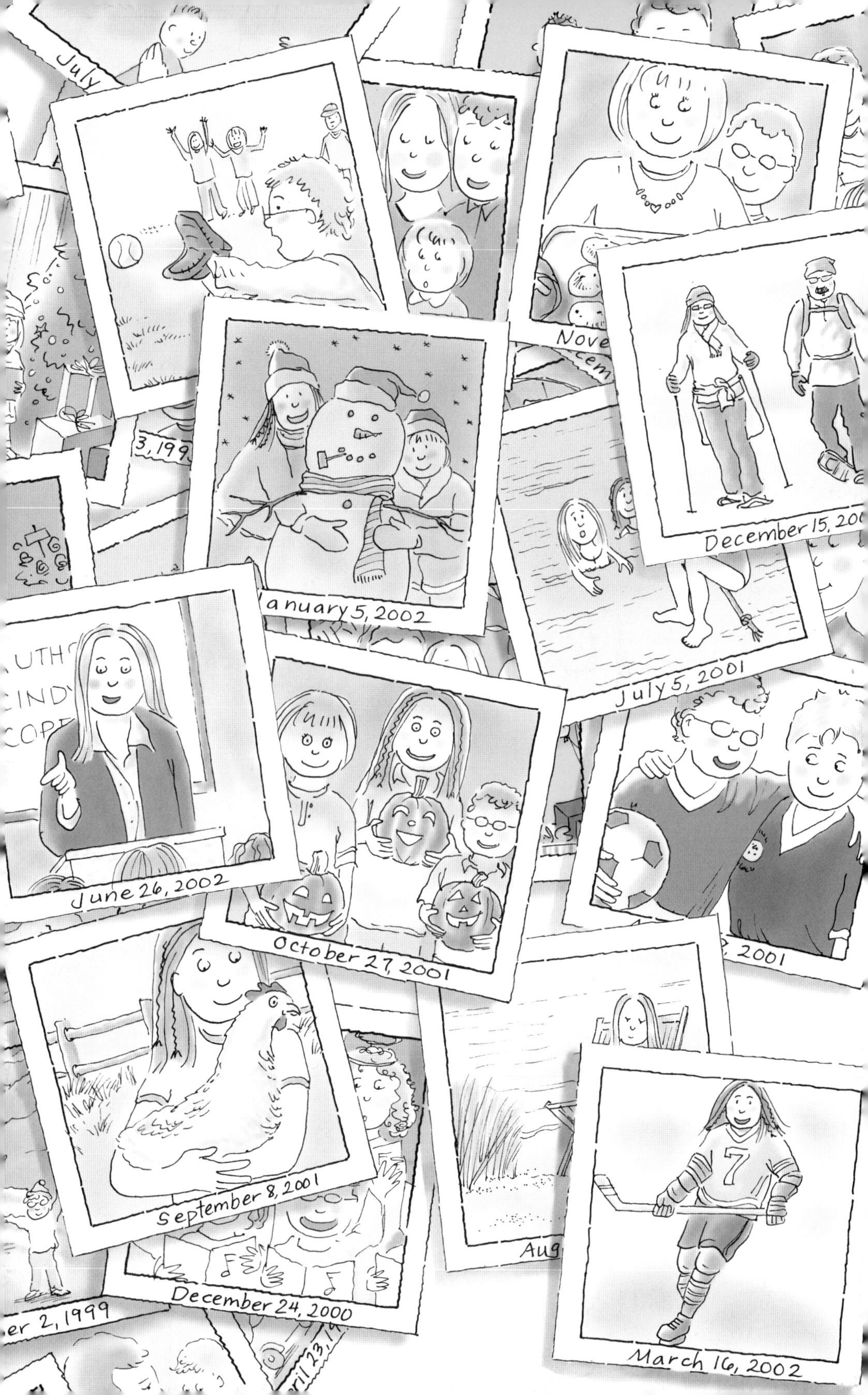
July
3, 199
Nove
cem
December 15, 20
January 5, 2002
July 5, 2001
June 26, 2002
October 27, 2001
2, 2001
September 8, 2001
Aug
December 24, 2000
er 2, 1999
March 16, 2002

I turned my attention away from men and toward my book projects. Recently, one of my books had been recommended by Ann Landers, selected for Oprah's "O List," and read aloud on T.V. by Regis Philbin!

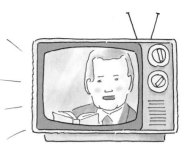

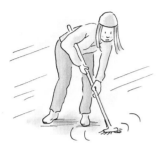

I had more time to write now because I'd stopped parenting like the sweeper on a curling team, furiously cleaning the ice sheet to create a perfectly smooth path for my children. It had exhausted me, and hadn't been helpful for them.

Annie, Emma, and Jack were bouncing admirably over the bumps. I'd noticed that they were actually reaping some benefits from going between two households. Because T.J.'s was not child-centered, they were forced to become more flexible and independent.

Here's Bunny Car... I'll dim the light and turn your fan on low...
me
My cousin is sleeping in your room, so you'll have to sleep on the couch. Ignore his dogs. They're friendly... but don't look directly at them.
T.J.

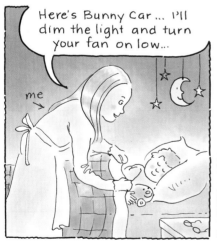

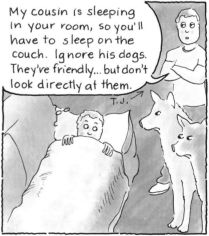

Not only did they learn to fall asleep anywhere and make a meal out of whatever was in T.J.'s refrigerator, they learned to fend for themselves and watch out for each other. They developed a much stronger bond because of their common experiences. They were Team Stewart.

The school year was coming to an end. I sent off the first draft of my new book, Annie started packing for a trip to tag loons in the Vermont wilderness, and Jack pledged to read 30 books over the summer (29 of which he would probably read the last week in August). Emma and I headed to our final parent/child book club.

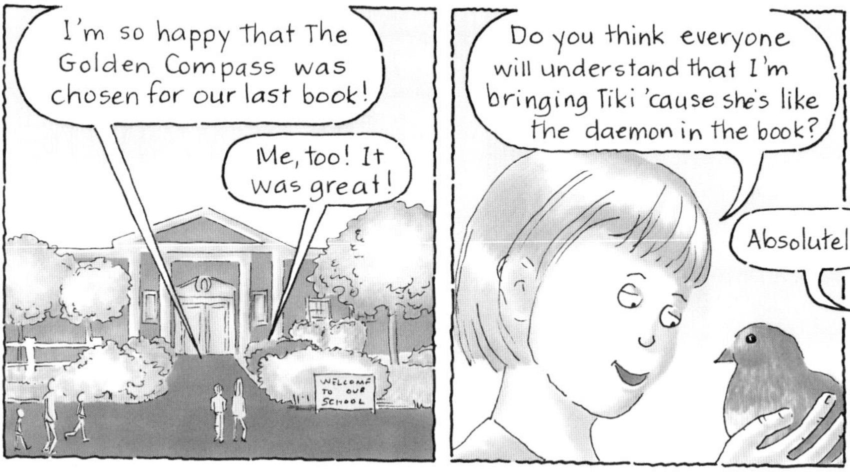
I'm so happy that The Golden Compass was chosen for our last book!
Me, too! It was great!
WELCOME TO OUR SCHOOL
Do you think everyone will understand that I'm bringing Tiki 'cause she's like the daemon in the book?
Absolutely!

Betsy, that month's leader, made an appropriate fuss over the pigeon before launching into the book discussion. Because it was our last meeting, everyone was more subdued than usual. Even Will, a former English teacher who often went back and forth with Emma on a book's merit, was unusually quiet.

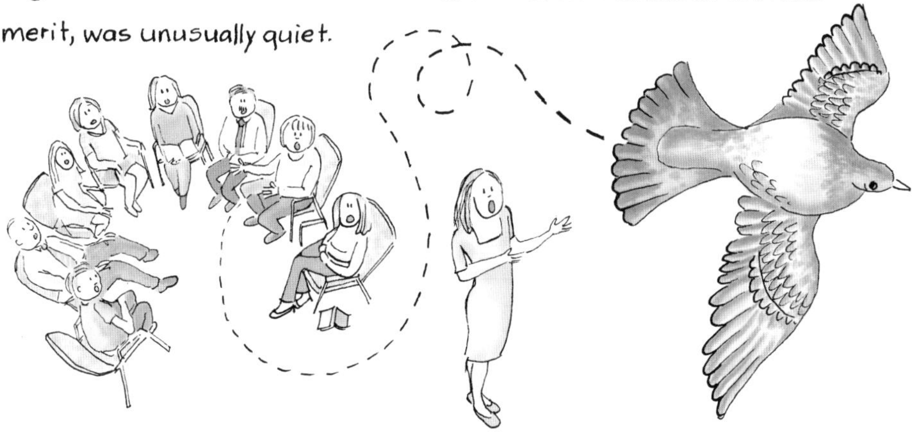

As Betsy stood abruptly to signal the end of the meeting, Tiki was startled out of her pigeon nap. She fluttered out of Emma's hands, flapped up to the ceiling, and landed on a fluorescent light fixture.

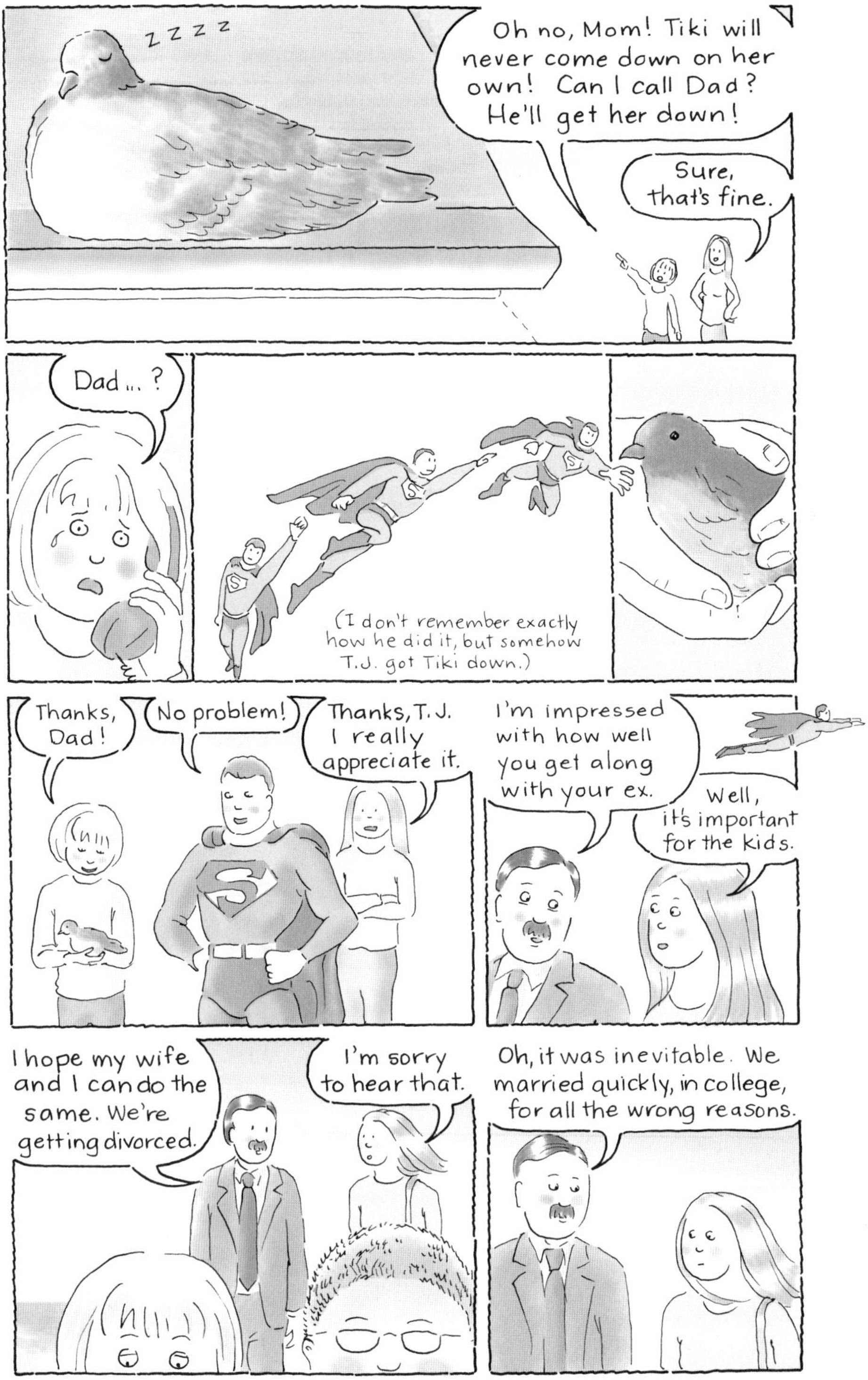
Z Z Z Z
Oh no, Mom! Tiki will never come down on her own! Can I call Dad? He'll get her down!
Sure, that's fine.
Dad... ?
(I don't remember exactly how he did it, but somehow T.J. got Tiki down.)
Thanks, Dad!
No problem!
Thanks, T.J. I really appreciate it.
I'm impressed with how well you get along with your ex.
Well, it's important for the kids.
I hope my wife and I can do the same. We're getting divorced.
I'm sorry to hear that.
Oh, it was inevitable. We married quickly, in college, for all the wrong reasons.

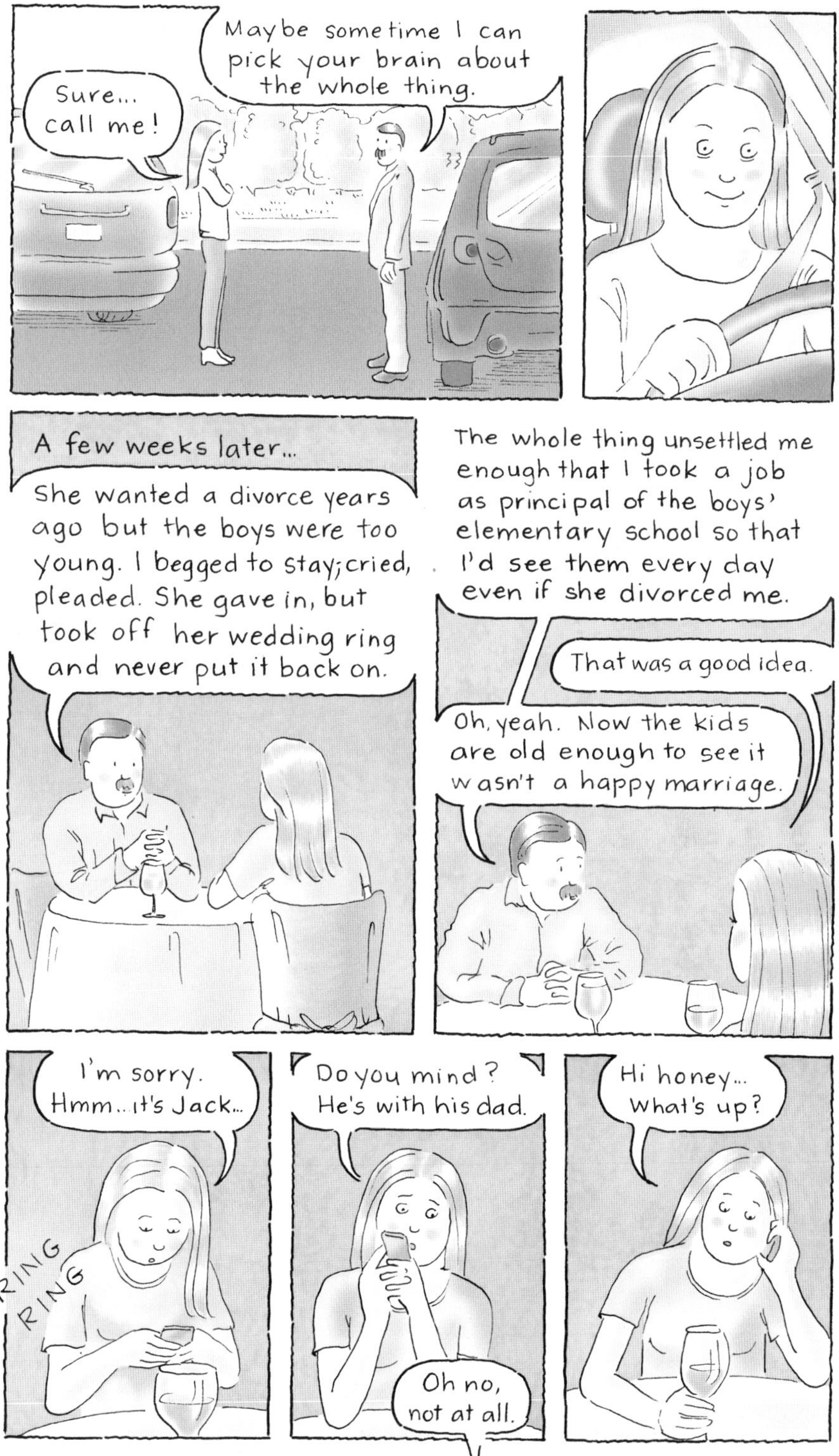
Maybe sometime I can pick your brain about the whole thing.
Sure... call me!
A few weeks later...
She wanted a divorce years ago but the boys were too young. I begged to stay; cried, pleaded. She gave in, but took off her wedding ring and never put it back on.
The whole thing unsettled me enough that I took a job as principal of the boys' elementary school so that I'd see them every day even if she divorced me.
That was a good idea.
Oh, yeah. Now the kids are old enough to see it wasn't a happy marriage.
I'm sorry. Hmm...it's Jack...
RING RING
Do you mind? He's with his dad.
Oh no, not at all.
Hi honey... What's up?

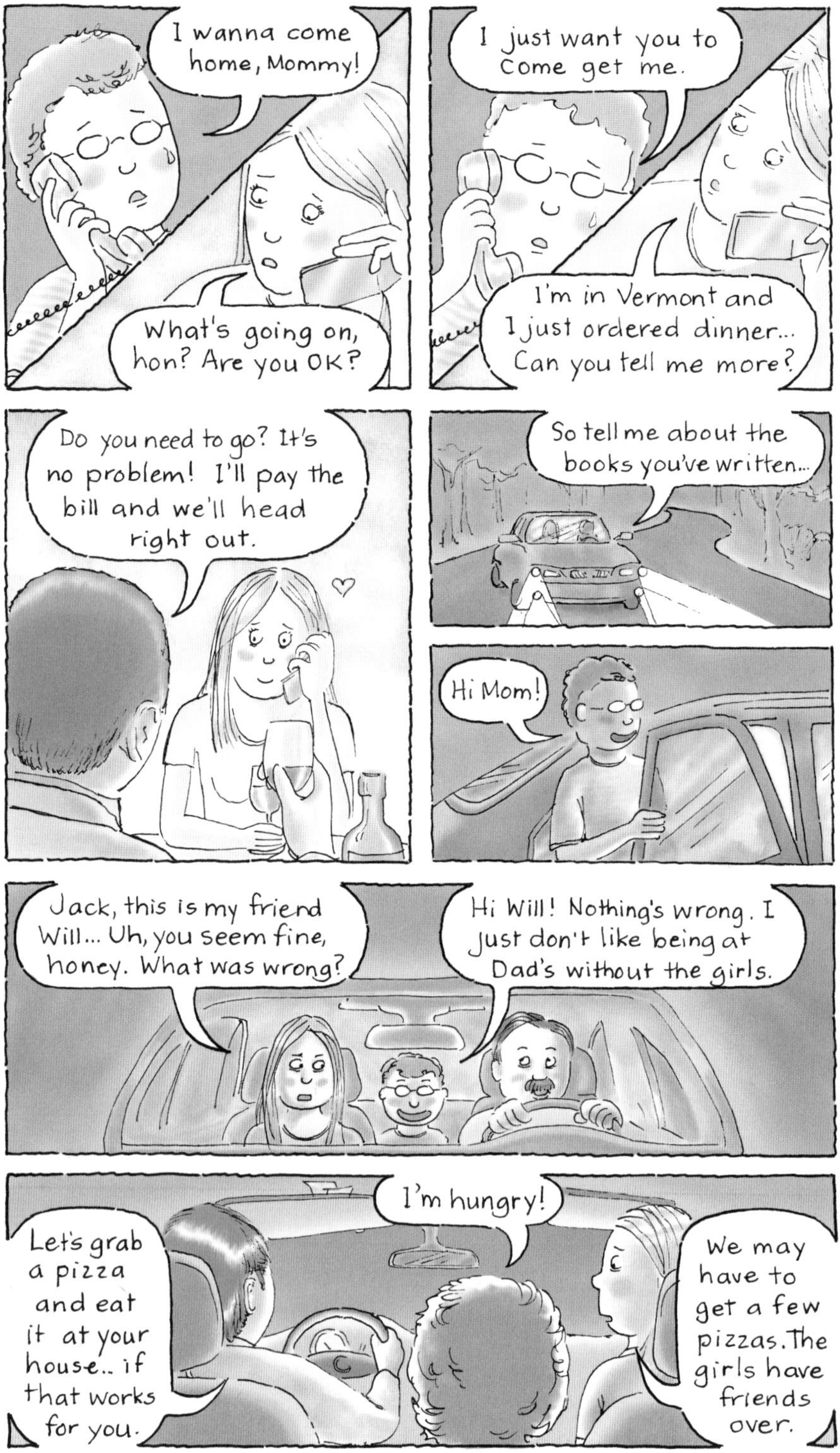
I wanna come home, Mommy!
What's going on, hon? Are you OK?
I just want you to come get me.
I'm in Vermont and I just ordered dinner... Can you tell me more?
Do you need to go? It's no problem! I'll pay the bill and we'll head right out.
So tell me about the books you've written...
Hi Mom!
Jack, this is my friend Will... Uh, you seem fine, honey. What was wrong?
Hi Will! Nothing's wrong. I just don't like being at Dad's without the girls.
I'm hungry!
Let's grab a pizza and eat it at your house.. if that works for you.
We may have to get a few pizzas. The girls have friends over.

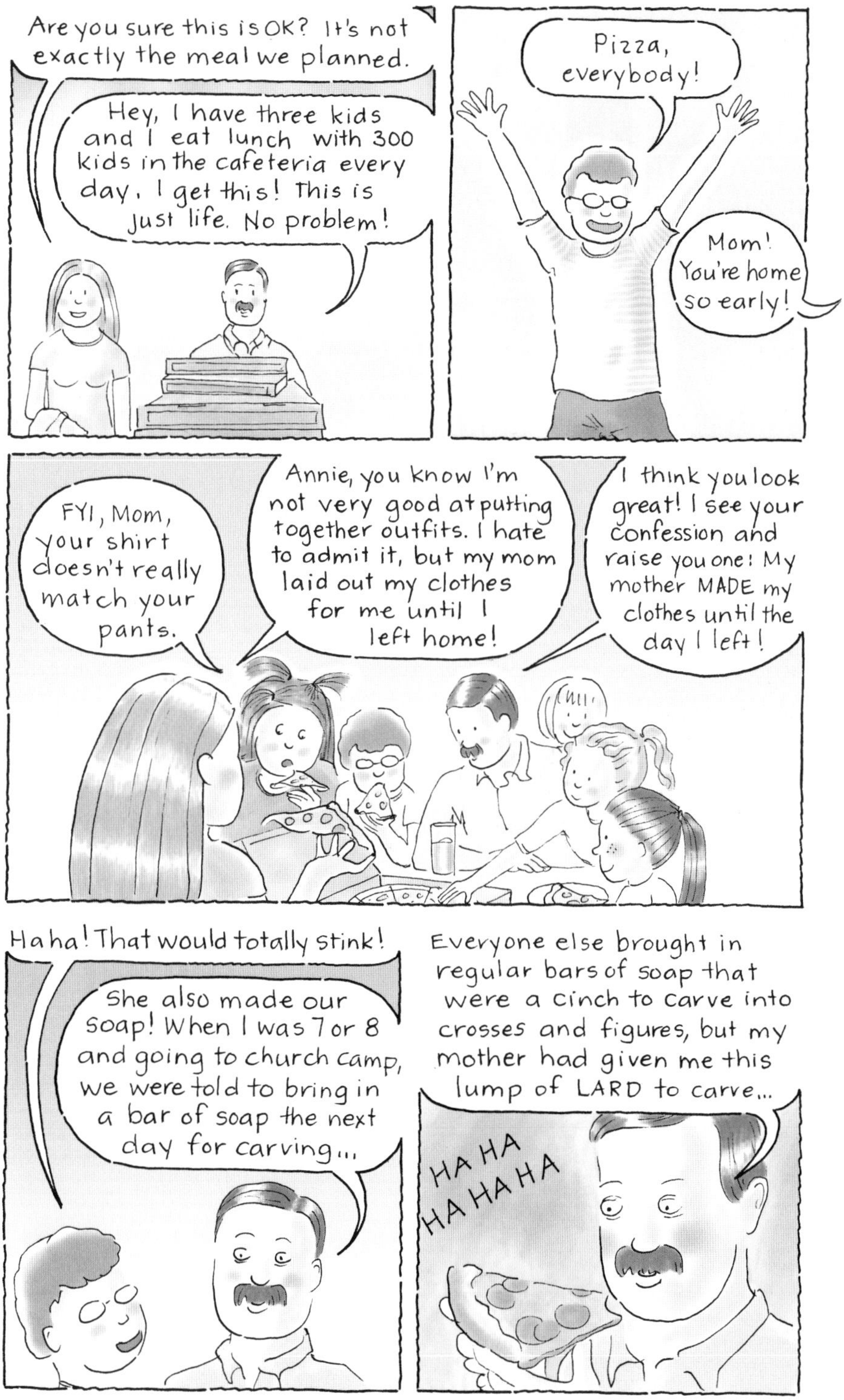
Are you sure this is OK? It's not exactly the meal we planned.
Hey, I have three kids and I eat lunch with 300 kids in the cafeteria every day. I get this! This is just life. No problem!
Pizza, everybody!
Mom! You're home so early!
FYI, Mom, your shirt doesn't really match your pants.
Annie, you know I'm not very good at putting together outfits. I hate to admit it, but my mom laid out my clothes for me until I left home!
I think you look great! I see your confession and raise you one: My mother MADE my clothes until the day I left!
Ha ha! That would totally stink!
She also made our soap! When I was 7 or 8 and going to church camp, we were told to bring in a bar of soap the next day for carving...
Everyone else brought in regular bars of soap that were a cinch to carve into crosses and figures, but my mother had given me this lump of LARD to carve...
HA HA HA HA HA

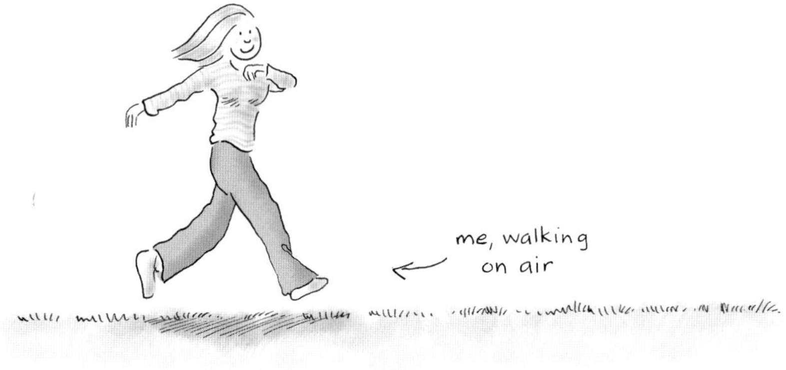
me, walking
on air

Sometimes it takes a while before you know that someone is right for you.
Sometimes it takes no time at all.

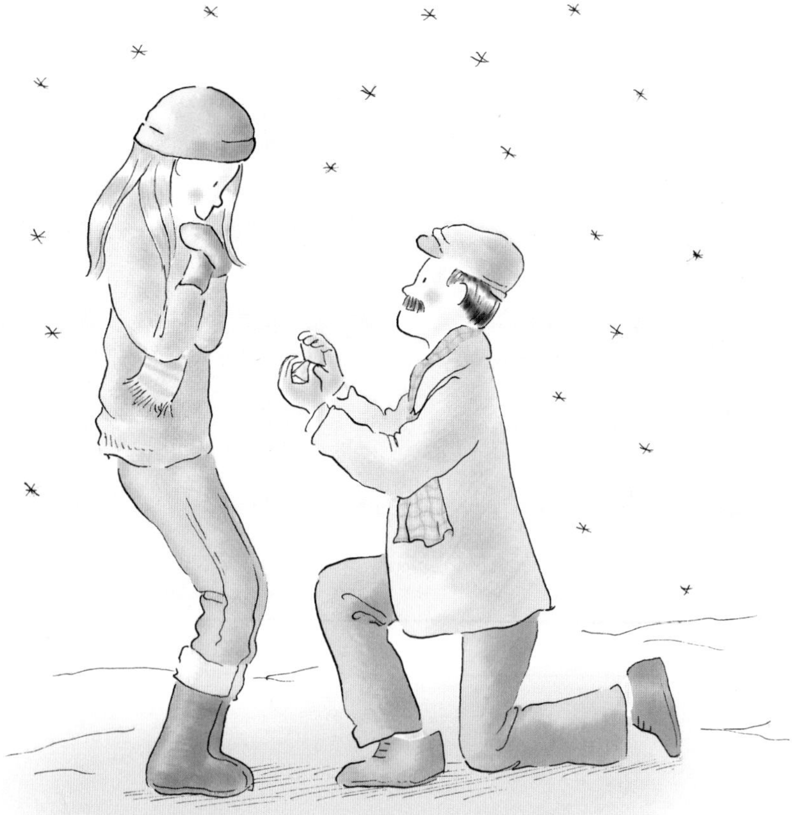

Will and I returned from a honeymoon in Hawaii with high hopes for our blended family. But knowing nothing about second marriages (other than what we had seen on TV), we were ill prepared for the messy world of steps and exes. Our Brady Bunch expectations did not line up with our Addams Family reality.

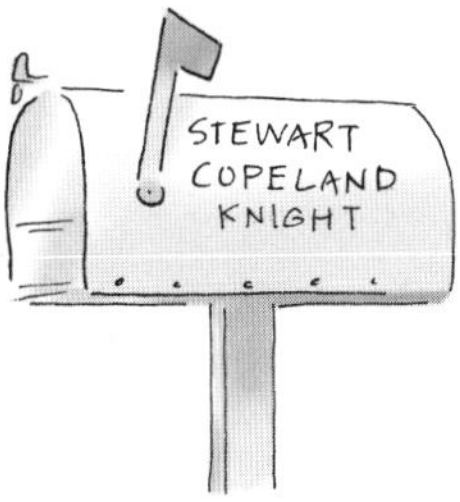
STEWART
COPELAND
KNIGHT

Among the curious assortment of people who constituted our inner circle were many who weren't exactly raising glasses and toasting our union...

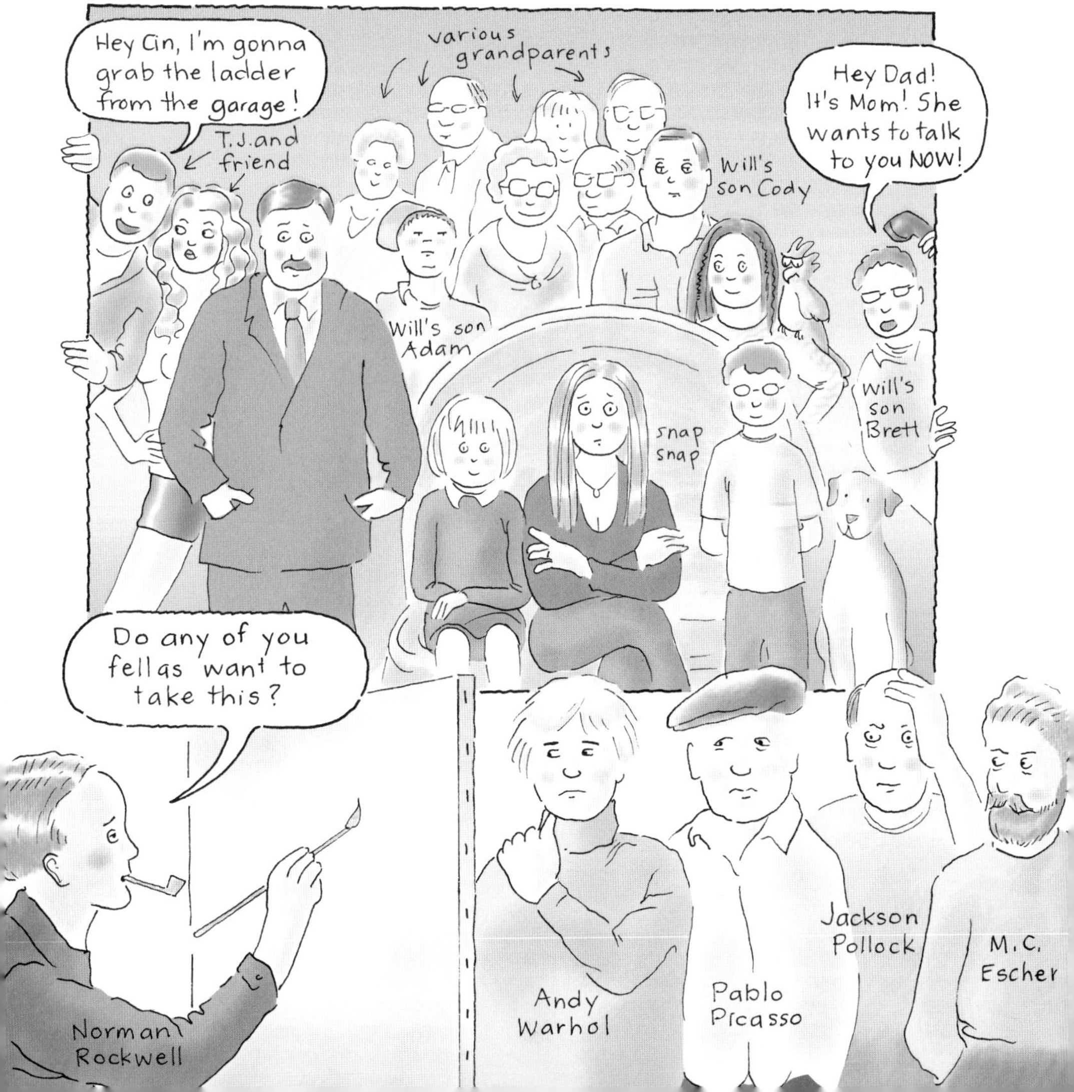
Hey Cin, I'm gonna grab the ladder from the garage!
T.J. and friend
various grandparents
Will's son Cody
Hey Dad! It's Mom! She wants to talk to you NOW!
Will's son Adam
snap snap
Will's son Brett
Do any of you fellas want to take this?
Norman Rockwell
Andy Warhol
Pablo Picasso
Jackson Pollock
M.C. Escher

Will and I struggled to find common ground. Everything—from our bank accounts to our kids—was either his or hers; nothing was ours.

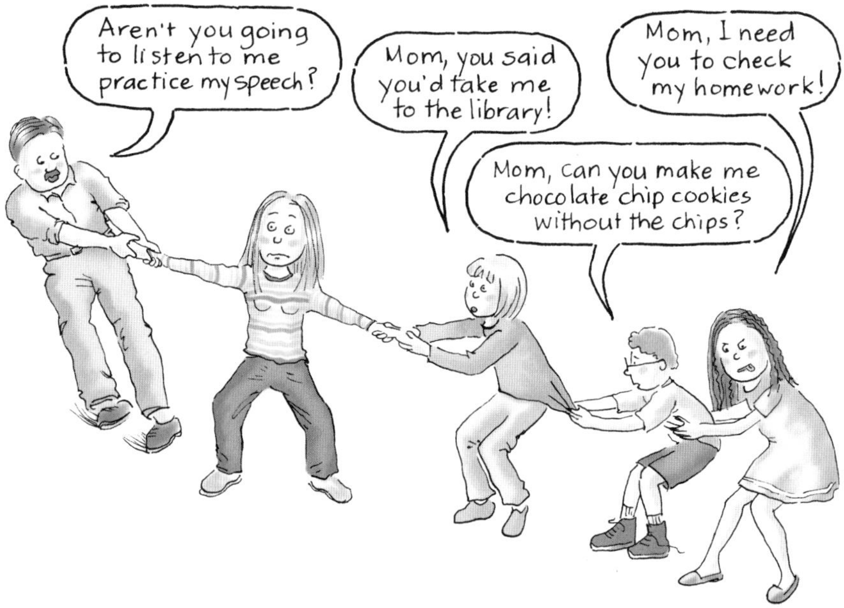
Aren't you going to listen to me practice my speech?
Mom, you said you'd take me to the library!
Mom, I need you to check my homework!
Mom, can you make me chocolate chip cookies without the chips?

Secretly, each of us felt a stronger bond with our biological children than we did with each other. It was a daily tug of war.

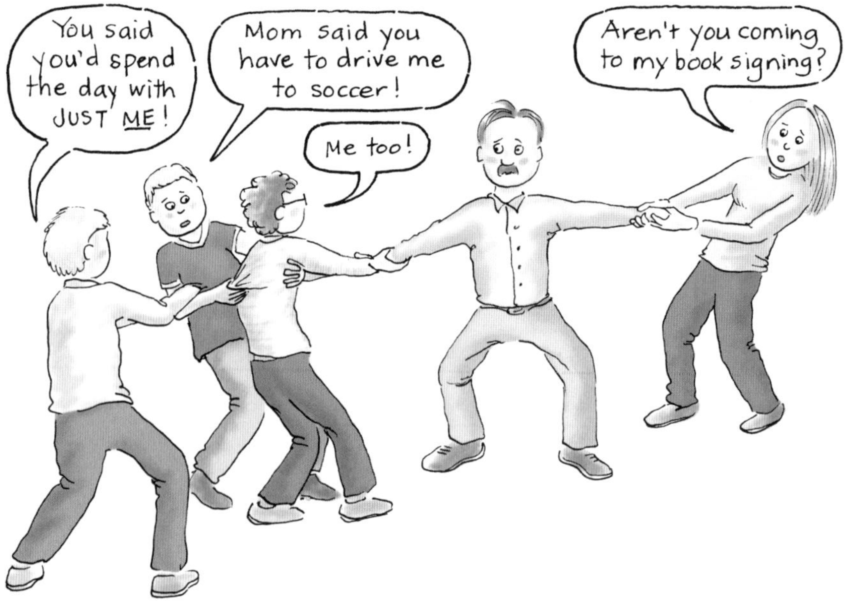
You said you'd spend the day with JUST ME!
Mom said you have to drive me to soccer!
Me too!
Aren't you coming to my book signing?

Will was afraid that once he gave up his apartment and moved in with me, his boys would be hesitant to visit him. So he threw out an exorbitant, indulgent welcome mat.

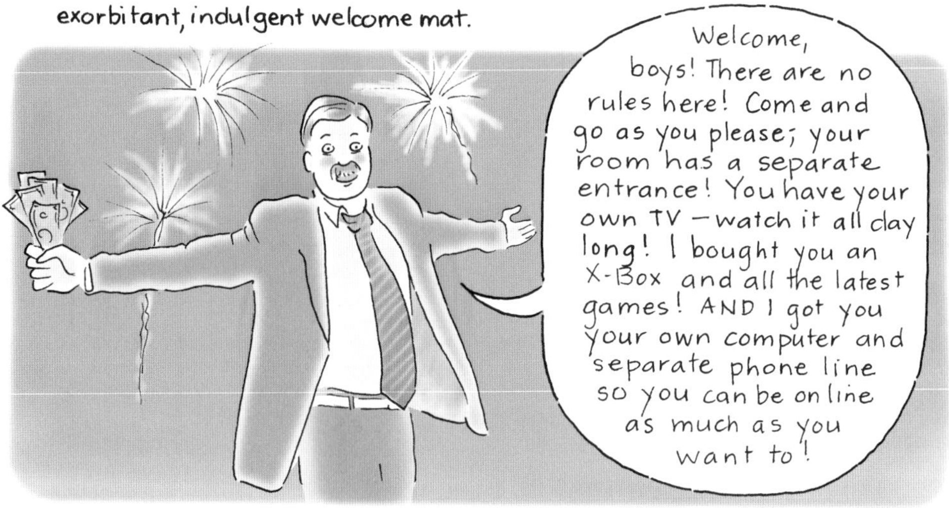
Welcome, boys! There are no rules here! Come and go as you please; your room has a separate entrance! You have your own TV — watch it all day long! I bought you an X-Box and all the latest games! AND I got you your own computer and separate phone line so you can be on line as much as you want to!

I was overwhelmed and baffled by teenage boys and everything that came with them:

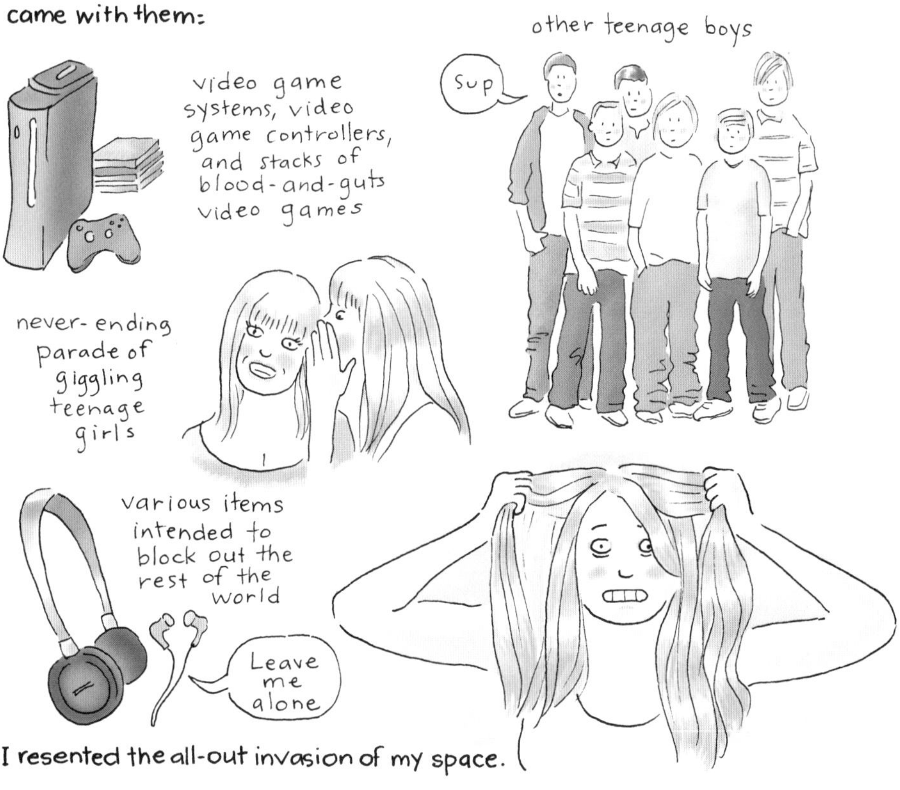
video game systems, video game controllers, and stacks of blood-and-guts video games
other teenage boys
Sup
never-ending parade of giggling teenage girls
various items intended to block out the rest of the world
Leave me alone

I resented the all-out invasion of my space.

Desperate to maintain some kind of control over my nest, I pushed back with the house rules that I'd had in place for years.

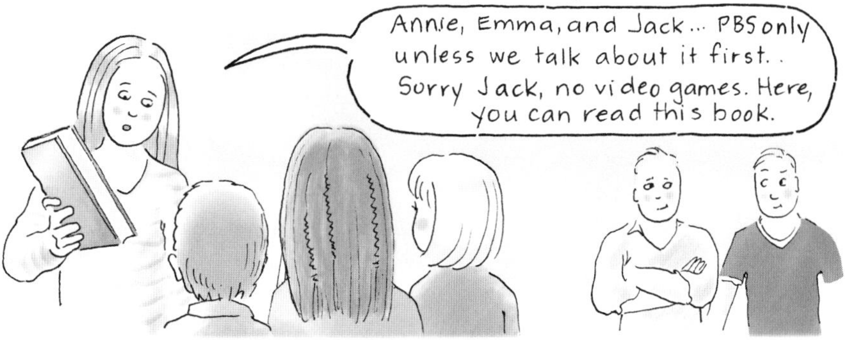
Annie, Emma, and Jack... PBS only unless we talk about it first.. Sorry Jack, no video games. Here, you can read this book.

It wasn't just the kids who came between us. We each spent more time placating our ex-spouses than the other one would have liked.

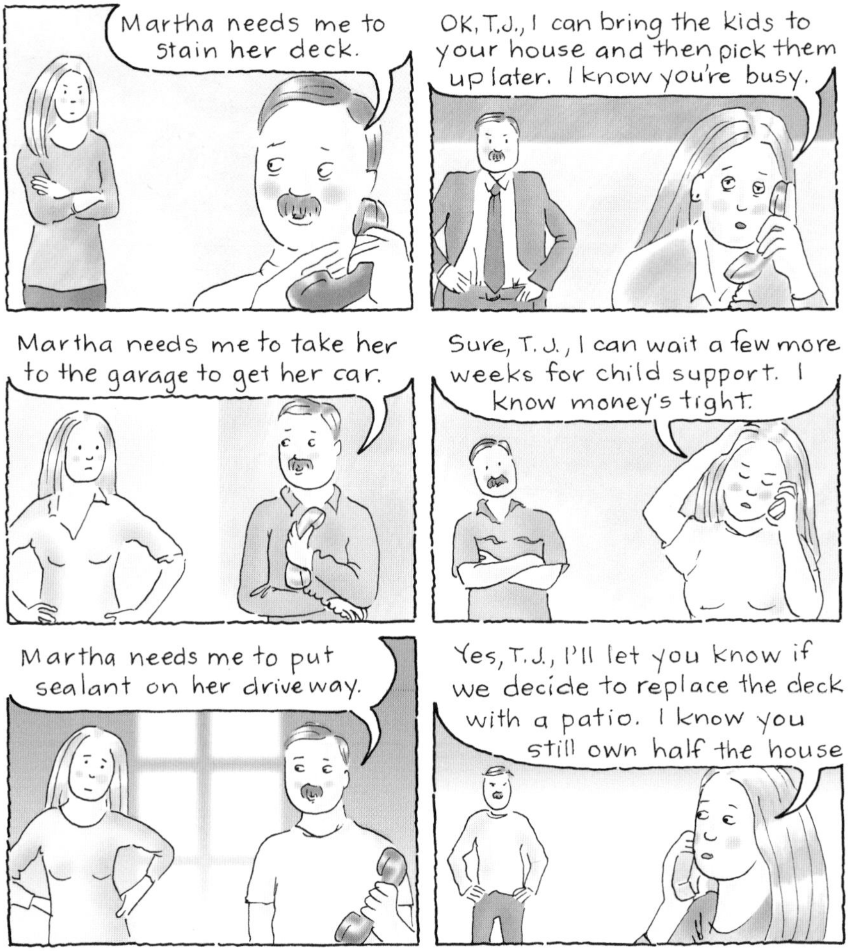
Martha needs me to stain her deck.
OK, T.J., I can bring the kids to your house and then pick them up later. I know you're busy.
Martha needs me to take her to the garage to get her car.
Sure, T.J., I can wait a few more weeks for child support. I know money's tight.
Martha needs me to put sealant on her driveway.
Yes, T.J., I'll let you know if we decide to replace the deck with a patio. I know you still own half the house

But despite the rocky start, there were signs that things would work out, if only we could hang on for the ride.

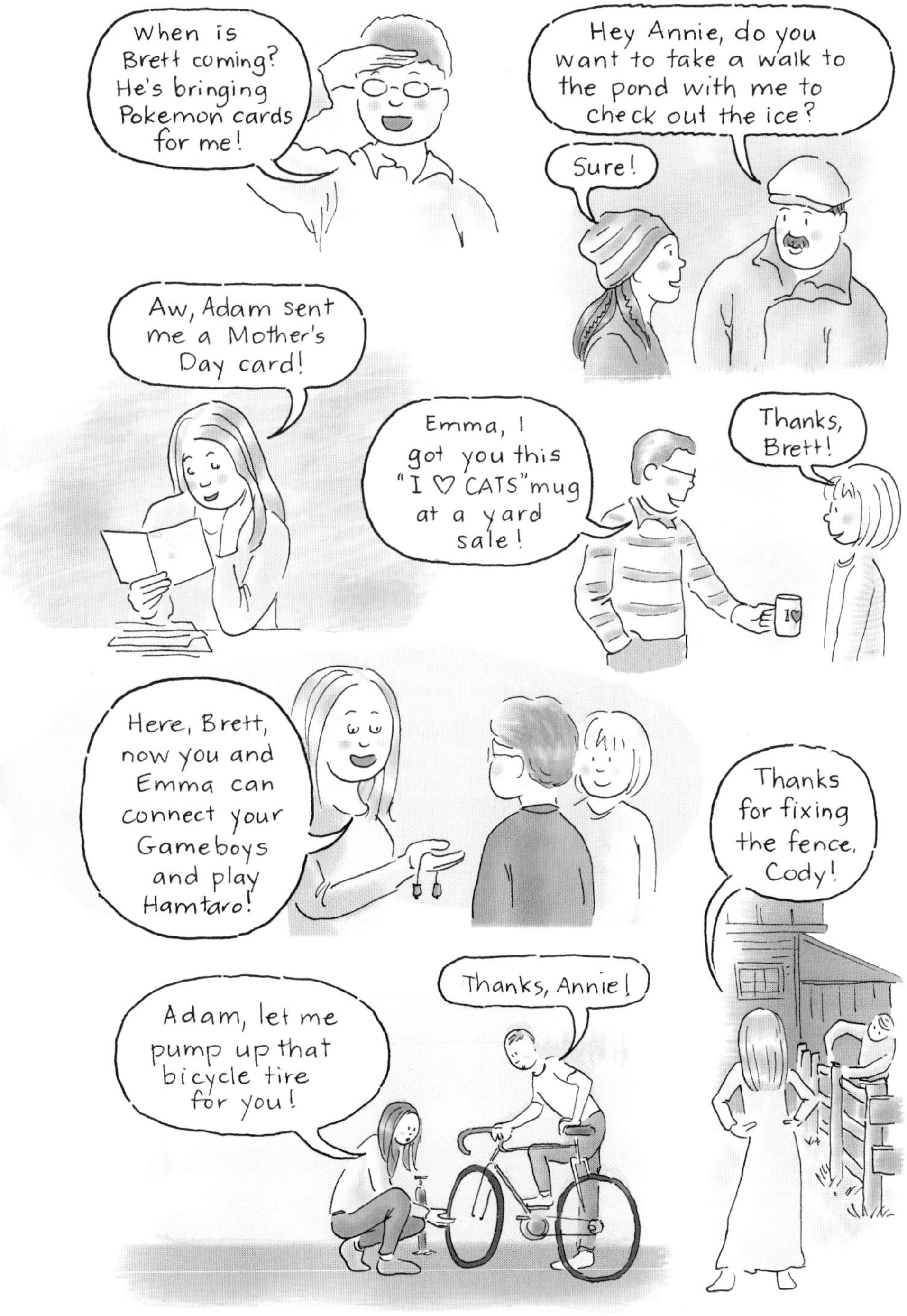
When is Brett coming? He's bringing Pokemon cards for me!
Hey Annie, do you want to take a walk to the pond with me to check out the ice?
Sure!
Aw, Adam sent me a Mother's Day card!
Emma, I got you this "I ♡ CATS" mug at a yard sale!
Thanks, Brett!
Here, Brett, now you and Emma can connect your Gameboys and play Hamtaro!
Thanks for fixing the fence, Cody!
Adam, let me pump up that bicycle tire for you!
Thanks, Annie!

Once in a while, Will and I got away by ourselves. In a second marriage, you're more respectful of the frailty of relationships and more aware that a marriage needs daily nurturing and tending to.

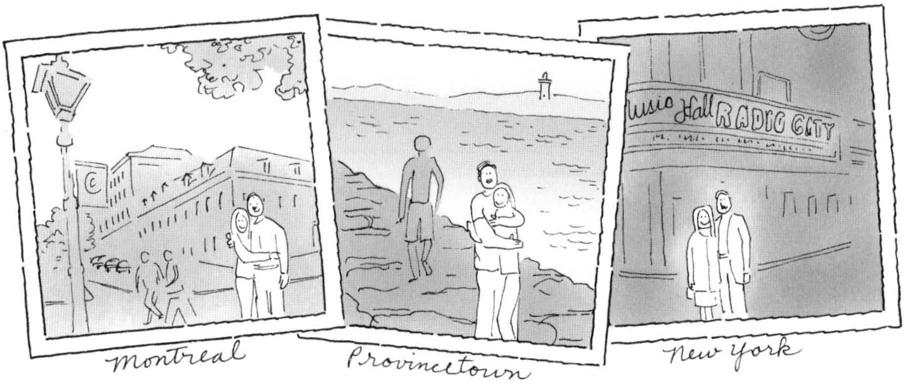
Music Hall RADIO CITY
Montreal
Provincetown
New York

Treading gingerly, we started to address our challenges and talk over some possible solutions.

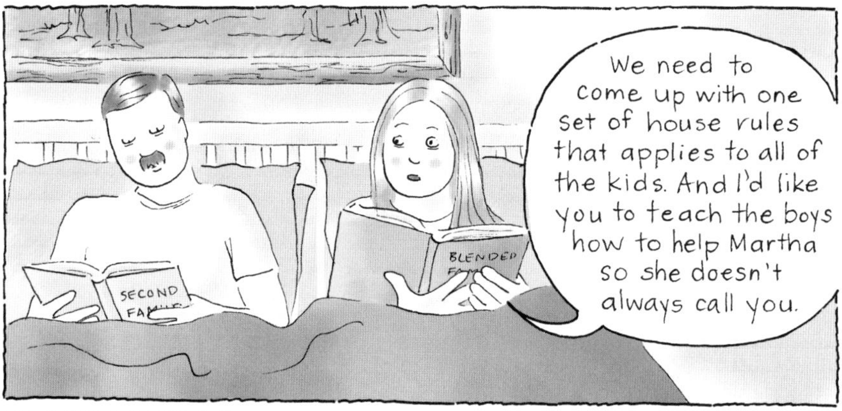
We need to come up with one set of house rules that applies to all of the kids. And I'd like you to teach the boys how to help Martha so she doesn't always call you.
SECOND
BLENDED

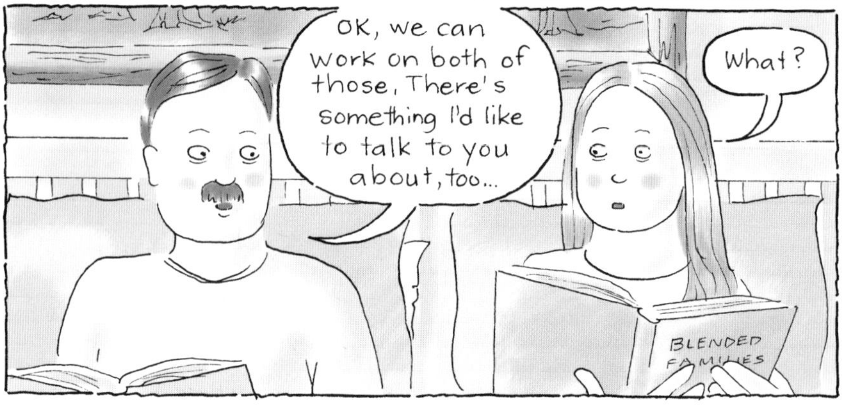
OK, we can work on both of those. There's something I'd like to talk to you about, too...
What?
BLENDED FAMILIES

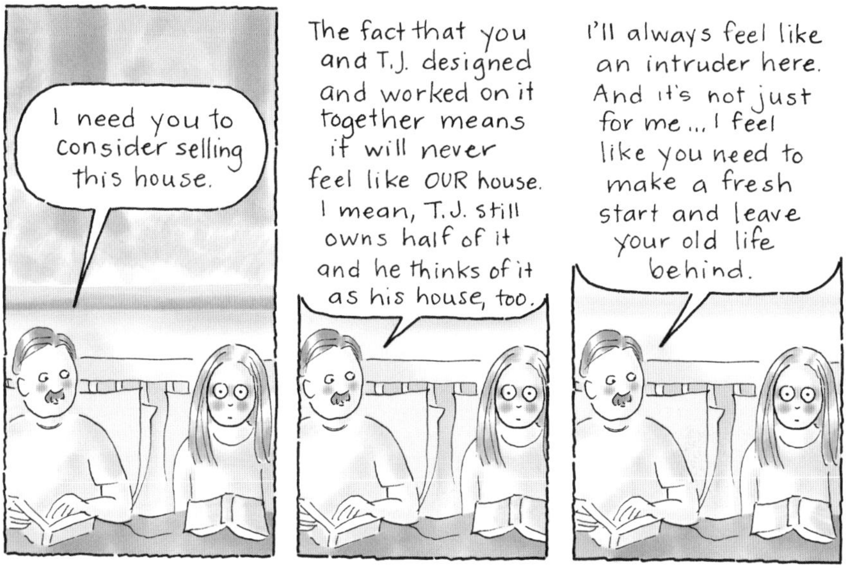
I need you to consider selling this house.
The fact that you and T.J. designed and worked on it together means it will never feel like OUR house. I mean, T.J. still owns half of it and he thinks of it as his house, too.
I'll always feel like an intruder here. And it's not just for me... I feel like you need to make a fresh start and leave your old life behind.

It's not that I didn't get it. I certainly wouldn't have been comfortable living in a house Will had built – and still owned – with his ex-wife.

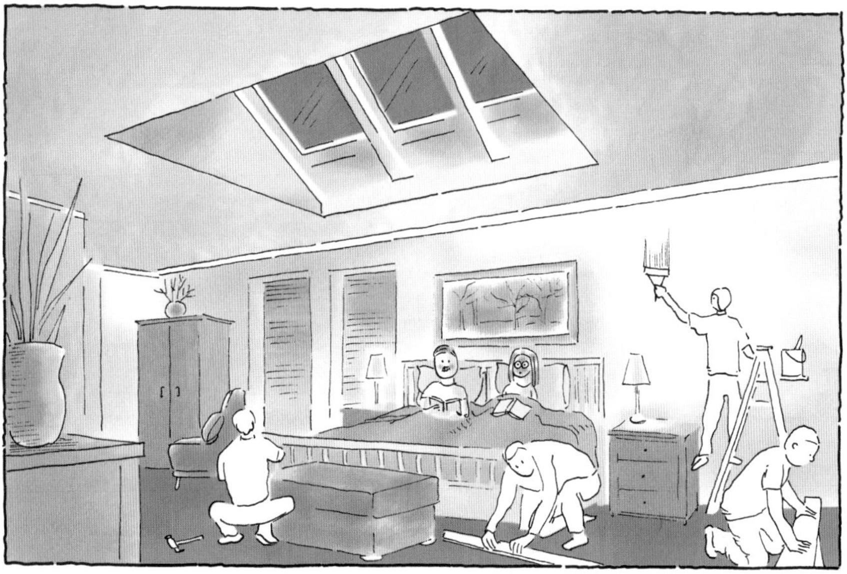

But reflections of T.J. in our house were a private comfort to me. We had been a happy family in this house. I liked remembering all of the years I was naïve enough to think that it would last forever. I just wasn't ready to give up this last tangible piece of my first family.

But once Will gave voice to the idea, it hung over us.

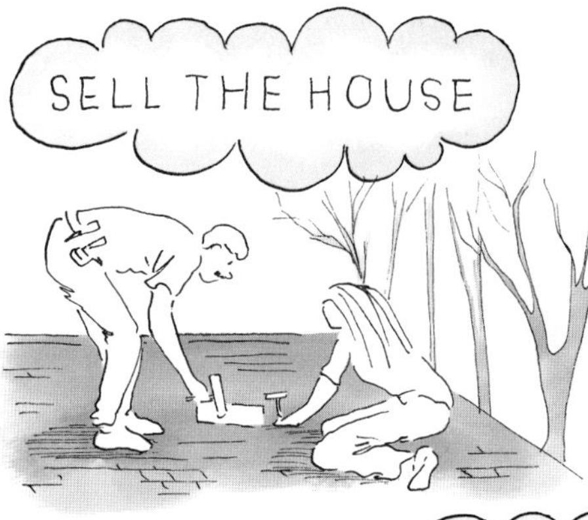
SELL THE HOUSE

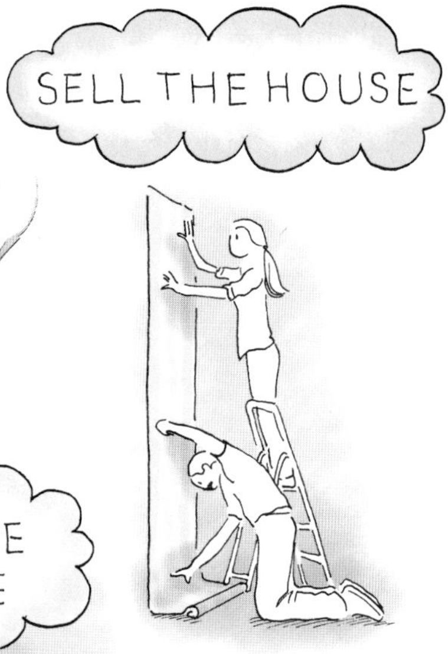
SELL THE HOUSE

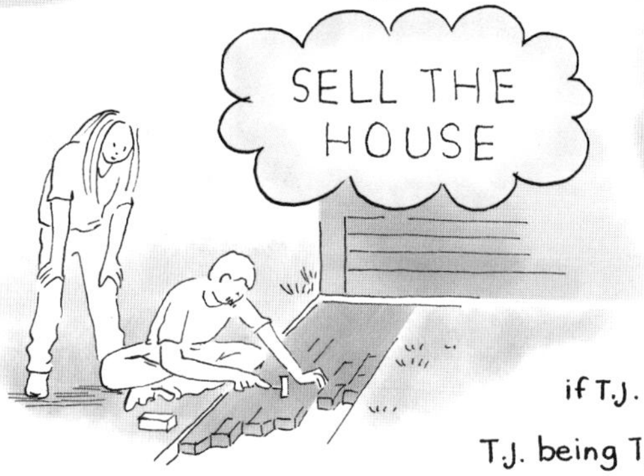
SELL THE HOUSE

For Will, it was as if T.J. were still there. And, T.J. being T.J., he often *was* there.

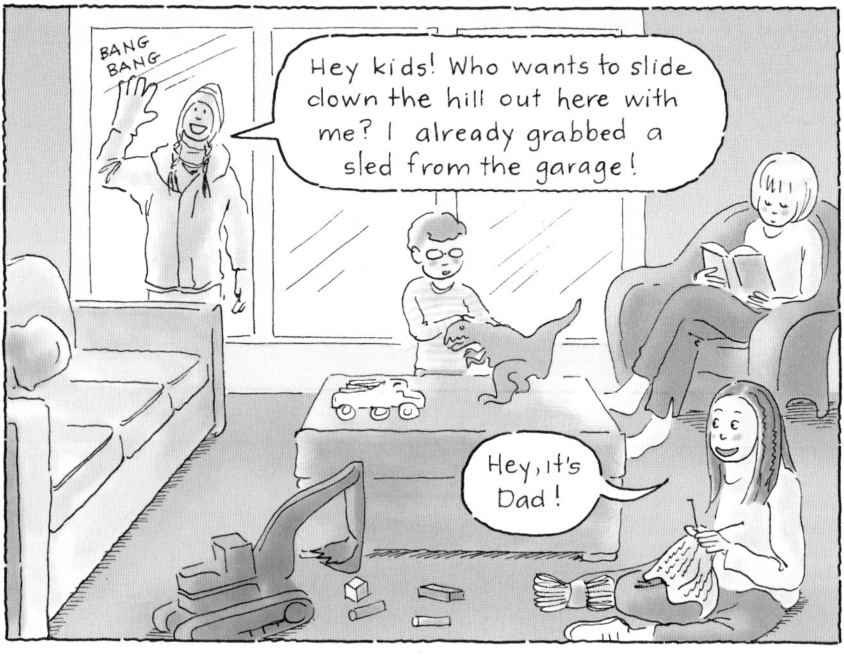
BANG BANG
Hey kids! Who wants to slide down the hill out here with me? I already grabbed a sled from the garage!
Hey, it's Dad!

Months passed; Will pressed. He felt it was a step we needed to take to commit to our lives together. I knew that our marriage had to be the priority.

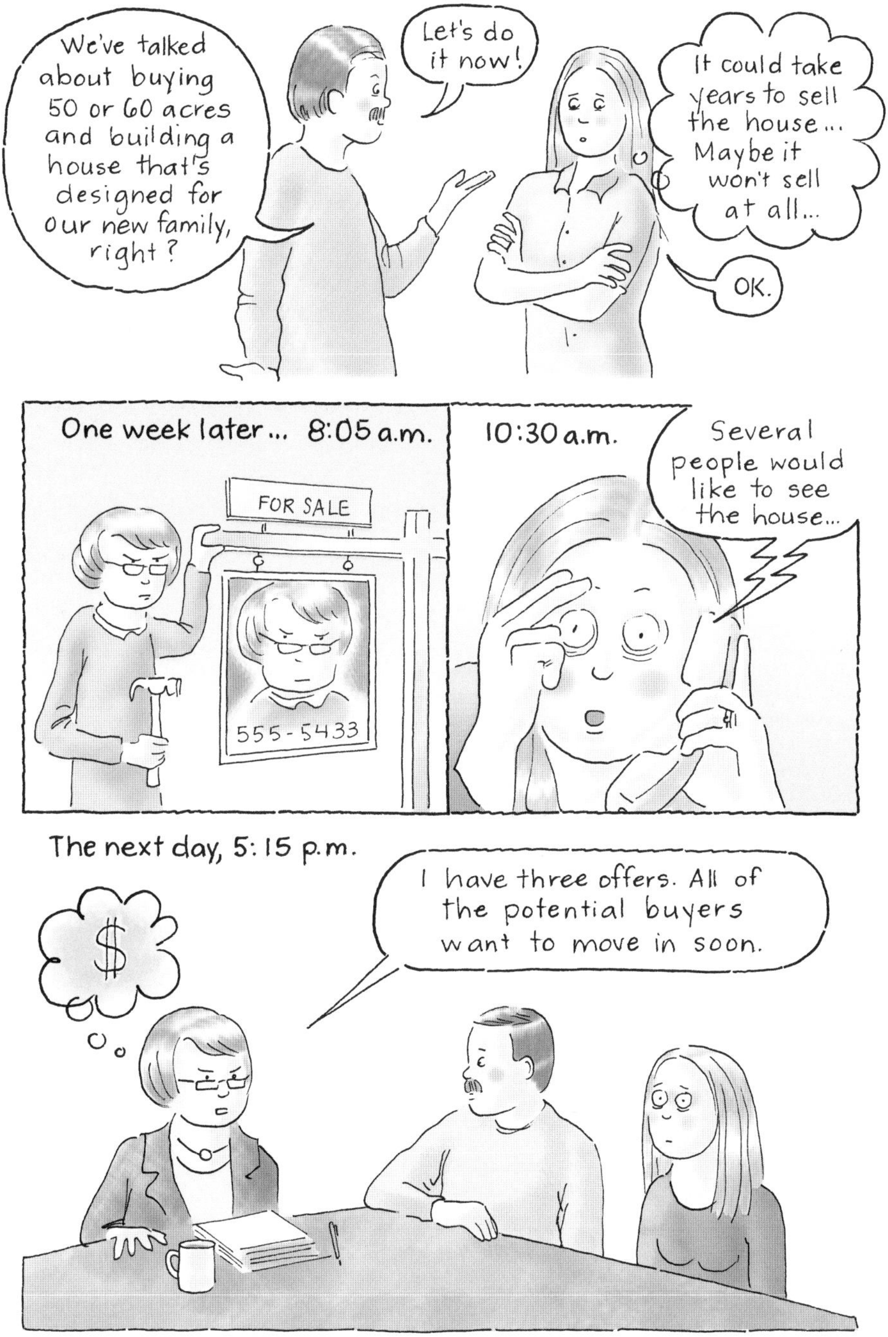
We've talked about buying 50 or 60 acres and building a house that's designed for our new family, right?
Let's do it now!
It could take years to sell the house... Maybe it won't sell at all...
OK.
One week later... 8:05 a.m.
FOR SALE
555-5433
10:30 a.m.
Several people would like to see the house...
The next day, 5:15 p.m.
$
I have three offers. All of the potential buyers want to move in soon.

I had very little time to adjust to what was happening. We scrambled to find a piece of land,

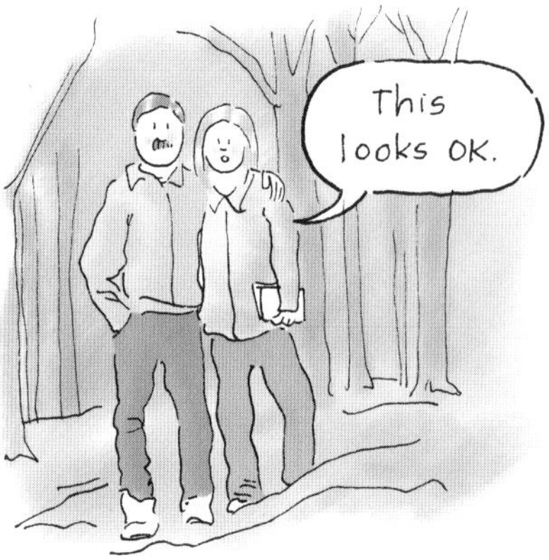
This looks OK.

an architect,

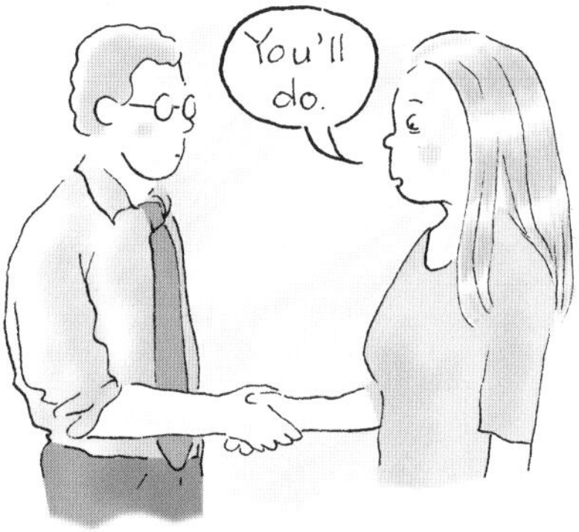
You'll do.

and a general contractor.

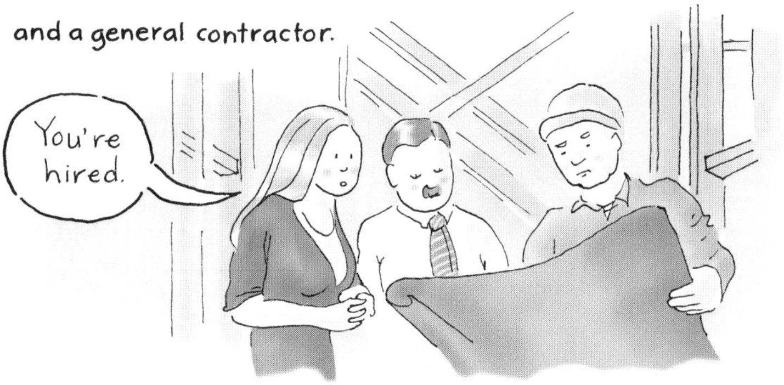
You're hired.

Then we searched for a house to rent in the meantime.

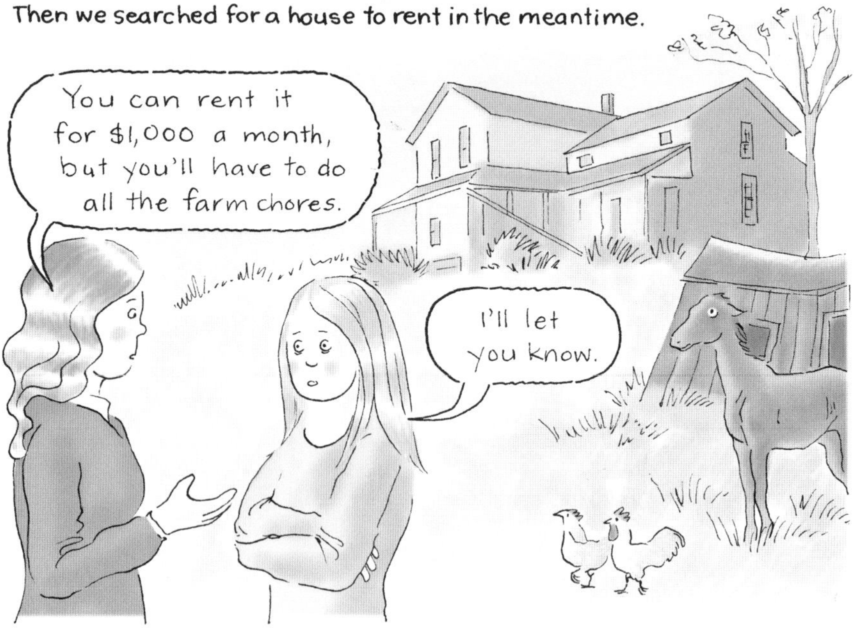
You can rent it for $1,000 a month, but you'll have to do all the farm chores.
I'll let you know.

Moving day was quickly approaching. I pretended it wasn't happening in the hopes that maybe it wouldn't.

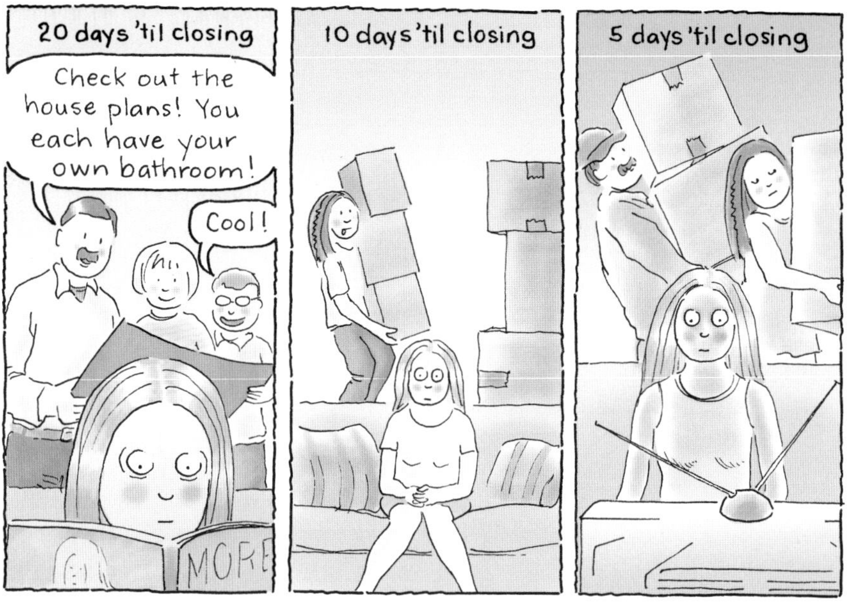
20 days 'til closing
Check out the house plans! You each have your own bathroom!
Cool!
MORE
10 days 'til closing
5 days 'til closing

Finally, with three days to go until the closing, I ventured into the attic with boxes Will had brought home.

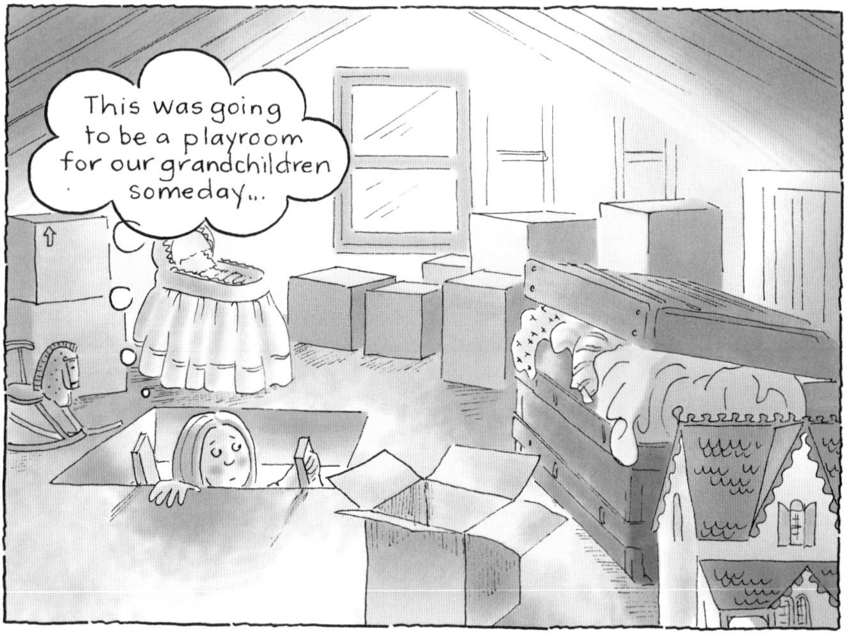
This was going to be a playroom for our grandchildren someday...

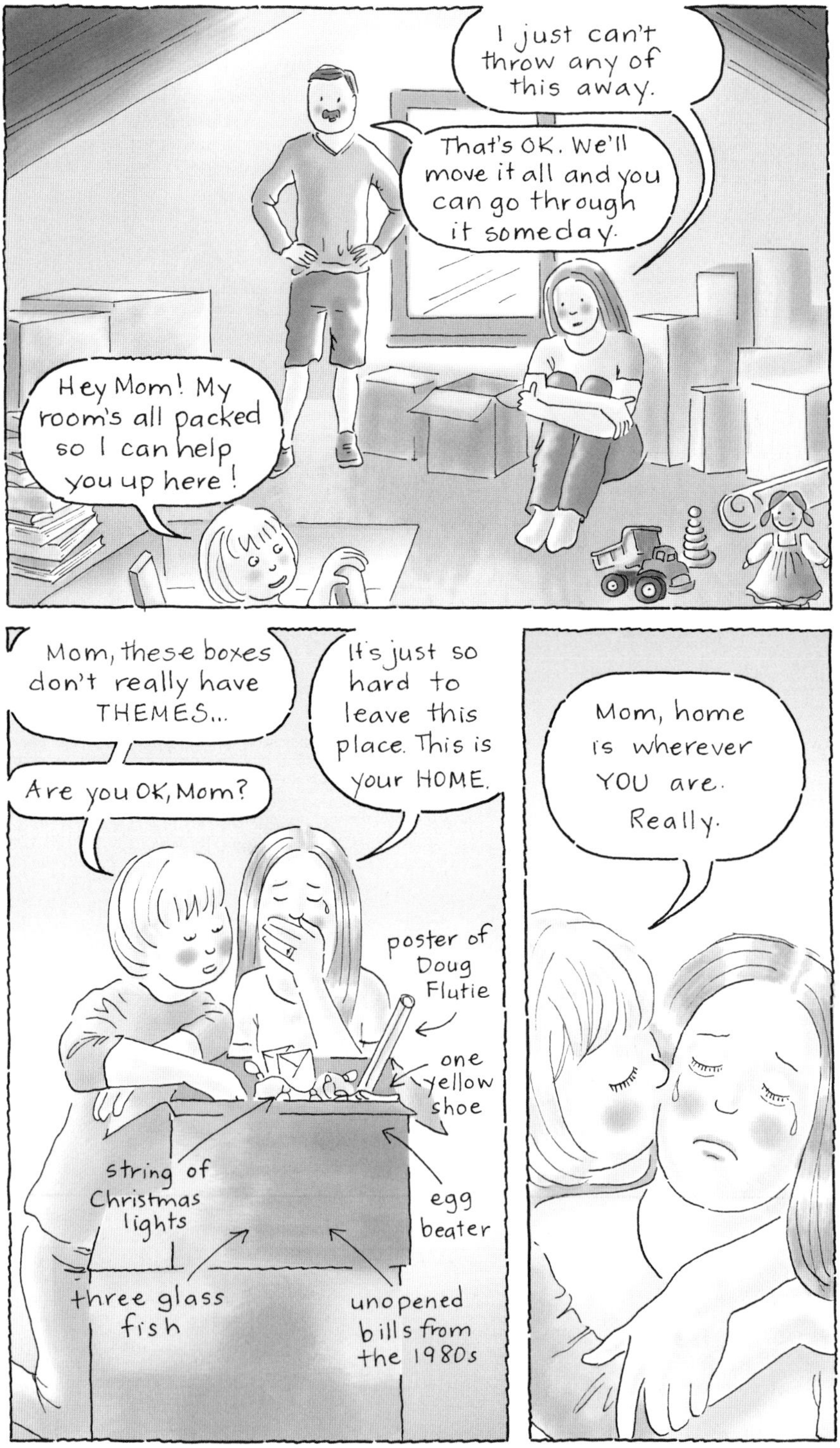
I just can't throw any of this away.
That's OK. We'll move it all and you can go through it someday.
Hey Mom! My room's all packed so I can help you up here!
Mom, these boxes don't really have THEMES...
Are you OK, Mom?
It's just so hard to leave this place. This is your HOME.
poster of Doug Flutie
one yellow shoe
egg beater
string of Christmas lights
three glass fish
unopened bills from the 1980s
Mom, home is wherever YOU are. Really.

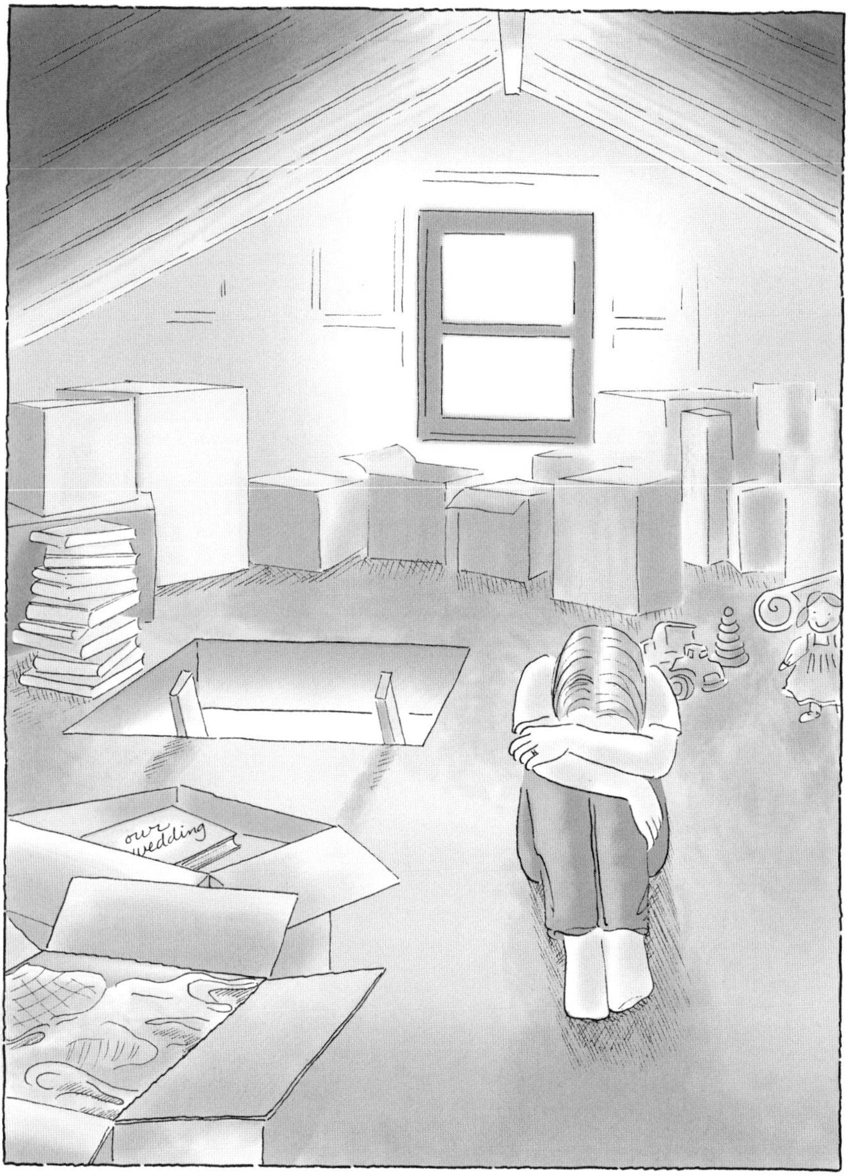
our wedding

Like most people, I hadn't saved any mementos of sad or difficult times. Instead I'd saved my first wedding dress, photos of family vacations, beloved toys, baby clothes, family heirlooms. All of these things I'd accumulated not only reminded me of our wonderful family history, but as I gently wrapped and packed each item, they began to shape it. Without even realizing it, I was mourning an ideal that never existed.

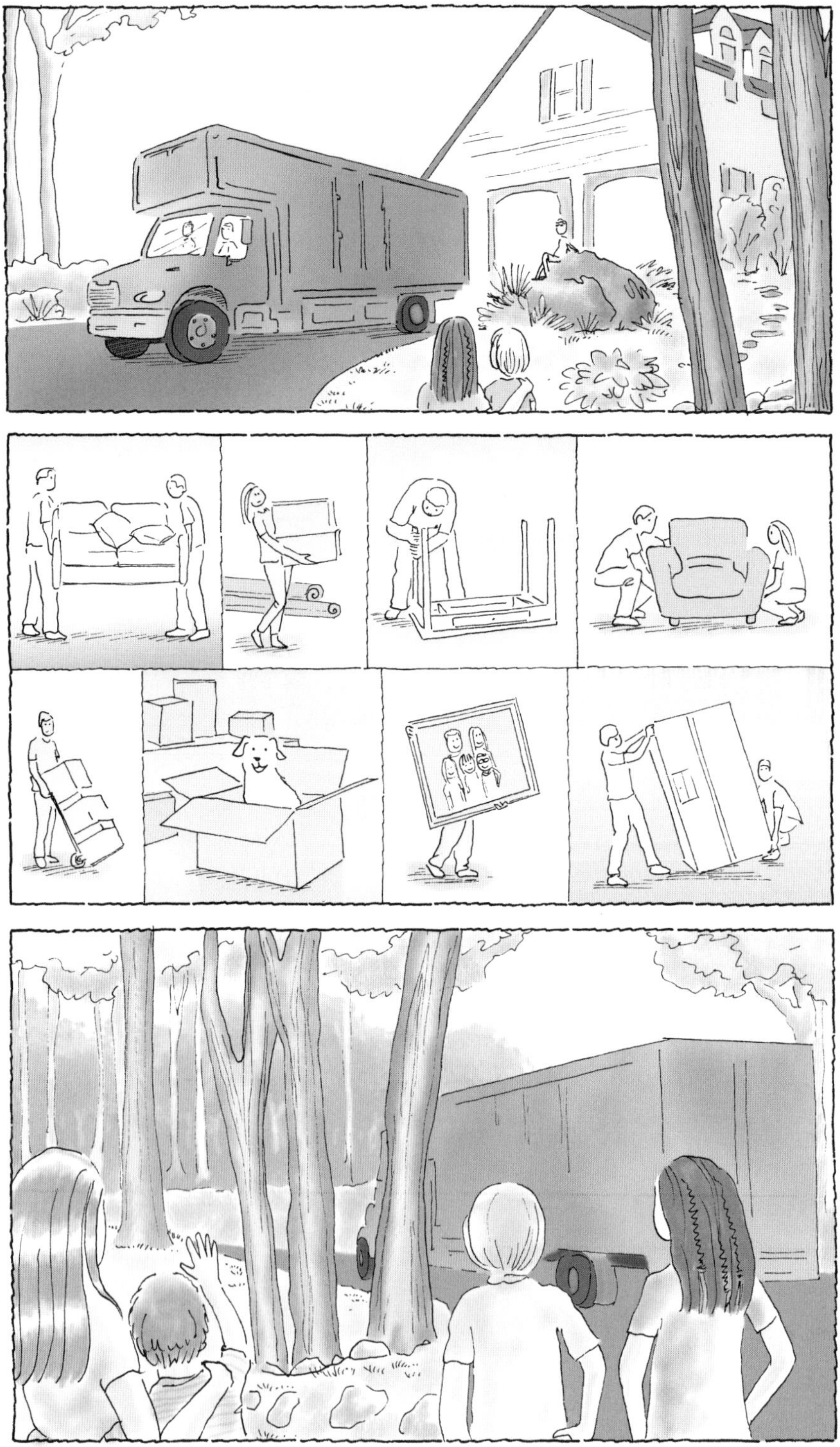

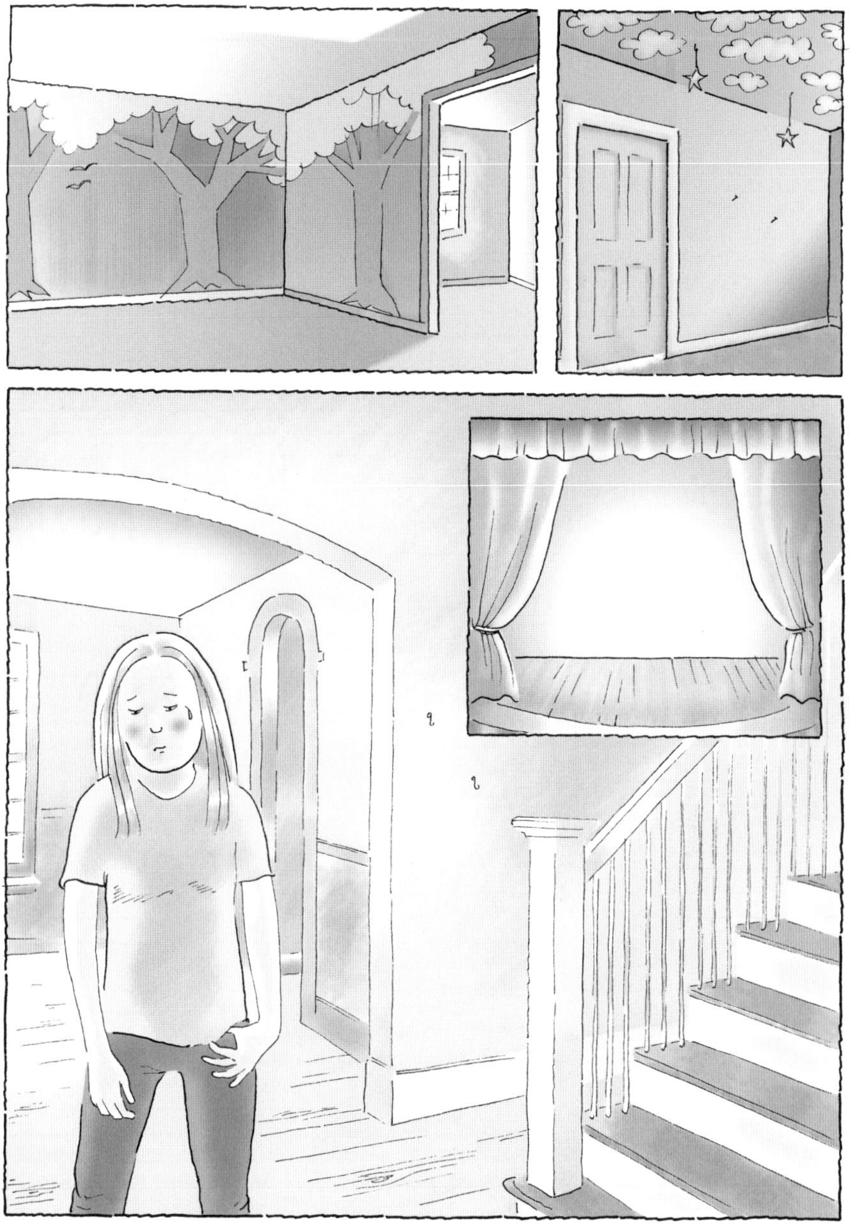

The thing is, you don't really get over a divorce. You just absorb it. It becomes part of your life story. Now and then, something triggers the sorrow and it overwhelms you.

The sadness can be spread out over many years.

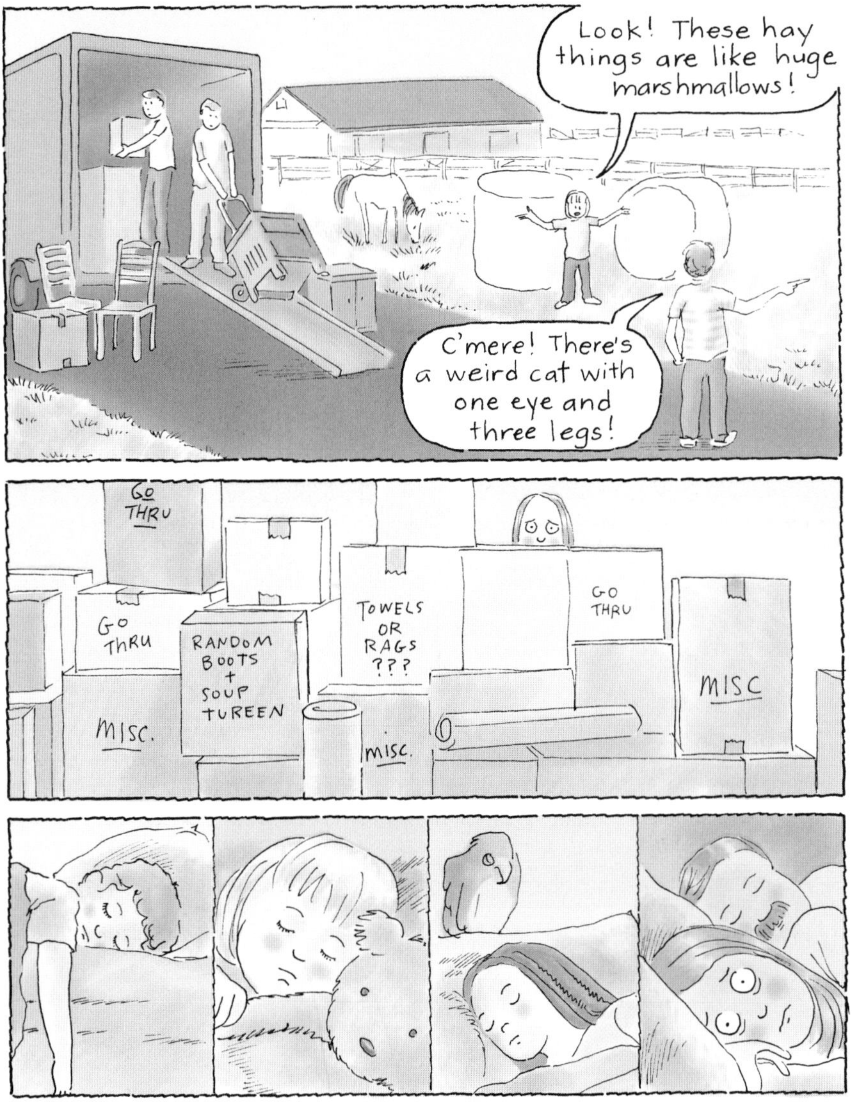
Look! These hay things are like huge marshmallows!
C'mere! There's a weird cat with one eye and three legs!
GO THRU
GO THRU
RANDOM BOOTS + SOUP TUREEN
TOWELS OR RAGS ???
GO THRU
MISC.
MISC.
MISC

The next morning, I woke up crying. The closing was in 2 hours.

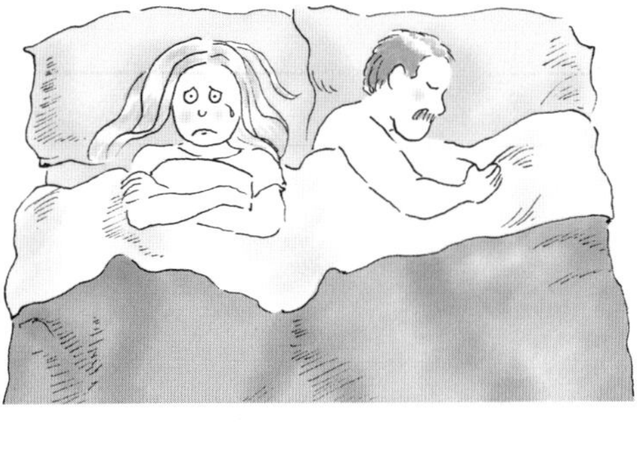

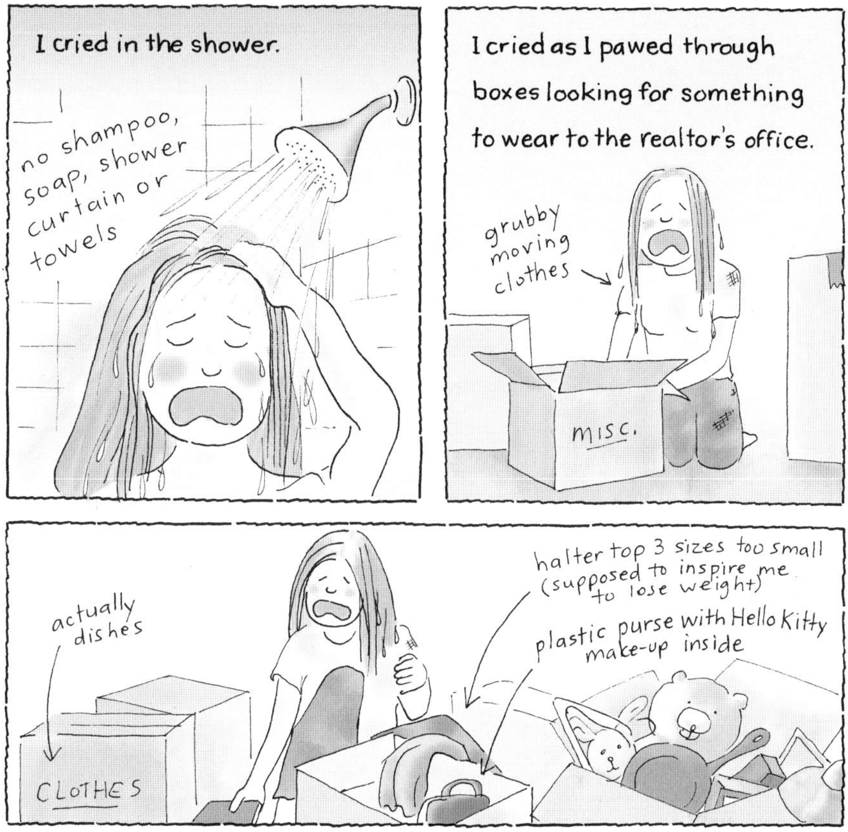
I cried in the shower.
no shampoo, soap, shower curtain or towels
I cried as I pawed through boxes looking for something to wear to the realtor's office.
grubby moving clothes
MISC.
actually dishes
CLOTHES
halter top 3 sizes too small (supposed to inspire me to lose weight)
plastic purse with Hello Kitty make-up inside

With no time left, I dabbed on some Hello Kitty eye shadow and sparkly lip gloss, tucked my wetted, unwashed hair behind my ears, stuffed myself into the sides of my halter top, and turned to Will.

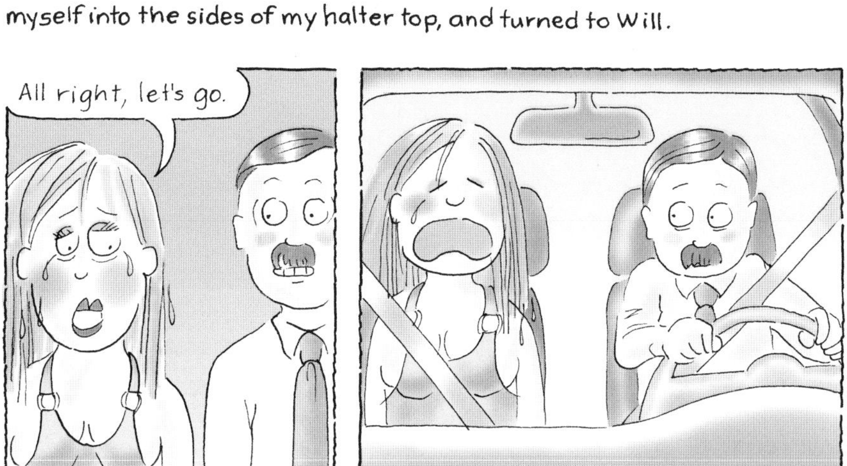
All right, let's go.

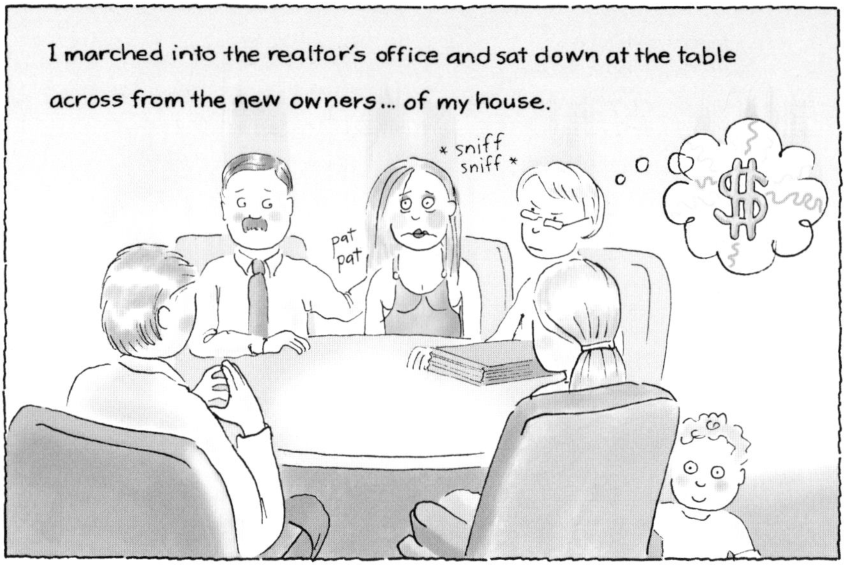
I marched into the realtor's office and sat down at the table across from the new owners... of my house.
* sniff sniff *
pat pat
$

Thankfully, their toddler took some of the attention away from me.

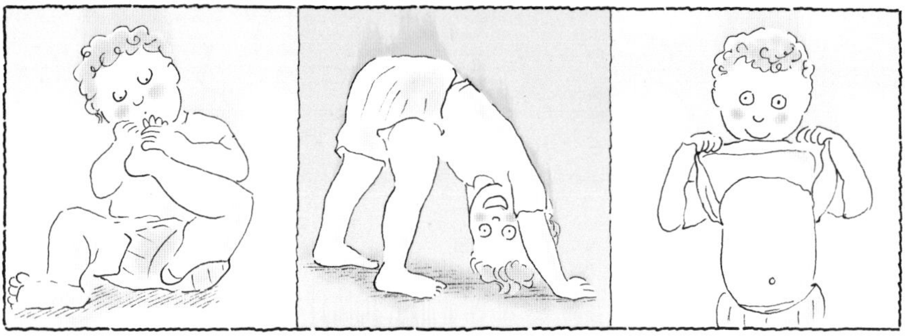

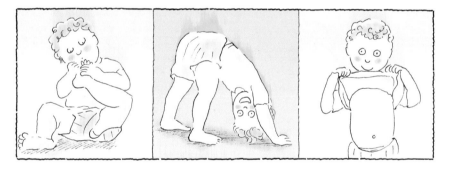

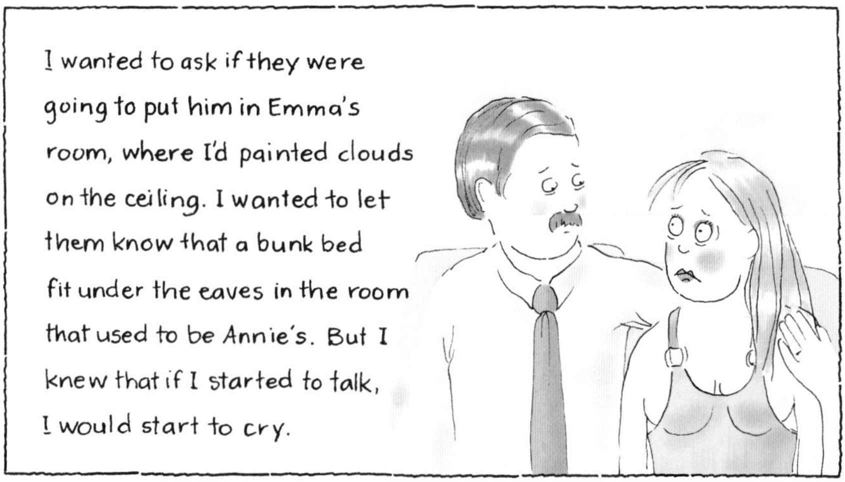
I wanted to ask if they were going to put him in Emma's room, where I'd painted clouds on the ceiling. I wanted to let them know that a bunk bed fit under the eaves in the room that used to be Annie's. But I knew that if I started to talk, I would start to cry.

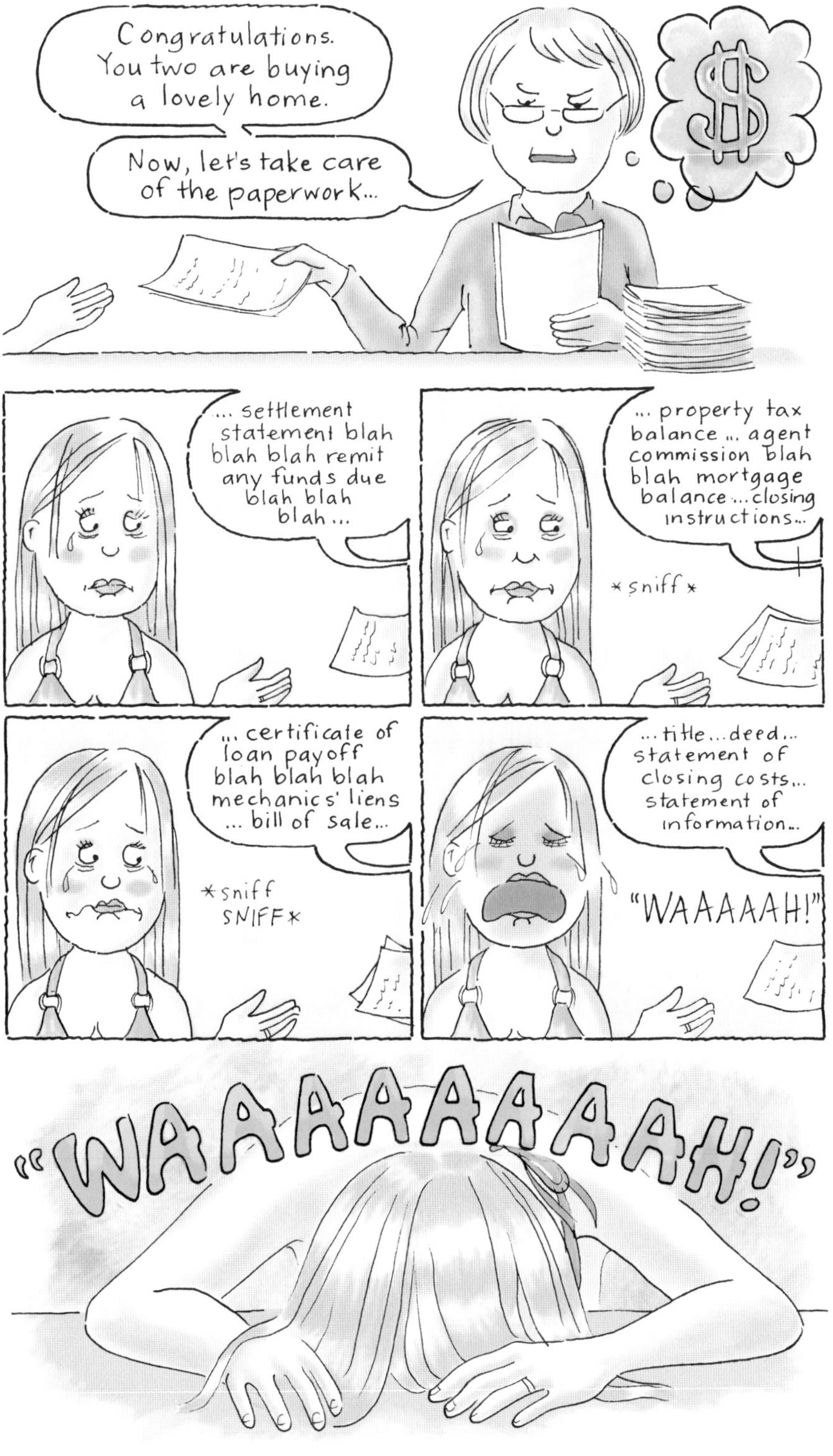
Congratulations. You two are buying a lovely home.
Now, let's take care of the paperwork...
$
... settlement statement blah blah blah remit any funds due blah blah blah...
... property tax balance... agent commission blah blah mortgage balance... closing instructions...
sniff
... certificate of loan payoff blah blah blah mechanics' liens ... bill of sale...
sniff SNIFF
... title... deed... statement of closing costs... statement of information...
"WAAAAAH!"
"WAAAAAAAAH!"

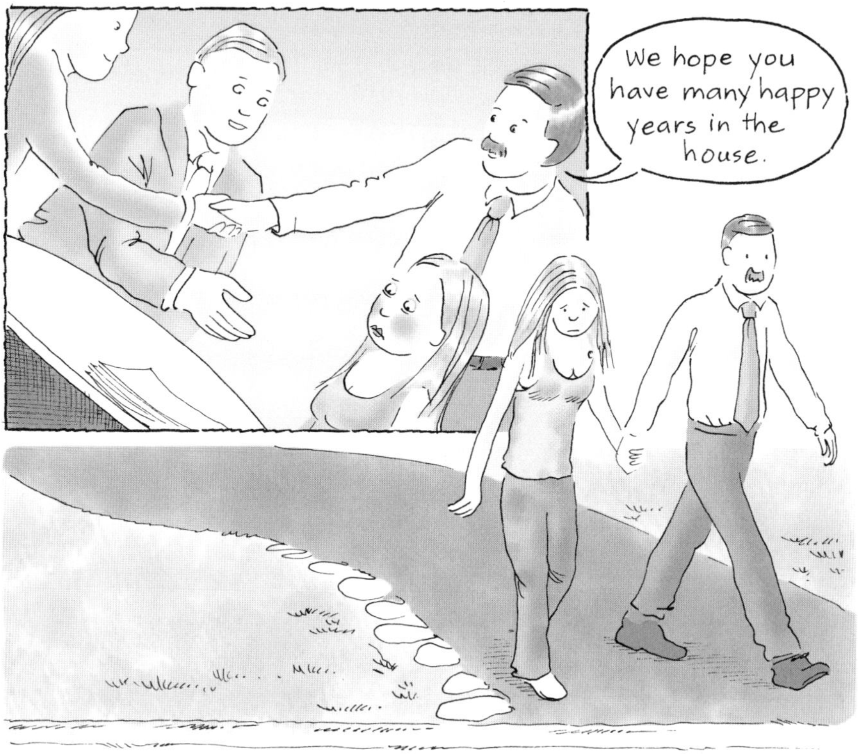
We hope you have many happy years in the house.

We all acquire scars as we make our way in the world, but these scars don't prevent us from living full and happy lives. Pain *can* be turned into possibility.

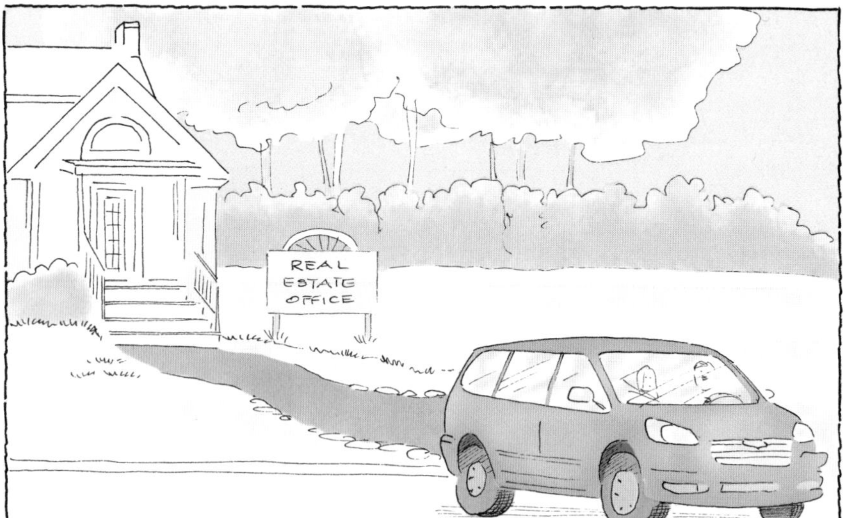
REAL ESTATE OFFICE

We can find a way to forgive and move forward, grateful for the blessings and good memories of the past and excited about the adventures to come.

When my children were little, I wrote a series of family hiking guides. After walking many hundreds of miles, I came to understand that the well-worn path holds few surprises. That predictability is certainly comforting.

But the side trails that aren't marked, the ones you follow when the blazed route to the mountaintop is closed, often lead to spectacular views.

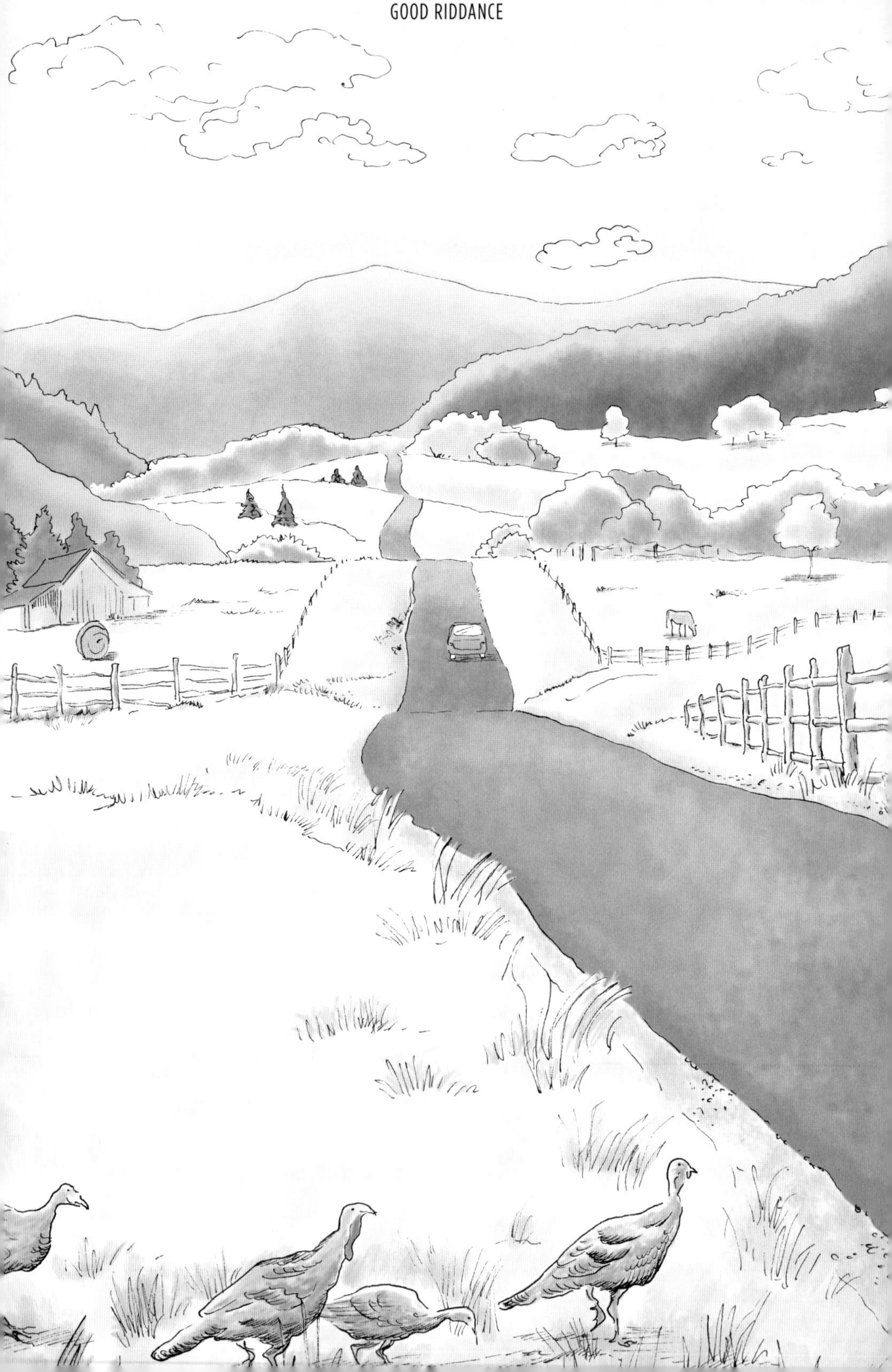

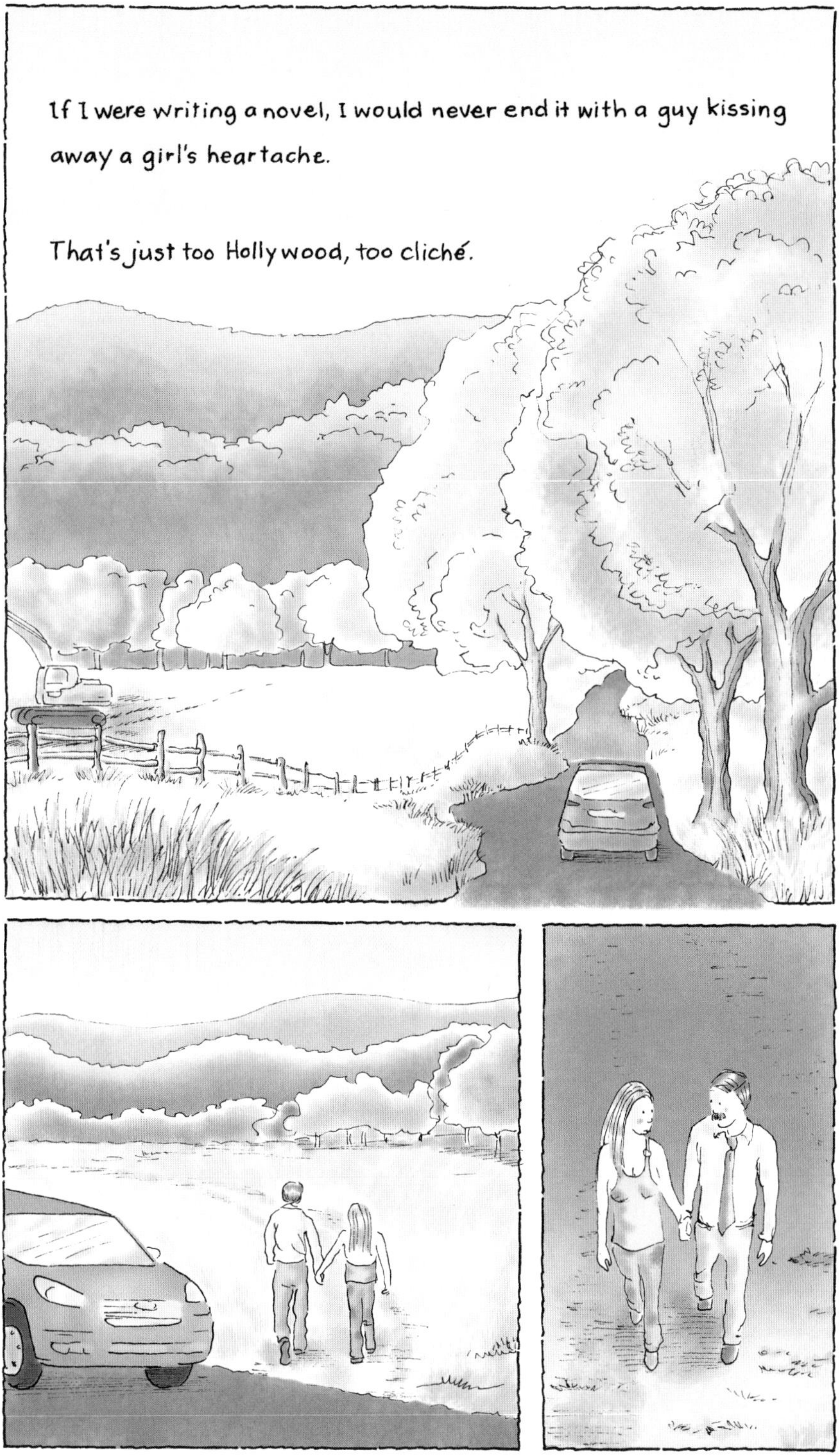
If I were writing a novel, I would never end it with a guy kissing away a girl's heartache.
That's just too Hollywood, too cliché.

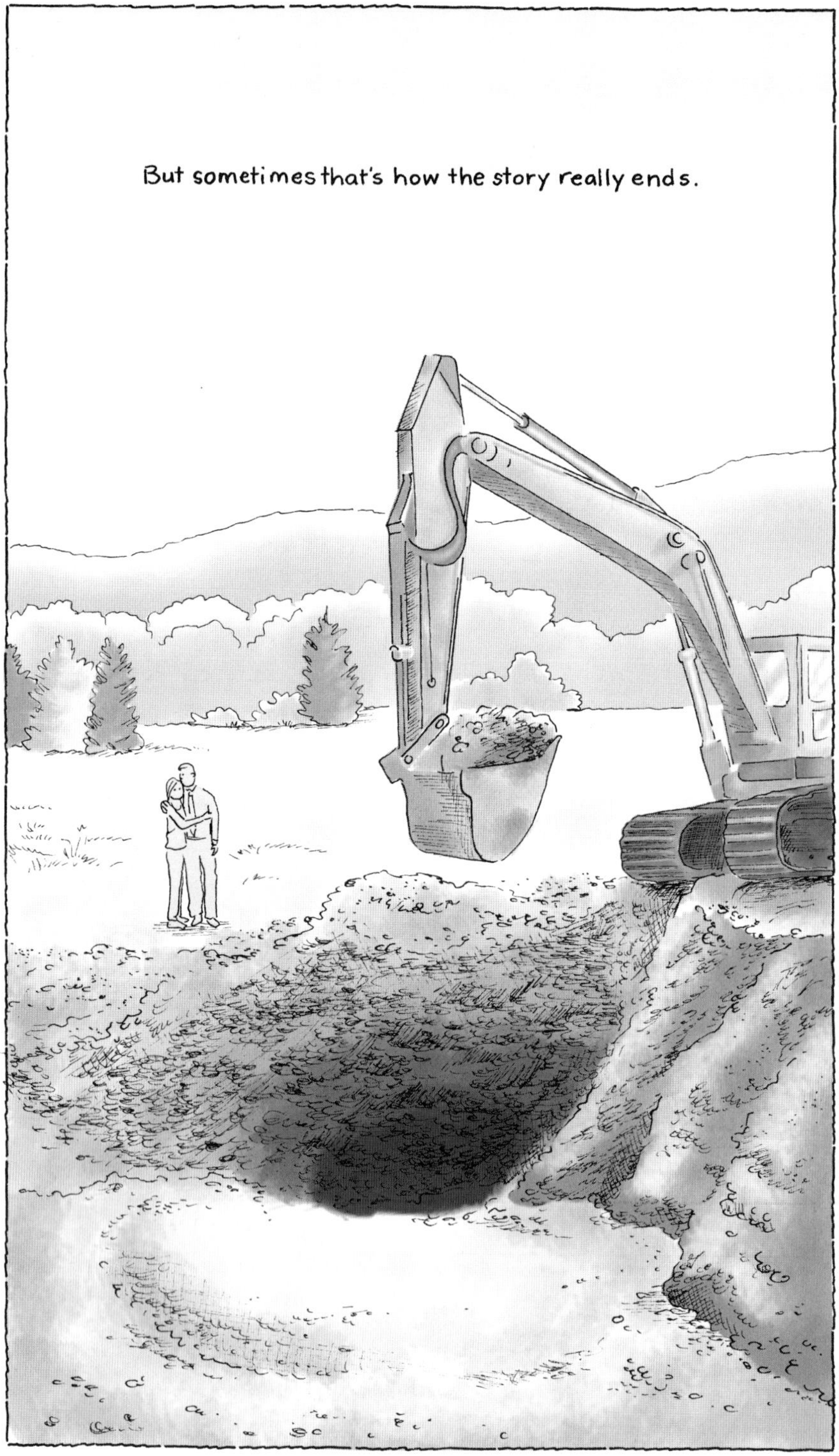
But sometimes that's how the story really ends.

Acknowledgments

irst of all, thank you to my extraordinary agent, Dan Lazar of Writers House, for encouraging me to tell my story as a graphic memoir and for helping to shape the book early on. This book exists because of his creative vision. I am so fortunate to be represented by someone with Dan's talent, insight, and work ethic.

Thank you to Frank Young, who did all of the coloring and shading on the interior pages (and fixed more than a few of my mistakes along the way). Frank is an accomplished graphic novelist in his own right, and I'm very appreciative that he was willing to work on my first graphic novel.

I am indebted to the clever and hard-working crew at Abrams. Sheila Keenan, my editor, has provided thoughtful and intelligent guidance for over a year as we've worked to focus the story and find the right balance of art and text. Respectful and patient, she helped shape the story without ever making me feel as if I'd lost control of it.

A heartfelt thank you to the incredibly talented and patient designer Sara Corbett, who held my hand through page uploads and cover changes and all sorts of complicated things. She is a rare combination of creative and concrete: She hasn't missed a thing or made a mistake in all the months we've worked together. And no matter what time of day or night I called the Abrams office, she answered her phone.

I'm very grateful for the support and encouragement I received from my friends and family, especially from Alex, who read the manuscript at every stage and offered invaluable advice, even though it was not an easy story for her to read.

And thank you to my sweet husband, who cheered me on, fed and watered me, and was even more ecstatic than I was when I finished the very last page. Now we can take that anniversary trip.

Editor: Sheila Keenan
Designer: Sara Corbett
Production Manager: Alison Gervais

Cataloging-in-Publication Data has been applied for
and may be obtained from the Library of Congress.

ISBN: 978-1-4197-0670-7

Printed and bound in the United States
10 9 8 7 6 5 4 3 2 1

Abrams ComicArts books are available at special discounts when
purchased in quantity for premiums and promotions as well as fundraising or
educational use. Special editions can also be created to specification. For details,
contact specialsales@abramsbooks.com or the address below.

115 West 18th Street
New York, NY 10011
www.abramsbooks.com